SM00003991
3/01
£14-95
KCR
(Pau)

THE RIGHT TO PRIVACY

052 178 6215

THE RIGHT TO PRIVACY

Edited by
**Ellen Frankel Paul, Fred D. Miller, Jr.,
and Jeffrey Paul**

CAMBRIDGE
UNIVERSITY PRESS

Published by the Press Syndicate of the University of Cambridge
The Pitt Building, Trumpington Street, Cambridge CB2 1RP, England
40 West 20th Street, New York, NY 10011, USA
10 Stamford Road, Oakleigh, Melbourne, Victoria 3166, Australia

First published 2000

Printed in the United States of America

Library of Congress Cataloging-in-Publication Data
The Right to Privacy / edited by Ellen Frankel Paul,
Fred D. Miller, Jr., and Jeffrey Paul.   p.   cm.
Includes bibliographical references and index.
ISBN 0-521-78621-5 (pbk.)
1. Privacy, Right of.   I. Paul, Ellen Frankel.   II. Miller,
Fred Dycus, 1944–   .   III. Paul, Jeffrey.
JC596 .R54   2000
323.44'8–dc21   00-035665
CIP

The essays in this book have also been published,
without introduction and index, in the semiannual journal
Social Philosophy & Policy, Volume 17, Number 2,
which is available by subscription.

CONTENTS

INTRODUCTION

The distinction between the public and private spheres of human life is a critical facet of contemporary moral, political, and legal thought. Much recent scholarship has invoked privacy as an important component of individual autonomy and as something essential to the ability of individuals to lead complete and fulfilling lives. However, the protection of one's privacy can interfere with the ability of others to pursue their own projects and with the capacity of the state to achieve collective goals. Developing an acceptable account of the right to privacy—one that provides satisfactory answers to both theoretical and practical questions—has proven to be a vexing problem.

The thirteen essays in this volume examine various aspects of both the right to privacy and the roles that this right plays in moral philosophy, legal theory, and public policy. Some of the essays discuss possible justifications for privacy rights, basing them on classical liberal principles or on considerations of moral pluralism. Other essays criticize prevalent foundational arguments for privacy rights, asserting that for various reasons the existence of a right to privacy as a fundamental right is dubious. Some of the essays examine the role that privacy plays in American constitutional theory, asking how various privacy rights have been justified by the U.S. Supreme Court and how privacy has generally been handled by prevailing methods of constitutional interpretation. Still others assess how privacy considerations affect certain issues in medical ethics, such as the proper extent of access to medical information and the normative status of the right to die.

Privacy rights are invoked in discussions of a vast array of issues, which leads one to wonder what the concept of privacy legitimately covers. Does contemporary usage of the word 'privacy' refer to things that actually are conceptually similar? In the first essay in this volume, "Deconstructing Privacy: And Putting It Back Together Again," Richard A. Epstein examines how consistent the contemporary law of privacy is with principles emanating from the classical liberal tradition. Epstein notes that cases involving privacy concerns fall into two general areas of common law: torts and contracts. With respect to torts, Epstein argues that privacy interests do emerge in considerations of several common law torts, particularly that of trespass. Yet certain actions do not fit cleanly into definitions of these torts. Developing new privacy protections against these actions will infringe upon the abilities of others to do as they wish. Yet if these limitations would lead to greater long-term benefits for all, Epstein claims, they are not inconsistent with a classical liberal approach. Epstein turns to contract law to discuss the privacy interests involved in consensual relationships. To the extent that freedom of contract provides controls on the transmission of information between consenting parties, the privacy interests protected are compatible with classical liberal principles. However, claims of privacy are often used to undercut the freedom of contract; for example, by limiting the types of information that employers may request from job applicants. Though public opinion may support privacy protections in these instances, Epstein maintains that such extensions of privacy are inconsistent with the sorts of privacy that are legitimately protected under the classical liberal framework. To the extent that one agrees with the principles of this framework, one ought to reject these extensions of privacy protection.

Yet tying privacy rights to classical liberal principles raises a more general problem. If privacy rights are justified via moral or political claims, then successful attacks on those claims will undercut the privacy rights that they support. This has led some advocates of privacy rights to claim that a right to privacy is grounded not in moral or political concerns, but in facts about man's nature as an autonomous agent. In "The Right to Privacy," Lloyd L. Weinreb questions whether autonomy itself can provide a root for privacy rights. He contends that assertions of privacy as a legal right, a natural right, or a civil right are unsatisfactory; invoking a theme also found in Epstein's essay, Weinreb suggests that confusion over privacy's various meanings may be the culprit. In one of its meanings, "the private" serves as a reference to autonomy itself, an essential characteristic of persons. Yet Weinreb argues that privacy, when understood in this way, is not itself a right; rather, it may be said to encompass rights that are normally subsumed under the rubric of liberty. More often, privacy refers to informational privacy, a person's control over disclosures about himself or herself. Various theorists have proposed accounts of informational privacy that link it to autonomy; such theorists argue that this link means that a right of privacy deserves recognition. In response, Weinreb notes that each of these accounts depends upon considerations of social good; none of them shows that a lack of informational privacy changes an individual's status as an autonomous actor. Therefore, each theory fails to show that autonomy requires privacy. Advocates of privacy rights may retreat to claims that a right to privacy is instead dependent upon social conventions. Yet consideration of this conventional right to privacy indicates that its contours do not resemble those of a right per se, but are instead highly dependent upon utilitarian considerations.

R. G. Frey is also critical of various accounts of informational privacy; Frey argues that the right of informational privacy is problematic because it depends, like negative rights generally, on assumptions of a sphere of noninterference. In his essay, "Privacy, Control, and Talk of Rights," Frey describes a basic format that characterizes several negative-rights theories. Rights theorists begin by asserting that some trait or value is essential to our status as agents or persons (self-direction of our lives, for example). They assert that this sphere requires noninterference, and then they give it a normative gloss, so that infringements upon the sphere may be portrayed as moral wrongs. Finally, rights theorists assert that rights of privacy are necessary to protect this sphere adequately. It is unclear, however, on what grounds we ought to accept the existence of this sphere of noninterference. Frey proceeds to assess several justifications that have been offered for such a sphere. For example, some theorists attempt to justify a sphere of noninterference with arguments based on principles of mutual respect, while others rely on accounts of human flourishing or human agency. However, analysis of these arguments reveals that, for various reasons, they are not successful in grounding the assumption that some sphere of noninterference exists that demands protection. The sorts of reasons that do support respecting a sphere of noninterference, Frey contends, are grounded in prudential/utilitarian concerns. This foundation, however, will not satisfy the rights theorist, because the protections that emerge from such concerns will not be rights that are independent of circumstances; rather, the protections will be subject to tradeoffs in the face of gains in collective well-being. Given these arguments, rights to informational privacy will be difficult to uphold, at least to the extent that they are based on general theories of negative rights. In closing, Frey argues that many of the concerns that give rise to justifications for spheres of noninterference can be adequately addressed by utilitarian perspectives.

Criticism of the philosophical foundations of the right to privacy also emerges from considerations raised by other fields of study. Evolutionary biology, for instance, may play a role in challenging assertions that privacy is ultimately a matter of morality or autonomy. In "Privacy as a Matter of Taste and Right," Alexander Rosenberg notes that "moral social psychologists" argue that privacy is a moral right because privacy is necessary for the expression of emotions and traits—such as love, friendship, and personal integrity—that are considered to have moral value. Yet such emotions and traits exist in societies where there is little or no privacy, suggesting that these accounts cannot be correct. Rosenberg proposes, instead, that a taste for privacy has emerged among humans and infrahumans as an evolutionarily adaptive trait: such a taste may help in the development of institutions and relationships that maximize reproductive fitness. This account provides a ready explanation for differing cultural norms of privacy: societies facing different environmental circumstances will express a generic taste for privacy in different ways. In situations where the economic value of information about others is rising and the costs of obtaining such information are falling, the incentives to obtain such material will increase. In these situations, privacy rights will emerge as a convenient, relatively unobtrusive method to protect ourselves from others. The result of this analysis, of course, is that privacy rights are a matter of prudential interest rather than a right backed by concerns of morality or autonomy. Rosenberg concedes that moral concerns seem to play a role in privacy rights (with respect to privacy of medical information, for example). He notes, however, that humans may have evolved with a predisposition toward recognizing other people's equality of opportunity to pursue their own interests. Privacy rights may be the most efficient tool to realizing this predisposition; privacy can thus be an institution of indirect, instrumental normative force.

The relationship between certain consequentialist moral theories and the right to privacy is the subject of Richard J. Arneson's essay, "Egalitarian Justice versus the Right to Privacy." Arneson begins by noting that our intuitions about the extent to which individuals should be subject to outside interference will influence our choices of moral theories; theories incompatible with our firm opinions on privacy issues ought to be rejected. Though many assert that consequentialism does not take rights— and, thus, a right to privacy—seriously, Arneson argues that certain consequentialist theories are compatible with privacy concerns (understood here as the right to be let alone). In particular, Arneson stresses the possibilities of "responsibility-catering prioritarianism." A form of egalitarianism, responsibility-catering prioritarianism directs that actions should be chosen and policies set so that moral value is maximized; moral value here is a function of individual well-being that gives priority to gains achieved by those who are worse off and by those who have behaved responsibly. This theory, however, faces criticism on several grounds. These range from general arguments against all consequentialist moral theories to arguments directed more specifically at responsibility-catering prioritarianism. Several of these critiques involve concerns about privacy. For instance, opponents of responsibility-catering prioritarianism note that to take agents' responsibility into account, facts about agents' lives will need to be uncovered; this may be quite detrimental to privacy. In response to these concerns, Arneson argues that assessments of moral value, properly understood, take care of these problems. To the extent that privacy plays a role in well-being, a proper assessment under responsibility-catering prioritarianism will incorporate privacy concerns as well as concerns for egalitarian justice.

It may be natural to think of privacy rights as a conclusion that is reached through the application of an accepted moral theory. In "Privacy and Limited Democracy: The Moral Centrality of Persons," H. Tristram Engelhardt, Jr., argues that privacy rights can also be viewed as the product of moral disagreements. Engelhardt observes that our secular moral knowledge is limited; no content-rich moral vision can legitimately claim to draw assent from all citizens. This carries consequences for political authority: given the absence of an accepted moral vision, governments cannot make appeals to moral authority that are based on any such content-rich view. Governmental authority must thus come from the consent of the governed. Rights of privacy, then, serve as recognitions of the limits of governmental authority. Engelhardt contrasts this portrayal of the state with those under which the state claims to represent a univocal moral vision. Under the latter, spheres of privacy, defined as areas in which individuals are free to pursue their own view of the right and the good, are problematic; spheres of privacy, here, would represent deficient deviations from the moral vision articulated by the state. Analyzing John Rawls's influential work on "public reason"—and, indeed, using it as a paradigmatic example of social democratic approaches to state authority— Engelhardt argues that even univocal accounts of democratic society that seem to allow for pluralism suffer from this problem. In closing, Engelhardt briefly discusses how provisions of the U.S. Constitution, specifically the Ninth Amendment, support a claim that—at least with respect to the United States—political authority is derived from the people's consent rather than from a particular moral vision.

While Engelhardt's discussion of the Constitution's relation to privacy is merely an addendum to his paper, the connections between privacy, the Constitution, and constitutional theory are the centerpiece of the next two essays in this volume. In "Legal Conventionalism in the U.S. Constitutional Law of Privacy," Mark Tushnet examines two lines of Court decisions: those involving reproductive freedom; and those concerning police searches and seizures. From this analysis, he concludes that the Court's idea of privacy finds its roots not in moral or political philosophy, but in what the Court considers to be the shared understandings of the American people. Thus, Tushnet notes, the basis of privacy in U.S. constitutional law is legal conventionalism. Yet legal conventionalism itself is problematic for several reasons. First, it is unclear whether the theory is compatible with theoretical principles—such as majoritarianism and federalism—to which we often profess allegiance. Furthermore, legal conventionalism may not be able to deal adequately with changes in the norms or technologies of a given society. A related set of questions involves the dynamic effects of Court decisions; the shared understandings of the American people may well be shaped by Court decisions themselves, introducing a problem of circularity into the theory's very core. While legal conventionalism may have the resources to deal with some of these problems, Tushnet concludes, it seems that proponents of the theory will ultimately have to look outside of legal conventionalism to find a solid basis for their judgments. This may lead them back to more controversial moral and political theories, an outcome that legal conventionalists had hoped to avoid in the first place.

While Tushnet illustrates a foundational problem with the Court's privacy holdings, the next author turns his attention to the hotly debated issue of constitutional interpretation and what various interpretive techniques reveal about a constitutional right to privacy. In "Privacy and Constitutional Theory," Scott D. Gerber examines the pivotal role that privacy rights play in modern constitutional theory. Gerber performs an exercise in "methodological self-consciousness," that is, he assesses how theories of proper constitutional interpretation affect theorists' assessments of privacy rights. In succession, Gerber examines how adhering to each of six major approaches to constitutional interpretation—textual, historical, structural, doctrinal, prudential, and ethical—impacts one's views about the constitutional status of privacy rights. Assessing the work of scholars who employ each of these methods, Gerber demonstrates that none of these techniques commits a person to a particular view on privacy rights. Each methodology can affirm or deny the constitutional status of privacy rights, depending upon how each practitioner interprets the evidence that is relevant under his favored approach. Given this methodological ambivalence, Gerber concludes that we must either admit that these interpretive theories are themselves impotent or that, with respect to highly charged issues like privacy rights, the ability of judges and scholars to apply these analytic tools is marred by ideological bias.

David Friedman moves the discussion of privacy from the philosophical and constitutional realms to the practical realm, focusing on people's ability to control access to information about themselves. In his essay, "Privacy and Technology," Friedman begins by assessing several arguments for the economic efficiency of privacy rights. These include arguments involving rent seeking, the efficiency of private markets for information, and protections against government interference. Each of these arguments is problematic, Friedman maintains, which suggests that the case for privacy rights—that is, for making it cheaper for individuals to control information about themselves—is dubious. Yet Friedman notes that these discussions of economic efficiency emphasize the role that technologies play in assessing the suitability of privacy rights, as these technologies affect the costs involved in hiding and collecting information. Following this lead, Friedman proceeds to assess three types of technological innovations. On the one hand, improvements in information processing have made privacy rights weaker by making it easier for organizations to collect data on individuals. On the other hand, developments in encryption—particularly public-key encryption—make it easier for individuals to enjoy a high level of privacy in on-line transactions, yet also allow for the development of cyberspace reputations as well as the benefits that such reputations allow. Finally, advances in surveillance technology, combined with public demands for effective law enforcement, are leading us toward a society in which our "realspace" privacy will be severely restricted. The upshot of these technological changes, Friedman concludes, is that we are moving toward a world where cyberspace will offer a great deal of privacy while realspace will offer very little. Overall, one's level of privacy will be determined by how much of one's life one chooses to spend in each realm.

The last four essays in this volume examine particular venues in which privacy is likely to be an ever-growing concern. In "The Priority of Privacy for Medical Information," Judith Wagner DeCew begins by noting that protecting the privacy of individuals' medical information is of critical importance to our freedom and independence. DeCew discusses three public policy approaches to protecting medical records. The first alternative involves reliance upon governmental guidelines. Though such a system would establish a presumption of privacy for medical information—and could lead to significant public health advantages—the centralization of records in the hands of a single public agency poses some privacy-related risks. The second approach is corporate self-regulation, in which the private sector would be the major force behind privacy regulations. Ideally, such a system would maximize consumers' choices about the extent of their privacy protection. However, allowing individual companies to implement differing privacy guidelines would lead to inconsistent levels of protection, a serious problem for patients. Finally, DeCew proposes her own "hybrid view" for consideration, which depends upon "dynamic negotiation." Under a dynamic-negotiation system, the default position would be that patients control their own records, and their records only could be released with their permission. This would lead to meaningful dialogue between patients and health care providers, protecting patients' privacy while allowing physicians to get the information that they need. This approach is not unproblematic; for example, problems that typically emerge when attempting to secure informed consent will arise under a dynamic-negotiation system. However, these problems must be weighed against the benefits. Indeed, DeCew concludes, the costs and benefits of each of these three approaches must be carefully considered by public policymakers when they discuss protecting the privacy of medical information.

While DeCew's essay focuses on medical information generally, recent advances in the study of the human genome raise a host of health and privacy issues. Of particular importance from a public policy perspective are the implications of genetic information for the insurance marketplace. A. M. Capron explores these implications in his "Genetics and Insurance: Accessing and Using Private Information." As scientific advances promise greater insight into individuals' genetic makeup, these same advances pose challenges to our capacity to lead self-determined lives. Not only can deterministic views of genetic test results undermine our conceptions of ourselves as the authors of our own lives, but access by others to this information may severely curtail our options. Of particular concern is how access to such information will affect the practices of insurance companies. Capron argues that, for reasons of practicality, principle, and policy, health insurance is unlikely to be affected by the dissemination of genetic testing results. Life insurance, however, is another story. Since life insurance is less essential to ensuring one's well-being than is health insurance, and because life insurance is issued to individuals rather than groups, life insurance companies may face competitive pressures to obtain and use the results of the growing number of genetic tests. Capron proposes that the best solution to this problem at the present state of our knowledge is a "don't ask, do tell" policy. Under such a policy, insurance companies could not mandate that individuals undergo genetic screening, because such data is still too new for us to assess its actuarial significance, and a mandate would tread heavily on privacy interests. Individuals would be free to inform insurance companies—the "do tell" component of the policy—of genetic testing results that demonstrated their luck in not inheriting a gene for a familial genetic disease. However, as an increasing number of validated gene tests become available, insurers should be afforded the option to require applicants to disclose any test information in their possession.

Privacy rights also play a part in some of our most traumatic life-and-death decisions. In "The Right to Privacy and the Right to Die," Tom L. Beauchamp begins by tracing the development of the legal right to refuse life-prolonging treatment. Between the mid-1970s and the early 1990s, courts justified this right by relying on previously established legal rights. Initially, privacy rights were the major source of justification, but liberty rights assumed greater significance in subsequent decisions. More recently, right-to-die issues have taken on the more active form of physician-assisted suicide and voluntary active euthanasia. Once again, legal rights are in dispute. Beauchamp begins his analysis by examining the moral status of a right to request active physician aid-in-dying; moral rights to privacy and liberty will justify these forms of aid-in-dying as well. Though the influential distinction between killing and letting die may seem to provide a moral justification for resisting acceptance of active forms of aid-in-dying, Beauchamp suggests otherwise, claiming that the morality of an act of physician aid-in-dying is determined entirely by the validity of a patient's authorization. Just as a valid refusal of treatment precludes a physician's moral culpability for a patient's death, so too a valid request for aid-in-dying should free a responding physician from culpability. Therefore, while there may be reasons why we ought not legalize active forms of physician aid-in-dying, these reasons can only be sought in the practical consequences of legalization, not in the moral status of the act itself, for privacy and liberty interests allow patients to validly authorize such acts.

The media is another flashpoint for privacy concerns, especially as new technology makes competition ever more cutthroat. Frederick Schauer's contribution to this volume, "Can Public Figures Have Private Lives?" examines how democratic theory interacts with the privacy rights of elected government officials and candidates for public office. Schauer begins by noting that arguments against the release of information about candidates or officials are typically phrased in terms of "irrelevance." Yet if by "relevant information" we mean information that is causally or indicatively related to traits that we want in our public officials, then the range of information relevant to voting decisions could be quite broad. Under democratic theory, people are thought to have a legitimate interest in knowing those facts that they consider relevant to the qualifications of candidates for public office. This applies not only to information that the majority finds relevant, but also to the informational preferences of minorities. Given the centrality of this right to know in democratic theory, candidates' and officials' abilities to restrict the amount of information about themselves that can be made public is severely circumscribed. In conclusion, Schauer notes that the right of nondisclosure, so often asserted by politicians against the release of embarrassing information, may be something that individuals must surrender when they choose to enter public life, just as they must sacrifice various other autonomy rights.

Privacy rights are an important mechanism by which individuals protect themselves from the prying eyes of others and from the intrusive state. These essays—written from a range of viewpoints by leading philosophers and legal theorists—offer valuable insights into the moral, legal, and public policy implications of these rights.

ACKNOWLEDGMENTS

The editors wish to acknowledge several individuals at the Social Philosophy and Policy Center, Bowling Green State University, who provided invaluable assistance in the preparation of this volume. They include Mary Dilsaver, Terrie Weaver, and Carrie-Ann Biondi.

We wish to thank Executive Manager Kory Swanson, for his tireless administrative support; Publication Specialist Tamara Sharp, for her patient attention to detail; and Managing Editor Matthew Buckley, for editorial assistance above and beyond the call of duty.

CONTRIBUTORS

Richard A. Epstein is James Parker Hall Distinguished Service Professor of Law at the University of Chicago. He is the author of *Forbidden Grounds: The Case against Employment Discrimination Laws* (1992), *Simple Rules for a Complex World* (1995), *Mortal Peril: Our Inalienable Right to Health Care?* (1997), and *Principles for a Free Society: Reconciling Individual Liberty with the Common Good* (1998). He is an editor of the *Journal of Law and Economics* and a member of the American Academy of Arts and Sciences.

Lloyd L. Weinreb is Dane Professor of Law at Harvard Law School, where he has taught since 1965. He teaches and writes in the areas of jurisprudence, moral and political philosophy, criminal law and procedure, and intellectual property. His books include *Denial of Justice* (1977), *Natural Law and Justice* (1987), and *Oedipus at Fenway Park: What Rights Are and Why There Are Any* (1994). He is currently working on a book about the nature of legal reasoning.

R. G. Frey is Professor of Philosophy at Bowling Green State University and a Senior Research Fellow at the Social Philosophy and Policy Center at Bowling Green State University. He has written numerous articles and books in moral and political philosophy, eighteenth-century British moral philosophy, and applied ethics. Most recently, he is the coauthor of *Euthanasia and Physician-Assisted Suicide* (with Gerald Dworkin and Sissela Bok, 1998).

Alexander Rosenberg is Professor of Philosophy at the University of Georgia. He is the author of many books in the philosophy of biology and the philosophy of economics, including *Economics—Mathematical Politics or Science of Diminishing Returns?* (1993) and *Instrumental Biology or the Disunity of Science* (1995). His most recent book is *Darwinism in Philosophy, Social Science, and Policy* (1999). He has received fellowships from the National Science Foundation, the American Council of Learned Societies, and the John Simon Guggenheim Foundation.

Richard J. Arneson is Professor of Philosophy at the University of California at San Diego, where he was department chair from 1992 to 1996. He has held visiting appointments at the California Institute of Technology, University of California at Davis, Yale University, and the Research School of Social Sciences, Australian National University. He writes mainly on social and political philosophy, with an emphasis on contemporary theories of justice.

H. Tristram Engelhardt, Jr., is Professor of Medicine at Baylor College of Medicine, Professor of Philosophy at Rice University, and Member of the Center for Medical Ethics and Health Policy at the Baylor College of Medicine. He is the editor of the *Journal of Medicine and Philosophy* and of the book series *Philosophical Studies in Contemporary Culture*. He is also coeditor of the journal *Christian Bioethics: Non-Ecumenical Studies in Medical Morality*, and of the book series *Philosophy and Medicine*. His recent publications include *Bioethics and Secular Humanism* (1991) and *The Foundations of Bioethics*, 2d ed. (1996).

Mark Tushnet is Carmack Waterhouse Professor of Constitutional Law at the Georgetown University Law Center. His books include *Red, White, and Blue: A Critical Analysis of Constitutional Law* (1988), *Making Constitutional Law: Thurgood Marshall and the Supreme Court, 1961–1991* (1997), and *Taking the Constitution Away From the Courts* (1999). He has written widely in the fields of constitutional law, constitutional theory, and U.S. legal history.

Scott D. Gerber is Senior Research Scholar in Law and Politics at the Social Philosophy and Policy Center at Bowling Green State University. He is the author of *To Secure These Rights: The Declaration of Independence and Constitutional Interpretation* (1995) and *First Principles: The Jurisprudence of Clarence Thomas* (1999), and is also the editor of *Seriatim: The Supreme Court before John Marshall* (1998).

David Friedman is Professor of Law and Professor of Economics at Santa Clara University. His current interests are in the application of economics to law and the implications of new technologies for law, economics, and society. His previous books include *Price Theory: An Intermediate Text*, 2d ed. (1990) and *Hidden Order: The Economics of Everyday Life* (1996). His next book, *Law's Order: What Economics Has to Do with Law and Why It Matters*, is forthcoming from Princeton University Press.

Judith Wagner DeCew is Professor of Philosophy and Associate Dean of the College at Clark University. She has previously taught at the Massachusetts Institute of Technology, and has been a Research Fellow at the Bunting Institute and at Harvard Law School. She is the coeditor of *Theory and Practice* (with Ian Shapiro, 1995) and the author of *In the Pursuit of Privacy: Law, Ethics, and the Rise of Technology* (1997). She is also the Secretary-Treasurer of the American Society for Political and Legal Philosophy.

A. M. Capron holds a University Professorship at the University of Southern California, where he is also Henry W. Bruce Professor of Law and Co-Director of the Pacific Center for Health Policy and Ethics. In addition to serving on the National Bioethics Advisory Committee and the Joint Commission for Accreditation of Healthcare Organizations, Professor Capron has written widely on the ethical and legal issues raised by developments in molecular genetics.

Tom L. Beauchamp is Professor of Philosophy at Georgetown University and is a Senior Research Scholar at the Kennedy Institute of Ethics. His research interests include applied ethics (particularly biomedical ethics and business ethics) and the history of modern philosophy. He is the coauthor of *A History and Theory of Informed Consent* (with Ruth R. Faden and Nancy M. P. King, 1986) and *Principles of Biomedical Ethics*, 4th ed. (with James F. Childress, 1994). He is also one of three editors of the *Clarendon Hume*, a critical edition of the works of David Hume.

Frederick Schauer is Frank Stanton Professor of the First Amendment and Academic Dean at the John F. Kennedy School of Government, Harvard University. He is the author of *Free Speech: A Philosophical Enquiry* (1982), *Playing by the Rules: A Philosophical Examination of Rule-Based Decision-Making in Law and in Life* (1991), and numerous articles on legal and constitutional theory. His work is the subject of Linda Meyer's collection, *Rules and Reasoning: Essays in Honour of Fred Schauer* (1999).

DECONSTRUCTING PRIVACY:
AND PUTTING IT BACK TOGETHER AGAIN*

By Richard A. Epstein

I. Beware of Conceptual Knock-Out Punches

It is a common conceit of academic writing to insist that progress in some given area of law or political theory is hampered by hopeless confusion over the meaning of certain standard terms. My usual attitude toward such claims is one of passionate rejection. Because the English language has served us well for such a long period of time, I bring a strong presumption of distrust to any claim of the conceptual poverty of ordinary language. The persistent fears of lack of understanding are in general refuted by the success of communication in ordinary life, as measured by the coordination of human behavior that language facilitates.

To be sure, it is easy to point to test cases carefully crafted to embarrass any general theory. But it is equally important to note the low payoff that attaches to the learned use of bizarre cases to confound general theories. Novel cases, almost by definition, occur infrequently in everyday life, so routine business can proceed apace without diversion or delay as the established rules yield clear outcomes in the large bulk of actual cases. Yet these routine cases are often neglected because litigation and philosophical discourse have at least this in common: they tend to focus on marginal cases whose intellectual difficulty exceeds their practical importance. Typically these cases can be decided either way, without upsetting the basic fabric of ordinary discourse.

Learned attacks on language, however, tend to go even deeper. It is often said that when we deconstruct language we unlock to our sorrow pervasive confusion that prevents us from working through the simplest of cases. At this point, however, the agenda is no longer politically neutral, as the terms singled out for attack are usually the staples of traditional legal discourse. Discrediting these terms counts as a conceptual victory over the critical components of the traditional legal order.

A couple of examples make the point clear. The frequent attacks on the central precepts of the law of tort, with its associated notions of individual responsibility, often begin with the observation that its core concept of causation defies rational explication. The issue arises with one of the central debates in the law of torts—that over the proper standard of

* I should like to thank Eric Rasmussen for his valuable comments on an earlier draft of this essay, and Laura Clinton and Jonathan Mitchell for their able research assistance.

liability in ordinary accident cases.[1] A strict liability standard holds a party liable for harm he caused even if he acted with all possible care and meant no harm to the injured party. The negligence standard requires the injured party to show in cases of accidental harm that the defendant could have avoided the harm he caused by acting with reasonable care. In *The Common Law* (1881), Oliver Wendell Holmes attacked the strict liability rule on the ground that causation was too malleable a concept to impose any limits to a defendant's potential liability; with his usual rhetorical flourish, he wrote: "nay, why need the defendant have acted at all, and why is it not enough that his existence is at the expense of the plaintiff?"[2] Holmes then claimed that by switching to a negligence system — where the foresight of the reasonable man could prevent the imposition of unlimited liability — that unappetizing result could be avoided. But he never examined any of the easy cases under strict liability, where the subsequent action of a third party breaks any causal connection between the defendant's action and the plaintiff's harm.[3]

Nor did this situation prove stable. What Holmes did to strict liability, the next generation did to the "reasonable foresight" test of negligence, whose own ambiguity in turn was used to justify resort to workers' compensation. Once again, it was easy to point out the linguistic confusions in the ongoing tort system without realizing that any newly minted substitute would be subject to similar objections. The basic test for liability under workers' compensation asks whether the employee's accident is one that "arises out of and in the course of employment." The test looks simple, but it also gives rise to its share of hard questions of coverage: should an employer be liable when a worker is stung by a bee on the premises, is engaged in horseplay, is injured while staying in a hotel on a business trip, or is stealing the employer's materials? The number of disputed cases is enormous, but the lesson is clear.[4] No matter what the direction of a proposed legal reform, marginal cases arise under every system.

The same claim of conceptual disarray has been used in constitutional discourse to undermine the system of property rights. The U.S. constitutional guarantees of liberty and property are stated in categorical terms in both the contracts and takings clauses of the U.S. Constitution. These clauses state, respectively, that "no state shall . . . pass . . . any law im-

---

[1] For discussion, see Richard A. Epstein, *Torts* (Boston: Aspen Law & Business, 1999), chaps. 2 and 3.

[2] Oliver Wendell Holmes, Jr., *The Common Law* (Boston: Little, Brown & Co., 1881), 95.

[3] Even under strict liability, the man who breaks into my house, steals my knife, and uses it to kill a third person has caused the harm, not I. I may be responsible if water breaks through the wall of my reservoir and floods a downstream neighbor, but I am not responsible if a stranger pumps my water into the basement of my neighbor, or stuffs my toilet with debris to flood a downstairs neighbor. See, e.g., *Rickards v. Lothian*, [1913] App. Cas. 263.

[4] See Arthur Larson, *The Law of Workmen's Compensation* (New York: Matthew Bender & Co., various dates).

pairing the obligation of contracts";[5] "nor shall private property be taken for public use without just compensation."[6] Yet in the relevant case law these basic guarantees are hemmed in by an acceptance of the state "police power," which allows for regulation to preserve (at the very least) "the safety, health and morals" of the public at large. These conventional accounts of the police power allow the state to enjoin without compensation the commission of a nuisance on public or private property. But in the first of the great zoning cases, *Euclid v. Ambler Realty Co.* (1926),[7] Justice Sutherland stretched the idea of a "nuisance" to cover the use of an ordinary apartment house in a residential area, so as to provide a margin of comfort for large single family homes nestled behind white picket fences. Put the term "nuisance" in quotation marks, and the constitutional barriers to the public regulation of private property quickly tumble. It is, therefore, no accident that the limited revival of the takings clause came in a decision, *Lucas v. South Carolina Coastal Council* (1992),[8] that looked to the *Restatement (Second) of Torts* to establish some definition of nuisance that predated legislative initiatives to extend the scope of land use control. Common law principles, thus, had their rebirth as constitutional doctrine.

In contrast, there are no similar conceptual deficits in First Amendment law, where the scope of the police power has been narrowly construed, lest the constitutional protection of freedom of speech follow the same dizzying descent that we have witnessed in the area of property rights. Now, in the context of defamation cases, the Supreme Court can speak about our "profound national commitment to the principle that debate on public issues should be uninhibited, robust and wide-open. . . ."[9] There is no skepticism here. Not surprisingly, the idea of a public nuisance has been confined to its common law boundaries in this setting.[10] The more that courts and scholars care about a subject, the more confident they are about its conceptual foundations.

The question that I wish to address is whether the law of privacy is also marked by dubious claims of conceptual incoherence that lead, as with tort and property, to a gradual erosion of the protection of the classical forms of individual rights. On this point, the answer is, to say the least,

---

[5] U.S. Constitution, art. 1, sec. 10.

[6] U.S. Constitution, amend. 5.

[7] *Euclid v. Ambler Realty Co.*, 272 U.S. 365, 394–95 (1926). Sutherland gives a set of reasons why apartment houses could be "parasite[s]" on the community, and concludes: "Under these circumstances, apartment houses, which in a different environment would be not only entirely unobjectionable but highly desirable, come very near to being nuisances."

[8] *Lucas v. South Carolina Coastal Council*, 505 U.S. 1003 (1992). *Lucas* struck down a state law that prohibited the owners of beachfront lots in hurricane-sensitive areas from building any structure at all. The case involved a so-called "regulatory taking," because the landowner was able to claim compensation for the loss in use value of the property even though the state did not actually occupy the land.

[9] *New York Times v. Sullivan*, 376 U.S. 254, 270 (1964).

[10] *Erznoznik v. City of Jacksonville*, 422 U.S. 205 (1975).

decidedly mixed. There is little question that *some* right of privacy forms an essential component of the classical liberal order. By the same token, the idea of privacy has been invoked to support a large number of other asserted rights that are in evident tension with the classical liberal view. For example, the right of privacy has been used to insist that individuals have a basic entitlement to keep private their own medical records from the prying eyes of employers and insurers. But it is not explained why this privacy right cannot be waived by contract. The right of privacy has also been invoked to justify the right of a woman to abort a pregnancy prior to term.[11] Yet it is not explained why the fetus does not count as a person who is protected by the general prohibition against the use of force. A more detailed explication of these claims is surely necessary, now that privacy has been subjected to conceptual overload by being pressed into defending such a heterogeneous set of rights.

My modest mission in this essay is to "deconstruct" the term privacy in order to reveal the present confusions in the use of the term. At first appearance, it looks as though I fall into the same skeptical camp as Holmes on torts, and Sutherland (whose politics make him an odd candidate for this position)[12] on zoning and private property. In this context, however, appearances are deceiving. My deconstruction of the multiple uses of privacy has a happy ending. Rightly understood, we can see light at the end of this conceptual tunnel. Some claims of privacy make perfectly good sense, even if others are profoundly misguided. In my view, deconstruction is not part of some occult literary theory of interpretation. It is just a matter of systematic disaggregation of disparate issues lumped together under a single term. In some contexts, privacy works hand-in-hand with the classical liberal conceptions of individual rights and responsibilities, but in other cases privacy claims are at war with these conceptions. Deconstruction of the term is a way-station toward its conceptual reconstruction, both for ordinary discourse and the hardier work of law.

II. The Conceptual Framework

The best way to understand the right of privacy is to place it within a larger conceptual framework. Although it is easy to identify countless

---

[11] See, e.g., *Roe v. Wade*, 410 U.S. 113 (1973).

[12] For a more detailed examination of his life, see Hadley Arkes, *The Return of George Sutherland: Restoring a Jurisprudence of Natural Rights* (Princeton, NJ: Princeton University Press, 1994). Sutherland was one of the conservative justices of the Supreme Court who resisted the encroachments of the New Deal. But he had a soft spot for zoning, which also imposes serious limitations on property rights. Arkes discusses *Euclid* only briefly (ibid., 70–71) as a sound embodiment of the police power. He does not note that the decision involved the deployment of a single 68-acre plot of land, which gave rise to none of Sutherland's concerns about the safety of children, the control of vehicular traffic, and the like.

variations on basic themes, it is convenient to divide the political theories into two large camps. The first of these is the classical liberal tradition that stresses certain ideas: private property, freedom of expression, and freedom of contract, coupled with a limited government designed to prevent the use of force and to supply the infrastructure (roads, courts, defense) needed for the protection of public life. On the other side lies the modern redistributivist state, which never fully denies the catalogue of individual rights and duties in the classical liberal state, but adds to them additional public functions: the elimination of (most forms) of discrimination not only in government affairs but also in ordinary market transactions between private individuals (as opposed to, say, the regulation of intimate personal affairs), and an extensive system of subsidies and restraints that allow for massive government redistribution of income or wealth from some groups to others. It is not as though this theory only allows for redistribution based on need, although that is surely the most justifiable case. More generally, the theory allows the political branches of government to decide who should subsidize whom: working-class families could be required to subsidize Medicare recipients; impoverished urban residents could be required to subsidize dairy farmers; well-heeled tenants could be "protected" against their landlords by rent control statutes, and the like.

In earlier work I have identified six key elements that mark the sensible classical liberal legal order.[13] Briefly summarized, the rules run as follows.

(1) The initial rule speaks in terms of autonomy or self-ownership. It excludes the possibility that any individual can be owned by another, or that the talents of all individuals belong in some social commons, to be taxed and regulated for collective purposes.

(2) The rule of first possession offers a relatively inexpensive means to link individual persons with external things. It allows individuals to assert ownership claims over previously unowned things, so that they can be used, consumed, developed, or traded in accordance with the fancy of their respective owners. It is not as though all resources should be removed from the commons with all possible speed; in some cases a regime of common use will perform better than one of limited ownership, as in the case of natural waterways. But for land and chattels, their cultivation and development depends heavily on the system of private ownership, which is most easily and directly achieved by taking things into possession.

(3) The protection of contract, or voluntary exchange, allows the transfer of services (ensured to an individual under the autonomy principle) and private property (initially acquired under the first possession rule). These exchanges allow property to move from lower- to higher-valued uses, so that one consistent legal focus should be to reduce the transaction

---

[13] Richard A. Epstein, *Simple Rules for a Complex World* (Cambridge, MA: Harvard University Press, 1995).

costs that slow down the otherwise sensible redeployment of social resources. In the ordinary case, a voluntary transfer produces mutual gains
between the parties, and these gains only accumulate as the velocity of
transactions increases. These transactions do have consequences on third
parties, but, as a first approximation, these externalities are more positive
than negative. The increased wealth of any individual will, on net, improve the trading opportunities of all other persons. The individual who
loses out because of his inability to secure gains in any single transaction,
therefore, has the comfort of knowing that other transactional possibilities
remain on which he can seize, perhaps by altering the mix of price or
quality of the goods and services provided.

(4) The law of tort prevents involuntary transfers of labor and property
by the use of force and fraud. These unilateral transfers always impose
losses on one side. Where these losses exceed the gains to the winners, the
transactions should be stopped altogether. Where the gains to the winner
exceed the losses to the other side, usually a voluntary transaction can be
arranged to secure the same result. Either way, there is a presumptive case
for voluntary over coerced exchanges.

(5) This presumption against forced exchanges may be overcome in
cases of necessity,[14] where the law creates a privilege to individuals stranded
at sea, in peril of their lives, to use the property of others without their
consent, conditional on payment for harm done. This privilege is hedged
in by sharp limitations so that one cannot simply decide to use a neighbor's bicycle because it is too hot to walk, or to cut the neighbor's lawn
in summer or shovel his walk in winter, simply because he is away for the
weekend. The necessity has to be imperative, and the compensation should
be as complete as possible once the peril has passed.

(6) The sixth rule, governing takings of private property for public use,
is, in a sense, a generalization of the necessity rule that allows for the
production and funding of a variety of public goods. Ordinary market
transactions require the consent of buyer and seller, and these work best
in a regime where each participant has multiple choices of trading partners. In contrast, the creation of a system of highways requires the unan-
imous consent of a large number of individuals, so that one holdout can
doom the common scheme. A forced purchase for compensation could
overcome that holdout problem.

Cash compensation, in contrast, is not needed within a general system
of reciprocal regulation. In this context, the in-kind benefits generated by
regulation serve as a compensation for the state-imposed restrictions. The
law prohibits me and my neighbors from building within five feet of the
boundary line. Each of us gains on net from this parallel set of restrictions,
just as we would all lose if the setback requirements were fifty feet. But
so long as all members of the community are equally situated, it is un-

---

[14] For discussion, see Epstein, *Torts*, 60–65.

likely that they would all vote to adopt schemes that worked against their individual interests. But in many cases the distribution of burdens and benefits is not so neatly correlated. Frequently, one segment of the community seeks to use its political power to gain at the expense of another. Abstractly conceived, therefore, it is not possible to assume that any system of comprehensive regulation supplies all regulated parties with the necessary compensation. In too many cases, a formally neutral system of state regulation is in reality nothing more than a disguised transfer of wealth from one individual or group to another. Thus, a rule that limits all subdivision members to the construction of a single family home on a single lot is far more likely to pass muster than a prohibition on new construction within the subdivision when all lots but one have been fully developed. The lone outsider is now forced to supply open space for his neighbors, even when he is left in possession of his land. The takings rule is meant to facilitate the orderly movement from less to more desirable social states whenever high transaction costs block voluntary movement in that direction. These rules are *not* designed to facilitate the covert transfer of wealth between individuals or interest groups. The provision of public goods is part and parcel of this scheme. The redistribution of wealth is not.

III. Tort and Privacy

It is important to see how this six-part framework applies to the law of privacy as it has developed over the past century. In dealing with this issue, it should be clear at the outset that the system will never operate as cleanly as do the rules governing property rights in land. For land, it is generally clear when one person has crossed the boundary that separates his property from another. The definition and identification of the appropriate boundaries is never as clear in disputes over privacy. Yet, even accepting these limitations, it is possible to make some measurable progress to a sensible end. In order to do so, it is best to divide the cases into two broad classes which track the familiar common law classification. The first of these, which I will examine in this section, deals with interactions between strangers, and situates the subject of privacy as a province of the law of tort. The second, which I shall discuss in Section IV, deals with the protection, if any, given to privacy in consensual arrangements between parties; this protection is a species of contract law.

A. Tort law and privacy rules

Our traditional legal system offers extensive protection to privacy interests even where they are not singled out by name for special protection. The ordinary rules of private property grant the owner the exclusive possession of land and the structures thereon. The owner's exclusive right of possession works in a sensible way to limit the intrusions that other individuals are able to make into one's private life. The people who cannot walk through someone else's grounds or lift up his window shutters will be much less likely to pry into his personal affairs. The ordinary rules of property allow a landowner to erect walls that keep other people out; these walls can also ensure privacy by blocking direct observation of what takes place on the land. Indeed, in one of the early cases dealing with concerns of privacy, the trespass action was allowed against a man who gained entrance into a woman's bedroom during childbirth when he pretended to be a doctor's assistant.[15] The defendant's fraud vitiated the consent given to his entry and thus exposed him to a trespass action, which included as damages the plaintiff's shame and embarrassment at having him watch the birth. It takes no great thinker to realize that protection of the privacy interest is "parasitic" on the commonplace tort of trespass, whose origins lie in the desire to protect individuals from neighbors who trample their corn, drive off their cows, or break down their houses.

It is equally important to realize the imperfect nature of this protection. To be sure, the system works very well when the rights of individual owners are respected so that there is no occasion to invoke the tort of trespass in the first place. But the rights of owners are subject to erosion when determined individuals seek to finesse the classical forms of protection. In a sense, the issue dates back to Blackstone in the eighteenth century, for the question often arose as to what sort of protection, if any, a landowner had from someone who eavesdropped on the conversations inside his house.[16] The term "eavesdropping," both in Blackstone and today, contains a certain built-in ambiguity. The term could refer to a trespasser who hangs from your eaves to listen to what goes on. The dictionary definition, however, skirts the trespass question by eschewing the literal definition—that is, a person who drops from the eaves—and, instead, moves smartly to a definition that implicates the modern definition of privacy: "To listen, or try to listen, secretly, as to a private conversation."[17] All of a sudden, the element of physical trespass does not loom large at all. It does not matter, as it were, whether the person who overhears the conversation hangs from his own eaves or from yours. The

---

[15] *DeMay v. Roberts*, 9 N.W. 146, 149 (Mich. 1881).

[16] "*Eaves-droppers*, or such as listen under walls or windows, or the eaves of a house to hearken after discourse, and thereupon to frame slanderous and mischievous tales, are a common nuisance and presentable at the court-leet: or are indictable as the sessions, and punishable by a fine and finding securities for good behavior." William Blackstone, *Commentaries on the Laws of England* (Chicago: University of Chicago Press, 1979), 4:169.

[17] *Funk & Wagnalls New Comprehensive International Dictionary of the English Language*, s.v. "eavesdrop."

"Eavesdrop: to stand within the 'wavesdrop' of a house in order to listen to secrets; hence, to listen secretly to private conversation. Also trans. To listen secretly to (conversation); formerly also, to listen within the 'eavesdrop' of (a house); to listen to the secrets of (a person)." *Oxford New English Dictionary*, s.v. "eavesdrop."

eavesdropping now offends a distinct interest in privacy. No longer does the faithful protection of land interests reflect the full set of ordinary expectations that people have about each other. The question, therefore, is how to think about the protection of privacy in those cases that go beyond the established forms of common law protection.

It is at this point that we have to recognize the limitations inherent in the normal libertarian rules that protect both person and property against the use of force and fraud. The facile explanation is that so long as there is no trespass, there is no wrong. But the correct response is to invoke the last of our simple rules and to fashion a generalized right of privacy that goes beyond trespass and works on average to the long-term benefit of all. Any creation of a property right necessarily imposes some limitation on the natural liberties of other individuals to do what they want with their own bodies or land. The justification for these limits comes from the greater long-term gains that a system of private property provides, which is why its defenders rightly rely on metaphors about the need to reap where one has sown. One key question is whether the last ounce of reciprocal net gains has been achieved by the trespass law. The insistent demands for, and the broad support of, a separate privacy interest give us good reason to think that it has not.

The intuition starts from the simple observation that the prohibition against eavesdropping and similar forms of behavior satisfies the condition of formal equality. There are no self-selected individuals who remain outside the prohibition. At one level, the rule embodies a strong reciprocal element, which is not found in skewed impositions that apply to some individuals but not to all. Standing alone, however, the condition of formal equality is also consistent with an outcome of dual ruin, in which both parties chafe under restrictions that each would like to remove.

In this instance, however, we can glean evidence against that unhappy outcome from another quarter, by looking to the analogous voluntary arrangements that govern the same issue. Thus we may ask whether a condominium association would pass some general rule to stop eavesdropping should it become a common practice. Or we can note, right now, the strong social custom that makes it inappropriate for individuals at one table in a restaurant to seek to overhear private conversations (the use of the phrase is suggestive) at another. The norm allows the removal of partitions that might otherwise be required and a reduced separation between tables, thereby lowering the cost of basic service. No one claims that this norm is perfect in all regards. One would not discuss highly confidential information about a desirable chemical formula nor announce the combination to a safe in a crowded restaurant, given the obvious risks. But we have, at the very least, a social norm that seems to improve the use of crowded spaces, both public and private, for less sensitive matters. The eager embrace of these practices accounts in large measure for the social recognition of the privacy interest.

This norm gives us a window into the general constitutional prohibition against unreasonable searches and seizures.[18] A quick inspection of the text of the Fourth Amendment shows how powerfully "thing-oriented" it is in its basic conception: "The right of the people to be secure in their person, houses, papers, and effects, against unreasonable searches and seizures, shall not be violated, and no warrant shall issue, but upon probable cause, supported by Oath or affirmation, particularly describing the place to be searched, and the persons or things to be seized." Both the global protection against unreasonable searches and seizures and the more particular protection of the warrant clause are clear that only places are searched, and only persons or things are seized. But what if the government decides to conduct its "search" not by entry but by eavesdropping, perhaps with powerful electronic equipment that operates at a distance? One possible response would be for the courts to wash their hands of the entire affair. If one concluded that this snooping counted as neither a search nor a seizure, then neither the question of reasonableness nor of warrants would arise at all. Yet this position could not be sustained in the long run, for the same transformation as in the private law of trespass took place in the public sphere as well. As a good rule of thumb, the principle of limited government should caution us against the creation of a "second set of books"—against, that is, giving ordinary terms special meanings—in developing on an ad hoc basis the relationship between the individual and the state. The possibility of slippage with the creation of ad hoc rules could usher in an era of serious abuse. That is one lesson learned from the elastic rendition of the police power.[19] Only when linked to the common law conception of nuisance does the police power offer a viable sense of what acts the government may enjoin without compensation. Unmoored from its private law background, just about anything can be deemed a nuisance, so that government supremacy in land planning is secured by what amounts to a play on words.[20]

In this privacy setting, we face exactly the same situation; the last of our simple rules has been extended in the private sphere to prevent intrusions through snooping and prying into individual space. The same restrictions could, and should, apply to the government. As a textual matter, that result is most easily obtained by recognizing that government searches of persons, houses, papers, and effects can take place from afar—as with a searchlight—without the need for any trespass to trigger the constitutional guarantee. These searches have long been regarded as improper

[18] U.S. Constitution, amend. 4.

[19] For recent Supreme Court expositions, see *Lucas* and *Dolan v. City of Tigard*, 512 U.S. 574 (1994).

[20] For discussion, see Richard A. Epstein, *Takings: Private Property and the Power of Eminent Domain* (Cambridge, MA: Harvard University Press, 1985), chaps. 9 and 10.

when undertaken by private parties,[21] and it is but a small giant-step, so to speak, to hold that a "search" under the Fourth Amendment is subject to the same transformation that animates the private law.[22] All this is not to say that devices may never search from afar: the basic text says that the individual right of "security" is only against "unreasonable" search and seizures. The government, therefore, should be able to show that certain searches are reasonable, for example, because of an imperative need to discover evidence that is about to be destroyed. My point here is not to explore the set of justifications that could be developed under this relatively open-ended constitutional norm. It is only to insist on parity between the two kinds of searches, thereby precluding a lower standard of justification for searches at a distance than for those that involve the direct entry onto someone else's property.

Up to this point, the notion of privacy extends the perimeter of rights around an individual in a manner generally consistent with the libertarian approach. The question now is how much further the law should extend the right of privacy. In this regard, it is useful to consider two possible extensions. The first concerns the preservation of the right of privacy within public space. The second concerns the extension of the right of privacy to cover cases where individuals say hurtful things about other individuals, without prying or spying into their lives.

B. Privacy on the commons

In speaking of the commons, I do not mean anything more complicated than an area, such as a highway or park, from which no one can be excluded but which no one is able to privatize. Within the commons, the danger of inconsistent uses is evident, and these can only be ironed out by a set of regulations that impose correlative limits on the rights of various users. To give a simple example, it is hard to justify any rule that prevents people from walking about naked in the privacy of their own homes. Yet it makes sense to impose limitations of this sort for people on public roads and, for the most part, public beaches. The danger of this rule is that it does not give any weight to people whose preferences run in the opposite direction; to accommodate them, it may be sensible to set aside some public beaches on which nude bathing is allowed. Indeed, in many European and Latin American countries the general social norms have switched enough to tolerate women going about bare-breasted on ordinary beaches, a practice that has not taken hold in the United States.

The same concern about use rights on the commons covers the question of privacy. Thus, one must ask to what extent individuals should be

---

[21] Two of the early cases were *Roach v. Harper*, 105 S.E.2d 564 (W. Va. 1958) (landlord used hearing device to listen to tenant's private conversations); and *Rhodes v. Graham*, 37 S.W.2d 46 (Ky. 1931) (tapping telephone wires).

[22] *Katz v. United States*, 389 U.S. 347 (1967).

forced to moderate their conduct in public spaces to respect the privacy of others. One obvious example is that it is generally regarded as wholly improper to closely follow another individual on the public sidewalk. It is probably actionable as a matter of tort law to "shadow" other individuals in public spaces, whether or not the event is observed by others. Thus, the "overzealous surveillance" of others, often public figures, has generally been treated as an invasion of privacy, even when it takes place on public streets. This conclusion holds even if (what is inescapable) "mere observation" does not create any liability.[23] The rule makes sense in light of the reciprocal nature of the rights and duties in question. A prohibition against looking at other individuals on a public street would impose limitations that ruin its utility for everyone concerned. If that prohibition is, however, confined to extreme and infrequent forms of conduct for which, at an intelligent guess, the balance of convenience supports restriction, then it makes sense. On one level, following closely on another person's heel looks a bit like an assault, and thus an ordinary common law tort, even if no physical contact is made. On another, if it is done in plain view, it partakes a bit of defamation, as though the shadower had some reason to follow the other person, which is then communicated to the rest of the world.[24] Even short of shadowing, the norm regarding taking pictures of other individuals in public places remains elusive. For the most part, tort law will not intervene, but some clear social sanctions will be invoked if someone purposively takes individual photographs of people walking down the street. The matter becomes the source of intense litigation when paparazzi go to inordinate lengths to bag their quarry.

C. Immunity from comment or criticism

There are, however, other instances where claims of reciprocal, long-term advantage fail to justify an extension of the right to privacy. To see where the breaking points develop, suppose that the claim of privacy is no longer tied to some particular invasion or intrusion by either the state or another individual. Thus, there are many things I might wish to keep private about my past or present activities, and it is seductive to claim, by way of analogy to cases of shadowing or snooping, that other people cannot speak of these things, either in public or in private, without my consent. This idea has its mischievous analogue in other cases. The idea of "harm" can be easily unlinked from its close connection with force or fraud to cover those cases where individuals suffer from the competition

---

[23] *Nader v. General Motors*, 255 N.E.2d 765, 771 (N.Y. 1970).
[24] *Schultz v. Frankfort Marine Accident & Plate Glass Ins. Co.*, 139 N.W. 386 (Wis. 1913), followed in *Restatement (Second) of Torts*, sec. 568, illus. 1 (1977).

of others.[25] In principle, these forms of competitive harms might become candidates for liability under some version of the harm principle. But this proposed transformation of the common law rules will fail, given the superior output that competitive markets yield over their economic rivals. A balkanized society, in which established players may block new entrants and thus continue to hold their customers in thrall, is a recipe for stagnation on a grand scale. The price of competitive harms in some transactions is paid to liberate the far greater productive powers of a free market system.

The extension of privacy to things about me that I would like to keep secret suffers, or should suffer, the same fate as the desire to expand the idea of harm to cover competitive losses. It is one thing to spy and pry on another individual. It is quite another to comment on his latest play, his new outfit of clothes, or his general health or pallor. Cumulatively, this information is of great value to all individuals in deciding whom to deal with and why, both in business and social settings. An organized society that allowed aggrieved individuals to ban the unfavorable comments of others comes close to being a police state. The liberty of conscience and thought depends on the free circulation of ideas, and it would create a nightmare of epic proportions to envision a system in which A gave consent to X to talk about his interactions with B, while B demanded silence on the same transaction: no one could ever complete the multiple transactions needed to unravel the legal knot. The right of fair comment had been established at common law long before the First Amendment was thought to control these things. The common law right was based in part on the commendable ground that the critic or commentator could be restrained in his pronouncements by the fact that his remarks in the public domain were subject to the like criticisms of others.[26]

Another way to see the same point is to note the twisted relationship between this form of privacy and the law of defamation, which makes it prima facie tortious to publish a *false* comment about the plaintiff to some third party that leads him to lower his estimation of her or otherwise refuse to do business with her.[27] Here we do not have to worry about any misapplication of the fundamental prohibition against force or fraud. The fact that the false statement of fact is made *about* the plaintiff to a third party, rather than *to* the plaintiff, only increases its danger. The plaintiff will be able to mount defenses when confronted with these false statements. But when these statements are part of a whispering campaign

[25] For my discussion of this theme, see Richard A. Epstein, *Principles for a Free Society: Reconciling Individual Liberty with the Common Good* (Reading, MA: Perseus Books, 1998), chap. 3.

[26] See, e.g., *Carr v. Hood*, 170 Eng. Rep. 981 (K.B. 1808).

[27] The classical definition of defamation is that of Baron Parke, which refers to a statement that "is calculated to injure the reputation of another, by exposing him to hatred, contempt, or ridicule." *Parmiter v. Coupland*, 151 Eng. Rep. 340, 342 (Ex. 1840). For the various limitations on the definition, see Epstein, *Torts*, 478–87.

behind her back, they may lead third parties to shun her so that she is unable to mount the deserved counterattack.

The risk of unmerited third-party shunning is far lower if the statements are true (and here for the moment, I shall assume that this means the truth, the whole truth, and nothing but the truth). Now all individuals are given better information to make more accurate choices about whether to do business with the criticized person or group. The key question is whether society in the aggregate flourishes with less information or with more information. Obviously, we shall have to make exceptions (as for military secrecy) when we move to a regime of open information. Yet there is little doubt that we are better off as a group in an open than in a closed society.

Thus, the right to privacy, sensibly construed, leads us one step past the common law rules of trespass by imposing restrictions on snooping. But the logic that allows for forced exchanges (under rule 6) does nothing to compel us to take the additional step of treating true but unflattering comments as invasions of privacy. The boundary line between truth and falsity becomes critical. The key question is how well that line can be policed.

At one level, the answer is: fairly well. The definition of truth that is used in ordinary two-party misrepresentation cases can easily be carried over to deal with the more complex tripartite scenario whenever publication is made about the plaintiff to a third party. At this point, it is easy to understand how the constitutional pressures now run in the opposite direction. No longer do we prop up the Fourth Amendment to expand claims of privacy. Now we invoke, under the First Amendment, a newsworthiness privilege that prevents the state from blocking the publication of any true account of matters of public interest and concern. Newsworthiness is defined not by the state, but by the individual or institution that publishes the true story in the first place.[28]

As with all privileges, it is possible to identify cases in which the assertion of newsworthiness leads to regrettable consequences. The cases that seem to call for the greatest unease are those in which newspapers reveal the names of rape victims available from the public record,[29] those in which gay activist groups or others choose to "out" people who otherwise wish to keep their sexual orientation private,[30] and those in which

---

[28] *Virgil v. Time, Inc.*, 527 F.2d 1122, 1128–29 (9th Cir. 1975). Once again, we see the same pattern that we saw in the nuisance cases. When the Supreme Court cares about constitutional doctrine, it migrates back to the common law baselines. In *Virgil*, the court announced that the provisions contained in the *Restatement (Second) of Torts*, secs. 652A–E, set out, albeit unintentionally, the First Amendment standard for the newsworthiness privilege. For an early recognition of the privilege, see *Sidis v. F-R Publishing Co.*, 113 F.2d 806 (2d Cir. 1940); adopted in *Restatement (Second) of Torts*, sec. 652D, illus. 19.

[29] *Cox Broadcasting Corp. v. Cohn*, 420 U.S. 469 (1975), accepted in *Restatement (Second) of Torts*, sec. 652D, cmt. d and illus. 12.

[30] *Sipple v. Chronicle Publishing Co.*, 201 Cal. Rptr. 665 (Cal. App. 1984).

individuals dredge up long-forgotten misdeeds of individuals who have made a return to respectability.[31] One point in favor of the broad newsworthiness privilege is that public reaction, often bordering on outrage, will lead to sensible forms of self-regulation. Today, most media outlets will not publish the names of rape victims, even if these names appear in other newspapers, until the matter becomes one of common notoriety. Similarly, "outing" can easily lead to a public backlash against the groups that engage in it. As matters stand, it is very difficult to identify any clear *content-based* limitation on the newsworthiness privilege in privacy cases.

D. Broadcast of illegally seized information

The most troublesome questions in the broadcasting of illegally seized information arise at the intersection of two rights: the one that prohibits trespass and the other that protects publication from suit. In cases where individuals trespass or eavesdrop merely for their own titillation, it becomes very difficult to assert any public interest in their conduct. The matter becomes much more vexed when the acquired information is then published to the world at large. To make the case most vivid, assume for the moment that the methods of acquisition involve a trespass (or some invasion of privacy that is for these purposes akin to a trespass). The critical question is whether the ends justify the means: does the public release of true information justify the trespass? Is the individual owner of the property entitled to damages that compensate, not only for any physical entry or property damage, but also for the consequential losses that follow from the publication of the information?

The legal response to this question has been divided, but the clear movement has been toward a greater recognition of a newsworthiness privilege even in trespass cases. The first judicial foray into this area was in a case decided in 1971, *Dietemann v. Time, Inc.*[32] *Time's* investigative reporters were in league with the local district attorney. Together, they went to Dietemann's home office, where they posed as patients for the plaintiff's quack medical treatment in which he put his hand on the breast of *Time's* female reporter. The entire incident was recorded by secret cameras. *Time's* publication of the photographs netted the plaintiff $1,000 in damages, as Judge Hufstedler took the hard line that nothing in the First Amendment either excused or justified the trespasses that had taken place. In my view, the simplest way to think of the issue is to ask whether or not the plaintiff could have enjoined the activities of the defendant's reporters if he had known of their true intentions. Given the right to

---

[31] For one early attempt at establishing liability for harmful but truthful disclosures, see *Melvin v. Reid*, 297 P. 91, 93 (Cal. App. 1931) (explicitly recognizing "the right to pursue and obtain safety and happiness without improper infringements thereon by others").

[32] *Dietemann v. Time, Inc.*, 449 F.2d 245 (9th Cir. 1971).

exclude, it seems clear that he could. That protection, however, does not insure him immunity against public revelation of information about his methods, if obtained by proper means. No doubt, the police could have obtained an appropriate search warrant if his conduct was illegal under some local law. It also seems clear that individual patients who entered for ordinary treatment are entitled to report about their treatment to others, including reporters, unless, perhaps, they sign some form of confidentiality agreement as a condition for treatment—a red flag that would send most customers scampering off in the opposite direction.

In this case, the use of hidden photographic equipment seems to extend beyond the implied license that most individuals extend for entry onto their property.[33] As that is the case, why should the defendants be allowed to benefit from their broadcast simply because their deception was successful in the first place? One possibility is to tie the damages awarded to an unjust-enrichment theory, so that the defendant has to disgorge all the profits that it obtained from the exercise. That remedy has the modest advantage of removing any incentive to engage in the wrong in the first place, on the assumption that a court or jury, after the fact, could tease out the portion of net profits that was attributable to this one article. In most cases, however, the plaintiff chooses the unjust-enrichment approach only when the defendant's gains from using the plaintiff's property exceed the plaintiff's losses.[34] But in the usual case where the damage to the plaintiff exceeds the gain to the defendant, then the plaintiff is entitled to insist on ordinary tort damages. In this instance, the plaintiff will urge that the appropriate baseline constitutes the state of affairs before the publication of the damaging report, which includes whatever peace and solitude that the plaintiff enjoyed. It was clearly this theory on which the plaintiff proceeded in *Dietemann*.

Subsequent cases have taken a dimmer view to protecting privacy from publication, but for reasons that seem far from overpowering. In *Howell v. New York Post* (1993),[35] the plaintiff, Howell, had been institutionalized at a psychiatric hospital with the knowledge of her immediate family, but no one else. The *Post* sent an investigative reporter to track down another patient. The reporter trespassed on hospital land and used a telephoto lens to take a picture of Hedda Nussbaum rehabilitating with friends, including Howell. Nussbaum had been the live-in lover of Joel Steinberg,

---

[33] Note, in dealing with this issue, I take the position that there is no class of private property that "is affected with the public interest" just because customers have been allowed to enter as a matter of course. That implied license is, of course, valid until countermanded. But it is not as though it converts the land to some form of quasi-public property. In order for that to take place, some form of a dedication is generally required, which might apply to a public way, but not to a closed office. Obviously, the entire civil rights movement is in tension with this view, at least where the denial to entry is done on grounds of race, sex, or national origin. See *The Civil Rights Act of 1964*, 42 U.S.C. secs. 2003 et seq.

[34] See, e.g., *Phillips v. Homfray*, 24 Ch. D. 439 (1883).

[35] *Howell v. New York Post*, 612 N.E.2d 699 (N.Y. 1993).

who was involved in a terrible killing of their daughter, six-year-old Lisa Steinberg. The medical director of the hospital begged the *Post* not to run the story with Howell's picture in it, but was rebuffed. The New York Court of Appeals held that the *Post* was within the newsworthiness privilege because a cropped picture, without Howell, would not have given the public an accurate impression of the course of Nussbaum's recuperation.

What is one to make of all this? No one questioned the right of the *Post* to publish public information about Hedda Nussbaum. But, ironically, the belated recognition of the privacy interest has led to an odd setback in the protection of privacy. Courts have learned the lesson that trespass is not critical to the issue, for indeed this situation would not differ materially if the defendant's reporter had stayed off the grounds only to use a stronger photographic lens, or had taken the picture from public airspace above the hospital. The sensible accommodation is to treat both forms of intrusion, trespassory and nontrespassory, as actionable, but the current view gives recourse against neither. Indeed, one frightening implication of *Howell* seems to be that if the hospital staff had discovered the intrusion before the picture was taken, they could not have prevented the reporter from taking his picture. So much for the right to be left alone.

Another case, somewhat closer to the line, is *Desnick Eyes Serv. v. ABC* (1995),[36] in which Chief Judge Posner refused to award damages for invasion of privacy against ABC's *PrimeTime Live*, which sent its reporters to secretly tape the defendant's practice of recommending unnecessary surgery to his patients. The case follows the familiar pattern of allowing parties to publish with impunity information that they had no right to obtain by deception in the first place. Here again, the principles of *Dietemann* seem to govern, for it hardly makes a difference in principle that one person operated his business out of his home while a second ran his in an ordinary doctor's office. To justify the result, Posner offers a set of flawed examples to show that fraud is sometimes acceptable in ordinary affairs. Thus, he notes that it is a common practice for restaurant reviewers to conceal their identity from the proprietors of the restaurants they review. But his point hardly suffices. If the restaurants were called in advance, and told that *Chicago Magazine* would only run anonymous reviews, I have no doubt that these restaurants would accept that condition. The negative inferences that could be drawn from a restaurant's refusal to allow any reviews would be devastating. Alternatively, if a positive review had first been cleared by the restaurant, it would be dismissed with contempt by readers—think only of the fierce customer reaction to Amazon.com's bright idea of taking a handsome fee for allowing publishers, unbeknownst to customers, to run favorable reviews of their own works. Customers demand and receive a bold set of assurances that the line between reviews and advertisements is scrupulously observed. So the secret restaurant critic,

---

[36] *Desnick Eyes Serv. v. ABC*, 44 F.3d 1345 (7th Cir. 1995).

who publishes an unbiased report, will receive a very different reception from the restaurant owner than will the investigative crew that will publish dirt if it finds it, and kill the story if it does not.

Posner's second comparison involves dinner guests who conceal their true opinion about their host's dinner party. The example is intended to bolster his argument that fraud is acceptable in a wide range of contexts. But again the argument overgeneralizes from a specific social practice with a discrete social function. We all engage in some white lies to ease social interactions and to avoid unnecessary embarrassment and pain. These social conventions are not done in order to cast public aspersions on the host; nor would it be considered good form to broadcast an honest critique of a private dinner party. This instance of fraud is not meant to berate the target, or to make him part with his money, but to smooth over interactions in the long haul. There is no anticipated harm from these white lies, and the situation thus bears little resemblance to the media publication of information obtained by illegal means.

The widespread publication of the information in *Desnick* takes the case out of the domain of intimate social interactions and into the world of mass publication, where, as with the tort of defamation, it looks as though the case pits the plaintiff's private interests against those of the public at large. But in one key particular these cases of intrusion-with-publication function quite differently from the ordinary defamation case. In defamation cases, the publication of *false* information is a harm not only to the person who is defamed, but also to the public at large who hears the defamation and becomes less informed in consequence. The modern view is to recognize a qualified privilege that, in cases involving public figures, can only be overridden by proof of actual malice (which, for these purposes, constitutes statements known to be false or made in reckless disregard as to whether they are true or false).[37] Even for private figures, some proof of negligence is required. The privilege is subject to attack on the ground that public debate is not enhanced by the dissemination of false information; such information only misleads the public. In the invasion-of-privacy cases, however, the information published by the defendant is *true* by assumption, so the inquiry comes down to this: is the asserted public gain from publishing truthful information sufficient to offset the loss sustained by the deliberate violation of private rights brought about by the fraudulent entry?

Making these judgments is tricky, because they cannot be vindicated in any obvious sense by showing that all individuals are on net better off by this deviation from the libertarian norms against force and fraud. Quite the opposite, a privilege of publication in cases of this sort will guarantee that one party suffers large uncompensated losses for the benefit of others. The loss can be minimized by announcing in advance a general rule that

---

[37] The key case on this point is still *New York Times v. Sullivan*, 376 U.S. 254 (1964).

places all parties on notice of the basic principle. But even so, the question remains whether the gains to the general public are sufficiently large to justify the creation of a privilege for a broadcaster to inflict substantial harm on the targets of its investigations. That question is genuinely close. One point against recognizing the privilege is that the publication of tortiously obtained information is not the only way for the press to investigate possible business irregularities. They can also use interviews with former customers. Parallel investigations may also be undertaken by public authorities with licensing power, or by private individuals who believe that they have been bilked out of money. Indeed, any absence of individual complaints is some evidence that the problem in the operation of Desnick's clinics might not have been as great as the *PrimeTime Live*'s broadcast suggested.

This last observation leads to the larger question of the definition of truth. Unlike the restaurant critic, investigative reporters by design publish only negative material. Often they package it in suggestive ways. Thus, suppose that reporters are tipped that the cleanliness at one XYZ restaurant is well below the average level of the chain. Investigative reporters then catch footage of rats and roaches on one of ten visits to that restaurant. They do not call health inspectors and no citations are issued; no customers report any ill effects. A publication that says that XYZ has rats in its restaurants is true in a sense. But it creates the systematically false impression that the condition in the worst restaurant represents the average quality of the chain. The question is whether this particular instance counts as the truth when the party who runs the story knows that it has not been duplicated in other situations. Matters are even worse if the broadcaster also knows that the rate of health violations in XYZ's competitors is the same as it is for XYZ. My own (minority) view is that the law of defamation should require, as it does not, that the defendant speak the truth, the whole truth, and nothing but the truth. If the publisher knows that its viewers will draw systematically misleading conclusions from the published stories, then it should be treated as telling false stories. The situation is in reality no different from a social scientist who runs one hundred regressions to examine the correlation between two variables, and chooses to publish only those results that support the connection that he wishes to establish. The nondisclosure of the other runs counts as a clear breach of scientific ethics. In dealing with cases of selective disclosure, lines have to be drawn, and the plaintiff should have the burden of showing that a story that is true in isolation is false in context. That standard is not insurmountable, for it is applied by courts to the incomplete statements that the issuers of new stock make in a securities prospectus. In those cases liability can be imposed for the nondisclosure of material facts, and often is.[38]

---

[38] See, e.g., *Texas Gulf Sulphur Co. v. J. R. Simplot Co.*, 418 F.2d 793 (1969).

Nonetheless, my preferred approach is not the law today, given the scope of the newsworthiness privilege, and the unwillingness of courts to weigh what is said against what has happened. As that is the case, we can no longer assume that these cases of investigative revelation pit a positive externality to the world against the negative aspects of the trespass to the plaintiff. Now, in cases of selective disclosure, the statement of "truth" has both negative and positive aspects, where the former could easily outweigh the latter. At that point, the case for the newsworthiness privilege on overall social grounds becomes far weaker. For myself, I think that on balance the view in *Dietemann*—that the publication of truthful information deceptively acquired is a fair shot for private damages—is troubled, but correct.

IV. Contract and Privacy

The issue of privacy must also be understood in relationship to the law of contract. Here the initial point of departure is that individuals by agreement can regulate the use of information that they share with each other. The common law position on trade secrets, for example, takes the position that individuals are allowed to keep quiet by contract such matters as formulas and trade lists.[39] The right to keep this information concealed means that the paradigmatic wrong is the disclosure of the information to the public at large or to competitors because of the loss of the competitive advantage that trade secrets normally secure.

It would be, however, a major mistake to assume that trade secrets are the only kinds of information that parties are allowed to keep private by contract. The ordinary interaction between patient and physician involves the transfer of sensitive information about the patient's condition to the physician, normally under a guarantee of confidentiality. That confidentiality is breached by *truthful* disclosures to third persons who are not authorized to receive the information in question. The clear upshot is that the scope of the duty of confidentiality is determined by contract, and that the duty normally follows the information into the hands of authorized third parties. Thus, researchers who receive information about individual patients are required to respect personal confidences and not reveal any names, in the publication of their overall reports. It follows, therefore, that the law of contract operates much like the law of trespass. Although contract's primary objective is to secure the exchange of property and labor between persons, it can easily be extended to protect the proper transfer of information in both personal and business contexts.

---

[39] *Ruckelshaus v. Monsanto, Inc.*, 467 U.S. 986, 1001 (1984), which relied on the definition of trade secrets in *Restatement of Torts*, sec. 757. The case offers (in addition to the definition of nuisance, and the scope of the privacy interest) a third instance where *Restatement* definitions end up doing double duty as constitutional norms.

Much of the modern concern with the right to privacy arises in these consensual situations. Information is easily divisible and reproducible; unlike land it can be given away with one hand and retained with the other. Its transmission can be welcomed for some purposes and feared for others. Only a strong system of internal controls can ensure that information is used for some purposes but not for others. Only a reliable system of contracts can devise the permissible splits: a law firm may use sensitive financial information to determine how to defend a corporation from a takeover bid, but not to allow its partners to trade in shares of the client for their own accounts.

At this point, privacy once again fits snugly within the framework of classical liberal values. Yet, some of the most controversial applications of the right of privacy seem to me to be deeply unprincipled. In dealing with privacy in the tort context, I indicated that any protection of privacy always raised the risk of fraud, and I tried to indicate the reasons why this form of fraud could be justified as a way to ward off media investigators and ordinary voyeurs. The situation becomes, however, quite different when claims of privacy are invoked not to support, but to override the principle of freedom of contract. Common illustrations of this come from many sources. A job applicant may have had a criminal record or may suffer from a serious medical condition. An employer might wish to know about these things in order to decide whether to make an offer, but the law may prevent him from inquiring. The general rule of freedom of contract says that, in competitive markets at least, a person may refuse to deal for good reason, for bad reason, or for no reason at all. The point of this rule is not to celebrate irrational behavior, but to avoid the morass that arises in deciding both the factual and legal questions as to which refusals to deal are for "good cause" and which are not.

In monopoly-type situations, a duty not to discriminate is introduced as a counterweight to monopoly power.[40] Yet most labor markets are highly competitive, so the original preference for freedom of contract holds, on the ground that the asserted irrationality of one party is best countered by taking one's business to another. It is a commonplace feature of modern life to regard this limitation on a firm's power as insufficient in a number of contexts. With respect to juvenile criminal records, it is said that the information should be concealed in order to encourage past wrongdoers to get a fresh start on a clean slate. The fear is that former offenders will not be able to gain jobs if dogged by their criminal record, thereby undercutting the incentives for rehabilitation.

The argument has some power, but it does not go far enough. The object of a system of criminal sanctions is to minimize the number of violations, cost of prevention held constant. The efforts to protect juvenile criminal records may enhance rehabilitation—which operates to the good.

---

[40] For a longer discussion, see Epstein, *Principles for a Free Society*, chap. 10.

But ex ante, the rule reduces the expected cost to the juvenile of the initial crime by lessening the social sting of a criminal conviction. The overall empirical argument depends on the relative strength of these two effects (before and after the initial incident), a proposition on which it is hard, to say the least, to obtain reliable evidence.

There is, however, a second feature of the practice of expunging criminal records that is more germane to the issue of contractual freedom. The information in question is surely material to the decision of any prospective employer. Past criminal conduct is correlated with the likelihood of future criminal conduct. The hiring could easily increase exposure to theft or personal violence for the employer and other employees, for which civil and criminal sanctions after the fact are at best imperfect remedies. The state-sanctioned concealment of this information thus works a material fraud on the employer for which the state offers inadequate compensation should matters turn awry. No longer are we dealing with the amiable white lies that people use to keep their indigestion secret from their hosts. Now, the object of the concealment is not defensive; it is not to be left alone. It is to give a false impression in order to gain an advantage that exposes the person and property of others to substantial risk. Context matters. When someone conceals illness to avoid a host's social embarrassment, little is lost. When he does so to obtain employment for which he is unfit, the resulting consequences could prove enormous.

My own view in these cases remains that of the unrepentant libertarian. The employer can ask any question of the prospective employee that she wants. The applicant may refuse to answer. In the end, the two can decide whether the information is more valuable when kept private or when shared. In many cases, the personal life of an employee will be regarded as information to which the employer has no right. If so, it will not be because of some high first principle, but because of the joint recognition that the information is worth less to the employer than its concealment is worth to the employee. Let the employee receive comprehensive benefits from the employer, such as health care, and the calculus may well shift radically: now it does matter whether the employee drinks, smokes, or exercises on a regular basis. If that information is relevant to an insurer in setting a risk, then it is relevant to the employer who has to foot the bill for the long-term health plan. The key point here is that there is no transcendent public-regarding view of what counts as relevant information for an employer. Even on such matters as intimate sexual practices, an employer could ask, for example, about the risk of AIDS. In most cases, however, it will be detrimental for the employer to ask about sexual practices because of the ill will such questions generate. But we should not confuse a social regularity with some hovering legal standard of privacy. Whatever regularities are observed in practice should not conceal the point that in each individual case we have only the exercise of the joint judgment of the contracting parties.

This position is, however, in massive disrepute today in large numbers of contexts.[41] The entire structure of the Americans with Disabilities Act of 1990 works on the premise that handicap discrimination is impermissible in employment relationships. That position is not enforceable if the employer is allowed to consider sensitive medical information in deciding whether to hire individual workers or in deciding whether or not to include them in the firm's health plan.[42] An overwhelming public consensus has erected an employee right of privacy around this information, so that strong civil and criminal sanctions are brought against any employer (and in some settings, any insurer) who seeks to uncover the risk and price accordingly.[43] Further proposals are afoot, for example, to make it impermissible to require the release of any sensitive information about employees' genetic predispositions to certain conditions, be it Huntington's disease or breast cancer.[44]

The implicit logic of this position is to reverse the classical rules of insurance contracting, which imposed on the insured a duty to disclose any risk or condition that might affect the insurer's risk.[45] The net effect of the new rules is to force employers and low-risk coworkers to undertake the high risk of certain employees, for which they receive no compensation at all. The practice will obviously encourage spirited efforts to

[41] Paul R. Billings, Mel A. Kohn, Margaret de Cuevas, and Jonathan Beckwith, "Discrimination as a Consequence of Genetic Testing," *American Journal of Human Genetics* 50, no. 3 (March 1992): 476–82. See also Joseph S. Alper and Marvin R. Natowicz, "Genetic Discrimination and the Law," *American Journal of Human Genetics* 50, no. 3 (March 1992): 465–75.

[42] I discuss the question at far greater length in Richard A. Epstein, *Mortal Peril: Our Inalienable Right to Health Care?* (Reading, MA: Addison-Wesley, 1997), chaps. 6 and 7. See also Richard A. Epstein, "The Legal Regulation of Genetic Discrimination: Old Responses to New Technology," *Boston University Law Review* 74, no. 1 (January 1994): 1–23.

[43] See, e.g., Me. Rev. Stat. Ann. tit. 24, sec. 5011(1)(A) (West 1997): "Rates for policies subject to this subsection may not vary based on age, gender, health status, claims experience, policy duration, industry or occupation."

[44] For recommendations on breast cancer, see, e.g., Barbara A. Koenig et al., "Genetic Testing for BRCA1 and BRCA2: Recommendations of the Stanford Program in Genomics, Ethics, and Society," *Journal of Women's Health* 7, no. 5 (June 1998): 531–45. "Privacy legislation must be strengthened as one part of a strategy to limit genetic discrimination. Employers and insurers should be prevented from making decisions based on genetic information by putting health professionals and others who have access to the information under an obligation not to disclose it." Ibid., 532.

The recommendation comes after this description of the sad state of medical services: "In addition, genetic services are delivered within a social context described by King as shaped by 'a paternalistic medical establishment, an opportunistic biotechnology industry and a malevolent insurance industry.'" It is nice to be among friends. The reality? One recent *New York Times* story on the managed care syndrome notes that the industry's efforts at cost-containment have lagged because of its utter inability to enforce any of the planned restrictions on coverage. See Michael M. Weinstein, "Managed Care's Other Problem: It's Not What You Think," *New York Times*, February 28, 1999, sec. 4, p. 1: "Rarely a week goes by without a health maintenance organization getting hammered in the press or in court for denying payment for the care of a gravely ill patient." But the diagnosis of the key problem? "That problem is too many medical treatments rather than too few."

[45] *Lindenau v. Desborough*, 108 Eng. Rep. 1160 (C.P. 1828). See also Lord Mansfield's earlier opinion in *Carter v. Boehm*, 97 Eng. Rep. 1162 (1766). For a statutory recognition of the duty, see Marine Insurance Act, 1906, 6 Ed. 7, chap. 41, sec. 18(1).

tailor coverage in ways that minimize the risk, even if it means abandoning or reducing coverage to other employees whom the firm is willing to insure. In this context, moreover, there is at least the glimmer of a respectable compromise that has the benefit of transparency appropriate for deliberative democracies. The level of subsidy required for high-risk employees is the difference between the price that the market charges for covering disabled persons and its ordinary rates. Nothing prevents that differential cost from being placed on the government's budget, where it can be covered in full or in part, depending on the preferences of the community as a whole. Yet this approach has public costs that would be very visible, so the preferred solution is to create rights that limit contractual freedom and require the creation of hidden subsidies that are borne by some but not all firms. Karl Llewellyn once said that "covert tools are bad tools." That maxim applies in this case.

V. Conclusion

Privacy today is one of our most newsworthy topics, but it suffers from regrettable overuse. Sometimes claims of privacy are invoked in order to keep people apart, thus recognizing and enforcing our right to be left alone. Even within this broad category, it is necessary to distinguish between cases. Snooping and prying are the most obvious candidates for legal and social sanctions. At the other extreme, claims of privacy should fall flat when invoked to immunize individuals from comment and criticism. In between lie difficult cases in which people try to preserve some semblance of privacy in public places, or deal with the wide-scale dissemination of information acquired by illegal means but of great value to the public at large.

On the other side, a very different type of privacy claim often arises in connection with various consensual transactions. In this context, it is again necessary to make one critical distinction between privacy claims that grow out of contract, such as those arising in confidential arrangements, and privacy claims that are raised in opposition to contract, such as those arising out of the operation of antidiscrimination laws. In my view, the treatment of these two types of claims should be determined by our attitude toward contracts in general. For someone who starts with a market-oriented, classical liberal perspective, privacy claims should be respected when created by contract, but emphatically rejected when invoked to limit the freedom of exchange of information between trading partners.

In the end, the debate over the use and limitations of the privacy concept folds back into the larger ongoing debate over the use and limits of government power. The deconstruction of privacy depends on our ability to isolate the individual pieces of the puzzle for separate examination and review. The successful reconstruction of privacy is not something beyond our capacity, but depends on linking the analysis of privacy to more general theories of rights and duties, both legal and social.

Law, The University of Chicago

THE RIGHT TO PRIVACY*

By Lloyd L. Weinreb

I. Defining the Issue

The question that I address in this paper is whether there is a right to privacy. It is not the question whether in the United States there is a legal right to privacy or, more particularly, a constitutional right to privacy. There are any number of ordinary legal rights and specific constitutional rights that might be so described, and the U.S. Supreme Court has referred also to a generic "right to privacy" that is implicit in the U.S. Constitution.[1] Nor is the question that I address whether persons have a moral claim to privacy that others ought to respect. I assume that in many circumstances, respecting a person's claim to privacy is productive of the good and, if so, that the claim ought to be respected. Rather, my question is whether persons have a right to privacy not dependent on positive law, such that it ought ordinarily to be respected without regard to the consequences, good or bad, simply because it is right.

In what follows, I shall take it for granted that although rights have normative implications, the existence of a right is a matter of fact. For example, it is a matter of fact, answered by reference to the positive law, whether there is or is not a particular legal right. The law answers the question whether there is a legal right, not whether there ought to be one. Similarly, whether there is a right to privacy independent of the law is a matter of fact, which is answered by reference to what is the case. The ground of all human rights is autonomy—the capacity for freedom and moral responsibility—which distinguishes human beings from other kinds of beings and things generally and qualifies them, and only them, as persons. The rights that human beings, as persons, have are, simply, the conditions of responsibility; they follow directly from the proposition—a noncontestable, structural fact of our experience—that persons are autonomous. Each of those propositions, I recognize, is difficult and controversial. I have explained and defended them at length elsewhere and shall, without more, rely on them here.[2] The close connection between a right to privacy (if there is one) and autonomy is generally conceded; a reader

* Richard Fallon gave invaluable assistance in sorting out the arguments contained herein, without necessarily subscribing to any of them. Jacob Tyler helped greatly with editing tasks.

[1] *Griswold v. Connecticut*, 381 U.S. 479, 486 (1965).

[2] See Lloyd L. Weinreb, *Oedipus at Fenway Park: What Rights Are and Why There Are Any* (Cambridge, MA: Harvard University Press, 1994).

may accept that connection, at least provisionally, without addressing the general argument that explains and justifies it.

The whole subject of privacy is considerably muddled by the convergence of claims and arguments of very different kinds: that the desire for privacy is a natural and universal human characteristic; that there are many legal rights to privacy or that there is one overarching legal right that takes many particular forms; that privacy is inherently good or is generally productive of the good. At least one important strand in the discussion, which is not always clearly distinguished from the rest, represents privacy as a right that is not in any way dependent on positive law but stands behind and justifies particular legal rights. So, for example, in *Griswold v. Connecticut* (1965), Justice William O. Douglas based the conclusion that married couples have a constitutional right to use contraceptives in their bedroom on "a right of privacy older than the Bill of Rights."[3] Although he cited some prior cases as evidence that there is such a right, he did not indicate its source, whether some law higher than the Constitution, the community's long tradition, or something else; but there was no doubt that it was not in any sense merely positive law. Since *Griswold*, the right to privacy there stated has been a litmus test of one's constitutional credentials as a scholar or (would-be) judge: liberal or conservative, activist or textualist, and so forth. The question whether there is such a right and the constitutional question are not just the same, however. For one might believe that there is a right but that it is not embodied as such in the Constitution. It is only the former question with which I am concerned here.

The question is more than a matter of conceptual clarity. What is at stake, at bottom, is the ground or grounds on which the various claims to privacy, those that are recognized as legal rights as well as those that are not, are based: whether it is more than convention, or one side of the imponderable distinction between self- and other-regarding conduct, or, more narrowly focused, a common human desire to conceal or withhold from others certain information that they have some reason to want. An interest in privacy may rest on any of those grounds and may be a sufficient ground of a legal right, as a matter of social policy. A legal right so justified, however, is vulnerable to opposing arguments: that the convention is otiose and ought to be discarded, or that significant other-regarding aspects of conduct have been overlooked or undervalued, or that information obtained by methods that are not themselves objectionable is generally available to all for their use. Even if the legal right withstands such arguments, it may fall short of the privacy that is claimed. Conventions are stretched by novel practices unknown when the conven-

---

[3] *Griswold*, 381 U.S. at 486. The reference in the opinion to "the sacred precincts of marital bedrooms" (ibid., at 485) has been taken to be a reference to the Fourth Amendment. But the passage refers explicitly to "the notions of privacy surrounding the marriage relationship" (ibid., at 486).

tions took shape and require justification for their extension. Changing technology and new information alter the balance between what is self-regarding and what is not. Information that previously was confidential as a practical matter is generated, collected, and disseminated with an efficiency that shatters old compromises, and to those who want to use the information, can implies ought. One way or another, the contingency of a merely legal right seems less than we need if privacy is to be preserved.

In such a situation, the likely recourse is some version of a "natural right"; nature, we are accustomed to believe, has the durability and permanence that, left to our own devices, we must do without. That position, however, has proved difficult to sustain, more difficult even than most other natural-rights arguments. For one thing, the claimed privacies, including some that are regarded as basic in one place or another, are too variable among different communities. Some privacies, on the other hand, although legally recognized, seem altogether too circumstantial and ad hoc to be cloaked in the universal mantle of nature. With respect to informational privacies in particular, it is difficult to find in the natural order any footing for a right to the ignorance of others, even about information that concerns oneself.

Nature failing, a more promising approach is to cast the right to privacy as a civil right. As Justice Douglas's argument in *Griswold* suggested, it shares some of the characteristics of what are commonly regarded as civil rights. Despite its manifest variability from one community to another, failure to respect the right to privacy is frequently a basis for criticism of positive laws. Like civil rights generally, which appear in some manner to be objectively valid, privacy has both descriptive and normative content. "That's private" is both a statement of fact and a prescription of how one ought to behave. Privacy seems thus, as I characterized civil rights on another occasion, "to occupy a murky middle ground between natural (or human) rights on one hand and 'positive' legal rights on the other."[4] Those who defend the right to privacy typically speak of it in this way, not merely as a matter of desirable social policy but as a right that ought to be recognized, considerations of the social good aside. Yet, if there is a civil right to privacy, the grounds for so regarding it have not been shown.

Not the least of the difficulties about privacy is that it is so elusive. Just about anything may be private: persons, places, things, actions, words, thoughts, emotions—"whatever," as Seinfeld likes to say. It is not apparent what might join, say, a retired schoolteacher, a family cottage, a monkey wrench, singing in the shower, an expletive, speculation about the quality of mercy, and a suppressed rage, under the common umbrella of privacy. Evidently it has to do with a connection to some definite person; for whatever it is that is private, the privacy at stake attaches not to it but

---

[4] Lloyd L. Weinreb, "What Are *Civil* Rights?" in Ellen Frankel Paul, Fred D. Miller, Jr., and Jeffrey Paul, eds., *Reassessing Civil Rights* (Cambridge, MA: Blackwell, 1991), 2.

to someone. It is far from clear, however, what that connection is, unless it is privacy itself. Privacy largely conceived readily encompasses the argument against regulation of self-regarding conduct that Mill made the cornerstone of his defense of liberty.[5] But it is just as easy to think of privacy as an aspect of liberty; efforts of the government to collect personal data are often decried as an attack on liberty.[6] Privacy may include shelter from the presence of others. Yet privacy is not solitude, and it becomes an issue only in relation to others. Certain activities, mostly sexual or bodily functions, which are anything but secret or unusual, are private if anything is, but in this instance, privacy is as much an obligation as a privilege or right. Included prominently within this hodgepodge is informational privacy, having to do with a person's control over what is known about him, which itself takes various forms. An invasion of informational privacy may involve observing or listening to a person without his consent, in which case the notion of privacy as shelter also may be involved. Much more generally, the invasion of informational privacy includes any manner, unauthorized by the person himself, of obtaining information about him or collecting or distributing it, even if there is no actual intrusion on him personally. The mere fact that a person prefers that information be unknown to others does not make it private. It is neither necessary nor sufficient that the information be secret, or embarrassing, or out of the ordinary, or, indeed, anything except private. But what makes it private is not evident.[7]

The situation is scarcely better in the law, in which the content of a right is, perforce, more definite. The privacies that the law protects are not all of the same kind. Civil laws protecting property against trespass or conversion and criminal laws prohibiting burglary and theft are the most

---

[5] John Stuart Mill, *On Liberty*, in Mill, *Utilitarianism, Liberty, and Representative Government* (New York: E.P. Dutton, 1951), 81–229. See *Eisenstadt v. Baird*, 405 U.S. 438, 453 (1972): "If the right of privacy means anything, it is the right of the *individual*, married or single, to be free from unwarranted governmental intrusion into matters so fundamentally affecting a person as the decision whether to bear or beget a child." In the wake of the decision in *Griswold*, a number of scholars objected to the inclusion of liberty from regulation within the ambit of privacy. See, e.g., Louis Henkin, "Privacy and Autonomy," *Columbia Law Review* 74, no. 8 (December 1974): 1410–33. As a matter of constitutional law, I agree. The due process clause of the Fifth and Fourteenth Amendments is the constitutional locus of protection of liberty. As a nonconstitutional matter, however, the abstract notion of privacy incorporates liberty without difficulty. Cf. Judith Wagner DeCew, *In Pursuit of Privacy: Law, Ethics, and the Rise of Technology* (Ithaca, NY: Cornell University Press, 1997), 34–45.

[6] In the 1930s the Federal Bureau of Investigation promoted a campaign for universal fingerprinting, which was finally defeated, in part by the efforts of the American Civil Liberties Union, which published a pamphlet called "Thumbs Down" in 1938. The debate about fingerprinting is being replayed for higher stakes in the controversy about the collection and filing of DNA samples from sex offenders, or all serious criminals, or all of us. See *The New York Times*, October 12, 1998, p. A1; December 13, 1998, sec. 1, p. 51; and March 2, 1999, p. A15.

[7] Judith DeCew identifies three broad categories of privacy: informational privacy; accessibility privacy, having to do with what I have referred to as shelter; and expressive privacy, corresponding roughly to liberty. See DeCew, *In Pursuit of Privacy*, 75–78.

obvious examples, but there are other privacies that do not have to do with property at all. It has been questioned significantly whether we have need of an independent legal notion of a right to privacy, rather than depending on the rights that protect property and the person.[8] If we do have such need, it is at least true that the right to privacy piggybacks a good deal on those other rights, not only for its definition but also, much more, for its protection.[9] On the other hand, when Samuel Warren and Louis Brandeis wrote their groundbreaking article about the right to privacy, their point was precisely that seemingly distinct rights in disparate areas of the law were better regarded collectively as constituting a right to privacy.[10] In *Griswold*, Justice Douglas found traces of a right to privacy in four different amendments to the Constitution and a number of constitutional decisions, dealing with subjects as various as the quartering of soldiers and the education of one's children.[11] Whether it be one or many, if all its protean guises are taken into account, the legal right to privacy, much like the notion of privacy itself, eludes the usual classifications. It may have the aspect of a claim based on property as, for example, under the Fourth Amendment.[12] It may have the aspect of a claim in tort that restricts specific conduct, like its prohibition of unwelcome commercial exploitation of one's persona.[13] It may have something of both property and tort, as in cases involving a tangible or intangible intrusion into space occupied by another. The right to privacy seems paradigmatically to protect against official encroachment on "private" lives. On another front, however, it calls for the government to prevent individuals from encroaching on the lives of others.

It is scarcely surprising that the right to privacy is problematic, if it is so uncertain what it is a right *to*. The matter is complicated further because the notion of privacy has a resonance that informs many of its particular concrete forms. With rare exceptions, we think of privacy as a

---

[8] See Judith Jarvis Thomson, "The Right to Privacy," *Philosophy and Public Affairs* 4, no. 4 (Summer 1975): 295–314, reprinted in Ferdinand David Schoeman, ed., *Philosophical Dimensions of Privacy: An Anthology* (Cambridge: Cambridge University Press, 1984), 272–89.

[9] See, for example, the discussion of the basis for an expectation of privacy that the Fourth Amendment will protect, in *Rakas v. Illinois*, 439 U.S. 128, 144 n. 12 (1978): "Legitimation of expectations of privacy by law must have a source outside of the Fourth Amendment, either by reference to concepts of real or personal property law or to understandings that are recognized and permitted by society. One of the main rights attaching to property is the right to exclude others . . . and one who owns or lawfully possesses or controls property will in all likelihood have a legitimate expectation of privacy by virtue of this right to exclude."

[10] Samuel D. Warren and Louis D. Brandeis, "The Right to Privacy," *Harvard Law Review* 4, no. 5 (December 1890): 193–220, reprinted in Schoeman, ed., *Philosophical Dimensions of Privacy*, 75–103.

[11] See *Griswold*, 381 U.S. at 484. The four Amendments are the First (right of association), Third (prohibition against quartering of soldiers), Fourth (prohibition against unreasonable searches and seizures), and Fifth (privilege against compulsory self-incrimination).

[12] See note 9 above. See also *Minnesota v. Carter*, 525 U.S. 83 (1998).

[13] See, e.g., *Waits v. Frito-Lay, Inc.*, 978 F.2d 1093 (9th Cir. 1992); and *Midler v. Ford Motor Co.*, 849 F.2d 460 (9th Cir. 1988).

good that *belongs* to someone. Unsurprisingly, those two characteristics, without more, are easily translated into a right. The aura of a right may surround any aspect of privacy, a tendency of thought that is encouraged by a distinct, wholly abstract conception of privacy, which has not to do with any particular form of privacy but is only a reflection, as it were, of personal autonomy. That abstract conception is the subject of Section II. Discussion of a concrete right to privacy typically is more narrowly focused on informational privacy. Shelter from others, including the privacy of sexual and bodily functions, is usually subsumed within the rubric of private property, which engages issues quite apart from privacy itself. Self-regarding conduct is ordinarily discussed not as a matter of privacy but under the rubric of liberty. Justice Douglas's departure from that was evidently dictated by the disfavor with which "substantive due process of law" was then regarded.[14] Regarding rights as such as a function of autonomy, the question to be answered, then, is whether it is a condition or a consequence of autonomy that information relating to a person, in some way yet to be ascertained, not be disclosed or disseminated without his consent. That is the subject of Section III. Finally, in Section IV, I consider whether a right to privacy can be founded directly on the settled conventions of the community, whatever their basis.

II. Privacy as Autonomy

Few aphorisms in political philosophy are repeated as often as Aristotle's statement near the beginning of the *Politics* that "man is by nature a political animal."[15] That perception, that human beings acquire their distinctive nature in the company of other human beings, has been echoed in various forms countless times. Hobbes, for example, whose stringent reductionism and rigorous logic carried the argument to its conclusion, famously observed that outside a community bound together by normative conventions, the life of man would be "solitary, poor, nasty, brutish, and short"[16]—that is to say, not (fully) human. Without a community, he argued, there is lacking the predicate for responsible action, which distinguishes a human being from all other kinds of being and makes him a

---

[14] See the opinion of Justice Stewart, concurring in *Roe v. Wade*, 410 U.S. 113, 167 (1973). In the wake of the furor over the Supreme Court's decisions striking down New Deal social and economic legislation, e.g., *Carter v. Carter Coal Co.*, 298 U.S. 238 (1936) (declaring unconstitutional federal legislation regulating wages and conditions of work in the coalmining industry), the Court retreated from using the due process clause to limit the objectives of legislation and for many years regarded the clause as limited to matters of procedure. So-called "substantive due process" was revived, albeit in a different context, starting in the 1970s. E.g., *Roe* (declaring unconstitutional state criminal law prohibiting abortion).

[15] The complete statement is: "[T]he state is a creation of nature, and . . . man is by nature a political animal." Aristotle, *Politics*, 1253a1, trans. B. Jowett, in Jonathan Barnes, ed., *The Complete Works of Aristotle* (Princeton, NJ: Princeton University Press, 1984), 2:1987.

[16] Thomas Hobbes, *Leviathan*, ed. Michael Oakeshott (Oxford: Basil Blackwell, 1957), 82.

person. Whether the source of moral principles is traced to some extra-human source or, as Hobbes asserted, is within the community itself, it is a condition of responsibility, in the specifically human sense of freedom, that there be the company of other likewise responsible (human) beings.[17]

A community, on the other hand, is made up of individual human beings and, without contribution from them, has no existence as more than an aggregate of individuals. Locke reduced the contribution to a minimum, but even that minimum was large.[18] Both fundamentally and at a more practical level, the individual and the community are inter-dependent. It is clear from actual cases that an individual who has once acquired the sense of responsibility can sustain it and can maintain his existence in isolation from other persons.[19] Barring such extreme examples, it is the human condition to live in a community, meaning only an organized mode of coexistence with other human beings.

There is, therefore, a realm of individual life—to use the broadest, most inclusive term—that is public, in the very general sense that the community may properly take an interest in it. The least that is within this public realm is that which relates to the community's survival as a community. But in any circumstances other than those in which survival is an over-riding issue, the public realm includes far more, not only those matters in which the community as a whole is involved, but also those that involve oppositional human interaction—other-regarding conduct, in Mill's account of liberty[20]—and call on the resources of the community as the source of law and authorized dispenser of force.

That there is also, necessarily, a realm of life that is not public is perhaps not so obvious. That too, however, follows from the same premise, that it is the nature of human beings to live in community. For although they are subject to the will of the community so far as concerns its public life, as self-determining and morally responsible beings, persons may be said also to inhabit a private realm, in which they are autonomous. In this sense, privacy might be regarded as the face that autonomy presents to others similarly situated in the same community, merely one side of the abstract dichotomy between public and private: Whatever is public is not private, and whatever is private is not public. Used in this way, the two terms have meaning only in opposition to one another. There is no pri-

---

[17] Without such company, a being might become aware of its causal agency and the causal agency of other beings and, taking itself as a model, might even conceptualize differential causal agencies as a contest of wills; but without communication with another being like itself, it is difficult to see how any normative understanding sufficient to sustain notions of freedom, responsibility, and desert—autonomy, in short—could arise. See Weinreb, *Oedipus at Fenway Park*, 142–46.

[18] See John Locke, *Second Treatise of Government*, in Locke, *Two Treatises of Government*, ed. Peter Laslett (Cambridge: Cambridge University Press, 1960), 283–446.

[19] There have been cases, for example, of Japanese soldiers who remained alone and in hiding for years after the Japanese military forces retreated from islands in the Pacific.

[20] See Mill, *On Liberty*, 95–96.

macy between them. If in the United States now, public life is considerably debased and encroachment on private life strenuously resisted, at other times and in other places, private life was regarded as the lesser of the two, as the obvious English derivative of the classical Greek equivalent of "private"—*idios*—makes plain.[21]

There have been some efforts to describe a society in which there is no nonpublic life. In George Orwell's *1984*, Winston is brought to Room 101 because everything, even his unexpressed thoughts and emotions, are deemed to be a proper object of concern to, and at the service of, the state.[22] Describing societies not intended to be dystopic, Plato and Rousseau reduced the private realm to far less than most of us regard as ordinary.[23] Some actual regimes have looked in that direction; Sparta is an example that, for all the obloquy since, was highly regarded in its own time.[24] But however far the imagination and theory may go, reality stops short. Completely to displace the private with the public would be to deny human autonomy, that is, to deny that human beings are persons; and without persons, there is not a human community.

Privacy in this sense is wholly abstract and says no more about what is private than does autonomy itself. Although, therefore, there are, necessarily, public and private realms of human experience, it has proved powerfully difficult to specify the content of the latter. According to Mill's principle, self-regarding conduct is private, so far as government regulation is concerned, but whether particular conduct is self-regarding is itself controversial and not easily determined. In any case, whether self-regarding conduct is private in any other respect is an open question. The government or other individuals may seek to inform themselves about personal conduct without intending or trying to affect it, for reasons having nothing to do with regulation of the conduct or from idle curiosity.[25] Mill himself did not think that conduct that is self-regarding is necessarily private in respects other than immunity from government

---

[21] See Barrington Moore, Jr., *Privacy: Studies in Social and Cultural History* (Armonk, NY: M.E. Sharpe, 1984), 82; and Arlene W. Saxenhouse, "Classical Greek Conceptions of Public and Private," in S. I. Benn and G. F. Gaus, eds., *Public and Private in Social Life* (London: Croom Helm, 1983), 365. For an insightful, more concrete discussion of the public and the private, see W. L. Weinstein, "The Private and the Free: A Conceptual Inquiry," in J. Roland Pennock and John W. Chapman, eds., *NOMOS XIII: Privacy* (New York: Atherton Press, 1971), 27–55. There are helpful essays discussing many aspects of the distinction between public and private in Benn and Gaus, above.

[22] George Orwell, *1984*, in *The Complete Works of George Orwell* (London: Secker & Warburg, 1986–87), 9:296.

[23] See Plato, *Laws*, trans. A. E. Taylor, in Edith Hamilton and Huntington Cairns, eds., *The Collected Dialogues of Plato* (Princeton, NJ: Princeton University Press, 1961), 1225–513; and Jean-Jacques Rousseau, *Considerations on the Government of Poland*, in Rousseau, *Political Writings*, ed. and trans. Frederick Watkins (Edinburgh, NY: Nelson, 1953), 157–274.

[24] See, e.g., Xenophon, *Constitution of the Lacedaemonians*, in Xenophon, *Scripta Minora*, ed. and trans. E. C. Marchant (Cambridge, MA: Harvard University Press, 1968).

[25] The effort to gather information may violate the proscription of regulation, but that is not inevitable.

regulation and was not averse to using nongovernmental pressure to change it.[26] Although it is not mistaken to locate liberty to engage in self-regarding conduct within the private realm and, therefore, to regard it as an aspect of privacy so considered, the reference to privacy adds nothing concrete to what is contained in the idea of liberty. Nor does it provide content for a right to privacy distinct from rights that are part of liberty itself. Its significance is only to relate liberty as a political ideal to freedom or autonomy as an ontological concept.

The privacy of some aspects of ordinary life has been thought to flow "naturally" from universal human characteristics. Sexual conduct may seem to be naturally private, because of the abandon or exclusivity of attention that sexual fulfillment typically requires. Similarly, excretory functions may seem to be naturally private for quite different reasons; the unpleasant sensory aspects of excretion readily lead one to avoid being observed. But although a few eccentric exceptions would not perhaps refute the argument that such privacies are inherent in the conduct in question, the exceptions are not so limited. There is far too much public sexual display, in live performances, movies, and so forth, and there are apparently far too many persons for whom public display is not only permissible but pleasurable to sustain a conclusion that sex is inherently private. So also, the privacy of excretory functions, although very common, is evidently culturally conditioned.[27] In any case, privacy of this kind typically is obligatory; common human impulse though it be, it is not a reflection of autonomy but an other-regarding aspect of conduct within the public realm.

A person's unexpressed thoughts, emotions, and attitudes may seem to be private if anything is. One's "interior" mental life is private as a practical matter, and its insulation from investigation by the government is widely regarded as a prominent aspect of liberty. From a practical perspective, however, the privacy of one's unexpressed thoughts and the rest is only contingent. Were human beings suddenly to acquire the power to "read minds," our behavior would likely be affected, and we might adjudge individuals' responsibility for their actions differently in some circumstances, but there would be no basis for concluding that human beings were no longer autonomous and that responsibility itself was overthrown. In the absence of such power, the methods that are, perforce, used to obtain such information involuntarily may assault the person physically or psychologically and, in view of their object, appear to intrude bluntly on privacy regarded as shelter. However, although the available methods may make investigation of what one keeps to himself especially objectionable, they do not make the information itself more private, except, again, as a practical matter; the methods themselves are

[26] See Mill, *On Liberty*, 96, 177–87.
[27] See Moore, *Privacy*, 59–71.

no more distinctly a matter of privacy than any assault. Liberty may well be involved and, were the privacy of private thoughts generally lost, the sense of individual responsibility might be affected. But unless the capacity for self-determination were eliminated altogether, personal autonomy would remain. A person's interior life may well deserve special protection, but so far as privacy itself is concerned, it falls within the general topic of informational privacy, which is discussed below.

Although it is common to speak of a private realm or domain in which a person's conduct of his life is his own business, the space so described is metaphorical only. The abstract notions of public and private are scarcely more than reminders that human beings are at one and the same time constituted as persons within a human community and autonomous. Strictly speaking, autonomy is not a right but rather is the condition of having any rights at all. Because it is possible at the limit, however, to deny personal autonomy, it is not seriously incorrect to speak of autonomy as a right. In the same way, one may speak of a right to a private domain, or to privacy, in the sense that, as a person, one has (a right to) a "space" in which he is autonomous. But the right thus identified does not specify at all the shape or dimensions of the space or what it contains. It adds nothing, except by way of metaphor, to a reference to autonomy itself.

III. Informational Privacy

When people speak of a right to privacy, they mostly have in mind informational privacy, a person's control over others' acquisition and distribution of information about himself. That is what the Supreme Court had in mind, for example, when it said that the Fourth Amendment protects a person's "legitimate expectation of privacy," whether or not there was a trespass in the ordinary sense.[28] Some other aspect of privacy, like shelter from the presence of others or the exclusion of others from some space, may also be involved, but the core of informational privacy and what the right to privacy most often concerns is simply a person's right to determine the distribution of personal information. (I shall hereafter refer to informational privacy simply as privacy, unless the context indicates otherwise.) Not all information, nor even all personal information, is private, however. Not the least of the difficulties confronting a defense of the right to privacy is specifying without circularity what information it shields.

A person may resist the disclosure of information because of its consequences. Although the Supreme Court has separated the right to privacy protected by the Fourth Amendment from the remedy for a violation of the right, the reason for asserting the right is almost invariably to avoid

---

[28] *Katz v. United States*, 389 U.S. 347 (1967). *Katz* is the source of the phrase "legitimate expectation of privacy," although not the precise words. See *Rakas*, 439 U.S. at 143.

the incriminating consequences of the violation.[29] But an invasion of privacy is thought to be wrong—an injury—in itself, even if there is no harmful consequence. Insofar as persons have a desire for privacy, whatever their reasons, satisfying the desire contributes to the social good. Insofar as other persons want to have information or would be pleased if they had it, however, satisfying their desire also would contribute to the social good. One may have little impulse to relieve the curiosity, prurient or otherwise, of readers of the tabloids, but calculations of the good do not discriminate. For most purposes, furthermore, in the absence of a special need for secrecy, the possession of information is regarded as empowering and its distribution, therefore, as desirable.

Seeking a foundation for the right to privacy that is not subject to the variable and changing practices of a community and its assessment of the good, defenders of the right have looked to personal autonomy as a quality of personhood itself, not dependent on local convention. Because privacy in all its forms attaches uniquely to persons and because the abstract notion of privacy, discussed above, is scarcely more than a reflection of autonomy, the connection of informational privacy in particular with autonomy has seemed attractive. Three theories that have made the connection in different ways illustrate its attraction as well as its weakness. In the end, the argument that informational privacy is an incident of autonomy does not succeed.

James Rachels has urged that the crucial importance of privacy as a value distinct from interests that we have in our persons and property is that it enables us to adapt our social relationships with other persons to the circumstances of the individual relationship.[30] A relationship is not simply an attitude toward the other person—affection, indifference, dislike—but is also dispositional; it is constituted in part by one's conduct toward and with the person. Privacy, Rachels argued, is, in effect, a sluice gate that allows a person to control what other persons know about him, raising or lowering the gate as he determines. Not only does the content of what he discloses affect the relationship generally, but more specifically, it enables him to maintain a relationship unaffected by what he has disclosed to someone else with whom he has a different relationship. The fact that one presents himself differently to different persons is not, Rachels observed, a regrettable lack of authenticity. For the persons with whom we deal, superficially or intimately, are different, as are the reasons for

---

[29] The usual, almost always the only, remedy for violation of a Fourth Amendment right is the suppression of incriminating evidence obtained by the violation. Only someone whose own right was violated has standing to obtain a remedy, however; and he may not move to suppress evidence against someone else. Accordingly, if the police violate Jones's right and thereby obtain evidence against Smith, there is typically no remedy. See, e.g., *Wong Sun v. United States*, 371 U.S. 471 (1963).

[30] See James Rachels, "Why Privacy Is Important," *Philosophy and Public Affairs* 4, no. 4 (Summer 1975): 323–33, reprinted in Schoeman, ed., *Philosophical Dimensions of Privacy*, 290–99.

which and occasions on which we deal with them. There are not one indisputably genuine person and a variety of more or less fraudulent variations; there are simply different relationships, which call for different behavior, including what we make known about ourselves.

Charles Fried had earlier defended a narrower version of this thesis, which located the value of privacy, or at least a very significant part of it, in a more limited range of special relationships.[31] Privacy, Fried argued, gives us the "moral capital" with which to have intimate relationships of love, friendship, and trust.[32] Intimacy, he said, "is the sharing of information about [oneself] which one does not share with all."[33] Had we no control over the disclosure of information about ourselves, our willingness to share it sometimes would count for a good deal less, and intimacy would, therefore, be devalued. Responding to Fried's argument, Jeffrey Reiman objected that there is something "hauntingly distasteful" about making intimacy dependent on something like market scarcity, a lover's revelations being prized only insofar as they are not available to others.[34] Intimacy, Reiman said, depends not only on how much is revealed but also on the spirit with which it is revealed. One may reveal more about some things to one's doctor, secretary, or tax accountant than to one's lover, and have a more intimate relationship with the latter nonetheless. Still, one of the cues by which we signal a desire for intimacy and intimacy itself is to let down barriers of all kinds and "hold nothing back." If privacy is not exactly the condition of intimacy, nevertheless, most of us would probably think of intimacy as a heightened form of privacy.

Rachels's broader thesis, which readily incorporates Fried's discussion of intimate relationships, describes an ordinary feature of most people's lives. Few of us would not resist being, as it were, permanently on camera, one's behavior with others, including revelations about himself, being disclosed on demand to persons not present, who could then compare—and contrast—his behavior with them. It would be a sadly limited person who treated everyone alike, whether too remotely or too intimately. Whether that provides the ground of a right is another matter.[35]

---

[31] Charles Fried, "Privacy," *Yale Law Journal* 77, no. 3 (January 1968): 475–93, reprinted in Schoeman, ed., *Philosophical Dimensions of Privacy*, 203–22.

[32] Ibid., 484.

[33] Ibid.

[34] Jeffrey H. Reiman, "Privacy, Intimacy, and Personhood," *Philosophy and Public Affairs* 6, no. 1 (Fall 1976): 32, reprinted in Schoeman, ed., *Philosophical Dimensions of Privacy*, 304.

[35] The title of Rachels's article is "Why Privacy Is Important," and he was mostly concerned to describe the interests that lead persons to want privacy. His thesis might, therefore, be regarded not as a defense of the right to privacy but as an argument that privacy is a particularly weighty element in the calculation of the good. He spoke also, however, of a right to privacy that is distinct from other rights to one's person and property (ibid., 331–33). Fried appears clearly to have regarded privacy as a right. He rejected an instrumental analysis of privacy and stated that it has "intrinsic value" (Fried, "Privacy," 477). He observed that because privacy is a necessary context for intimate relationships, "a threat to privacy seems to threaten our very integrity as persons" (ibid.).

A good deal of social interaction is sustained simply as a matter of fact, by our capacity to seek or avoid the presence of others. Were there no normative restriction on the acquisition and disclosure of information about other persons, there would still be occasion and opportunity for differential relationships. No doubt behavior would be affected. People would probably be more circumspect in some of their relationships, depend more on mutual advantage to avoid unwanted disclosures and less on common normative understandings. They might find it necessary to dissemble more than they do or to check carefully to ensure that they were not observed. In many situations, privacy would give way to secrecy. Especially for those who had previously relied on privacy, there would probably be a loss of well-being.

All the same, were privacy gone, persons would remain able to determine their conduct for themselves and be responsible for it. Although it is true, as Rachels and Fried strongly argued, that without the cloak of privacy we should not be able to differentiate relationships with others so easily as we do now, the inability to control what others know about oneself, as such, would no more be a derogation of autonomy than is the inability to alter one's appearance at will or make oneself invisible. The former circumstance no less than the others would simply be part of the conditions in which one acts. Autonomy does not require that one's self-determined actions be exercised in an undetermined context; one must determine his actions for himself, but he is not and need not be free to determine all its consequences. On the contrary, autonomy is consistent with, even in the end dependent on, a determinate—that is to say, not self-willed—background order. The exercise of freedom and responsibility as we know them requires that one's actions have consequences. Absolute, unconstrained choice negates freedom and responsibility, because in the absence of all constraints, no choice is necessary or possible.[36] Some constraints are antithetical to self-determination, of course. But no principle excludes the awareness of others from the conditions in which acts may be freely chosen. The fact that in this case the condition may be subject to the will of others rather than the impersonal natural order does not make a difference. If self-determination means *responsible* choice rather than simply randomness, the usual principle that one ought to acknowledge responsibility for one's acts strongly suggests otherwise.

Stated clearly, and separated from the abstract notion of privacy as autonomy, on one hand, and the undoubted value of privacy for the maintenance of satisfactory personal relationships, on the other, the point is indeed obvious. It is not the case that whenever a person is not in private, he ceases to act autonomously and does not determine his con-

---

[36] In Camus's play *Caligula*, the emperor tests the limits of freedom by acting without any constraints. See Albert Camus, *Caligula*, in Camus, *Caligula and Three Other Plays*, trans. Stuart Gilbert (New York: Vintage, 1958), 1–74.

duct for himself; he acts differently, perhaps, but he is no less responsible for what he does. That is as true of personal relationships as it is of other conduct. Rachels and Fried amply explain the importance that we attach to privacy, although it should be added that even that may depend significantly on contingent, if deep-rooted, social conventions rather than universal human characteristics. They provide a strong argument for legal rights that support the normative understanding. They do not establish a right to privacy standing by itself.

Grounding the right to privacy on respect for persons, Stanley Benn proposed as a general principle that "any man who desires that he *himself* should not be an object of scrutiny has a reasonable prima facie claim to immunity."[37] The basis of the principle, Benn argued, is that to acknowledge someone as a person is to recognize him as a self-determining actor who attempts "to steer his own course through the world."[38] Respect for someone as a person requires that one take into account how one's own conduct might affect the person's course and his attempt to steer it. To scrutinize someone without his consent denies him this respect, because it obliges him to perceive himself as an object (of the scrutiny) and alters his sense of himself as an actor. (If he is the object of secret scrutiny, he is also denied respect, in another way; he is made a fool, because he steers his course under a mistake.)

This right to privacy, Benn said, is prima facie only; it can be overcome by utilitarian arguments. The good of protecting a child from abusive parents, for example, would overcome their objection to having their conduct found out. The good of full and open public debate outweighs some—but not all—objections of public figures to scrutiny by the press. Benn maintained that there is a burden of justification in such cases, which depends only on recognition of the person whose privacy is at stake as autonomous. Although occasions when a claim to privacy is overcome by considerations of the good are likely to be more evident and numerous than occasions when other rights are similarly overcome, the claim to privacy, he believed, also qualifies as a right, albeit perhaps a weak one.

Benn did not assert that scrutiny of any information at all against a person's will violates his privacy. His principle is limited to scrutiny of the person himself and what is conventionally accepted as an extension of his self—family members, some property, and so forth. Reiman objected that without such a limitation, Benn's principle would be too broad to be at all plausible—as indeed it would—but that the limitation presumes the very notion of privacy that it purports to explain.[39] Benn might respond that scrutiny of a person is uniquely significant, because it not only dis-

[37] Stanley I. Benn, "Privacy, Freedom, and Respect for Persons," in Pennock and Chapman, eds., *Privacy*, 12, reprinted in Schoeman, ed., *Philosophical Dimensions of Privacy*, 232.
[38] Ibid., 9.
[39] Reiman, "Privacy, Intimacy, and Personhood," 37–38.

regards his purposes, opposing one's will to his, but actually makes *him* an object in his very capacity as an actor. That response leaves a difficulty about scrutiny of a person when he is not an actor, for example when he is sleeping. But passing that, it seems sufficient to meet Reiman's objection.

The larger difficulty is that the "objectification" that Benn's principle is intended to avoid does not undermine the conception of a person meriting respect, as he asserts it does. The same response to Rachels's argument with respect to the conditions of autonomous action applies here with respect to the actor himself. We are alike part of nature and apart from it. It is the human condition to be at one and the same time subject and object, self-determining actor and causally determinate being. So also it is the human condition to live in the community as part of, yet apart from, it. Although assessment of a person's responsibility focuses on his role as actor, it does not ignore the limitations to which he, as actor, is subject. Nor is he, determining his action, likely to be unaware of or to disregard those limitations. That we are subject to the scrutiny of others does not contradict our autonomy any more than does our inability to fly, although a particular means of becoming informed about a person may be objectionable for other reasons. All one can say is that *if* respecting another's privacy is regarded as a mark of respect for his person, then to invade someone's privacy denies him respect. There is, however, no valid objection grounded simply in respect for persons as autonomous to others' awareness of information about them.

Responding to the theses of Benn and Rachels, Reiman argued that the justification for informational privacy is not that it protects a person's ability to enter into differential relationships with others or respects him as a person, but rather that it contributes significantly to the person's perception of himself as autonomous and is actually constitutive of him as autonomous. Privacy, he said, "is necessary to the creation of *selves* out of human beings, since a self is at least in part a human being who regards his existence—his thoughts, his body, his actions—as his *own*."[40] The creation and maintenance of a sense of oneself as a self-determining agent requires, Reiman argued, the experience not only of actual agency—control over one's thoughts, body, and actions—but also of privacy—control over "cognitive appropriation" of one's self.[41]

Acknowledging that the significance that he gave to informational privacy was speculative, Reiman relied on studies of "total institutions," like prisons and mental hospitals, in which deprivation of privacy is a "means to mortify the inmate's self—that is, literally, to kill it off."[42] This limited empirical verification for his theory, he believed, together with the fact that it establishes privacy as a fundamental right for all human beings—

---

[40] Ibid., 39 (footnote omitted).
[41] Ibid., 42.
[42] Ibid., 41.

the concrete content of which is fixed by social practices—makes a convincing case.

The argument that the sense of oneself as autonomous depends on social practices rather than on some innate, self-prompted necessity recalls the argument in Section II above that the human condition is to live in community with other human beings. It supports the fundamental dichotomy between public and private and the abstract notion of privacy that reflects that dichotomy. Nothing in that argument, however, supports Reiman's specific justification of informational privacy. Rather, that portion of his argument, although admittedly speculative, rests on empirical evidence, which is, however, very limited. The examples of prisons and similar institutions provide little support for the universal proposition of his thesis. Although there is typically a loss of privacy in such institutions, it is, after all, also a feature of them that ordinary agency itself is severely restricted, sometimes by close confinement in a small space from which most opportunities for normal activities have been removed. In many institutional settings, inmates who are subject to constant surveillance evidently retain a strong sense of self, which they express by giving heightened importance to the limited opportunities for agency that they are allowed. So also, outside an institutional setting, the range and extent of privacy varies according to circumstances. In the wake of a natural disaster, for example, people may live in conditions affording little or no opportunity for ordinary privacy. Even if those conditions persist, the sense of self is not invariably lost; rather, it is sustained in other ways, for example by an affectation of anonymity by both observer and observed. More generally, although there is anthropological evidence that some forms of privacy or its surrogate can be found in all societies, the range and extent of privacy vary widely. Reiman's argument seems to suggest that personhood itself is diminished where privacy is relatively slight. That seems incorrect, not merely "politically" but as a matter of fact. Very general observations of this sort are not firm ground on which to stand, but they are no more infirm than the contrary observations on which Reiman relies.

The transition from privacy as an experienced phenomenon to privacy as a normative validation of selfhood is made by postulating that persons perceive the social practice of privacy and take it to be confirmation of their status as a moral agent.[43] That may be so. Since the argument does not depend, nor could it, on concrete personal testimony, it is no easier to prove than to disprove. One can say at least that such an inference is probably beyond the capacity of children at the stage when their sense of agency and moral responsibility begins to take hold. There is a much more direct and obvious source of the awareness of oneself as autonomous. Moral responsibility depends on agency. Responsible conduct *is*

---

[43] Ibid., 42–44.

self-determined conduct. Learning when it is appropriate to assign responsibility and when not, through the practice of praising and blaming, and that one is oneself responsible is, it seems likely, all that is needed to mark the divide between persons and things and to recognize oneself as a person. Neither extrapolation from such concrete evidence as we have nor abstract reflection about the concept of personhood warrants giving privacy the fundamental importance that Reiman's theory dictates.

The three theories that I have discussed are insightful examinations of the importance of informational privacy in the conduct of ordinary lives. They show how privacy can enhance one's sense of his own potency as an autonomous actor living in community with others like himself. None of them, however, makes the case for a right to privacy independent of its value as a social good. At bottom, the case fails because in each instance it *directly* concerns only what *others* know. Although the context in which he acts has changed, the person whose privacy is invaded is, *qua* actor, the same after the invasion as before; or if he is not, it is because of *his own* reaction to the fact that others have acquired the information in question about him.[44] Although there are certain conditions of autonomy that are conditions of personhood and attach as rights to all human beings, they do not qualify the contingent, determinate circumstances in which persons act.[45]

This conclusion is manifest from the fact that in the end none of the theories is able to specify what is private, except by reference to persons' ordinary expectations, confirmed by conventional understandings. Rachels and Fried passed by this difficulty by focusing attention on relationships and assuming that something in them must be private, if only because it is not told to others. Fried especially made the nature of the private seem obvious by emphasizing intimacy; the intimacies in question, one supposes, must perforce be private. Benn made a person's physical being central, because of "[t]he very intimate connection between the concepts of *oneself* and *one's body*,"[46] and adds to that culture-variant extensions of the self. There too, however, the strength of the connection between autonomy, or self, and privacy is only its familiarity. Reiman made no effort to specify what is private; rather privacy "is a social practice," the content

[44] One might posit a case in which a person's awareness that others had acquired certain information about him operated so forcefully on him that it affected him, as it were, directly and not through the intermediary of his own will and reason. That kind of psychological determinism would go much further than, and would be different in kind from, the not so unusual case of someone who is very much affected by some disclosure about himself and takes an otherwise unlikely action in response.

[45] Elsewhere, I have identified five conditions of autonomy that qualify as human rights: "[t]he right not to be subjected to constraints on autonomous action too great to be resisted," "[t]he right to physical and mental well-being," "[t]he right to education," "[t]he right to moral consciousness," and "[t]he right to moral opportunities" (Weinreb, *Oedipus at Fenway Park*, 117–21 [italics omitted]). See generally Lloyd L. Weinreb, *Natural Law and Justice* (Cambridge, MA: Harvard University Press, 1987).

[46] Benn, "Privacy, Freedom, and Respect for Persons," 12.

of which is whatever social practice says it is. The practice of privacy, Reiman argued, is also the source of the autonomous self. Although privacy may strengthen one's sense of autonomy and afford scope for autonomous action, autonomy as a human characteristic is the predicate of privacy, not its consequence.

IV. A RIGHT TO PRIVACY GROUNDED IN CONVENTION?

The defense of a right to privacy need not, however, end there. Suppose it be conceded that autonomy is not contingent on privacy and that privacy is conventional only, a construct of social practices. Suppose that what is private is not universal or necessary but is contingent. Provided that the convention is more or less settled, so that the proposition that something is private has the aspect of a statement of fact, is that not enough to sustain a right to privacy, not only in law (if there happens to be one) but in fact? A right requires a factual predicate, but unless it is a *human* right, pertaining to all human beings as such, it need not be a necessary predicate. The right to privacy would then be contingent on the existence of social practices sufficiently settled within the community in question to be regarded as a matter of fact, albeit variable from one community to another. But that is true of civil rights generally, which depend on the settled conventions of the community. Is that not enough to establish the right to privacy as a civil right?

It is true that in ordinary discourse, the adjective "private" is commonly used as if it states a matter of fact. "That's private" is a predicative statement grammatically and would typically be received as such. It has also normative force, which is not a matter simply of approval (or, possibly, disapproval), but includes a prescription of how one ought to behave. That combination of fact and norm is an essential characteristic of rights. Furthermore, privacy is commonly expressed in ordinary discourse as a matter of right, without discrimination among its various aspects or meanings. Nevertheless, there are persuasive reasons why informational privacy in particular should not be so regarded (except, of course, insofar as it may be a legal right). Rather, on close inspection, informational privacy appears to be grounded on utilitarian considerations and its protection in a particular instance to depend on a judgment, often inexplicit, that it will serve the social good or, perhaps, is dictated by a rule that serves the social good.

In a large number of familiar situations, information about a person that would ordinarily be regarded as private is not so regarded, because, in the circumstances, its disclosure is thought to serve the proper interests of others or of the public generally. The assertion that some information has significant other-regarding consequences, if accepted, is ordinarily a full response to a claim of informational privacy. So, for example, if a woman asked her would-be lover or fiancé whether he was HIV-positive or had been promiscuous without protection in the past (or if, as is not uncommon, she insisted that he be tested for the AIDS virus), it would be odd indeed to berate her for invading his privacy. On the contrary, even if he were not asked, he would be criticized if he failed to disclose such information. Similarly, the fact that a man is homosexual, or likes kinky sex, or is impotent is surely private; but it is highly relevant to his fiancée and well within the range of information that she ought to and is entitled to know before they marry. She might be criticized if she went around to his former girlfriends and asked if any of those propositions were true. But criticism on the ground that her desire for the information did not respect his privacy would surely be misplaced. Likewise in the public arena, debate about the disclosure of facts about the "private life" of a candidate for public office focuses on their relevance to his ability to perform his duties; if it is agreed that the facts are relevant—that is, have other-regarding significance—objections to their disclosure fade. So long as the conclusion that information is generally not other-regarding is accepted, a person's privacy with respect to that information may have the aspect of a right, because the possibility of harmful consequences to others is not in issue. Once that possibility is raised, however, and is seriously in issue, privacy loses its quality as a right and is decided as a matter of the good.

In ordinary discourse, there is no need for a sharp distinction between the right and the good; all that needs to be said is that, in view of the circumstances, the person's privacy is not a barrier to disclosure. If the kind of information that is at stake generally is regarded as private, the situation may be described as one in which the person does indeed have a right to privacy but has waived it—by becoming engaged or running for office—or his right is overcome by the good of disclosure, rather than as one in which he has no right to waive or to be overcome in the first place. The so-called "waiver," however, which rarely is explicit,[47] consists of nothing but the fact that the information is not, in the circumstances, regarded as private. Although a rare departure from a right in especially exigent circumstances need not defeat its quality as a right, it is the very essence of a right that it does not depend on a calculation of the good and ordinarily prevails despite the harm that its exercise may cause others. "I have a right to . . ." is not an assertion that the contemplated course of action is morally correct or will not have unfortunate consequences; rather, it is an assertion that even if it be otherwise, it does not matter.

The recognition of a person's privacy is not, as is the application of a right, independent of circumstances. On the contrary, it is freighted with

---

[47] Imagine the man saying to his fiancée, "Of course, your question violates my right to privacy, but I do love you and I hereby waive my right." Or imagine the candidate for office saying to his constituency, "In truth, it is none of your business, but I shall sacrifice my right to privacy and tell you whatever you want to know." In all likelihood, the former would find himself unattached and the latter would be looking for a job in the private sector.

assumptions about circumstances and varies accordingly. The particular circumstances may be disregarded if there is a rule favoring privacy in some category of cases to which the instance in question belongs. Nevertheless, the justification for privacy in that instance is not the person's right but the social good. One who believed that privacy ought not be respected would argue, on grounds of the good, either that the rule was not applicable in that instance or that if it was, the rule was mistaken in that respect or generally. If his argument prevailed, there would be no residue of a personal right.

If it is correct that informational privacy is conventional only, grounded in the practices and normative understandings of the community and variable from one community to another, then it is reasonable to suppose that within a community as well, it may depend on circumstances. To think of informational privacy in this way gives up the rhetorical advantage of associating it with rights generally and with the demands of individual autonomy or liberty in particular, in exchange for a sharper, clearer understanding of its true value. In an age when, as we are told, information is the key to social well-being and wealth, insistence on privacy will look increasingly like Luddism. The march of technology creates uses for information that was previously random data or makes available information that was unknown and even unknowable—in a sense, therefore, inviolably private. A response that does no more than assert a right to privacy may prevail for a time, but only so long as the benefits that it opposes are small. Eventually the debate will be about the good. That does not mean that privacy must always be the loser. It does mean that those who would defend privacy as we know it will have to provide a convincing account of the human good that overshadows the material rewards that are offered in its place. It will not be easy.

Law, Harvard University

PRIVACY, CONTROL, AND TALK OF RIGHTS

By R. G. Frey

I. Introduction

An alleged *moral* right to informational privacy assumes that we should have control over information about ourselves. What is the philosophical justification for this control? I think that one prevalent answer to this question—an answer that has to do with the justification of negative rights generally—will not do.

My concern, then, is not with some *legal* right to privacy; with how such a right is to be construed; with its derivation from some more-embedded, constitutional right; with the scope and extent of what falls under such a right; with any broad or narrow construals of privacy and/or legal privacy; or with any of the specific issues (such as sexual orientation or genetic inheritance) that today are alleged to fall under such a right. Rather, my concern is a more general one, which has to do with one alleged ground of schemes of negative rights—a ground that seems at the same time very tempting to give as the ground for the control that some putative right to privacy is supposed to confer upon us. Equally, my concern is not with an analysis of rights, as, for example, Hohfeldian bundles of powers, privileges, liberties, etc.;[1] for I take it to be obvious that to provide an analysis of rights is not the same thing as to provide a ground for them. I do not deny that much interesting work can be done in moral/political theory simply upon granting the assumption that rights claims can be properly grounded. Judith Jarvis Thomson's *The Realm of Rights*,[2] Hillel Steiner's *An Essay on Rights*,[3] Ronald Dworkin's *Taking Rights Seriously*,[4] and Robert Nozick's *Anarchy, State, and Utopia*[5] show this possibility to be a real one.

What I want to explore instead is the philosophical issue of what grounds schemes of negative rights, including schemes that contain or acknowledge a right to privacy. (Why I frame the issue in terms of negative rights

[1] See Wesley Newcomb Hohfeld, *Fundamental Legal Conceptions as Applied in Judicial Reasoning* (New Haven, CT: Yale University Press, 1919).
[2] Judith Jarvis Thomson, *The Realm of Rights* (Cambridge, MA: Harvard University Press, 1990).
[3] Hillel Steiner, *An Essay on Rights* (Oxford: Basil Blackwell, 1996).
[4] Ronald Dworkin, *Taking Rights Seriously* (Cambridge, MA: Harvard University Press, 1977).
[5] Robert Nozick, *Anarchy, State, and Utopia* (New York: Basic Books, 1974).

will emerge below.) First, however, it is necessary to locate the discussion more exactly.

II. Information and Control

There are things about ourselves that we would like others not to know; life, we judge, would just go better for us if this information were kept to ourselves and, say, to those bound to us by some professional obligation. Our welfare or well-being would be adversely affected, we think, if certain things about us became known. We fear, for example, that such information might be used to deny us a job or insurance; we dread the embarrassment and shame that we would experience if others came to know these things about us; we suspect that, in a very direct manner, we would suffer loss of respect or repute in the eyes of others if they knew these things. Since there appears to be no inherent limit on what individuals can think will adversely affect their well-being, there appears to be no easy way to circumscribe the kinds of information that individuals want kept to themselves.

Given the right set of circumstances, virtually anything—if it became known—may be judged by us to pose a threat to our well-being. General knowledge of her age can be seen by the Hollywood star as a threat to her well-being, as judged, subjectively, by her; knowledge of weight can be judged to pose a threat to the airline steward; and knowledge of gender and race can pose a threat to a white male seeking admission to a university. Obviously, denial or loss of job or insurance through the use of knowledge of one's sexual orientation or genetic profile appears in a similar light to those who suffer such denial or loss.

Similarly, to adapt an example from Thomson's paper "The Right to Privacy,"[6] my well-being might well be judged by me to be adversely affected if it came to be known that I kept pornographic pictures locked up in my wall safe and took them out at night to look at them. This kind of example sets up the issue of privacy in terms of what others may do in order to find out that I am looking at pornographic materials at night. May they break into my wall safe? May they peek through the cracks in my blinds? May they train high-powered binoculars on me from afar in order to see through the cracks in my blinds? And so on. In her paper, Thomson brilliantly teases out of a series of examples every last ounce of philosophical import for privacy issues, without, it seems to me, ever addressing the most striking feature of all the cases that she discusses: her assumption that the individual in each case enjoys from the outset a right to privacy, and so an entitlement to keep certain things about himself

---

[6] Judith Jarvis Thomson, "The Right to Privacy," *Philosophy and Public Affairs* 4, no. 4 (Summer 1975): 295–314, reprinted in Thomson, *Rights, Restitution, and Risk* (Cambridge, MA: Harvard University Press, 1986), 117–34.

from others. There are subsidiary issues that strike one as well, such as how we determine which things to keep private. The most striking as well as the most interesting aspect of Thomson's examples, though, lies in the assumption that the individual in each has an entitlement to keep certain things about himself from others, without it ever being explained how he came to get this entitlement and, indeed, what demonstrates that he has it in the first place. (Thomson, it might be urged, doubtless does not see herself as in the business of seeking grounds for entitlements to privacy.)

Yet, discussion of the invasion of privacy only makes sense against the backdrop of a presumption of privacy, and it is this presumption that is at issue. To raise the question of what others may permissibly do in order to find out (and to use) information about oneself that one wants to keep to oneself presumes privacy, in that others now have to undertake some sort of (moral) justification of the methods that they employed to find out the information in question and, indeed, some sort of (moral) justification for even trying to find out the information at all. In this sense, Thomson's examples presume (a right to) privacy; the individual has the presumption of an entitlement to rebut intrusions into his life that he deems to be detrimental to his well-being. (I leave aside any question about whether what he deems is accurate or not; I simply assume that he deems correctly.)

Of course, if the invasion of privacy takes the form of breaking and entering to get at my wall safe or of trespass to look through the cracks in my blinds, then we can use violation of property rights as a basis to object to what was done, independently of any presumption about things about ourselves that we are entitled to keep to ourselves. This whole way of approaching privacy, however, shifts the burden of argument over the important issue from the individual to others. It makes it appear that what really must be justified is what others may do in order to find out information about me, when the really interesting issue, I think, is what exactly it is that confers upon me the entitlement to privacy that such a discussion presumes. This presumed entitlement is not a matter of law. The presumption in Thomson's examples does not flow from the legal system; if anything, it is what, by giving legal recourse to those who suffer intrusions, grounds this presumption of privacy. In this sense, some notion of legal privacy cannot be the crux of the matter (and Thomson rightly does not treat it as such). For that matter, the entitlement that the presumption of privacy involves is not itself a legal entitlement, though we may go on to enact laws that legally serve to protect that entitlement. We need some reason to be persuaded that there is a presumption of privacy.

To say that our lives would go better if certain things about ourselves were not known does not show that we enjoy an entitlement concerning such information; it does not even establish a presumption of privacy. Suppose it were true that one's sexual orientation would be used against one in the job market: this does not show that one enjoys the requisite moral entitlement or presumption. It simply shows that one could suffer denial or loss of a job, if one's sexual orientation became known. Suppose, therefore, we put in place a policy that forbids employers from using one's sexual orientation against one in hiring: this, too, would not show that one had the requisite moral entitlement or presumption. It would show only that there exists a policy that prohibits employers from using certain information about an individual while hiring.

Notice, then, why rights theorists typically cannot be content with policies instead of moral rights; for what policies can all too easily do is transfer control over what happens to you from yourself to others. If I control what information can be released about me, then I am not dependent upon others to observe prohibitions on using that information. This makes the issue of such control vital.

Again, rights theorists cannot be content with our acknowledgment that privacy is an important issue that seems to be part of any viable conception of the good life. For so long as there are other values recognized in a conception of the good life, or so long as there are competing conceptions of the good life held by others within the same community that vary with respect to the importance and/or extent of privacy claims, it can remain unclear where operative control over what finally happens to information about one lies. In such settings, tradeoffs between values can occur, and it may well turn out that what one wants kept private becomes public. Placing control in one's own hands, the way entitlements do, seems a surer path to keeping the information in question away from others.

Moreover, this issue of control is a general one, since there is no specific subject matter that we can identify as all and uniquely the domain of the private. Sexual orientation, genetic inheritance, age, religion, or socio-economic class—all may be held by one to be detrimental to one's well-being, if known publicly. Sometimes, it can turn out that what one wants kept from others can vary between individuals, even within the confines of the same case. Thus, in admission to graduate school, one party may want the characteristics 'black' and 'female' known, while another may want the characteristics 'white' and 'male' not known. I take it that this sort of contrast is possible in each and every case where privacy concerns are thought to be at issue, so that it is not by any specific content (e.g., having to do with sex, religion, etc.) that we can identify the domain of the private.

Furthermore, were we to endorse the notion that an individual has control over what information about him could come into the public sphere, yet concede that this information may vary over any and all subject matters, then any point of contrast between private and public would seem in jeopardy of being lost. Everything could potentially fall into the private sphere. Of course, information widely thought to be to our credit or advantage, such as high IQ, is not usually something that we want to be kept from others, but circumstances are easily imaginable in which we consider knowledge of even this information to be detrimental to our well-being. (Remember, I am not inquiring about the individual's accuracy in gauging how knowledge of information about him affects his well-being; I simply assume that he is correct in his assessment.) Going too far down this road could cause just about everything to be the subject of privacy claims, but not to go down this road at all leaves the crucial issue of control over information about oneself in the hands of others. For rights theorists, this represents a fundamental tension in acknowledging a right to privacy within the system of rights.

The ancillary issue of whether one may voluntarily relinquish this element of control over information about oneself is not to the point here. In the famous story of the Duke of Wellington, the Duke responds to his mistress's threat to publish her memoirs and thus to make their affair public with the remark, "Publish and be damned!" Here it may be tempting to hold that the Duke has voluntarily relinquished any element of control that may remain in his hands over knowledge of the affair. Even if one grants this, however, I take this overt relinquishing of control to be comparatively rare and, at least in part, alien to the usual sort of strong concern with control that motivates so much contemporary discussion of privacy. Nothing here determines the issue, if one accepts a case for privacy, of how extensive that privacy should be; it merely indicates that I shall not assume either that anyone is voluntarily relinquishing control over information through overt disavowal or that anyone does so through implicit disavowal.

One way to move forward the discussion concerning privacy, then, is to inquire after this notion of control over information about oneself. To assume that such a prerogative to keep certain information to oneself is there from the outset provides no justification of it, and a part of any justification must surely involve specifying what the ground of such control is. In virtue of what have we come to enjoy such a prerogative?

III. Negative Rights and Control

If we think of positive rights as imposing duties upon others to assist one in certain respects, we can think of negative rights as imposing duties upon others not to interfere with one in certain respects. Positive rights tend to be a battleground today, even amongst rights theorists, who differ over their endorsements of rather extensive schemes of socioeconomic or welfare rights and extensive schemes of human rights generally; these theorists also disagree about the extent to which we may impose duties on others to assist us in all these various respects. Accordingly, we can see negative rights as providing some measure of agreement amongst rights theorists. For, on the whole, positive-rights theorists endorse schemes of negative as well as positive rights, and thus think of individuals as having justified claims or entitlements not to be interfered with in certain respects. In a sense, negative rights may even seem more "fundamental" than positive ones, if, indeed, it is true that they secure one the opportunity to select for oneself some conception of the good life, to live out that conception, and to lead one's life as one wishes.

In turn, it is not difficult to see one's wish that certain information remain under one's own control as part of the life one wishes to live and, therefore, to think that one has a negative right, or at the very least a rebuttable presumption, against invasion by others, so far as this information is concerned. Certainly, it is not implausible to assume that all of us would want domains of privacy in our lives and that we have selected conceptions of the good life which contain these. But this does not show that we have any claim or entitlement in the matter; it only shows that we think our lives would go better, that we would have a better chance to live out our conceptions of the good life, if we get to keep certain information from others. All kinds of things, both by way of assistance and by way of noninterference, would make our lives go better, from the point of view of our individual well-being; but we have no reason to think that wish is father to the right.

Of course, it might be urged that *this* is all that privacy is about, namely, our desire to keep from others certain information about ourselves that we think likely to impair our well-being and to retain control over whether and when this information gets disseminated. This view of privacy, however, is perfectly compatible with a thoroughgoing utilitarianism in which, ultimately, one's individual privacy gets traded off for the collective well-being. Therefore, to have a right that bars such a tradeoff would be a powerful thing, indeed. Put differently, if one associates privacy with negative rights, in the way and for the reason that I have suggested, and if one then goes on to take these rights of noninterference to resist very fiercely intrusions by others on behalf of the collective well-being (except at the proverbial level of catastrophe), then one might claim truly to have a powerful instrument on behalf of living out the life of one's choice. It is not surprising, then, that the pictures of such powerful rights that we associate with Dworkin and the early Nozick recur in the contemporary debate on privacy, since deep resistance to utilitarian sacrifice is an important part of each picture. Since these pictures are very familiar today, I shall not bother to sketch them in great detail; what I want from them, so far as my discussion of control over information about ourselves is concerned, will become apparent.

IV. Normativity and a Core of Noninterference

Rights theorists today put into the moral picture what they want to get out. They do this in two ways. First, they put into the individual, or, in contemporary jargon, the 'flourishing individual', by postulation that which they will find needs protection by a rather fierce scheme of negative rights of noninterference. Second, they hold that only rights can fully serve to protect what has been postulated. I do not claim that every rights theorist makes these moves, but such moves do represent a very pronounced tendency in modern rights theorizing.

The rights theorist reflects upon what makes us moral agents or fully persons (looked at normatively) or what constitutes our individuality, finds or postulates some kernel or core of relevant features, and then ascribes rights the role of protecting this core or sphere, over which a normative gloss is then cast. The job which rights of noninterference are ascribed flows from their treating the core normatively, as of the very essence of what makes us moral beings, or, in contemporary jargon, what makes us fully 'persons', 'agents', or 'individuals'.

Take self-direction of our lives: when this notion is given a normative gloss, it then comes to be treated not just as being a feature of some or many human lives but as a feature absolutely crucial to our standing as persons, agents, or individuals. Loss of self-direction or interference with it is then held to pose a threat to our very standing as persons, agents, or individuals. Therefore, we must be given the normative equipment with which to rebut intrusions by others into this thing (namely, self-direction) the protection of which is vital to our core, and this normative equipment takes the form of a rather strong scheme of rights of noninterference.

It must be *rights* that do the protecting, and this is the case for two reasons. First, if the job of protection can be done by something else, say, by claims about what is right and wrong and what ought to be done, then rights would lack any *distinctive* work to do in the picture. Without distinctive work to do—if we could, without loss of meaning or import, eliminate rights and simply talk in terms of what it would be right and wrong to do—rights run the danger of being regarded as unnecessary. With distinctive work to do, with work that only rights can do, they appear necessary. Second, it must be rights that do the protecting because anything else would not be faithful to the core that the theorist has postulated as that which is vital to our standing as persons, agents, or individuals. Anything else and we will lack tools appropriate to the task of *our* repelling intrusions into *our* core, since rights of noninterference, unless we relinquish, waive, or forfeit them, give *us* the power to rebut intrusions. If the theorist now adds that these rights cannot be relinquished, waived, or forfeited, protection of our core is left entirely up to us. We can keep people at bay from the core of what, normatively, is crucial to us as persons. To leave this protection solely in the hands of others is not to give us appropriate normative equipment with which to defend our core against the intrusions of others.

If, then, rights are to have distinctive work, they must be found a job that only they can do. With core-views, this job consists in using strong rights of noninterference as protective devices of the core of our person-hood, agency, or individuality, which in turn is held to be fundamental to our status as moral beings. Finding or postulating this core, then, is a requirement for the distinctive work that rights do. Much of contempo-rary philosophical agonizing over personhood, agency, and individuality can be traced to this mission of locating a core in each of us, protection of which would then be essential to regarding and treating people as moral beings.

Of course, it is up to each rights theorist to say what he takes this core to be, but that a negative-rights theorist will find or postulate a core is certain. The nature and scope of this core can and does vary among theorists, but there will be a core. It will take the form of a feature or set of features the loss of, diminution in, or interference with which will affect fundamentally what is taken normatively to constitute our core as persons, agents, or individuals. The contemporary debates surrounding the personhood of fetuses and the normative status of animals illustrate precisely this point, as does another contemporary debate on the possible loss of personhood, agency, or individuality of those suffering from senile dementia or anencephaly.

To speak either of "finding" or of "postulating" this core strikes me as amounting to the same thing. For it is up to the individual theorist to identify what comprises the core, and he is at liberty to find or deem anything to constitute it, though some things will be more believable or plausible than others. To repeat, without the core, rights lack distinctive work to do, and what counts as the core is up to each rights theorist to indicate. This is what I mean by getting out what one puts in: what one deems the core to be will determine which rights we have. We will have strong rights of noninterference with respect to precisely those features of ourselves that the particular theorist has deemed to constitute the core of personhood, agency, or individuality. Rights are only required at bottom to serve the instrumental task of protecting the core, and each theorist is at liberty to make the core out to be anything he wants—though some things will be more believable or plausible than others.

A normative gloss on the core is necessary; otherwise, it will simply consist in natural characteristics and capacities that humans have and that can be described naturalistically. A normative gloss on the core con-fers normativity upon it, and so enables the theorist to cast intrusions by others into it in a negative moral light. It is what lets the theorist treat interferences into the core as something other than socially occurring phenomena; it enables the theorist to treat interferences as moral evils. Rights, then, are protective devices that enable us, in our own right and with control left in our own hands, to guard against this moral evil.

In short, a rights theorist typically finds or postulates a core to human personhood, agency, or individuality, casts a normative gloss over this core, and then treats this core as protected by a scheme of rights. In this way, rights are seen both to be necessary and to be doing distinctive work. Within reason, however, anything can serve the rights theorist as the core of human personhood, agency, or individuality; he can pick what he likes. This raises the question of whether or not the core is arbitrary, that is, dependent upon whatever the particular theorist deems to be the relevant characteristics and capacities. (It is important to note, as we shall soon see, that theorists do not agree as to what these characteristics and capacities are.) Without the normative gloss, these characteristics and capacities would be just that—characteristics and capacities. The normative gloss enables us to treat interferences by others with these characteristics and capacities as moral evils, which our rights enable us to repel. Rights, on this view, play the instrumental role of protecting the core or sphere of noninterference. Accordingly, rights theorists, such as Dworkin, the early Nozick, and John Finnis,[7] are committed to coming up with a core. As far as privacy is concerned, the question would then be whether a particular theorist thought that a right to privacy protected some characteristic, capacity, or interest that was so important as a good that he deemed it to be part of the core. A right to privacy would then refer to simply another piece of the core picture.

The real problem in all this, of course, is that there are no defeasibility conditions. Nothing serves as a check on the correctness of what is being asserted as an element of the core. A rights theorist postulates a core, protects it with a scheme of strong rights of noninterference, and adds for good measure that these crucial rights cannot be relinquished, waived, or forfeited. These matters in essence become unarguable, in that nothing serves to defeat or rebut the claims at issue.

Notice here as well why it matters that moral rights are involved; for it might be argued that, with regard to legal rights, matters are different, since a check of sorts—say, conformity with constitutional practice— might be thought to exist. Constitutional practice, however, is irrelevant in the case of these deeper, moral rights, which no future constitutional convention could revoke, even if its acts could be legally binding.

V. Spheres of Noninterference

Negative rights, rights of noninterference, are natural rights. By this, I mean three things. First, they are not contingent upon specific social structures and political institutions but rather serve as checks upon the kinds of structures and institutions that can justifiably exist. Second, they are not conventional and social in character, that is, they are not conferred upon individuals by government or society. Third, if they are not given by the state, they cannot be taken by the state or by any other grouping of individuals. The question arises: what is the ground of these rights? I am

---

[7] John Finnis, *Natural Law and Natural Rights* (Oxford: Clarendon Press, 1980).

not here concerned so much with any detailed answer to this question as I am with the similarities between two main pictures within which rights claims have been located and with a common claim that lies at the base of each picture. Following the literature, we can think of these as the liberal and classical liberal pictures within which rights claims function and find their home. Each takes the relationship between the individual and the state, collective, or society to be the ultimate datum of political theorizing; each vigorously affirms that the individual should prevail in the struggle between living one's life as one wishes and the demands of the collective well-being and the projects and concerns of other people.[8]

In the liberal picture, each individual is viewed as having a certain private realm or sphere of noninterference that is protected by a rather strong concatenation of rights that trump, among other things, considerations of the general welfare and the deep intrusion into one's life of other people's projects and concerns. These rights are required, and are as powerful as they are, because they are what ensure that we can not only choose a conception of the good life for ourselves but also live out that conception, free from the interference of others who do not share and are hostile to it or to the way that we conduct our lives in pursuit of it. Deep hostility to certain kinds of lives and to the activities that fill them is endemic to all but the most homogeneous—and small—communities, so possession of the means by which to repel assaults upon one's kind of life and one's activities seems fundamental to having a conception of the good life. For to have a conception of the good life but to be unable to live it out, because one lacks the theoretical wherewithal to resist claims of interference in one's activities, is in effect not to be permitted to adopt a conception of the good life for ourselves at all. The choice of how we are to live our lives and the activities that we engage in to fulfill that choice are integral parts of our individuality, which individual rights protect and preserve. (Below, I turn to another way of developing this focus upon individuality, through the notions of flourishing and human agency.)

As a result, certain things fall out on the liberal picture. The state or the collective must be neutral with respect to conceptions of the good life. Different conceptions of the good life are possible, and one is free to choose among them. If the state or collective were to foster some conceptions and to suppress others, it would fail to take seriously each individual's right to equal concern and respect. This right is crucial, if one is to resist intrusions by the state or others into one's life. In Dworkin's own work, this right is taken to be "fundamental and axiomatic" and so is not argued for,[9] though it seems to be part of what is implied by some deep sense of equality that he believes we find in ourselves. What the right to

---

[8] In this and the next section, I adapt material from my "Ethics, Politics, and Negative Rights," *American Philosophical Association Newsletter* 88, no. 1 (November 1988): 24–30.

[9] Dworkin, *Taking Rights Seriously*, xv.

equal concern and respect betokens is an individual trump over decisions justified collectively. Moreover, we cannot balance benefiting one person against harming or imposing burdens on another, if the person adversely affected had his right to equal concern and respect violated. A violation of this right is not undone through conferring benefits upon another person.

The sense of autonomy that the whole picture relies upon is, first, *individualist*, in the sense that it stresses individual choice, self-direction of one's life, and so, in the sense intended, self-creation of one's life. Second, it is *active*, in the sense that it stresses agency and construction of a life for oneself. Autonomy has been variously conceived of as (i) personhood and acting as a person; (ii) taking one's own decisions, at least in the important affairs of life, and directing one's own life; (iii) constructing or building a life of value for oneself; and (iv) adopting or living out a life plan: each conception is individualist and involves agency. Agency in turn allows one to make one's life into a thing of value, by allowing one to choose a conception of the good life for oneself and to mold one's life in ways that are appropriate to living out that conception. One is in this way the author, in part, of the value of one's life by, as it were, constructing one's life in accordance with the conception of the good life that one has chosen.

Though the liberal picture does emphasize equality, through the importance placed upon the right to equal concern and respect, it is quite clear that the assumption of a sphere of noninterference surrounding individuals gives pride of place to autonomy and self-direction. Put differently, at the deepest level, we may think of a right to equal concern and respect as protecting individual autonomy, as manifested in our choice of a conception of the good life and in the activities that we select in order to live out that conception.

Matters are very similar in the classical liberal picture. Once again, we are held to have a certain sphere of noninterference that is protected by a rather strong concatenation of rights that resist considerations of the general welfare. These negative rights resist the encroachment of others in our lives, as we seek to live out our different conceptions of the good life that we choose for ourselves. Such interference, whether by the state or others, cannot be justified by the collective good. Of course, if I consent to such interference, that is one thing, but I am perfectly at liberty not to consent. For the state or collective to impose its views, values, and conceptions of the good upon me is to violate these rights of noninterference I hold against the state and all others.

In this classical liberal picture, it is autonomy around which the picture explicitly revolves, and this value is held to be very sensitive to coercive intrusions by others. Whereas the liberal picture might take it to be permissible to use taxation to redistribute wealth in the name of equality, the classical liberal picture resists such policies, since, among other things, they impose upon one, without one's consent, 'end-state distributive schemes' (in Nozick's felicitous phrase) that violate one's autonomy to dispose of one's labor, earnings, and property as one sees fit. Even if most of us were to agree that such policies were a good thing, to violate a person's autonomy in order to bring them about—something which util-itarians might be prepared to do—is simply wrong. Here, as in the liberal picture, harms and benefits do not offset one another: to benefit one person by violating another's autonomy does not undo the wrong done the person whose autonomy is violated.

Taking negative rights seriously can seem to require only a minimal state and limited coercion, whereas taking positive rights of assistance seriously—something which most defenders of the liberal picture do— seems to require a more substantial and active state and more generous doses of coercion. If we are to assist others, and if gifts and charity cannot ensure that others' claims to assistance are met, then the coercive powers of the state may be required to meet them, since there seems, in the absence of further charity, no other feasible way to ensure that assistance is forthcoming. On the classical liberal picture, the expanded role of the state that positive rights and their enforcement require will be resisted, since coercion in this context inevitably and inseparably involves infringe-ment of the coerced individual's autonomy. This is not to say, of course, that negative rights are cost-free; clearly, they are not, and for reasons other than those having to do with enforcement mechanisms. All rights impose duties upon others, and, at the very least, there is the cost to consider of others not being able to engage in the activities of their choos-ing, as well.

A central point of intersection between the liberal and classical liberal pictures—one that bears directly on their reliance upon a sphere of non-interference surrounding individuals that is protected by a scheme of strong, individual rights—is resistance to utilitarianism. This resistance manifests a number of fears. First, there is the fear that utilitarianism allegedly fails to take seriously the separateness of persons, their sepa-rateness being a cardinal feature of the noninterference assumption. No argument is supposedly needed to show this: summing utilities across persons, it is alleged, just is to ignore the separateness of persons, and so runs up against the noninterference assumption. A second fear is that utilitarianism can demand the sacrifice of one individual's interests and well-being in the name of the collective good, which fails to treat every-one with equal concern and respect and fails to take seriously each per-son's autonomy. Since all forms of democratic government wherein some individuals do not accept the sacrifices imposed upon them by the ma-jority in the name of the good of all would seem guilty on these counts, one can appreciate why the liberal wants individual rights held against the state or collective to be virtually inviolable, and why the classical liberal is suspicious of the state per se. A third fear about utilitarianism is that it is a theory about tradeoffs of values, wherein such tradeoffs are seen as the very stuff and substance of social/political life. In a society in which there are diverse peoples with different interests, goals, and conceptions of the good life, compromise can seem inevitable, and utilitarianism is a theory that can be used for reaching compromises. It takes values, all values, to be capable of being traded off against each other, whereas the liberal and classical liberal pictures deny, respectively, that the right to equal concern and respect or the right to autonomy can be traded off in favor of other values. No concatenation of other values, no matter how weighty, can justify treating someone with less concern and respect than others or justify usurping someone's autonomy. (It is not obvious that laymen would, all other things being equal, choose either the liberal or the classical liberal picture in preference to utilitarianism, when living in harmony among diverse peoples with different ends and accounts of the good is at issue.) This third fear gives further content to the separateness of persons claim. By having a system of individual rights that resist appeals to the general good, by trying to ground these rights in a deep sense of equality or individual autonomy, and by regarding this sense of equality and autonomy as integral to fleshing out the assumption of a sphere of noninterference that surrounds individuals, both sorts of liberals reject some tradeoffs of values that some utilitarians accept. They reject tradeoffs that permit others to invade the sphere of noninterference in the name of the collective good (or some concatenation of other values).

VI. NONINTERFERENCE AND CONVENTION

Why should we accept the assumption that there is a sphere of noninterference surrounding individuals? Negative rights protect this sphere—which in turn supplies their ground—but why should we make the initial assumption? Again, if we were to grant the sphere and the fiercely protective rights that surround it, if we were to think that only the consent of the person in question could make interference permissible, and if we were also to take the right to privacy to be one of these negative rights surrounding this sphere of noninterference, then we would have a ground for control over information that we believe would be detrimental to our well-being if that information were made public. For without control over (what counts as a permissible) intrusion into this sphere of noninterference, it could be invaded whenever the collective good dictated that it should be. Thus, without the control that the right to privacy presumes the individual to have, the collective good could amount to a case for having the information made public.

Why, though, should we grant the assumption of a sphere of noninterference surrounding individuals, upon which we then hang a scheme of negative rights? There are some good prudential/utilitarian reasons that at first blush appear to be weighty. After all, part of how we determine whether our lives are going well or badly is by the extent to which we can satisfy our desires and pursue and fulfill our projects and commitments (about which we have desires as well). But our desires, projects, and commitments are not the end of the matter, since we live among other people who have their own desires, projects, and commitments. What do we do when all these conflict? This is, or certainly seems to be, a condition of social/political life, and utilitarianism is a theory for achieving trade-offs. The point is not that social/political life is inevitably communal and that this demands that our sphere of noninterference be progressively invaded and restricted; it is that we need an argument for granting this sphere of noninterference in the first place.

One argument for such a sphere is this: others will only respect my autonomy, projects, and commitments if I respect theirs, so that, suitably developed, this *mutuality condition* provides each of us with grounds for acknowledging a sphere of noninterference in our respective lives. There are two problems with this argument, however. First, it assumes that all that moves us to noninterference in the lives of others is fear of interference in our own, and this view already assumes a preexisting autonomy out of which we bargain or contract our way to specific agreements. We need an argument, though, for this preexisting autonomy, individualistically conceived and self-interestedly oriented. For what, except an assumption of self-interest by some and rational self-interest by others, tells one from the outset that fear of loss to oneself motivates noninterference in the lives of others? Do we not already have to assume that agents come to the bargaining table with the desire to preserve noninterference in their lives as their most powerful desire? Anything less than this would be compatible with agents desiring noninterference in their lives but desiring something else more, such as something that interference in their lives can make possible (for example, road construction paid for by the interference of compulsory taxation).

An answer to the bargaining situation that the mutuality condition brings to mind is to redraw the scope of what will count as an unwarranted interference in one's life. At least in many of the affairs of life, what one will regard as an unwarranted interference will depend not upon some consuming desire not to be interfered with, but upon one's conception of the good life. A person's conception may strike us as severely individualistic, embodying autonomy of an extremely individualistic kind, and it is easy as a result to believe that almost all kinds of interference in that person's life will be regarded by him as detrimental to his well-being and, thus, as unwarranted. But not all conceptions of the good life are of this order. Thus, to an environmentalist, cleaning up and preserving the environment are important things; he sees these things, and the way in which they can enhance animal and human lives, as great goods, and he is prepared, for example, to be taxed in order to bring them to pass. Even though he could do other things with the money taxed away from him, he does not regard this tax as an unwarranted interference in his life. Whether he regards the tax as unwarranted interference or not cannot be determined from the outside without knowledge of how he structures his life in accordance with his conception of the good life. The fact that money is taken from him does not justify the conclusion that he regards the taking as unwarranted.

There are good utilitarian and prudential reasons for assuming that a sphere of noninterference surrounds individuals. But these reasons do not establish the assumption in the way the rights theorist requires. For either they do not bar utilitarian sacrifice in the way and to the degree that the rights theorist requires, or else they make the weight of other people's ends, projects, and commitments count in the balance along with one's own prudential concerns. To be sure, social/political life is inevitably communal and appears to involve tradeoffs between values, and utilitarianism is a theory of tradeoffs. The assumption of a sphere of noninterference is the first step in trying to resist utilitarian tradeoffs, and if the reasons for making the assumption are themselves compatible with such tradeoffs, then that first step is in jeopardy. Certainly, exclusive control over what befalls one will be lost, since utilitarian tradeoffs imply that, for example, one's desire that information one considers to be detrimental to one's well-being be kept private can be frustrated in the name of the collective well-being. However the assumption is defended, it has to be by means of an argument that blocks utilitarian tradeoffs, if the rights theorist is to be satisfied.

Utilitarianism infects another way of looking at this attempt to establish a sphere of noninterference. Suppose that it is agreed on all sides that mutual forbearance is a good thing, that it gives us all the best chance of living out our conceptions of the good life, and that, as a result, we mutually agree to refrain from interference in other people's activities in pursuit of the good life. A utilitarian of the most extreme form can agree to this much. Notice two points. First, if such a policy maximizes utility, then a utilitarian will adopt it. He will not think that there is any natural right involved in the matter, but so long as utility continues to be maximized overall, he follows the policy. (This permits him to adhere to a policy that maximizes utility overall even when on a particular occasion utility might not be maximized.) The problem for the rights theorist is that this kind of construal of the policy does not leave control over what happens to information that is deemed detrimental to one's well-being in one's own hands. Control is effectively left in the hands of those who decide to deviate from the policy, for whatever reason. In other words, the problem is that, even if this policy were truly effective in producing mutual forbearance and, thus, noninterference in the required respects, it would not do so in a way that an entitlement does. An entitlement leaves control in the individual's own hands. Mutual forbearance leaves control in other people's hands. To be sure, such a policy, because of the good consequences it has, is better than no policy, but it cannot provide the security for individual control that an entitlement can. The assumption of a sphere of noninterference protected by a series of rights of non-interference—including noninterference in carrying out one's decision to keep certain information about oneself to oneself—provides what a policy, even a good policy, cannot.

Second, suppose that the agreement on mutual forbearance—because it holds out the prospect of inter- and intracommunal harmony in living out various conceptions of the good life—itself issues in a right or an entitlement of noninterference: the problem would then be a different one. For now, while we might accept, for the sake of argument, that we have a right, it does not appear to be a right of the right kind. That is, it appears to be a *conventional* right, the product of human agreement, in aid of desirable consequences. It is not a *natural* right, that is, it is not independent of human agreement. This matters for three reasons. First, what agreements bestow, agreements can withdraw. This destroys the security of control over what befalls us that the rights theorist seeks. Second, agreements in aid of desirable consequences can come unstuck when less-than-desirable consequences result, again destroying the security of control over what befalls us. Third, it is not obvious that conventional rights resist considerations of utility to the same degree as natural rights are alleged to resist such considerations. The institution of promising is a human contrivance devised for social convenience, yet promises are broken on particular occasions for the sake of utility. This, also, leaves too much of one's fate in the hands of others, so far as the natural-rights theorist is concerned.

Famously, Hume saw clearly that certain rules and conventions are required in order for us to live our lives among others, not all of whom may share the same goals or ends. This is especially true since many goods are scarce and conflicts over scarce goods seem inevitable. Human contrivance comes to the rescue: ". . . a convention enter'd by all members of the society on the possession of those external goods, [leaves] every one in peaceable enjoyment of what he may acquire by his fortune and industry. By this means, every one knows what he may safely possess. . . ."[10] Clearly, for Hume, the rules of justice and the right to property, and the subsidiary rights that a right to property involves, are social conventions and so do not exist in the absence of social agreement on the institutions in which they figure. While self-interest first leads people to form societies, social conventions, he saw, lead to rules of property and justice within those societies.

No natural-rights theorist, in the sense I earlier specified, can possibly be content with this view of the ground of rights, even if it is true that the

---

[10] David Hume, *A Treatise of Human Nature*, ed. L. A. Selby-Bigge (Oxford: Clarendon Press, 1888), 503.

rules and conventional rights so grounded have immense utility, for the reasons given above. Hume's picture of the ground of rights, that is, human agreement, does not assume that there is a sphere of noninterference surrounding individuals that it is the job of rights to protect. Indeed, in Hume, even the right to private property, which he takes to be absolutely crucial to human society, is the product of human contrivance, and it is devised in order to aid ease of living, the prevention of quarrels, and the production of a good life for all. There is no thought that something of immense importance—namely, the security of control over one's fate that natural rights are supposed to convey—has been lost to human society, no thought that the individual has been deprived of something that is his by antecedently existing right.

Any conventional rules agreed to over privacy issues show only that ease of living, prevention of quarrels, and production of a good life for all obtain over these issues as over others. These rules (and rights) may be overcome by utility, since were good consequences not produced by a *continued* observance of the rules, it would be time to change the rules, with consequent effect, perhaps, upon matters that some people want kept private. In this regard, we would do well to remember that even those who used to call themselves "rule utilitarians" were utilitarians.

VII. Noninterference and Human Flourishing

The way forward, it may be thought, is to go down the path of human flourishing and human agency. That is, perhaps the way to defend an assumption of a sphere of noninterference surrounding individuals is to try to defend it as part of an account of rights that focuses upon human flourishing and the development and manifestation of human personality in the form of agency. But an assumption similar to the assumption of a sphere of noninterference surrounding individuals arises here as well.

Suppose we agree, following Finnis in *Natural Law and Natural Rights*,[11] that a certain list of human goods is required in order for humans to flourish, that we can know what is on this list (if not exhaustively, at least pretty fully), and that we can agree on how much or little of each one of these goods a human must have in order to flourish: it might then be claimed that an individual has a right to precisely that level of each good that is on the list. This in turn may mean that, for whatever reason on the individual's part, we may have to provide that level of each good to him or, at the very least, to remove barriers in the way of his providing that level of each good for himself. Accordingly, if we can know what is on the list, then we can determine the scope of our rights. It used to be said that a right to subsistence that was held against those who could provide that subsistence was of this sort, since, under some heading or other, food

---

[11] Finnis, *Natural Law and Natural Rights*.

almost certainly was on the list of goods. (I leave aside here any concern as to whether some scheme of negative rights has to be augmented, in cases where removal of barriers does not suffice to put individuals at the right level, with some scheme of positive rights.)

Now, what is of interest in all this is not whether there is such a right to subsistence (based, perhaps, simply upon someone lacking enough of the relevant good to rise to the minimal threshold of flourishing), but how one determines what things to put on the list to begin with and whether privacy is on it. Finnis, for example, gives his list, which is based upon those things he identifies as human goods, possession of which to some specified degree is required for human flourishing. These goods, when fully manifested in a functioning human agent, partly identify what we take the fully realized human to be. Other theorists provide their lists. The problem is to try to figure out what makes the list and exactly how to determine what makes it.

For example, consider human flourishing: can a person flourish while having it known that he looks at pornography at night? Yes. Can a person flourish while having it known that he is homosexual or has a certain genetic predisposition? Yes. Can a person flourish while having it known that she is 'black' and 'female'? Yes. If we change the issue, it is not always the case that the answer changes. Can a person flourish while remaining comparatively ignorant? Why not? Can a person flourish while becoming comparatively nonautonomous in the important decisions of life? Why not? Monks who entered medieval monasteries—and so surrendered their lives in important respects to the Church and the abbot—did not take themselves not to be flourishing or to cease being human agents, nor did those who wrote about the monks' lives take them to be living lives that were less than "fully" human. Of course, it all depends upon what you mean by flourishing and the point at which, of any characteristic required for flourishing, one defines the minimum that must be possessed; these decisions lie in the hands of the theorist who is drawing up the list.

Moreover, if the list includes more than self-preservation, as does every list-view with which I am familiar, then we have constantly to face the question of whether tradeoffs are possible between items on the list and whether, after tradeoffs, an individual would still be judged as flourishing. For example, suppose a monk cares very little about his autonomy but cares passionately about his happiness, and both are on the list: surely he continues to flourish when he enters the monastery.

What list-views presume is that there is a level of human flourishing and human agency that is the minimum necessary in order to be considered a fully functioning, fully human agent, and that nothing should be permitted (whether it involves transfers or the removal of barriers) to get in the way of having each human placed at that minimum. This minimum sets up a sphere of noninterference, in the sense that it is that minimum that needs to be protected, preserved, and not allowed to diminish. It is tempting to hold, then, that one has rights to that minimum—as defined by the theorist in terms of the conditions and goods (and the requisite degree of them) that need to be in place—in order to satisfy what the theorist sees as the condition of full human flourishing. Everything turns upon where the minimum is drawn, what the conditions and goods are (in terms of which flourishing and full agency are defined), and, as I have explained, how one determines what gets on that list of conditions and goods.

What matters here is simply that the minimum is treated as definitive of what individuals may not be deprived of or prevented from acquiring, which in turn gives them the kind of control over their lives that I earlier noted. Whenever the minimum is not met, the individual can point this out, and this ensures that he must be brought back up to the minimum level of the good in question. In this sense, the minimum sets up a sphere of noninterference surrounding him, at least with respect to how others may behave toward him. Without this kind of assumption—that the minimum serves as a normative marker of outcome or treatment below which the individual may not go or suffer—utilitarian sacrifice of an individual's well-being for the sake of collective well-being would be possible. If we do not grant the assumption, or if we reject the alleged normative character of the minimum that the theorist wants us to accept as definitive of human flourishing, then such sacrifice can occur, and control over one's life is not left fully in one's own hands. The fate of privacy concerns would be swept away in the wash, so far as control is concerned; what would remain would be that element of control over information one deems detrimental to one's well-being that was consistent with the maximization of utility—and no more.

Notice here that another possibility for grounding privacy arises. A move can be made to try to wedge some level of privacy into the minimum by suggesting that privacy is a part of autonomy or that having privacy to some degree or other is a necessary condition of autonomy.[12] Unless this level can be specified rather exactly, though, the claim seems false on the face of it. For, as indicated above, it seems wrong to suggest that I cease to be a self-directed individual if others find out my sexual orientation, my secret hopes for the future, or my age. To be sure, I may regard my well-being as diminished if others come to know these things, but it is misleading to suggest that knowledge in and of itself by others of these things turns me into a non-self-directed individual. Indeed, it may even be true that certain choices may be denied me that, were others not to know these things, would be open to me, but only if the ability to make any and all choices is required in order for me to be fully autono-

---

[12] See, e.g., Elizabeth Beardsley, "Privacy: Autonomy and Selective Disclosure," in J. Roland Pennock and John W. Chapman, eds., *NOMOS XIII: Privacy* (New York: Atherton Press, 1971), 56–70. See also Joseph Kupfer, "Privacy, Autonomy, and Self-Concept," *American Philosophical Quarterly* 24, no. 2 (January 1987): 81–89.

mous am I any less autonomous for others knowing these things. My claim is not that privacy is not related to autonomy; it is only that, unless some minimum of privacy can be specified as required for autonomy, the fact that some choices are now not open to me that otherwise would have been does not show that I am not autonomous. Even to say that I am "less autonomous" in this situation strikes me as wide of the mark, unless one assumes that the ability to make and carry out just any choice is required for full autonomy. If not, then one must specify which choices are the ones required for being autonomous.

VIII. Noninterference and Self-Ownership

One interesting suggestion is that the notion of self-ownership may provide us with what we want, at least if this notion is understood in a particular way. If we own ourselves—if, that is, we have a private property right in ourselves, and if a right to private property were taken to entail the right to exclude others from using our property—then it might be thought that this gives us what we want, that it gives us our core as persons, agents, or individuals, and from that a right to privacy. If we own our core as persons, then we can repel others' intrusions into our core. Such intrusions would violate our private property right, and in so doing would fail to respect our right to exclude others' intrusions into the core. All that a right to privacy would amount to, on this view, is a version of a right to private property, construed as entailing a right to exclude others from use. While this is an interesting line of argument, it is hard to see how it hangs together.

Does it make sense to talk of owning one's core? Have we not just made the sphere of noninterference that rights theorists have taken to surround us part of the extension of our right to private property? Where the flow of information is concerned, it is hard to see how boundaries operate. To say that I have a private property right in the information that constitutes my birth date—I surely do not have a private property right in the fact of it being a particular day and month of the year—is hard to fathom from the perspective of initial acquisition. How do I acquire the right in this information? It seems silly to say that I acquire the right by being born on that date. Other considerations seem even less plausible.

Suppose that I have a certain illness and do not want the fact of my having it to be released: how do I acquire a private property right in this information in such a way that the fact that I have this illness becomes, as it were, mine? For, notice, anything less than owning the fact—as it were, owning the information that I have the illness—would be compatible with others learning this information but violating no private property right of mine. However, if I own the fact, if I own the piece of information that is constituted by the fact that I have the illness, then presumably I can exclude others from the use of this information. But how do I acquire ownership in this case? Do I acquire ownership merely by it being true that I have the illness in question, or merely by it being true that I do not want the information that I have the illness to be released? This is to broaden the scope of "what is mine" in all kinds of ways, since there are countless things that are true of me, in any number of respects, that I do not want to be known by others. Merely by it being the case that something is true of me that I do not want known, surely this does not confer ownership of that something on me. I have bought nothing, sold nothing, traded nothing, and bartered for nothing.

Again, exactly how strongly will this kind of private property right resist appeals to utility? My point is not the thought that, at some level of necessity in others, my private property rights yield to them, though this may well be true; it is rather that the rights theorist who wants privacy to be part of the core seems confronted with a choice. On the one hand, if the theorist stipulates that this private property right to privacy, located in the core, is not to yield at all to utilitarian concerns, then it seems unlikely that informational privacy would fall within the core. It does not seem as sufficiently important to warrant absolutely no intrusion by others *no matter what the consequences*. Otherwise, we should have to tolerate contagions and the rapid spreading of disease. On the other hand, if the theorist stipulates that at least some ground can be given to utilitarian concerns, then we are back where we were in earlier discussions of rights, that is, trying to decide whether this or that case is sufficiently weighty to override the right, for consequentialist reasons, to informational privacy.

Of course, the rights theorist might claim that the right does not yield to utility but to a concatenation of other people's rights claims, but then the additive feature that is supposed to haunt utilitarianism will haunt the rights theorist as well, as one person's right to privacy is balanced against two people's rights in other respects. And if the claims are not additive, so that the situation is one right versus one right versus one right, then it is not clear that we have any way of deciding what to do at all, any way, for example, of preventing the spread of contagion and disease. Any claim that negative rights are compossible in a way that positive rights are not is affected by an obvious fact: two people's lives and well-being can be adversely affected by one person's assertion of a private property right over the information that he is contagious.

IX. UTILITARIAN SACRIFICE AND INDIRECT UTILITARIANISM

To be sure, I have discussed utilitarian sacrifice because that notion, historically, where rights theory is concerned, has been taken to threaten the very control that a concern with natural rights was supposed to locate in the individual. It is obvious, though, that another utilitarian line on the matter is possible, as Hume rightly saw and as virtually all utilitarians today advocate. For one might well hold that utility would stand the best chance of being maximized in social/political life not by postulating in people spheres of noninterference that natural rights can then protect, but rather by ensuring, through a series of institutions and policies, that all people are secure in their persons and their possessions. This could well mean that a strong sense of self-ownership and a relatively strong right to private property are the best ways of achieving maximization of utility. But the notion of self-ownership would not extend to the postulation of a sphere of noninterference in order then to attach a scheme of rights as protective devices to that sphere. There would be no need for such a sphere. One would be taken to own one's own body, one's talents, one's labor, and so on—all things that do not antecedently exist prior to one's coming into existence. Nor would a strong right to self-ownership be utterly immune to the demands of utility, though it certainly could be made to resist mere marginal increases; massively significant increases in utility would carry the day, hopefully with—but also ultimately without— one's consent. There would not be a sphere of noninterference that such increases in utility violated. The same would hold true of a right to private property.

In my opinion, this indirect or two-level form of utilitarianism is, when suitably developed, the only plausible form of utilitarianism. While this is not the place to develop it, it does serve radically to reduce the incidence of utilitarian sacrifice, and it does provide one with good utilitarian reasons to adhere to the institutions and practices in place, even when utility on some particular occasion might be maximized through departing from them. The picture of the utilitarian engaging constantly in utilitarian sacrifice—one of the fears that modern rights theory was developed to still—is an alien one today. However, that such sacrifice remains a possibility, when massive utility could be achieved or massive disutility avoided, is certainly the case.

The fate of utilitarianism is not to the point here. The concern, rather, is with rights theory and the postulated core to persons, agents, or individuals that all such theories assume. Even if utilitarianism were shown utterly deficient as a normative ethical theory, nothing would have been achieved thereby toward showing that a moral right to privacy exists as part of a postulated core.

X. Privacy and the Good Life

As far as I can see, the right to informational privacy finds its philosophical home in this kind of debate about my control over my life and my ability to resist the interference of others with my pursuit of activities that comprise my conception of the good life. Privacy is not special in this regard. It is a part of the general discussion both of those things that go toward making up the good life and of the tension that this in turn creates between my activities in pursuit of the good and the presence of others with different ends and different conceptions of the good. What is worrisome in this debate is that many theorists assume what has to be shown and then go on to find that a right to privacy just follows in the wake of what they have assumed. The assumption of a sphere of noninterference over which I have control is just too accommodating an umbrella under which to place a right to privacy to let its role in the discussion of privacy pass unnoticed.

Philosophy, Bowling Green State University

PRIVACY AS A MATTER OF TASTE AND RIGHT

By Alexander Rosenberg

I. Introduction

Privacy is something we all want. We seek privacy to prevent others from securing information about us that is immediately embarrassing, and so causes us pain but not material loss. We also value privacy for strategic reasons in order to prevent others from imposing material and perhaps psychic costs upon us. I use the expression "securing information" so that it covers everything from the immediate sensory data that a voyeur acquires to the financial data a rival may acquire about our businesses. In the degenerate case of the Peeping Tom's invasion of our privacy, suffering is caused just by the voyeur's having acquired the information, even if nothing is ever done with it beyond the voyeur's recalling it from time to time. In all other cases, privacy prevents others from imposing costs or harms on us in ways that require that they secure information about us.

Since we all want privacy, it is natural to assume that it is something we have a right to. If it is something we all have a right to, then surely it must have moral value. This is the beginning of both the interest in and a certain amount of confusion about the political philosophy of privacy. For now the philosopher is obliged to define privacy, identify its moral value, and show why privacy is ours as a matter of right. But the more one thinks about privacy, the less confident one can be that privacy is a distinctively moral desideratum, as opposed to a largely prudential one, when it is anything more than a matter of widely shared taste. I shall argue that our interest in privacy is mainly a matter of taste and prudence. I say mainly, because in the end there appears to be a normative component in our thinking about privacy that seems resistant to this account of privacy as a matter of taste and prudence.

II. The Moral Social Psychology of Privacy

Instead of beginning with the obvious point that we seek privacy to prevent others from securing information about us that is embarrassing to us or of strategic value to them in their interactions with us, moral philosophers have sought some positive moral value that privacy plays. They have done so owing to a suspicion that if privacy is just a matter of hiding the truth from others, it cannot be a good thing from the moral point of view. But the weaknesses of the arguments for the moral value of privacy suggest that privacy's importance rests on other, largely prudential considerations.

Most of those who have worked in this area have attempted to develop or presuppose a moral psychology or, more exactly, a moral social psychology for privacy. *Moral psychology* is the study and theorizing about those psychological factors that either make normative principles binding or allow us to exercise moral judgment. By analogy, *moral social psychology* deals with the social relations that may do either of these things. Thus, moral social psychologists have widely agreed that some sort of privacy is a requisite for the full range of normal or healthy social relations. However, they have not been able to agree on what privacy is or exactly what human personal needs privacy fulfills. For example, political scientist Robert Gerstein argues that "intimate relationships could not exist if we did not continue to insist on privacy for them."[1] Part of his argument is that the presence of unwanted spectators would turn the participants in an intimate experience into spectators, whose self-consciousness would so distract them from the experience that it would be impossible to consummate the experience. Gerstein illustrates the point by describing how the presence of observers to a sexual relationship can destroy many of its most important qualities, when it can proceed at all.

In the same vein, law professor Charles Fried argues that privacy is important to a range of human relationships:

> It is my thesis that privacy is not just one possible means among others to insure some other value, but that it is necessarily related to ends and relations of the most fundamental sort: respect, love, friendship and trust. Privacy is not merely a good technique for furthering these fundamental relations; rather without privacy they are simply inconceivable. They require a context of privacy or the possibility of privacy for their existence.[2]

Similarly, philosopher James Rachels argues that privacy is a necessary condition for other socially valuable ends. Unlike Fried and Gerstein, Rachels explicitly recognizes the connection between privacy and information:

> I want to give an account of the value of privacy based in the idea that there is a close connection between our ability to control who has access to us and to information about us, and our ability to create and

[1] Robert Gerstein, "Privacy and Self-Incrimination," in Ferdinand David Schoeman, ed., *Philosophical Dimensions of Privacy: An Anthology* (Cambridge: Cambridge University Press, 1984), 252.
[2] Charles Fried, "Privacy," in Schoeman, ed., *Philosophical Dimensions of Privacy*, 205.

maintain different sorts of social relationships with different people. According to this account, privacy is necessary if we are to maintain the variety of social relationships with other people that we want to have, and that is why it is important to us. By a "social relationship" I do not mean anything especially unusual or technical. I mean the sort of thing which we usually have in mind when we say of two people that they are friends or that they are husband and wife or that one is the other's employer.[3]

According to Rachels, each of these (and other) social relations is characterized by "an idea of . . . what information it is appropriate for them [the parties to the relations] to have."[4] If we could not maintain these relationships, we would have good reason to object. But maintaining them requires that we differentially control access to information about ourselves, owing apparently to the fact that differential access is a key determinant of what sets different relationships apart. In a similar vein, philosopher Ferdinand Schoeman noted the wrong that is done to others when unsought intimate information is imposed on them. "It is . . . very awkward to be going about one's business and be confronted with a plea or expectation for personal involvement which by hypothesis is unoccasioned by the relationship. Although occasionally welcome, generally such pleas are disturbing for they seem to give us less control over where we will expend our emotional resources."[5]

All of these authors express noble sentiments about friendship, love, intimacy, and the importance of privacy to their maintenance. But is privacy really necessary to the establishment and maintenance of social relationships characterized by intimacy, friendship, and love? "Really necessary" here can mean "logically or conceptually necessary" or "necessary as a matter of fact about *Homo sapiens* in groups" or "necessary as a matter of fact about us in contemporary society." On the first interpretation, the claim that privacy is necessary would require a great deal of further argument and a good deal of consensus about the meaning of fundamental concepts in moral philosophy. On the second interpretation, the claim requires a great deal of empirical (as opposed to armchair) social science to establish. On the third interpretation, the claim may have little universal normative significance.

To move from these claims of moral social psychology, even if they are true, to the conclusion that privacy is, therefore, a moral value, requires that social relationships of intimacy, friendship, and love have a more fundamental moral value from which the value of privacy as a means can

---

[3] James Rachels, "Why Privacy Is Important," in Schoeman, ed., *Philosophical Dimensions of Privacy*, 292–93.

[4] Ibid., 295.

[5] Ferdinand Schoeman, "Privacy and Intimate Information," in Schoeman, ed., *Philosophical Dimensions of Privacy*, 404.

be derived. Endowing these relationships with intrinsic moral value seems far-fetched. Intimacy, friendship, and even love are not of intrinsic moral value: each of them can prove to be a means to moral ills or in themselves contribute to the badness of a state of affairs they characterize. When these three features characterize the relationship between people engaged in heinous crimes against humanity, they certainly do not detract in any way from the badness or wrongness of the actions. When their presence is causally necessary for such acts, some might hold that the presence of intimacy, friendship, or love among the perpetrators increases the badness or wrongness of their acts. For example, war crimes committed by a group of soldiers might be in part the result of zeal inspired by their friendship, intimacy, or love for one another.

For all their desirability, could a just society get along without intimacy, friendship, and love? We can perfectly well imagine a desert island society and a scenario of impeccable justice and moral probity in which the inhabitants have no interest in the sort of social relations that moral social psychologists extol. Like the emotionally controlled society of Vulcan in *Star Trek*, it might not be a society creatures like us would want to live in, but it might well be devoid of injustice. Such a society would have no need for the sort of privacy that moral social psychologists seek to justify. Alternatively, we can imagine a society replete with friendship, intimacy, and love, but without privacy, although the agents in that society would be differently situated than us. Anthropologists have even reported the existence of societies of this latter sort. For example, various Eskimo and Inuit peoples live in harsh environments that make privacy impossible, but make friendship, intimacy, and love necessary for survival and emotional health.

No one doubts that we all want to have a full range of normal social relations, but it is not clear what is so morally special about this range of social relations that might underwrite the *intrinsic* moral value of privacy. Bear in mind that doubts about the moral value of X can be compatible with the recognition that people like us find X psychologically indispensable for normal human life in our society. But for X to have intrinsic moral value, it must have cross-cultural force. Thus, X must transcend present social arrangements of any one society and, also, transcend doubts born of ethical relativism.

As Fried develops his argument for the necessity of privacy for intimate social relationships, he connects privacy to a distinctive quality that is much more well accepted as genuinely and distinctively morally significant than intimacy, friendship, or love: our integrity as persons.

> To make clear the necessity of privacy as a context for respect, love, friendship and trust is to bring out also why a threat to privacy seems to threaten our very integrity as persons. To respect, love, trust, feel affection for others and to regard ourselves as the objects of love,

trust and affection for others is at the heart of our notion of ourselves as persons among persons, and privacy is the necessary atmosphere for these attitudes and actions, as oxygen is for combustion.[6]

Similarly, Schoeman argued that

the respect for privacy marks out something morally significant about what it is to be a person and about what it is to have close relationships with another. . . . [R]espect for privacy reflects a realization that not all dimensions of self and relationships gain their moral worth through their promotion of independently worthy ends.[7]

If some dimensions of self and some relationships have moral worth independent of the worthy ends that they may promote, then they must have intrinsic moral worth. The conception that we have of ourselves as persons of integrity does seem a stronger candidate for something having intrinsic value than do various social relationships. But then the problem becomes one of showing that privacy is in fact indispensable to personal integrity. The claim that privacy is, in Fried's words, "the necessary atmosphere" for personal integrity seems empirically false. It is clear that actual and hypothetical scenarios obtain in which respect, love, friendship, trust, and the greatest personal integrity are possible though there is no scope for privacy.

Consider, for example, the unprivate prison career and personal relationships of Nelson Mandela and his fellow prisoners of the South African apartheid regime, or the personal integrity of the political prisoners whom Solzhenitsyn described in *The Gulag Archipelago*. Even if love, trust, and affection are crucial to regarding ourselves as persons, the fact that they may exist and even flourish in the absence of privacy makes moot the controversial claim that personhood is impossible without privacy. Again, no one should question the claim that in this day and age, we may have great difficulty, as a matter of fact, in actualizing our potential to be moral agents without the support of these social relationships. But from this it no more follows that these social relationships are themselves of intrinsic moral value than that oxygen is of intrinsic moral value because it is necessary for actualizing our potential to be moral agents.

Thus, the moral social psychologists of privacy disguise a lack of argument with pious assertions. Even if they are correct about the connection between privacy and relationships that are important to us, these considerations will not underwrite the claim that privacy is either intrinsically morally valuable or an indispensable means to ends that are in-

[6] Fried, "Privacy," 205.
[7] Schoeman, "Privacy and Intimate Information," 404.

trinsically morally valuable. Privacy does not after all have any intrinsic moral value. It is just a matter of withholding information from others.

III. Evolution of a Taste for Privacy

Though they do not suffice to ground a right to privacy, all these accounts do touch on something significant about privacy itself. Behind these forays into moral social psychology, there lies an obvious and very plausible explanation for the origin of a universal taste for privacy: a felt need for privacy which, however, has different content in different environments. The division of social roles and specialization in a society is like the division of labor, adaptive for the individuals within it. Thus, the argument for privacy as valuable reflects an essential component of an evolutionary explanation of how a sense of privacy might have arisen among interacting humans and indeed infrahumans. Given hunter-gatherer organisms like us, geared to maximize reproductive fitness, the advantage to be secured by friendship and love is evident. There is much evidence that both cooperation and the division of labor are highly adaptive strategies among hunter-gatherer peoples competing against megafauna in the savannah. Cooperation and trade of the sort required under the circumstances for survival and flourishing will require social institutions and these in turn may well be fostered by privacy. If some sort of privacy is essential for friendship and love, its adaptive value is manifest.

This argument for the necessity of privacy is more compelling as an evolutionary explanation than as a piece of philosophical analysis. Note that this evolutionary argument does not mean that the felt need for privacy will always arise in human societies. The argument is compossible with the recognition that there are or can be societies in which environmental circumstances either discourage or obviate cooperation and with it social relationships that require privacy. There may have been and still are societies in which these relationships obtain with little or no privacy of the sort we recognize. A range of privacy-securing institutions, roles, and rules that differ from one another depending on a society's environment—from the Kalahari to the Arctic, from the Stone Age to the postmodern age—is just what we would expect if the acceptance of privacy is a disposition selected for and shaped by evolutionary adaptation to different environments. Additionally, though privacy may foster social relationships that are adaptive to a particular environment, in its absence other social arrangements will emerge that are equally adaptive. Nature always has more than one way of skinning its cats.

The anthropological literature suggests that almost all societies honor some sort of personal sphere for each individual. But the literature also shows that such spheres differ substantially from culture to culture, even in regard to human behavior paradigmatically marked out as private in our culture. What our society counts as paradigmatically indecent action—

intrusion on people engaged in basic biological functions, disrobed, or in sexual relations—other societies treat as acts of no moral importance. Among the Dobe Ju of East Africa there are no latrines, and sexual relations are conducted in the presence of children. Apparently, neither the Tiwi nor the Mardu of Australia wore clothing of any kind when they first met Europeans, and still remove them in their absence.[8] Even among modern industrialized societies of the same general culture, there is a wide diversity of standards of privacy. Americans traveling to Europe in the fifties and sixties were shocked at the lack of privacy in public rest rooms. Today, acceptable styles of bathing costume on the two sides of the Atlantic reflect significant differences over where the private sphere ends. Indeed, even in American society, while most of us will assert a right to privacy to prevent others from "indecently" observing portions of our anatomy, some assert an equal and opposite right to impose information on us about portions of their anatomy: hence nudist camps and topless protests. Even the most commonly private acts—sexual relations—are not universally private in all cultures, ours included.

The fact that territoriality and other claims of personal space obtain among a wide variety of infrahumans reinforces the attractiveness of an evolutionary explanation of our culturally variable desires for privacy.[9] The universality of our acceptance of and provision for personal space, coupled with the high variability of what acts, parts of the body, or physical space count as personal space, strongly suggests that there is an adaptational process operating to create differing spheres of privacy in differing environments. This adaptational response to differing environments operates to select for a generic taste for privacy in all human environments. Of course, it is possible that human concerns with bodily privacy may be "holdovers" from a territoriality-seeking disposition that was adaptive in our evolutionary ancestors. More likely, it is not a holdover. It is like the incest taboo, the conscious expression of a behavioral constraint selected for up and down the phylogenetic tree. Overcrowding and lack of privacy in animals is known to reduce populations, and both the symptoms which result from it and the mechanisms by which it is reduced are common among humans and nonhumans.

If privacy is adaptive for creatures like us, over the long term it will be selected for and will either become something that gives us psychological satisfaction or become closely tied to something that does. Thus, individual creatures will be selected for wanting it and for having taken steps to insure it. If the most efficient way for each to insure its own privacy is

[8] See Richard B. Lee, *The Dobe Ju/'hoansi*, 2d ed. (New York: Harcourt Brace, 1993); C. W. M. Hart, Arnold R. Pilling, and Jane C. Goodale, *The Tiwi of North Australia*, 3d ed. (New York: Holt, Rinehart, and Winston, 1988); and Robert Tomlinson, *The Mardu Aborigines: Living the Dream in Australia's Desert*, 2d ed. (Fort Worth, TX: Holt, Rinehart, and Winston, 1991).

[9] Edward O. Wilson, *Sociobiology: The New Synthesis* (Cambridge, MA: Harvard University Press, 1975), 256–78.

to adopt a rule enjoining privacy violations by all, then such a group norm may emerge as a "focal point" or as an evolutionarily adaptive strategy. Philosopher Brian Skyrms has shown that private property may evolve naturally as an adaptation that reduces conflict and encourages cooperative outcomes.[10] To the extent that privacy is a matter of restricting rights of others to informational resources, it could emerge along with other privatized resources. Even where property institutions do not emerge, privacy may evolve as a device for apportioning space or territory in ways that are mutually advantageous and so require little or no enforcement.

The trouble with this hypothesis, as with all such evolutionary theorizing, is its resistance to testing.[11] We can certainly imagine scenarios in which there is no taste for privacy and plenty of friendship, love, and other prosocial adaptive institutions. But the cross-species prevalence of territoriality and privacy makes evolutionary adaptation or sheer coincidence the best available explanation for the emergence of universal generic privacy, which differs widely in its specific content in different environments. The crucial thing to see is that if privacy is necessary for certain social relationships, this is only in virtue of other contingent facts about a society and the environment in which privacy's necessity is claimed. Someone might reply that since we are engaged in developing a moral philosophy for our actual society and not for a toy-society or a Robinson Crusoe island, the environmental contingency of privacy's importance makes no difference. But this misses the point: if the content of our desire for privacy and the desire to accord it to others is contingent on features of our society, and will be quite different for other actual and possible social arrangements, then any claim that privacy has special moral standing is seriously reduced.

For one thing, privacy becomes a relativistic concept. On the anthropological evidence and from the evolutionary perspective, it is clear why the extent and categories of the private sphere tend to differ so broadly across cultures. If what constitutes the private differs from culture to culture depending on other contingencies about these cultures and their environments, there may be little if anything that the concept of privacy covers that is common and peculiar across them all. If privacy is a concept with no common core, there may not be a single reason for any putative generic right to privacy across changeable social arrangements. In different societies, there may be different grounds for the same right. This will make privacy and any right to it quite a different notion from, for example, the classical civil rights of life or liberty, which many of us hold to obtain not only in our own society but cross-culturally as well. If even

[10] Brian Skyrms, *Evolution of the Social Contract* (Cambridge: Cambridge University Press, 1996), chap. 4, esp. 76–79.

[11] See Alexander Rosenberg, "The Biological Justification of Ethics: A Best-Case Scenario," *Social Philosophy and Policy* 8, no. 1 (Autumn 1990): 86–101.

within our culture the functions which privacy serves are contingent, variable among individuals, and changeable over time, then its nature and the putative right to it will not be provided by some very neat and simple theory. For example, a default right to privacy would be of great value to you in the face of an intrusive and coercive government, but it would be an annoyance to merchants when it prevents them from accessing information about your Internet purchasing preferences. If privacy is in the end a matter of individual taste, then seeking a moral foundation for it—beyond its role in making social institutions possible that we happen to prize—will be no more fruitful than seeking a moral foundation for the taste for truffles.

Finally, if the taste for some degree of privacy and for according the same to others are traits selected for and widespread, then the taste for privacy probably needs less protection than other things that we value. Only the odd mutant will seek to invade our privacy or wish us to invade his. A right to certain privacies that no one in his right mind would transgress is hardly a right that we need trouble ourselves much about, even if we grace it with the title of a right.

Privacy will begin to be something protected with rights only when the relative costs of invading it decline and the relative benefits of doing so increase. Therefore, privacy will not be a moral right at all, but rather a prudential one.

IV. Judith Jarvis Thomson on Privacy

I began this paper with an implicit definition of privacy: prevention of others from securing information about us that is immediately embarrassing (and so causes us pain) or of strategic value to others in their interactions with us (and so imposes on us other material costs). But this definition is controversial. Indeed, it is controverted by perhaps the most well-known philosophical treatment of privacy: Judith Jarvis Thomson's influential paper, "The Right to Privacy." [12]

Thomson begins her analysis by acknowledging that "perhaps the most striking thing about the right to privacy is that nobody seems to have a very clear idea about what it is." [13] Presumably the uncertainty revolves around the concept of 'privacy', not the concept of 'right'. In her inimitable way, Thomson then proceeds to sketch some imaginary cases in which her clear intuitions enable her to draw conclusions about the right to privacy. The conclusion to which she comes is that there really is no

---

[12] Judith Jarvis Thomson, "The Right to Privacy," *Philosophy and Public Affairs* 4, no. 4 (Summer 1975): 295–314, reprinted in Schoeman, ed., *Philosophical Dimensions of Privacy*, 272–89. Subsequent page references are to the reprinting.

[13] Ibid., 272.

distinct right to privacy, as opposed to other, presumably more fundamental, rights:

> The question arises, then, whether or not there are any rights in the right to privacy cluster which aren't also in some other right cluster. I suspect there aren't any, and that the right to privacy is everywhere overlapped by other rights. . . . The right to privacy is derivative in this sense: it is possible to explain in the case of each right in the cluster [of privacy rights] how come we have it without ever once mentioning the right to privacy.[14]

What Thomson means is that the right to privacy is "overlapped" by other rights in the sense that each privacy-right violation is in fact the violation of some other right, and the wrongness of the privacy-right violation is exhausted by the wrongness of the violation of the other right. Thus, it seems to me, "the right to privacy" will be at most a sort of convenient expression for packaging together all of these other rights. This will explain why it seems difficult to carve out a distinct right to privacy, for example, by identifying a moral desideratum that privacy is extrinsically good for. If this is Thomson's claim, then we need to ask why we find it convenient to employ the notion of a right to privacy, since the motley of other rights that it protects have nothing in common. As we shall see, the answer will vindicate the implicit definition of privacy in terms of information, a claim that Thomson denies.

Thomson's cases are all ones in which it may look initially tempting to say that a right to privacy has been violated, but which, she argues, in the end are violations of either property rights or rights over our persons/bodies. Summarizing these cases does her discussion a certain amount of injustice. Thomson's argument proceeds by appealing to our intuitions about the nature of the wrongness of certain privacy-rights violations. If I circumvent the steps a person takes to keep his face from view or his voice from hearing, I have violated that person's rights over his person. "These rights—the right not to be looked at and the right not to be listened to—are analogous to rights we have over our property."[15] If I circumvent the steps a person has taken to keep her pornographic picture's existence and nature from others, then I violate that person's property right, "specifically the negative right that others shall not look at the picture."[16] Although Thomson does not go on to make the claim, we may argue not for analogy but for the assimilation of a right over the person to a species of property rights—all persons being the owners of their bodies. This would reduce the cases in question exclusively to violations

---

[14] Ibid., 286–87.
[15] Ibid., 280.
[16] Ibid., 278.

of property rights. If all privacy-rights violations were property-and-body rights violations, then the right to privacy would just be an aspect of the right to property in a broad enough sense of the term to include ownership of the body. If privacy rights are a species or subset of property rights, they will require and submit to the sorts of arguments available for justifying private property.

Thomson does go on to address the claim that is of central concern to us, that is, the claim that privacy is about information. But having entertained the thought, she emphatically rejects it:

> I should say straight away that it seems to me none of us has a right over any fact to the effect that fact shall not be known by others. You may violate a man's rights to privacy by looking at him or listening to him; there is no such thing as violating a man's right to privacy by simply knowing something about him.[17]

Again, according to Thomson, examining cases of putative privacy violation shows that there is a right that people not take certain steps to acquire information about us—by looking at us or our property, by listening to us when we do not want them to, by torturing us, or by extorting information. Doing these things violates our property rights or our other rights. But there is no distinct right to keep information secret from all. Or again, there is a right that people not use acquired information to our disadvantage, but according to Thomson, this right is based on a right not to be caused distress. She proceeds in a similar fashion to dismiss other cases in which privacy violations are wrong because they violate the right to be free from annoyance in the home or in a public place, or the right that if famous the public not press one too closely, or the right that our liberties not be infringed in the absence of a compelling need to do so.[18]

But if Thomson is right about these cases, then there is an outstanding question that she does not answer: the question of why we invoke a privacy right at all if "the wrongness of every violation of the right to privacy can be explained without ever once mentioning [privacy]."[19] One attractive answer is that the right to privacy is an instrument, a convenience, a right we introduce and invoke because it is the best or most efficient or most convenient way to assure the protection of other rights of ours, including the motley of mainly property rights in the privacy-rights cluster.

Consider the following: in order to violate property or bodily rights we need to acquire information about the agent that the agent wishes us not

---

to acquire. Even the degenerate case of merely peeping is the acquisition of information. The case is degenerate in the obvious sense and also in the sense that pain is caused to the victim even if acquiring the data has no further causal upshot. The violations Thomson envisions of particular property rights—rights over the person, rights not to be annoyed, and rights not to be pressed too closely—require the acquisition of information that the subjects wish others not to acquire. There are other rights violations that require information, but these are violations that require information that we otherwise would not sequester, for example, wrongfully killing me requires information about where I am, which is the sort of information that is normally not considered private.

Invoking a privacy right in mainly property cases is effective and efficient because it requires the least interference with the actions of others that might infringe the mainly property rights in question. Suppose that information about us is available to others and could be exploited by them to arrogate our property or cause us nonmaterial harms like shame or embarrassment. Then, protecting property rights against violations would require constraints on others' exploitation of information about us. This would involve more interference with others than merely preventing them from securing information in the first place, whence the greater efficiency and effectiveness of an enforceable right to privacy.

Thus, privacy-rights violations are rights violations that are most effectively and efficiently prevented by restricting information (including mere sensory data). Yet, Thomson writes, "there is no such thing as violating a man's right to privacy by simply knowing something about him."[20] This will be so even though simply knowing something about a person may harm that person. For, as Thomson makes manifest in another justly famous paper, "A Defense of Abortion," causing someone harm may violate no right of that person.[21] Yes, but . . . it is the nature of the information and the inevitability that people will make use of the information that comes to them that makes it convenient or expedient to invoke a right to privacy.

Consider two alternatives. In one case everyone knows many embarrassing or discreditable things about everyone else, though no one realizes that anyone else does so. Suppose further that this knowledge has no effect whatsoever on people's actions and behavior. In the second case privacy rights are completely respected. Never mind that no actual human beings could realize the first case: we are all of us too sensitive to the information that we pick up about others (especially discreditable information) to be completely poker-faced about it. The question is whether there is a morally significant difference between the two cases: complete

[20] Ibid., 282.
[21] Judith Jarvis Thomson, "A Defense of Abortion," *Philosophy and Public Affairs* 1, no. 1 (Fall 1971): 47–66.

nonexploitation of widely disseminated, discreditable information about others or strict privacy. Note that in the first case, the invasion of everyone's privacy causes no one pain or loss because the invasion is undetected and unexploited. I suggest that there is not a morally significant difference between the two cases. From this equivalence, I infer that privacy is an instrumental good that we invoke because people as we know them are not immune to the effects of changes in the information that they acquire about others. Even in the degenerate case of the Peeping Tom, what troubles us is that the data remains accessible in the mind of the voyeur and can be accessed at any time. Even this "use" causes us pain.

Owing to our evolved taste for privacy and for according privacy to others, we need invoke no right to it until the value of information rises and the costs of securing it fall. When the costs to others of acquiring information that we wish to keep secret fall, and the value to them of this information rises, the incentives to invade privacy increase, and we begin to seek means of protecting it. A right to privacy emerges as the most convenient protective device.

V. Privacy and the Economics of Information

The right to privacy turns out to be a natural right to the extent that the preferences that lead to wanting it and granting it were selected for as evolutionary adaptations. But it is at the same time a prudential right, the sort that will arise as a matter of institutional design among rational agents bargaining over a set of rules to govern themselves for mutual advantage. Rational bargainers will adopt prudential rights in information that are distinctive and separate from rights to property and person, largely owing to the character of information as a commodity. To see this requires only a little pure theory of the economics of information.

Economists recognize that information is a commodity, but it is not like other goods we want. Information is abstract, in a sense familiar to philosophers, as opposed to concrete. It can be expressed in a variety of physical representations, various kinds of writing (print, digital coding), and most important for present purposes, it can be represented in people's brains under the label 'beliefs'. But we need to distinguish a piece of information from any of its representations for the same reason we distinguish numbers from numerals. However, for information to be a commodity it must be physically represented at least somewhere—in a brain or elsewhere. Economically valuable information has come to be labeled "intellectual property," but information is a commodity that is different in important ways from other kinds of property.

Perhaps, most obviously, unlike physical goods, information is not appropriable, even though it must be represented physically (in our brains or elsewhere). It is inappropriable because it can be perfectly and almost costlessly duplicated. If I have information and I give it to another, or another takes it without permission, I still have the information. If I give it away or sell it, I have further information about who else now has it. In many cases, we need to keep information in other forms than memory; we need physically to represent it—on paper, electronically, etc. But then it can be copied. If it is taken by copying without my knowledge, then unlike other property, I will not be able to tell that someone else has taken it simply by inspecting my store of intellectual property. Nothing will appear to be missing. In most cases, there is no mark on my representation or copy of the information that shows it has been copied. Only if I apprehend the other individual acquiring the information or if that person's use of the information comes to my attention will I acquire the information that it is no longer exclusively mine. Of course, at that point it may be too late to stop the use or avoid its effect on me. Moreover, because information is abstract, it is sometimes impossible to establish that it was my (copy of the) information that was misappropriated.

Consider the fate of an invention in a regime of perfect competition and no rights of ownership of information. The inventor has in effect acquired some information about how to make something or make it better or cheaper, etc. The inventor cannot surrender the sheer information by selling or giving others (copies of) the information. But economically valuable information like this, which may have cost a great deal to acquire, can be sold (nonexclusively), then resold very cheaply, or even given away. The incentives to sell useful information that you have bought will be very great just because selling the information often does not reduce its usefulness to you, and selling it enables you to reduce your net costs of acquiring the information or even to profit from your original investment. Consider the black market in software, which is easy to copy at very low cost. These two features of the information mean that those who created it originally and, indeed, those who purchased it from the owners cannot secure anything close to the total market revenue that will be produced through its legal and illegal sale. More generally, information cannot be fully appropriated by a purchaser because the seller still has the information, nor can any seller—neither the original owner nor the subsequent purchaser—secure full revenue in the market price charged for selling a copy or representation of the information. Consequently, in a perfectly competitive market without rights over information, no one will have an incentive to invest in the creation of new information, and all will have an incentive to acquire it without payment from those irrational enough to invest in its creation. As a result, there will be underinvestment in new discoveries, that is, below the level that would be repaid by returns on improvements in production or utility gained through the market. Alternatively, if information once acquired through original discovery is effectively kept secret and not sold, the increasing returns to scale for the owners might provide so great a competitive advantage that inventors would duplicate one another's efforts and there would be overinvestment in research and development. Thus, in a competitive economy, investment in the original acquisition of information like inventions will always be suboptimal. Moreover, as the costs of copying information fall, costs of new discoveries rise, and as the difficulty of enforcing secrecy increases, investment in new discoveries will decline further and further below the optimal level. The nonprivacy of information is a classical example of market failure. In our day, the cheap photocopier, the reliance on unencrypted electronic information storage, and the powers of reverse engineering would make the degree of market failure catastrophic.

Fortunately, this problem of market failure was long ago solved through the institutions of patent and copyright. These devices do not quite ensure an optimum level of investment in information, because they allow for economies of scale (and, hence, monopoly rents), but they enable markets more nearly to approach it. A patent in part solves both the potential underinvestment and overinvestment problems. On the one hand, it solves the underinvestment problem by giving the first owner of the information an enforceable right to charge for each "copy." On the other hand, it solves the overinvestment problem by requiring the owner to make the information public, so that all who might be able to use it can learn of its existence and purchase "copies." Though patents and copyrights were hardly the result of an explicit social contract, rational agents faced with the general problem presented by the socially nonoptimal provision of new information would endorse a system of rules that make information more like nonabstract property, over which privacy can be better retained.

Consider, as another complication, the economic problem of positional information: unpatentable information a firm may have about its own state and plans. For example, company secrets like financial position, merger and acquisition strategies, and other economically valuable information could be of great benefit to a competitor. Given imperfect patent laws, or imperfect enforcement, an original owner of information may wish to retain it as a piece of positional information, forgoing the returns from sale in order to reap greater rewards from exclusive use, if exclusivity can be enforced. A trade secret could be positional information as well.

Suppose that, as rational agents contracting a legal environment for ourselves, we are faced with the choice between establishing an environment in which such information can be kept enforceably secret and one in which all such positional information is fair game to commercial "espionage." Roughly, we are in the situation of card players contemplating whether or not to have a rule that players may surreptitiously look at one another's cards or not. We can allow it, but then we will be playing a quite different game than a traditional card game. The game may be interesting and diverting, but it will no longer be a test exclusively of our knowledge of probability theory, human psychology, and facial gestures; it will be a test of all of these plus our powers of surreptitious observation. Since our objective is a game of skill at cards rather than furtiveness, we choose to prohibit looking at one another's cards. A game in which looking at other players' cards is permitted is not a morally inferior game to one in which it is forbidden—it is just less fun.

Similarly, rational agents could contract into an economy in which there are no restraints on the acquisition and use of positional information, but the result will be suboptimal for most of us most of the time. Without enforceable privacy of positional information, the price signals can be employed to deceive others about one's knowledge of their private affairs and one's willingness to trade. If most players know this, then market-pricing as a device for efficiently exchanging commodities will be threatened. For a graphic example, consider what happens in an auction when the buyers learn the sellers' real reserve price (as opposed to the one sometimes quoted in the catalog) or the sellers know the buyers' maximal price or both. If both parties know that this scenario is likely, the auction may collapse. Indeed, a nonperfectly competitive market (i.e., any real market) may grind to a halt altogether, leaving everyone worse off, including those who seek and secure positional information.

As with card games, the choice between privacy and no privacy is not between morally superior and morally inferior options. Rather, it is a pragmatic decision about which alternative is more likely to leave us better off. As with patents and copyrights, the abstract problems described were long ago solved in principle in the legal theory of contracts. As technology makes information acquisition, duplication, and transmission more and more inexpensive, ways are sought to adapt these principles of contract to preserve rights to retain information or to recover the gains from trade in information.

The important point about patents, copyrights, and positional information is that regulations that govern information reflect the nature of information as an unusual commodity, as well as the costs and benefits that accrue among agents in a market from various regimes for the control of information. Moral or normative considerations do not seem to enter into the matter.

Now, consider two scenarios. In the first case, there is information about me that has a value that is not measured in dollars but rather in units of utility. If someone acquires the information, I will suffer pain owing to the sheer embarrassment that the other's knowledge produces in me or because the other will use the information to my disadvantage. In the second case, there is either little or no information about me that is embarrassing or useful against me or the cost of effectively protecting embarrassing or useful information is low and the cost of securing it is high. No one will need a very strong privacy right in the second case. This situation characterizes most pre-Western societies. Social groups in which there is extreme equality, both of resources and power, and high homogeneity of tastes, preferences, and mores, will not trouble themselves to establish rights to privacy (though they will honor privacy mores shaped by evolutionary adaptation). The reason is that information about members will not have any value in extracting advantage from them. But as inequalities and differences among people arise, so do opportunities for exploiting such information for material and nonmaterial reward. Because of its unusual character, so different from other commodities, information about people, especially information that they do not want others to have, is versatile. Often, the acquisition of compromising information will be an effective tool to enable its user to extract almost anything from a subject, while retaining a high degree of anonymity for the user (no fingerprints, no DNA traces on copies). Thus, information can be effectively employed to acquire almost anything protected by property and self-ownership rights. If at the same time technological change makes the cost of securing information fall and the cost of protecting it rise, then the search for ways of controlling the use of such information will intensify. The best and most effective way to control use of information, without interfering with the conduct of others, is to prevent it from ever coming into others' hands. This is the essential function that a right to privacy serves, and that right will be strengthened and entrenched as the cost of securing information falls and its value rises.

Justice Louis Brandeis, who served on the U.S. Supreme Court from 1916 to 1939, in a way recognized this instrumental role of the right to privacy. Although he is widely credited with the view that the right to privacy is the right to be let alone, in fact his argument for the latter right rests on its instrumental role in securing the former. Writing of "the makers of our constitution," Brandeis held that "[t]hey conferred, as against the government, the right to be let alone—the most comprehensive of rights, and the right most valued by civilized men. To protect that right, every unjustifiable intrusion by the Government upon the privacy of the individual, whatever the means employed, must be deemed a violation of the fourth amendment."[22]

The upshot of this discussion is that whether rational agents seek to establish privacy rights will depend on cost/benefit calculations that change over time. It will be no surprise if privacy rights are highly variable between cultures and levels of technology, as these factors affect the value, storage, costs, and control of information.

VI. Credit and Genetic Testing: Efficiency v. Equality

Yet all these cost/benefit considerations seem to come up against a major piece of irrationality about privacy, so large a bit of irrationality as

---

[22] *Olmstead v. U.S.*, 277 U.S. 438, 478 (1928) (Brandeis, J., dissenting). Thus, the criticism advanced by William A. Parent, for instance, that Brandeis unwarrantably assimilated privacy to the more general right to be let alone, seems mistaken. Brandeis rightly saw that a privacy protection was the most effective way of ensuring "the most comprehensive of rights." See William A. Parent, "Privacy, Morality, and the Law," *Philosophy and Public Affairs* 12, no. 4 (Fall 1983): 271.

to undermine this whole approach, or at least suggest that it misses something important about privacy.

An example will illustrate my point. In the system of health insurance in force in the United States, individuals usually secure coverage through their employers, though occasionally it is obtained through insurance companies. In the former case, health insurance rates are determined by the cost of providing care to large groups brought together for reasons which have nothing to do with their actual health. When a group is large enough, this practice of "experience-rating" ensures that aggregate health care costs are predictable to the insurer and affordable to employers and participants. Experience-rating of groups provides no incentive for insurance companies to secure information about individuals.

Until the advent of the computer, information about people's medical conditions was lodged in files in doctors' offices, clinics, and hospitals, and it was difficult to gain access to such information. Once this information was put on networks, in order to facilitate, for example, the detection of dangerous prescription drug interactions, it became literally a matter of a bit of clever computer hacking to gain access to almost anyone's medical records. Additionally, an important change in the nature of medical information has arisen with the developments that have occurred in genetic testing. Such testing enables individuals to learn relatively early in life the likelihood that they might fall victim to late-onset, genetically based diseases. Since the late 1980s literally a score or more of such diagnostic tests have become available. Within a decade that number will have expanded manyfold. Because most people in the United States who are likely to take advantage of such testing are provided with health insurance by their employers, or by insurance companies, it is widely recognized that these corporations have a strong incentive to acquire aggregate information about the long-term health risks of these people in order to minimize business risks. More importantly, in the future, the greater availability of predictively useful information about each individual who seeks to participate in an "experience-rated" group, coupled with the dramatic declines in the cost of storing and using such information, is expected to give health insurance providers overwhelming incentives to move to a system of individualized actuarial risk. Life insurance is underwritten in this way. Especially as more individuals begin to seek long-term disability insurance with the aging of the baby-boom generation, individualized risk-assessment strategies will become not just attractive, but will also become business necessities for commercial insurance companies.[23]

---

[23] See, for example, Larry Gostin, "Genetic Discrimination: The Use of Genetically Based Diagnostic and Prognostic Tests by Employers and Insurers," *American Journal of Law and Medicine* 109, nos. 1 and 2 (1991): 135; and Robert J. Pokorski, "Use of Genetic Information by Private Insurers," in Timothy F. Murphy and Marc A. Lappé, eds., *Justice and the Human Genome Project* (Berkeley, CA: University of California Press, 1994), 103.

In anticipation of this predicted shift in insurers' underwriting practices away from group risk assessment to individual risk rating, there has
emerged a demand on the part of insurance clients that their privacy be
protected against disclosure of the findings of genetic tests. It should be
borne in mind that insurance companies have always sought confidential
health information about prospective life insurance clients, that medical
records even in the pre-computer age have sometimes been accessible to
unauthorized inspection, and that people always have been able to some
extent to predict their own health risks. Thus, recent developments in
genetic testing do not pose a genuinely new problem, but rather an es-
calation of a long-standing one. But hitherto, the availability of reliable
information about long-term health risk was low, the cost to insurance companies to avoid "adverse selection" by acquiring information was high,
and feasible treatments were nonexistent or inexpensive and cost insurance companies little. In recent years the cost to the insurance companies
of securing this information about people has gone down, the cost to the
insured of the undesired dissemination of this information has gone up,
and the risk to insurance companies of failing to secure this information
has increased. All these trends will accelerate over the next few decades.
The result is that insurance companies will increasingly want the information, while the potential insured will want to hide the information.

Let us consider the consequences of two alternative scenarios: in the
first, strict privacy is the rule for individuals; in the second, medical
information is widely disseminated. How will insurers and individuals
rationally respond to these alternatives? Privacy of medical records can
be and is strictly enforced; that is our assumption in the first case. The
result will be ever-increasing adverse selection. People who know that
they are at high risk will insure more heavily, while people who know
that they are not at high risk will reduce their insurance coverage. In the
long run, as diagnostic tools increase in number and accuracy, large sections of the hitherto insured population can acquire information about
their genetic disposition to health risks, and then seek to tailor their
insurance expenditures to these risks. As a result, insurance companies
will eventually be forced to curtail and eventually withdraw health insurance protections because the costs of treatment will grow rapidly, the
base of customers may decline, and the size of the premium required to
make an acceptable return may rise beyond the ability of enough people
to pay. The result will be the withdrawal of private insurance companies
from health care insurance and a much stronger and more univocal demand for public health insurance. With a government program, problems
of adverse selection will decline because everyone will have health insurance, but problems of moral hazard, such as irresponsible behavior
prompted by the safety net of insurance, will increase. Note that the
substitution of universal public health care for private health insurance
may reduce the quality of everyone's health care—witness the quality of

medicine in the United Kingdom. Finally, those people who are more risk-averse than others, or otherwise are prepared to pay for a higher-than-minimal provision of health care by purchasing supplementary insurance, will be unable to do so, because there will be no suppliers of such insurance products under the privacy conditions assumed in our first case. Thus, strictly and effectively enforced privacy rights will make most people worse off: insurers and their employees; people of average means and average health; all those who now provide themselves with private health insurance; and those with above-average aversion to health risks. Those who will be advantaged in this scenario will include people susceptible to late-onset genetic disorders that can be detected, and those not now insured by private insurance who will secure public health care.

Let us next consider the likely outcome in the second case, where medical information is widely disseminated. If insurance companies have the right to secure information about late-onset early diagnoses, they will craft health insurance prices to reflect risks. Individuals will have strong incentives to minimize risks by taking precautions and avoiding conditions that will further increase risks, as well as undertaking preventative treatments. Insurance companies will be in a position to offer people incentives by special pricing—on the model of "good driver" car insurance rates—to minimize risk. But if testing for a wide variety of late-onset genetic disorders becomes widely available, many people may turn out to be privately uninsurable through no fault of their own. Companies will withdraw their health insurance products from these individuals, and the result will be greatly increased demands for public health insurance. However, in an environment of widely available information about all or most individuals' susceptibility to late-onset genetic disorders, both the provision and enforcement of steps to minimize health risk will be easier to effect. In exchange for free health insurance, the government could require the insured to take steps to minimize risk and avoid environmental factors which together with gene defects produce these late-onset disorders. For example, those with genetic susceptibility to lung cancer might be required to avoid cigarette smoking in exchange for public health insurance. The result of this enforcement regime would be to the advantage of the recipients and those who pay for such a system of free health insurance, that is, everyone. As a side-benefit, general disclosure of information about genetic traits in the population and their correlation with various diseases will provide a powerful database for medical research that could produce a wide variety of improvements in treatment and enhanced longevity.

If agents are rational, problems of adverse selection will disappear and problems of moral hazard will be minimized. There may even emerge a market for private supplementary health insurance for those especially risk-averse or those wishing to devote larger portions of their resources to health care.

If anything like these two projected scenarios is accurate, then the privacy of medical records does not seem to be a right worth having. Agents in possession of these facts, when bargaining over a social contract, may well forgo these privacy rights. At a minimum, this would suggest that privacy—at least of medical records—does not have intrinsic moral value. Indeed, in a society like ours, claiming a right to privacy may be harmful and irrational.

Yet the trend in demands for privacy of genetic testing information does not appear to be moving in this direction. Rather, demands for such protection are growing. This may be owing to widespread irrationality, to the failure of people to foresee the near-term future, or to some factor that my analysis has failed to take into account. Or it may be that privacy is not to be understood exclusively on the model of a prudential property right.

Compare another area in which the demand for privacy is quite different: credit reporting. Credit reporting agencies solicit, collect, store, and disseminate credit records on consumers, and the agencies sell these records to any authorized business entity prepared to pay their price. Buyers include potential lenders, employers, landlords, and insurance companies. As with medical records, the cost of maintaining such records and transmitting them has decreased, while the range of reports, the rate of updating, and the level of accuracy has increased over time. By and large, the only regulatory demands that credit reporting companies have had to honor are ones which ensure accuracy and give subjects the opportunity to correct and comment on, but not keep private or otherwise control, credit records. These agencies do not need our permission to solicit, record, and store financial, other personal, and sometimes even medical information about us. The only way that we can prevent release of this information is by declining to deal with the companies that utilize such services before offering us loans, employment, insurance, housing, etc. It is clear that the advantage that each of us gains from giving credit reporting companies the right to solicit, record, store, and sell such records is cheaper access to and more available credit. The cost is the availability of our records to an employer, insurer, lender, or landlord willing to pay for information about our credit records, creditworthiness, insurability, and purchasing patterns.

Why is privacy less of an issue here? Why do consumers not protest when creditors, banks, and others report on their credit histories to credit reporting agencies, while at the same time many wish to prohibit the central collection of their medical histories? Why do we permit the transmission of information about our credit histories to current and potential employers, landlords, and insurance companies, while it is not permissible to transmit information about our medical histories to the same agencies? The answer is obvious: were the same strictures that surround medical records to be enforced about creditworthiness, the cost of loans, and the risks facing employers, landlords, insurers, and others would greatly increase. In the extreme, the market for loans would rapidly disappear; interest rates required to compensate lenders for risk resulting from their ignorance of creditworthiness would become too high for borrowers to bear. The result would be the disappearance of credit to the disadvantage of all. Yet it is doubtful that most people accept the nonprivacy of credit reporting on this basis.

People do not think about these issues the way economists do or the way economists assume that people do. Rather, one reason that they may accept nonprivacy for credit reporting is that people believe that except for misfortunes we have earned our credit history and creditworthiness by our own choices, decisions, actions, etc. We deserve the credit rating that we have, assuming it is accurate, of course.

By contrast, we have not earned our "genetic load," the burden of deleterious hereditary dispositions with which we were born. In addition to not earning our genetic load, we did not earn and do not deserve the standards of decorum and taste or the public/private distinctions of the societies into which we were born and socialized. We cannot help it if we are embarrassed by some things which members of other cultures do not find embarrassing. This suggests that among those attributes the knowledge of which can be employed by others to our disadvantage, those that are unearned and undeserved are the ones for which we are more likely to crave privacy. At any rate, we find them suitable candidates for protection from others by the invocation of a right to privacy.

It is here that moral values may finally enter the story. Along with a desire for privacy and for according privacy to others, there is good reason to think that *Homo sapiens* evolved with a predisposition to fairness in the division of resources, a predisposition that translates into equality of opportunity to pursue our interests.[24] Whatever equality of opportunity comes to, it requires at least that individuals not be disadvantaged by unearned burdens imposed upon them. Some traits are uncontroversially burdens for which society should equalize: others are more controversial. Thus, much greater debate rages in the United States about affirmative action policies than about the Americans with Disabilities Act of 1990. Those traits of ours and facts about us that we seek privacy for are like disabilities, which the polity tries to compensate for in order to ensure some level of equality of opportunity. These traits are unearned obstacles to equality of opportunity: unearned because we have no choice in our nature or our nurture, our genes or our socialization; obstacles to equality of opportunity because they provide others with information useful to control our access to opportunities. The cheapest way to avoid the threat of unfairness that information about unearned differences poses is by privatizing the information.

[24] See Skyrms, *Evolution of the Social Contract*, chap. 1.

Although privacy is a matter of taste or prudence, we have seen how it becomes an institution of indirect, instrumental normative force because, given human behavior as it is (and not as it ought to be), ensuring privacy of information is the most efficient means of attaining outcomes prized for their intrinsic moral value. "Being let alone" in Justice Brandeis's words, or equality of opportunity as adumbrated in the Fourteenth Amendment, are different ways of expressing intrinsic moral value. On this understanding at least, privacy might even provide some basis—albeit indirect—for some of the uses to which it has been put in American constitutional law. For example, in *Roe v. Wade* (1973), the U.S. Supreme Court's majority opinion cast about for a constitutionally entrenched "right of personal privacy or zones of privacy":

> In varying contexts the Court or individual justices have indeed found the root of that right in the First Amendment, . . . in the Fourth and Fifth Amendments, . . . in the penumbras of the Bill of Rights, . . . in the Ninth Amendment, . . . or in the concept of liberty guaranteed by the first section of the Fourteenth Amendment. . .
>
> This right of privacy, whether it be found in the Fourteenth Amendment's concept of personal liberty and restrictions on state actions, . . . or . . . in the Ninth Amendment's reservations of rights to the people, is broad enough to encompass a woman's decision whether or not to terminate her pregnancy.[25]

Much of the legal controversy surrounding *Roe* reflects the tortuous character of the Court's alleged discovery of a right to privacy as implicit in constitutional amendments in which the word 'privacy' does not figure. But if the right to privacy about information has the prudential character that I accord it—in virtue of the nature of information and the special potential for information's misuse, by contrast to other commodities—then there can be a firmer foundation for a right to privacy than "penumbras" of various U.S. constitutional amendments. That firmer and less controversial foundation can be found in privacy's role in securing other rights that are not merely prudential.[26]

Philosophy, The University of Georgia

---

[25] *Roe v. Wade*, 410 U.S. 113 (1973), reprinted in Tom L. Beauchamp and LeRoy Walters, eds., *Contemporary Issues in Bioethics*, 4th ed. (Belmont, CA: Wadsworth, 1994), 313.
[26] For extensive comments and criticism of previous drafts, I owe thanks to Clark Wolfe, Roberta Berry, Kristin Shrader-Frechette, Judith Jarvis Thomson, and Ellen Frankel Paul.

EGALITARIAN JUSTICE VERSUS THE RIGHT TO PRIVACY?

By Richard J. Arneson

I. Introduction: Broad Privacy

In their celebrated essay "The Right to Privacy," legal scholars Samuel Warren and Louis Brandeis identified as the generic privacy value "the right to be let alone."[1] This same phrase occurs in Justice Brandeis's dissent in *Olmstead v. U.S.* (1927).[2] This characterization of privacy has been found objectionable by philosophers acting as conceptual police. For example, moral philosopher William Parent asserts that one can wrongfully fail to let another person alone in all sorts of ways—such as assault—that intuitively do not qualify as violations of privacy and thus cannot be violations of the right to privacy.[3]

The right to privacy that was claimed to have constitutional status by the U.S. Supreme Court in *Griswold v. Connecticut* (1965) has also attracted objections, to the effect that the conception of privacy defined by the justices was constructed by misclassification and confusion. Griswold, an officer of the Planned Parenthood League of Connecticut, had been convicted as an accessory under a Connecticut statute that prohibited any person from using "any drug, medicinal article or instrument for the purpose of preventing conception." Griswold's specific act had been to counsel married couples regarding contraception. The Court reversed his conviction on the ground that the Connecticut statute as applied to his case violated a right of privacy that was within the "penumbras, formed by emanations from" specific guarantees in the Bill of Rights.[4] This decision has proved controversial on several counts, one being that the Court was really protecting a liberty or autonomy interest, not anything that could properly be called "privacy." Among those who have pursued this line of criticism, academic lawyer Hyman Gross warns that "there is some danger that privacy may be conceived as autonomy," a danger to

---

[1] Samuel D. Warren and Louis D. Brandeis, "The Right to Privacy," *Harvard Law Review* 4, no. 5 (December 1890): 193.

[2] *Olmstead v. U.S.*, 277 U.S. 438 (1927).

[3] William A. Parent, "Privacy, Morality, and the Law," *Philosophy and Public Affairs* 17, no. 4 (Fall 1983): 272.

[4] *Griswold v. Connecticut*, 381 U.S. 479, 484 (1965).

which "[t]he United States Supreme Court succumbed completely in 1965 in its opinion in *Griswold v. Connecticut*."[5] The error, according to Gross, is that "[i]n the *Griswold* situation there had been an attempt by government to regulate personal affairs, not get acquainted with them, and so there was an issue regarding autonomy,"[6] which the Court confounded with privacy.

In fact, there is a plain and simple construal of "the right to privacy" for which "the right to be let alone" is a good paraphrase.[7] All societies enforce rules and conventions that carve out a boundary between matters that are socially regulated (i.e., public) and those left to individual discretion and control (i.e., private). The boundary is multidimensional: in different contexts of choice or spheres of social life, the line between what is public business and what is not may be drawn in different ways. The right of privacy in a particular society is fixed by the ensemble of the protections against social regulation and control that are established by the society's current rules and conventions. Alongside this sociological usage we can find a critical or philosophical ideal of privacy. The right to privacy in the critical sense is the right to privacy that morally ought to be accepted and enforced in a particular society.[8]

When private and public are contrasted in this way, the private sphere is not a sphere of anarchy. If the individual is to be free to do what she chooses and not to be accountable to society for the exercise of discretion over some range of decisions, then other persons must be prevented from interfering.

Taken by itself, the right to privacy that is equivalent to the right to be let alone is an empty shell, purely formal, and lacking in substantive content. Content is filled in by some normative theory or set of principles that specify where boundary lines between public and private should be drawn. This may be part of what law professor Harry Kalven meant when he suggested that the right of privacy might be a "residual."[9] Writing about the right of privacy regarded as having constitutional standing, Kalven observes that the content of this right to privacy may be whatever is left over when everything that is legitimately a matter of public business is subtracted from whatever one might be inclined to hold to be normatively private. In other words, Kalven's suggestion is that the

---

[5] Hyman Gross, "Privacy and Autonomy," reprinted in Joel Feinberg and Hyman Gross, eds., *Philosophy of Law*, 3rd ed. (Belmont, CA: Wadsworth Publishing, 1986), 296.

[6] Ibid.

[7] Of course, this point has no particular bearing on the question of whether or not the *Griswold* majority opinion by Justice William Douglas was a reasonable constitutional interpretation.

[8] In the sociological sense, the morality of a society at a time is the set of norms actually accepted and enforced as morality. In the critical sense, the society's morality is the set of norms that ought to be accepted and enforced as morality.

[9] Harry Kalven, "Privacy in Tort Law—Were Warren and Brandeis Wrong?" *Law and Contemporary Problems* 31, no. 2 (Spring 1966): 327.

ideal of privacy sets no constraints on what legitimately may be regarded as public business. One could just as easily say that what is legitimately a matter of public business is a residual category; it is what remains when all matters that normatively belong to the private sphere are subtracted from whatever one might be inclined to hold to be normatively public. At any rate, bare appeal to the right of privacy as the right to be let alone will not do any work in arguments for or against any law or policy. The work is done by principles—libertarian, communitarian, totalitarian, etc.—that give specific content to the idea of privacy by specifying the extent to which people should be let alone.

Broad, diffuse, and contentless, the right to privacy construed as the right to be let alone does not capture all that one might have in mind in invoking a public/private distinction in political argument. That distinction is between behavior that is considered appropriate in private places, such as within private homes, and behavior that is deemed appropriate in public spaces, such as streets, parks, and businesses that are open to the public.[10] A society might have different codes of behavior for public and private spaces without endorsing the idea that individual discretion should reign in the private spaces. Individual conduct might be strictly regulated in both spheres, but differently in each. Rules that specify appropriate behavior in public and private might take the form of rights, conferred on persons, that others behave in public and private in these approved ways. In this way, when a couple that is romantically inclined makes love in a public park, this is an invasion of the privacy of those who wish to use the park without being distracted by this sight, or rather, an invasion of the public sphere by conduct that ought to be done in private. An example of intrusion of public behavior into the private sphere would be my launching into a sermon, as though to my Sunday congregation, at a private dinner party.

Privacy is often understood in another way that is narrower than the broad notions we have canvassed. In this sense an individual enjoys privacy when she is not accessible to others. Access can be variously understood. One kind of access to a person is gained when others learn facts about that person. Another kind of access is physical proximity, or perhaps physical proximity accompanied by the direction of attention toward the person.[11] Much ink has been spilled in the analysis of this family of notions. Often the analysis is guided by the polemical aim of showing that only one of the candidate interpretations of the narrower

[10] Avishai Margalit recounts hearing an elderly Englishwoman remonstrating at the sight of a woman sunbathing in a park in bra and panties. A query to her about whether this was more objectionable than sunbathing in a bikini elicited the reply, "That's different. Underwear is private." See Margalit, *The Decent Society*, trans. Naomi Goldblum (Cambridge, MA: Harvard University Press, 1996), 202.

[11] Here I follow the analysis in Ruth Gavison, "Privacy and the Limits of Law," *Yale Law Journal* 89, no. 3 (January 1980): 421–91. There is a voluminous literature devoted to the analysis of the concept of privacy.

notion is legitimate or that no broader usage of the notion than one being analyzed by the writer is conceptually licit.

I shall leave aside this literature on accessibility and ponder broad privacy as the right to be let alone. If a moral theory would have it that I should be let alone along some dimension of conduct, to some extent, then bringing it about that I am in fact let alone would require much stage-setting, only some of which would get associated with privacy. If I am to be free to X or not as I choose, others must be prevented from interfering with my choice. If I am to be free, the government must neither force me to X nor prohibit me from Xing. It will be useful for me to be able to assure myself of seclusion by placing myself where I will not be disturbed by anybody who is not coordinating with me in Xing. If my doing X is something I would prefer others not to know about, the cost to me of doing X is lessened if I can keep the fact of my Xing secret. There is a strong affinity between privacy in this broad sense and private property. Suppose that I want to assure myself the freedom to X without disturbance, in seclusion, and with the freedom to keep detailed knowledge about my doing X from becoming widely known. A good strategy for accomplishing this is to inhabit a regime that does not ban Xing, own some property in land, retire to it with persons who want to do X with me and agree not to publicize our doing it, and carry on Xing with means to X that I own or use with the consent of their owners.

II. Egalitarian Consequentialism and Orwellian Worries

I have urged, thus far, that talk of privacy and of rights of privacy lacks determinate normative content in the absence of some theory or set of moral principles capable of fixing and justifying lines of division between public and private. Yet appeals to privacy surely function as a constraint on the acceptance of moral theories. We have intuitions about ways in which individuals should be left free from certain sorts of social interference, and these intuitions serve to test proposed moral theories. The theories that are incompatible with our firm privacy intuitions must be rejected. Perhaps the firmest such privacy intuitions reflect the twentieth-century experience with totalitarian governments and with the type of totalitarianism as represented, for example, in George Orwell's *1984*.

In this essay, I shall explore the suspicion that maximizing consequentialist moralities cannot adequately reflect the depth of our commitment to rights to privacy. This worry that consequentialism cannot take rights seriously haunts discussions of utilitarianism. In the face of these worries, the strategy I shall follow is to argue that an egalitarian version of utilitarianism generates a plausible approach to issues of privacy.

John Stuart Mill's utilitarianism holds that institutions and policies should be set and actions chosen so as to maximize the aggregate sum of human pleasure. Mill has a complex story to tell about pleasure, but the complications, to my mind, do not overcome the difficulty that the human good is not plausibly identified with pleasure: quality of life does not reduce to quality of experience. For Millian consequentialism to be plausible, it must incorporate as the goal to be maximized whatever is picked out by the soundest theory of human well-being. (One can regard Mill himself as having taken incomplete steps in this direction when he proposed that pleasures differ in quality as well as in quantity.) For the sake of the argument, let us suppose we have done our homework and have that soundest theory at hand.[12] From now on, I will identify the human good to be maximized as well-being rather than pleasure, without supposing that I have done more than give a name to a problem that eventually must be solved.

In his detailed political theory and policy recommendations, Mill consistently tilts toward equality, a tilt he claims to have derived from neutral utilitarian summation. But he never squarely addresses the critical issue of the distribution of well-being (utility): he does not consider whether we should have a preference between any of many possible future states of the world that have the same net sum of utility, yet have very different distributions of utility across persons. I endorse amending Mill's utilitarianism by incorporating a preference for equality directly into the fundamental principle. This yields what nowadays is called *prioritarianism*: this is the claim that institutions and policies should be set and actions chosen so as to maximize moral value, with the moral value of a gain in well-being for a person being greater, the greater its size and the lower the person's prior lifetime expectation of well-being.[13] Prioritarianism is sometimes referred to under the heading "weighted well-being." The prioritarian aims to maximize not well-being in the aggregate, but well-being weighted by giving priority to the worse off.

Contrasting prioritarianism with utilitarianism clarifies the former idea. For the utilitarian, the right policy is the one that maximizes the sum of utility (human well-being). For the prioritarian, the right policy is the one that maximizes the sum of moral value. Moral value accrues from utility (human well-being) gains obtained for persons, but the moral value of each gain is adjusted depending on its size (other things being equal, more utility is better than less) and also depending on the prior utility level of the recipient (other things being equal, utility to a badly off person is better than a similar gain obtained for an already well off

---

[12] For some discussion, see my "Human Flourishing versus Desire Satisfaction," *Social Philosophy and Policy* 16, no. 1 (Winter 1999): 113–42.

[13] On prioritarianism, see Derek Parfit, *Equality or Priority?* The Lindley Lecture (Lawrence, KS: Department of Philosophy, University of Kansas, 1995); and Dennis McKerlie, "Equality and Priority," *Utilitas* 6, no. 1 (May 1994): 25–42. To the best of my knowledge, the first philosophical discussion of the idea is in Paul Weirich, "Utility Tempered with Equality," *Noûs* 17, no. 3 (September 1983): 423–39.

person). The extent to which prioritarianism in practice would yield recommendations for policy that are different from those that utilitarianism would recommend depends on the specific degree of priority to the worse off that is assigned. Prioritarianism encompasses a family of principles that give more or less priority to the worse off.

Prioritarianism attracts some criticism that is similar to attacks leveled against utilitarianism and egalitarianism. Prioritarian accounts of justice are faulted on the ground that they fail to distinguish between deserving and undeserving, responsible and irresponsible agents. One line of response is to stiff-arm the criticism. If arranging institutions to reward undeserving or irresponsible agents establishes perverse incentives that operate over time to lower productivity to the point that the weighted well-being sum is less than it could be if incentives were better structured, then prioritarianism demands the better structure of incentives that would result in maximization over the long run. Prioritarianism, like utilitarianism, accommodates deservingness and responsibility as instrumental values. This degree of accommodation may be insufficient, however. If we must choose between providing a gain (or avoiding a loss) for a saint or a sinner, where the weighted well-being gain would be the same whichever person we favor, and there are no further consequences to consider, it might seem intrinsically more valuable to achieve the gain for the saint. Think of the saint as someone who fulfills her moral obligations and within these moral constraints uses her well-being opportunities efficiently for her advantage, while the sinner squanders well-being opportunities for others and for himself.

To take this line would be to hold that rewarding the deserving is intrinsically morally worthy. One might also hold that considerations of responsibility affect what distribution of well-being should be promoted. Here the idea would be that it is morally more important to help someone who is badly off than to help someone who is equally well off but could have avoided her present plight. Without trying to be more precise about responsibility—I will assume that it matters morally—we should amend prioritarianism to yield *responsibility-catering prioritarianism*.[14] On this view, the moral disvalue of imposing a loss on a person or transferring benefits from her is greater, the greater the person's degree of responsibility for the well-being expectation that she currently enjoys (if it is high, she is among the fortunate). Similarly, the moral value of conferring a gain on a person or transferring benefits to her is greater, the lower the person's degree of responsibility for the well-being expectation she currently enjoys (if it is low, she is among the unfortunate). This yields a version of weighted well-being in which the moral value of well-being increments that we

---

[14] I believe that one should modify prioritarian principle to cater for the concern about responsibility but not for the concern about deservingness, for reasons I do not articulate in this essay.

might obtain are adjusted twice—once to give priority to the worse off, and again to reflect the degree of responsibility of each individual for her present condition (whether she is well off or badly off in well-being prospects).

Taken as a standard for assessing the laws, practices, and social norms of modern democratic societies, responsibility-catering prioritarianism might appear to be preposterous. The idea that we might adjust our distributive-justice system based on our estimation of persons' overall deservingness or responsibility seems entirely chimerical. Individuals do not display responsibility scores on their foreheads, and the attempt by institutions or individuals to guess at the scores of the people they are dealing with would surely dissolve in practice into giving vent to one's prejudices and piques. The criminal justice system has a difficult time making reliable determinations of an individual's guilt or innocence with respect to the charge that she committed a particular criminal act; the thought that we could construct a distributive-justice system that assesses people's lifetime responsibility is surely a nonstarter.

The prioritarian component of responsibility-catering prioritarianism, which says that social policy should tilt toward the worse off, also looks problematic on its face. Should we adjudicate conflicts of interests among citizens based on hunches about their comparative welfare as well as about the rights and wrongs of their disputes? Should we have one law for the rich (who are presumed to have a better quality of life on average) and another for the poor?

These doubts echo familiar right-wing suspicions that left-wing egalitarian goals are incompatible with the firm respect for individual rights that is the indispensable ground of decent social relations. Economist Friedrich A. Hayek once warned that "any policy aiming directly at a substantive ideal of distributive justice must lead to the destruction of the Rule of Law."[15] The argument is straightforward. Individuals are different and circumstances vary continuously, so to bring it about that the outcomes individuals reach match the outcome specified for them by distributive justice, no set of laws that is specified in advance, firmly adhered to, and applied uniformly across persons can be embraced. Either the laws would have to change capriciously, or they would have to give so much discretion to officials that individual citizens would not be able to predict how the laws would be applied; the ideal of the rule of law would be defunct in either case. In a similar spirit, philosopher Robert Nozick has observed that "[p]atterned distributional principles do not give people what entitlement principles do, only better distributed."[16] The "rights" that one is assigned as means to egalitarian goals are always

---

[15] Friedrich A. Hayek, *The Road to Serfdom* (Chicago: University of Chicago Press, 1944), 79.

[16] Robert Nozick, *Anarchy, State, and Utopia* (New York: Basic Books, 1974), 167.

liable to disappear whenever a marginally more efficient method of fulfilling the goals requires the alteration or abolition of these individual
rights. From this we get Nozick's charge that the realization of any pattern of egalitarian justice in distribution requires continuous and wrongful interference with the liberty of individual persons to live their private
lives as they would choose.

In responding to these criticisms, the egalitarian can learn lessons from
the history of similar criticisms of the general family of consequentialist
views, of which egalitarian-justice views are members. (Mill anticipates
these lines of criticism in *Utilitarianism* and *On Liberty*.[17]) The lesson is
that a consequentialist moral principle is to be understood as a criterion
of right conduct and the right arrangement of social practices, not necessarily as a decision procedure or as a practical guide to deliberation and
policy choice. Given the limited knowledge, limited intelligence, and limited altruism of actual human beings, the social rules that it would make
sense, on consequentialist grounds, to teach them to obey will need to be
more rigid, more specific, easier to grasp and apply, and more resistant to
biased misapplication than are very general and abstract principles. Given
the importance of the stability and predictability of laws, and of providing assurance to individuals that if they build a house today, others will
not have the right to tear it down or occupy it tomorrow, it makes sense,
on consequentialist grounds, to implement a legal code that achieves the
values of the rule of law and avoids perverse incentives. Given that
people need liberty and privacy to have good lives, liberty and privacy
must be secured. Consequentialist principles that are successfully applied
would not give rise to Orwellian totalitarianism, so opposition to the
latter is not any sort of reason for rejecting the former.

How far can the consequentialist go in promoting stability and assurance in the development of legal and social rules? (The consequentialist
obviously will not make a fetish of specifically legal stability. A war,
natural disaster, severe economic shock, or other sudden large changes in
circumstances can upset people's reasonable expectations and prudent
plans just as a change in the tax laws can.) In *On Liberty*, Mill proposes
that we ought to conform conduct and social policy to his Liberty Principle, absolutely and without exception—even in circumstances when we
reasonably foresee that violating the Liberty Principle will produce better
consequences.[18] His argument is that we cannot reliably distinguish the
situations in which it would be best to violate the Liberty Principle from

[17] J. S. Mill, *Utilitarianism*, in Mill, *Collected Works*, vol. 10, ed. J. M. Robson (Toronto: University of Toronto Press, 1969), 203–59; and Mill, *On Liberty*, in Mill, *Collected Works*, vol. 18, ed. J. M. Robson (Toronto: University of Toronto Press, 1977), 213–310.

[18] Mill's Liberty Principle states that "the sole end for which mankind are warranted, individually or collectively, in interfering with the liberty of action of any of their number is self-protection." Mill immediately restates the principle in these words: "the only purpose for which power can be rightfully exercised over any member of a civilized community, against his will, is to prevent harm to others." Mill, *On Liberty*, 223.

other seemingly similar situations in which adherence to the principle, despite appearances, would be best. Given this, treating the Liberty Principle as an absolute and exceptionless rule predictably does more good than any policy of partial compliance that we could devise and implement. In other words, we cannot devise any fine-grained policy for carving out categories of exceptions to the Liberty Principle that would have greater expected utility than would following the Liberty Principle without exceptions, so strict adherence to the principle is best.[19]

Suppose we say that if some person has a moral right to get X, then it must be the case that somebody is under a duty either to allow the person to act to get X or to provide X to the person; the person who has the right is wronged if this duty is not fulfilled. In Mill's terms, the idea of a right involves both the idea of a claim that should be honored and the idea of a specific person who is wronged if the claim is not honored. We might impose as an additional constraint that if someone has a moral right to X, then she does not cease to have a right to X just because the denial of her claim to X would produce the best consequences. Moral rights so construed can be justifiable in a consequentialist moral theory. The lessons of *Utilitarianism* and *On Liberty* apply. If the best consequences would flow from guaranteeing individuals a certain right, then consequentialism endorses the establishment of that right, which should be upheld even when cancelling the right in specific circumstances would on that occasion produce the best consequences. As with the Liberty Principle, we would respect the right without exception because of our inability to distinguish reliably between cases in which utility would actually be maximized by violating the right and cases that falsely appear to be such justified exceptions.

Philosopher David Lyons has argued that the reconciliation between consequentialism and rights countenanced above is unsuccessful.[20] If Mary has a moral right to use her car as she chooses, then she is morally at liberty to carry out any acts with her car that do not wrongfully injure others or otherwise violate their moral rights. But consequentialism as a moral theory asserts that one should always do whatever will produce the best consequences. Applied to Mary, consequentialist morality implies that she is not morally at liberty to carry out any of a wide variety of innocent acts with her car after all, because she morally ought to do only one of the acts that would produce consequences as good as any alternative available to her. Consequentialist moral principle is thus incompatible with recognition and endorsement of moral rights.

---

[19] This reading of Mill's argument is presented in John Gray, *Mill on Liberty: A Defence*, 2d ed. (London and New York: Routledge, 1996). The Liberty Principle that Mill actually defends is subtler than what I present in the text, but this does not affect the point that Mill argues for a Liberty Principle, to be accepted as an exceptionless rule, as a strategy for promoting utility.

[20] David Lyons, *Rights, Welfare, and Mill's Moral Theory* (New York: Oxford University Press, 1994), 147–75.

A reply is available to defend the consequentialist against Lyons's argument. The reply begins by distinguishing, perhaps artificially, between (1) the act that it is right to do, that one morally ought to do, and that one has the most reason to do, and (2) the act that one is morally obligated to do and that if one fails to do, one incurs blame or other punishment. The consequentialist can hold that an act is right (one morally ought to do it) just in case doing it would produce consequences that are at least as good as those that would be produced by any alternative act that one might choose. At the same time, the consequentialist can stipulate that an act is morally obligatory (one would be blameworthy for failing to perform it) just in case it is a member of a class of acts such that a social practice of punishing people for failing to perform them would produce the best consequences.

Now back to Mary. We were wondering whether a society run on consequentialist principles could coherently accord her a moral right to use her car as she pleases. Suppose the society does accord her such a right. What would this amount to? Despite the assignment to her of the right to use her car as she chooses, it remains the case (let us say) that there is some unique act she could perform with her car that would produce the best consequences, so this is the act that she morally ought to do. Yet it could be the case that she is under no moral obligation to perform this optimific act, and would not be blameworthy if she did not. If punishing a person for doing a nonoptimific act with her car would be counterproductive, then she should not be punished in any way for this innocent act. If there are many such acts, Mary is in a sense morally at liberty to perform any of them, in that she would not suffer blame or reproach from herself or others if she did any of these innocent nonoptimific acts with her car.

The point can be put in terms of socialization practices in a consequentialist society. We are imagining that the social-training practices that would produce the best consequences, and which a consequentialist society would implement, would bring it about that well-raised individuals would not be morally obligated always to choose the act, of those available, that would produce the best consequences, and would not feel blame or otherwise suffer punishment if they failed sometimes to do the act that consequentialism singles out as best. In such a society, Mary's moral right to do as she chooses with her car (so long as she does not harm others) is derived from (1) the fact that she is not morally obligated to do whatever act with her car would produce the best consequences in the circumstances, and (2) facts about the obligations of other people not to interfere in various ways. Why shouldn't the socialization practices be ratcheted up so that the Marys of the world are morally obligated to do whatever would be optimific in the circumstances? The answer is: if the society is already run according to consequentialist principles, then the level of obligation has been optimally set, and any raising or lowering of it would dampen the production of good consequences.

III. Prioritarianism and Paternalism

These comments on the structure of consequentialist moral theory leave untouched the more specific suspicions that are provoked by egalitarian consequentialism. One suspicion is the idea that guiding social policy by measurements of individual responsibility would be disastrous. Another suspicion is that tilting social policy toward the worse off, as prioritarianism bids us to do, conflicts with the principles of equal treatment and equal protection of all citizens under the law that are important aspects of the ideal of the rule of law.

Regarding responsibility, I simply maintain that it is intrinsically morally more valuable to secure a benefit for a person in bad straits if the person is not reasonably deemed responsible for bringing about her plight. The extent to which actions or social policies could be guided by this principle depends on what the best account of individual responsibility turns out to be and the degree to which the information needed to apply this account can be made available to decision-makers in ways that do not cost more, in moral terms, than they are worth. There is also an issue about the extent to which indirect policies (that is, policies that achieve responsibility-catering goals without directly making use of information about individual levels of responsibility) can be devised. For example, it might be possible to construct educational policies that tend to foster individual responsibility of the kind we seek to promote. I take no stand here on these difficult issues. If it turns out empirically to be the case that the information relevant to assessing responsibility is unavailable and that useful indirect policies are not to be had, then responsibility, though important in principle, would become irrelevant in practice.

It might turn out that in some circumstances it would be empirically possible to cater to the responsibility element in responsibility-catering prioritarianism, but only at great cost to prioritarian values. That is to say, one could to some extent channel benefits toward people according to their differential degrees of deservingness, but this would be very costly, and would lead to there being far fewer resources available to improve the condition of the worse off. One would then need to decide what weight to accord the responsibility element, as opposed to the prioritarian element, in responsibility-catering prioritarianism.

Regarding tilting toward the worse off, I do not see a conflict between doing this and following requirements of stability, good order, and the rule of law. If one's goal is a regime that maximizes the achievement of prioritarian values over the long run, arrangements that would undermine social stability and trigger perverse incentives and the like would not qualify. It is surely not the case that choosing prioritarianism impedes the choice of sound institutions to implement this conception of justice. One should also note that the prioritarian requirement—that institutions and practices should be set so as to maximize a sum of human well-being that is adjusted to give greater weight to gains for the worse off—is a requirement on the system as a whole. Thus, a prioritarian conception of justice might not necessarily involve instituting policies that explicitly tilt toward the worse off in every sphere of social life. For example, if a "nontilting" tort law system, in concert with some overall package of institutions, would maximize weighted well-being, then that would be preferable to a similar system with a tort law system tilted to favor the worse off. The same point holds for individual actions. If individual actions in some domain (for example, promises and contracts) would do better for the worse off in the long run than a system that deliberately tilted in favor of the worse off, then nontilting actions would satisfy prioritarian morality in that domain. I do not mean to do more here than raise a possibility; I do not intend for this discussion to settle any substantive issues.

In fact, though, I suspect that the shape of laws and institutions that would satisfy prioritarian principles often would have to be designed with special consideration for their impact on the worse off. Consider Mill's nemesis, paternalism—the restriction of someone's liberty against her will for her own good. The Liberty Principle espoused by Mill holds that the only good reason to restrict individual liberty is to prevent harm to nonconsenting others, which appears to rule out paternalism absolutely. Some of Mill's detailed discussions, however, suggest qualifications. If one lacks access to facts that are relevant to a self-regarding decision, or one is in a poor condition to make competent decisions from one's own standpoint, some restriction of liberty may be acceptable to Mill. Also, the Liberty Principle is intended to apply only to sane, nonfeebleminded adults. Mill holds that the principle against paternalism should be qualified along these lines, but that this qualified principle should be followed strictly and without exception. According to Mill, adherence to such antipaternalism would maximize the sum of utility in the long run. I have no idea whether or not Mill's speculation on this point is correct. For the sake of the argument, suppose it is. This would not settle the issue of whether paternalistic policies are ever morally justified. Mill's argument ignores the distribution of utility. For all that he has claimed, it could be the case that strict adherence to his version of antipaternalism would maximize human utility because the costs that it inflicts on badly off persons are more than offset by gains for already better off persons. Indeed, if Mill's conjectures are correct, this may be likely.

Human beings, no doubt, vary in their ability to determine where their good lies, to choose actions well calculated to gain their good as they see it, and to execute their choices. For simplicity, divide the population into good and bad choosers. I submit that it is plausible to hold that on the whole and on average, bad choosers will lead worse lives in terms of well-being than good choosers. Luck and favorable initial circumstances do interact with the degree of one's prudential ability to determine one's life prospects; other things being equal, however, those with greater talent for prudential choice and conduct will do better. Paternalistic restriction of liberty will never benefit well-informed, ideally good choosers, who will choose only options that are prudent. But paternalistic restriction can improve the life prospects of bad choosers, because subtracting options that are tempting but bad for them can render them likely to make choices that are more conducive to their well-being. An example would be paternalistic laws restricting people's liberty to consume dangerous recreational drugs. Without such laws, good choosers will use drugs only when doing so works to their long-run advantage, whereas bad choosers may opt for drug use that is self-destructive overall. If this is so, then the policy choice of whether or not to enact paternalistic drug-control laws presents conflicts of interest between good choosers and bad choosers, and ultimately between relatively advantaged and disadvantaged persons. Even if Mill is correct that paternalism cannot maximize human well-being over the long run, this is fully compatible with paternalistic drug-control laws being justifiable according to prioritarian principle, because prioritarianism gives greater moral weight to achieving gains and avoiding losses for those whose well-being expectations are low.

In theory, one could imagine policies that distinguish good choosers from bad choosers and provide freedom for the former and restriction for the latter. Recent proposals to render physician-assisted suicide legal in a limited range of cases gesture toward this strategy. Proponents propose that assisting someone's suicide be permitted only in cases in which suicide is almost certainly in the interest of the person who dies. However, the attempt to separate good and bad choosers sometimes generates extra costs. It can heighten the insult of paternalism by imposing the authoritative judgment of another person or, even worse, a state agency on you with the implication that you are not competent to run your own life. Paternalism imposes a stigma on its intended beneficiaries, and the costs of the stigma only increase with the effort to discriminate good from bad choosers.

In some cases, the costs of a stigma may be worth bearing, all things considered, so that the best policy choice is paternalism targeted toward the class of bad choosers. In other cases, the costs of a stigma tip the balance against paternalism, so that refraining from paternalism is best. In a third class of cases, the costs of a stigma might tip policy toward blanket paternalism that treats good choosers and bad choosers alike and makes no effort to distinguish between them.

"Get the state off our backs!" is a perennially popular cry. No doubt state intervention to help prevent people from suffering self-inflicted harm is often misguided, incompetently administered, or generated by the policymakers' failure to imagine and empathize adequately with the lives and outlooks of people different from themselves. Yet prioritarianism alerts us to the possibility that denunciations of paternalism reflect the self-interest of the already advantaged.[21] If we should care about the distribution of human well-being, then debates about this region of the line between public and private should be reconfigured.

IV. Privacy and the Need for Theory

Conflicting recommendations regarding privacy require some theory, consequentialist or otherwise, for their resolution. Examination of the starkly opposed opinions on privacy advanced by Warren and Brandeis, Richard Posner, and Thomas Nagel illustrates this point.

Arguing for a legal right of privacy in the sense of a right against publication of personal facts about an individual without his consent, Warren and Brandeis asserted that gossip in the press is corrupting and serves no significant and rational interest of its readers. Responding almost a century later, Judge Richard Posner proposes rational purposes that gossip might serve.[22] Posner's discussion is hamstrung by his assumption that the satisfaction of any desire that a well-informed agent chooses to pursue must increase rather than lessen the agent's welfare. Even if one were to reject that assumption, it is still an open question what substantive value should be assigned to the interests that gossip serves and frustrates. One needs a full assessment of the moral costs and benefits of possible privacy regimes to know whether or not the position of Warren and Brandeis is acceptable.

Writing in favor of more expansive and stringent informal privacy norms in the contemporary United States, philosopher Thomas Nagel cites three putative benefits of strengthening these conventions.[23] First, since divulging irrelevant personal matters in the context of schemes of cooperation tends to be distracting and divisive, cooperative enterprises will function more efficiently if privacy norms inhibit such divulging. Second, norms that require reticence about personal matters in social interactions also protect the inner mental life of individuals, which Nagel claims to be the source of individuality and the site where much that is valuable in individual life occurs. Finally, Nagel notes that conventions of privacy facilitate the selective disclosure of personal information in ways

---

[21] What about the responsibility element in responsibility-catering prioritarianism? It complicates, but does not undo, the prior discussion. The principle bids us to tilt toward action in favor of the worse off, and also in favor of those whom it would not be reasonable to hold personally responsible for their worse-off plight.

[22] Richard Posner, "Privacy, Secrecy, and Reputation," *Buffalo Law Review* 28, no. 1 (Winter 1979): 23-24; and Posner, "An Economic Theory of Privacy," *Regulation* 2, no. 3 (May/June 1978): 19-26.

[23] Thomas Nagel, "Concealment and Exposure," *Philosophy and Public Affairs* 27, no. 1 (Winter 1998): 3-30.

that enable intimate friendships to flourish. Nagel stresses that conventions of privacy that limit candor are needed in varying degrees in all types of social interaction, even in the most intimate personal relations.

The considerations that Nagel cites can pull together, but they sometimes tug apart. Nothing guarantees that the privacy conventions that would best enhance the efficiency of cooperative enterprises would coincide with the privacy conventions that would best protect the sphere of individuality constituted by the inner thoughts of each individual. Perhaps in some settings, insistence on divulging what are ordinarily thought to be legitimately personal and private matters does promote group productivity. Perhaps the privacy norms that best promote the appropriate degree of candor in personal friendships would conflict with the needs both of social productivity and of the flourishing of individual thought. Where such conflicts occur, how should the balance be struck? Nagel argues that conventions of reticence are needed because in a diverse modern society, people inevitably will disagree widely and deeply about how to live, so an increase in candor increases tension, hostility, and conflict. But if people in diverse democracies disagree about the right and the good, surely one such important sort of disagreement is how to draw morally legitimate boundaries between public and private in both the legal domain and in the sphere of informal social norms.

Nagel confidently pronounces that the considerations that he adduces justify strengthening the existing informal privacy norms. This may be so, but to decide whether or not privacy norms should be strengthened, weakened, or left alone, some further argument must be supplied that involves an overall assessment of the moral costs and benefits associated with the alternatives that one might choose. I do not mean to imply that an inclusive argument need be consequentialist. One might instead identify all the distinct deontological considerations that bear on the privacy issue, according to one's preferred deontology, and come to an all-things-considered judgment. But some theoretical perspective is needed.

Consider the practice of outing—the public revelation of the homosexuality of a prominent person who wishes to keep her sexual orientation a secret and who has worked to keep this aspect of her romantic life from becoming public knowledge. I focus on outings carried out by people who believe that they are striking a blow for tolerance of homosexuals and who do not aim to call down hostility and prejudice on the figure who is exposed. If there is a right not to have personal facts about oneself made public without one's consent, it is plausible to suppose that this right includes the right that one's sexual orientation not be disclosed against one's will. If there is such a right, what are its basis and justification? One might think that moral analysis here bottoms out in a deontological judgment, but surely the consequences of outing will be a big part of the basis for moral judgment in this case, even if one denies that consequences are the sole basis of judgment.

In some historical contexts, being identified publicly as a homosexual rendered one susceptible to the gallows, the dungeon, or violent death at the hands of an angry mob. In the contemporary United States, prejudice and discrimination against homosexuals are variable and waning, though still virulent. Active political movements combat discrimination against gays and lesbians, and many homosexuals in recent years have "come out of the closet," openly affirming their sexual orientation and no longer making a secret of it. I suppose the case for outing would go as follows. Let us suppose that at this time in the United States, the greater the number of homosexuals who openly affirm their sexuality, the lesser the stigma that attaches to openly acknowledged homosexuality and the easier it is to lead a life that eschews sexual secrecy. The open acknowledgment of homosexuality by one individual thus confers a benefit on all others who also openly acknowledge their homosexuality. Although this is less clear, I will assume that the open acknowledgment of homosexuality by some does not have any impact, positive or negative, on the life prospects of those homosexuals who continue to keep their sexual orientation a secret. I assume, furthermore, that the more generally well known the individual who reveals his sexual orientation, the greater the impact of the revelation on the disposition of public opinion toward tolerance of homosexuality. A celebrity has more clout in this regard than someone who is less well known.

The advocate of outing envisages a desirable future state of American culture in which being lesbian or gay is not regarded as shameful or sinful, no stigma attaches to nonheterosexuality, and no one has any reason to be secretive about one's sexual orientation. The outing advocate's claim, then, must be that the costs to self versus the gains to others of openly declaring one's sexual orientation if one is well known and gay are such that the prominent gay is morally obligated to take this course. Therefore, forcing this course on the unwilling is at least morally permissible. I have no idea whether the advocate wins or loses the argument because I have no clear idea as to the likelihood of the truth of the several empirical claims that the argument presupposes. What does seem true to me is that the characterization of an act as an invasion of privacy, even in this extreme case, does not settle its moral status, which requires here (as always) a calculation of consequences and a set of principles for weighting their moral value or disvalue.

V. EGALITARIAN OBJECTIONS TO RESPONSIBILITY-CATERING PRIORITARIANISM

Perhaps it is a sign that the brand of egalitarian justice that I favor fails to accommodate morally legitimate individual rights of privacy that this very complaint has been forcibly asserted by some egalitarians. In a nutshell, the problem is that versions of egalitarianism that seek to accommodate concerns of personal responsibility and deservingness appear to require for their implementation vast amounts of what would otherwise be private and merely personal information about people's lives. Suppose we say that justice requires equalizing people's opportunities for well-being. On this view, if one person is badly off now because she never had any opportunity to achieve a decent quality of life, there is a justice-reason to compensate her for her misfortune, whereas if another person is equally badly off now because she squandered the rich opportunities that were available to her, there is no justice-reason to compensate her. (There may even be a case for transferring resources away from the second person in order to improve the opportunities of those whose initial options were bleak.) Upholding egalitarian justice in this way requires that agents of society ferret out information about individuals that will enable their classification into different levels of responsibility for their current fate. Moreover, agents of society must make complex and discriminating moral assessments of people's conduct of their lives. To some, theories of distributive justice with these implications amount to rationalizations for a "Big Brother" state.

Philosopher Jonathan Wolff imagines an individual who cannot secure employment, even in a tight labor market.[24] Economic conditions are favorable, so in order to plead that, despite appearances, he has no genuine opportunity for employment and the improved quality of life that employment would bring, he has to demonstrate that his personal deficiencies interact with the favorable economic conditions in a way that renders his continued unemployment an affliction that is beyond his power to control. In this type of situation, opportunity-oriented versions of egalitarian justice impose on people a requirement of shameful revelation. One must explicitly confront in one's own mind, and then openly acknowledge to others, facts about oneself that one regards as deeply shameful. In modern democratic culture, where a competent adult is expected to be self-supporting, personal deficiencies, such as an abject lack of talent relevant to employment, qualify as deeply shameful. The individual who must shame himself in this way in order to be eligible for state income support will find it difficult to sustain his sense of self-respect and his belief that he is fundamentally an equal among equals in his society.

According to Wolff, a similar problem arises when considering a government bureaucracy that is charged with the task of administering resource transfers to aid the disadvantaged. The problem is that such a bureaucracy's institutional-security measures can express strong distrust of those who are being monitored. An individual who is able to view

[24] Jonathan Wolff, "Fairness, Respect, and the Egalitarian Ethos," *Philosophy and Public Affairs* 27, no. 2 (Spring 1998): 97–122.

himself as sharing a status of democratic equality with all others in society will regard himself as entitled to a presumption of trustworthiness.
If one's conduct is monitored by state authorities, whereas ordinary, non-
poor citizens are not subject to this degree of monitoring and scrutiny, one
reasonably feels distrusted. Here again, state action menaces one's sense
of self-respect and one's belief in one's fundamentally equal status in
society. To invoke an old example, the knock on one's door in the dead of
night may not be the Gestapo or the police. Rather, it may be one's
social-service caseworker, checking on the truthfulness of one's declaration that one is living alone, supporting one's children, and not cohabiting
with a boyfriend who should be counted as an extra source of income that
would reduce one's need for state support.

Wolff suggests a moderate response to these difficulties. Alongside
distributive-justice principles of fairness, we should embrace a principle
of respect, which forbids treating people in disrespectful ways or in ways
that threaten their self-respect. Sometimes fairness should give way to
respect when the two values conflict. Without directly discussing purported flaws in egalitarianism, philosopher Avishai Margalit identifies
"the decent society as one whose institutions do not humiliate people,"
where humiliation involves banishing someone from the human com-
monwealth or denying a person control over her vital interests—in short,
treating someone as a nonperson or as less than fully human.[25] Margalit
discusses invasions of privacy as one type of humiliation that the decent
society avoids. His book *The Decent Society* conveys the impression that
maintaining the decent society is morally a more urgent matter than
establishing justice. Even if decency is part of justice, it is the preeminent
part.

Philosopher Elizabeth Anderson emphasizes the disrespectful, negative judgments about the traits and lives of individual persons that egalitarian institutions convey to those who are classified as deserving of aid
as well as to those deemed undeserving. Her target is a family of views
of distributive justice that she calls "luck egalitarianism."[26] According to
the luck egalitarian, the problem of social justice is that people suffer from
undeserved bad luck, and what justice requires in response is that compensation and transfers be implemented so that the good and bad fortune
that each person gets through no fault or choice of her own is the same for
all. Anderson objects that the attitude that lies behind this conception of
justice is an unsavory disrespect—a disrespectful pity toward those la-
belled unfortunate—and a presumptuous hectoring of those deemed at
fault and, hence, responsible for the mess that we think they have made
of their lives. In the same vein, criticizing a luck-egalitarian essay by G. A.

---

[25] Margalit, *The Decent Society*, 1.
[26] Elizabeth Anderson, "What Is the Point of Equality?" *Ethics* 99, no. 2 (January 1999):
287–337.

Cohen,[27] Christine Korsgaard expresses a preference for conceptions of distributive justice that allow us to "avoid having to make moralizing judgments about individual cases."[28]

Anderson raises a further objection against luck egalitarianism, one that partly explains its tendency to promote offensive moralizing and paternalistic invasions of privacy. She holds it to be a mistake to include natural as well as social inequalities within the scope of social justice. According to luck egalitarianism, it is unfair that some are born handsome and charming and some plain and uncharming. Given this, perhaps the state should investigate, assign romantic-endowment scores to persons, and organize compensation for those destined to be unlucky in love (unless their misfortune along this dimension is outweighed by good fortune along other dimensions). According to Anderson, once the domain of inequality with which justice is supposed to deal is erroneously extended to natural inequalities, the social-justice principles that underwrite the extension are bound to go disastrously wrong in setting boundaries between public and private. Thus, the social agencies assigned to dispense egalitarian justice in these circumstances will inexorably trample on people's private lives in the name of public business.

All of these arguments claiming that egalitarian systems of justice cannot accommodate privacy rights sound plausible, but none is correct. Or at least, none makes serious trouble for responsibility-catering prioritarianism. First of all, we need to keep straight at what level of abstraction the discussion is supposed to proceed.

A counterexample to a moral principle envisages the successful implementation of the principle in specified circumstances, and argues that the implications of accepting the principle in these circumstances are morally unacceptable; thus, to block these implications, we must either reject or qualify the principle. As we have just seen, the arguments of the critics of egalitarian justice are supposed to demonstrate that values such as privacy and self-respect have weight independent of human well-being, and that perhaps the former values should be accorded predominant weight. However, the scenarios conjured up by the critics' arguments, as I read them, tend to be ones in which ham-fisted institutions smash privacy and human well-being as well. Read that way, the arguments cannot succeed. You cannot refute a moral principle that tells us we ought to achieve a certain aim to the greatest extent that is possible by pointing out (what is surely true) that some seemingly sensible ways of trying to achieve this aim would be counterproductive. Such a refutation only shows that the policies proposed for fulfilling the principle would be unsuccessful. They leave the principle untouched.

[27] G. A. Cohen, "Equality of What? Of Welfare, Goods, and Capabilities," in Martha Nussbaum and Amartya Sen, eds., *The Quality of Life* (Oxford: Clarendon Press, 1993), 9–29.
[28] Christine Korsgaard, "Commentary [on essays by G. A. Cohen and Amartya Sen]," in Nussbaum and Sen, eds., *The Quality of Life*, 61.

In order to ensure that we are not slipping into this unhelpful construal of the critics' objections, we will concentrate on examples in which it is clear that egalitarian justice as responsibility-catering prioritarianism is best fulfilled by means that the critics deem repulsive and immoral. Then the conflict will be squarely posed. The critic invokes a deontological standard for what counts as a violation of privacy; this standard is taken to be independent of the consequences of violating privacy (as privacy is construed according to the standard).[29] The critic seeks our agreement that if the facts fit a certain characterization, then conduct so characterized is morally wrong, regardless of its consequences (at least up to some threshold level of consequences).

Let us consider a drug-control policy in a world troubled by child abuse and human disarray, in which families have adult guardians who overuse recreational drugs, including alcohol, heroin, and cocaine. The state's policy is to encourage children to inform on their parents. Here we have Big Brother with a vengeance. We might imagine that such a family-splitting policy could yield bad results with no offsetting benefits, but then consequentialist views such as prioritarianism would condemn the policy, so on this characterization of the facts, this is not a good test case for assessing the independent moral weight of privacy. To isolate the moral urgency of the right to privacy per se, let us stipulate that the policy has unequivocally good results when these are assessed by the criteria of responsibility-catering prioritarianism. The policy predictably corrodes family ties and mutual trust among family members, and these effects are worse in families in which parents accused by their own children are either entirely innocent or are guilty of only some minor peccadillo that is disproportionate to the suffering that they, along with their children, are made to undergo. The policy puts state officials in the uncomfortable position of training children to be snitches, a task that the officials find odious, and which exposes the children to increased risk of physical and emotional harms. Let us suppose, however, that over time the policy does more good than harm, as weighted by consequentialist principles, and indeed maximizes moral good by comparison with any alternative policy. What are the net results? Social workers, an already well off group, are made slightly worse off, and parents of targeted families are on the average neither better off nor worse off. Children, though some gain and some lose, are substantially better off overall, and the gains are concentrated among the children whose ex ante prospects of living in miserably

---

[29] Another possibility is that the critic holds that the standard for good consequences set by responsibility-catering prioritarianism is inadequate. The critic may hold this because he thinks that responsibility-catering prioritarianism fails to recognize fully the value of privacy. The critic might also hold that one or more of the values of increasing human well-being, giving priority to the worse off, or adjusting priority by people's differential responsibility for their condition is flawed. Comments in the next paragraphs respond to these criticisms.

abusive settings placed them badly off even within the class of impover-ished and disadvantaged children. Weighted well-being is thus substan-tially increased.

My response to this imaginary case is that privacy values have already been included in the calculation that establishes people's overall increases and losses in well-being, so giving further weight to a purported "right of privacy" in a moral assessment of the policy involves illegitimate double-counting. Privacy, like many important human values, might be an in-strumental value; its importance would then be derivative. Privacy of various sorts contributes to human flourishing in many settings, so we honor it. Rights of privacy, to the extent that they are defensible, are tailored to conduce to well-being, just as healthy diets are designed to secure weight loss and other health goals, and a "good diet" that does not contribute to weight loss or other health values has no independent claim on our allegiance. Privacy might well figure into the weighted well-being approach in another way, as a constituent of well-being rather than as a means to it. Achieving certain privacy values might in and of itself, other things being equal, make one's life go better. But to the extent that privacy is rightly regarded as a component of well-being, then a principle that urges us to maximize human well-being as weighted by fair distribution considerations already incorporates adequate concern for privacy. If it turned out that we can maximize weighted well-being by violating pri-vacy, this is no more problematic, and no more an objection to weighted well-being, than discovering that in many circumstances we must endure or produce some physical pain in order to maximize weighted well-being, notwithstanding the fact that pain avoidance is no doubt a component of well-being. Thus the undoubted importance of privacy need not impel us to postulate privacy as a distinct and independent moral value. Everyone agrees that privacy conventions differ greatly from one culture to another. Do we really have a grip on how to evaluate these various privacy con-ventions apart from assessing their effect on the sum and distribution of well-being?

Whether well-being and its distribution could credibly serve as a single fundamental value in a theory of justice depends in part on how well-being is conceived. In this essay, "well-being" serves as a placeholder; how it is best conceived is a topic for other occasions. The reader should substitute the best account of well-being into the prioritarian proposal in order to give the proposal a fair hearing. If a perfect implementation of a prioritarian principle would bring it about that people are leading de-based and miserable lives, then we are deploying an unsatisfactory con-ception of human well-being. For example, if well-being is conceived as preference satisfaction, then the society that achieves the prioritarian goal might be one in which people overwhelmingly are satisfying benighted and foolish preferences that would not withstand reasonable critical scru-tiny. If this outcome strikes us as morally unsatisfactory, the likely culprit is the conception of well-being as preference satisfaction, not the principle of prioritarianism.

Notice that my example of the privacy-destroying state policy that maximizes weighted well-being—and should thus be regarded as morally satisfactory—requires that egalitarian justice at the fundamental level be concerned with individual well-being. Suppose, instead, that egalitarian justice were conceived as fundamentally requiring a fair distribution of resources. For simplicity, let us suppose that egalitarian justice requires an equal distribution of resources according to some standard for determining, given that different individuals hold different amounts of different resources, their overall or all-things-considered level of resource holdings. We then confront this conception of justice as equal resource provision with the objection that the most efficient means to bring about the achievement of social justice might involve cruel violations of privacy, as in the example of state encouragement of children to inform on their parents. The reply is that however morally bad we regard privacy invasion to be, there is no problem, because in the example the privacy invasion is required in order to secure egalitarian justice, and we are supposing that egalitarian justice is the moral value that takes priority over all others. Absent this privacy invasion, an equal distribution of resources to people could not be secured. The trouble with this line of response is that the distribution of resources—the stuff that people can use to help in achieving their goals—is not per se something that anybody should care about. We will want to look beyond the equal resource distribution to see what it does for people and whether it enhances the quality of their lives. Nothing guarantees that it will do so. Getting the postulated equal and fair share of resources may not do anything for my life, or may not do much. In this case the response to the privacy objection looks fetishistic. We suppose, plausibly, that the invasion of privacy that we are considering has significant negative costs on people's lives: values that matter to the good life are being corroded and destroyed. One cannot reasonably assuage this worry by cheerfully remarking that the costs incurred as a result of the loss of privacy are more than counterbalanced by the distribution of resources, such as bank-account wealth, that could not be achieved (so well) if the privacy loss were not accepted. For all that has been said so far, it could be the case that no one regards the loss of privacy as fair compensation for the extra piles of resources that are offered as compensation, and everyone might be entirely reasonable in rejecting this trade-off. In order that social justice can plausibly be regarded as a preeminent moral value, one that trumps all others, the currency of justice must be well-being rightly construed.

A fundamental moral principle that tells us to maximize weighted well-being will not be operationalizable; one cannot directly apply it as a guide to policy and law. One will need intermediate principles that posit measurable proxies for the weighted well-being that we really care about, which, even if measurable in principle, will not be directly measurable in practice. But the resultant moral structure, with its varying levels of abstraction (from fundamental principles to applicable policy guides), must be anchored in a credible understanding of what we think really matters from the moral standpoint.

I want briefly to tout another virtue of responsibility-catering prioritarianism that is manifest in the discussion of egalitarian justice versus privacy. This virtue can be claimed for prioritarianism only if it is bounded in some respects. Prioritarianism holds that the moral value of securing a benefit (or avoiding a loss) for a person increases as the affected person's prior level of well-being decreases; this level of well-being is measured on an absolute scale rather than a comparative one. (This last point means that the moral value of gaining a particular benefit for a person at a particular level of well-being does not vary depending on whether other people are better or worse off. Prioritarianism's judgments are not directly comparative. Thus, if Smith is worse off than Jones, conferring a one-unit benefit on Smith rather than Jones has greater moral value.) By how much does the moral value of providing a benefit get increased weight in this way? At one extreme, very little extra weight is assigned, and prioritarianism with almost no weighting becomes hardly distinguishable from straight utilitarianism. At the other extreme, the extra weight assigned in this way is always infinite, which renders prioritarianism a leximin doctrine.[30] This is an implausibly stringent reading of giving priority to the worse off. Prioritarianism as leximin would hold that if we have a choice between bringing it about that a worse-off person gets a small benefit or that a better-off person gets a larger benefit, priority to the worse off always takes priority over the size of the benefit, so we should opt for getting the tiniest increment of benefit for the worse-off person no matter how enormous the gain could be for the person who is better off. (Or at least, this is the case if either the benefit we can confer is a lump that cannot be divided into components or the shift in benefits would not render the previously worse off person better off after the change than the person who was previously better off.) When I appeal to prioritarianism, I have in mind some version of it that stipulates a "middling" weighting rule that avoids both extremes, but I have no precise proposal for identifying the best version. Thus, in what follows, I identify prioritarianism with a middle-range weighting rule.

With this proviso in place, prioritarianism yields plausible results in its application to policy when competing policy proposals involve gains and

[30] A leximin principle of distribution holds that as a first priority, one should maximize the benefit level of the worst-off person; as a second priority, one should maximize the benefit level of the second-worst-off person; and so on, up to the best-off person. In each instance the priority is absolute, so that one should seek even the slightest gain that can be made to improve the condition of (for example) the worst-off person no matter what costs this would pose to the condition of the second-worst-off person (so long as she remains second-worst-off) or to the condition of any better-off persons.

losses to better-off and worse-off persons. In the stylized invasion-of-privacy example discussed above, we supposed that already well off social workers find their position, on average, worsened by the shift to an aggressive drug-control policy that encourages children to inform on their drug-abusing parents. For this consequence to be tolerable, it is important that the potential gains and losses of the better off are not virtually disregarded by being discounted by an extreme weighting rule. If the policy choice affects an equal number of social workers and children, and the gains to the worse-off children are worth one penny, whereas the losses to the better-off social workers are worth millions of dollars, the social workers have a reasonable basis of complaint. If the ratio of the costs-to-the-worse-off to the benefits-to-the-better-off is sufficiently small, the morally preferable policy choice is the one that secures the benefits to the already better off.

Some might respond to my example by denying that it is empirically plausible to suppose that in circumstances modern societies are likely to face, egalitarian-justice principles could be efficiently served by gross intrusions on privacy. I have no quarrel with this response. The relevant facts are hard to discern. My goal is to urge that for various sets of circumstances, both likely and unlikely, that we can envisage, the implications of egalitarian justice, when thought through carefully, will make good sense.

The complaint that egalitarian justice should be limited to ending man-made oppression, and is not reasonably conceived as striving to undo all cosmic bad luck, requires more discussion than I can give it here. Very briefly, I would hold that if Smith is born blind or talentless, and will lead a miserable life unless society helps him, but could be enabled to lead a good life if he were to be helped, then there is just as much reason to aid Smith as there would be if he had been made equally badly off by human intervention. But I agree that one's view on this point will greatly affect one's view of the legitimate scope of social action to achieve egalitarian justice.

Let us return to the objection that egalitarian justice in its prioritarian guise compels individuals to engage in shameful revelation and that this constitutes wrongfully disrespectful treatment of persons or (what I shall argue is quite a different matter) treatment of persons that undermines their self-respect. The thought, here, is that as a condition of getting aid I must acknowledge to state officials that I am incompetent in ways that render me a failure, a "no-account" in my own eyes and in the eyes of observers.

I will forgo the response that, in the circumstances described, one is not compelled to undergo shame because one could refuse to engage in the self-revelation and refrain from taking the state aid. In some cases, one's material need might be so dire that one has no other options but to submit to shameful revelation or endure personal disaster. In some cases, one might feel such a strong obligation to ensure support for one's children by any morally legitimate means, that distasteful self-revelation becomes the sole recourse. Let us accept that in the case we are imagining, shameful revelation is in effect compelled. Must this be wrongful?

In passing it should be noted that the implementation of responsibility-catering egalitarian justice need not necessarily force individuals to reveal personal information about themselves to aid-dispensing government agencies. We may be able to succeed in devising policies that target the badly off for aid and the well off for provision of aid without requiring an intrusive examination of individual cases. A very simple example is a tax law that imposes progressively higher rates of tax as one's income rises. Such a tax, to a very rough degree, imposes burdens on the more talented and fortunate, who on average will tend to have higher income than others. Another example would be the provision of aid to the needy able-bodied by offering low-skill public sector employment at low wages. The aid would be open to anyone physically able to work who has low income, but it would tend to be more attractive to those low-income citizens who are less able and have fewer marketable skills. Talented individuals who have low income because they have a strong preference for leisure over work will have access to more skilled and highly paid part-time employment and will not want public sector employment. These examples show that it is not the case that egalitarian policies automatically and inherently require individualized "shameful revelation." The social planner may devise other means of appropriately targeting transfers to the truly disadvantaged.

Other things being equal, a society trying to implement responsibility-catering egalitarian principles of distributive justice will prefer policies that precisely target the needy for benefits and the advantaged citizens for burdens, and will, thus, prefer policies that elicit whatever information is needed to secure this targeting. If the gathering of information causes losses of well-being, because individuals find it offensive or shameful to reveal the needed information, then, provided that these responses are reasonable, other things being equal, society will prefer policies that economize on information extraction and protect individual privacy.

A successful policy optimizes the attainment of these sometimes conflicting goals: information extraction and individual privacy. In a similar fashion, other things being equal, a society prefers greater compliance with its just rules, and, hence, favors the monitoring of individuals to ensure a high rate of compliance. But monitoring itself generally imposes costs, including the feeling on the part of the monitored individual that she is not trusted by her fellow citizens; this may engender an atmosphere of suspicion and mistrust rather than one of solidarity. The best policy will again be a compromise that balances these conflicting goals. The issue becomes whether responsibility-catering prioritarianism provides the right norms to assess these tradeoffs. This principle will give weight to privacy, individual freedom, and other values only in a subordinate role, as instrumental to weighted well-being. Some may feel that this gives insufficient weight to the subordinated values, to which they attribute intrinsic value in their own right. However, this position must confront the plain fact that not all invasions of privacy are created equal, and some do not seem offensive at all. The responsibility-catering prioritarian theorist has an explanation for this: the intrusions on privacy that intuitively strike us as wrongful invasions do not serve to bring about a fair distribution of well-being. Intrusions on privacy that are effective means to achieve this fair distribution are not viewed as wrongful.

The critic might reply that privacy violations that are productive in this way are still wrongful because they undermine the self-respect of those whose privacy is violated or they manifest disrespect for persons.[31] These are two quite different objections, not alternative formulations of the same one. The worry about undermining a person's self-respect is that self-respect is something good that the individual has, which the privacy-violating act dictated by consequentialism might have the effect of destroying. In contrast, the imperative not to behave in a way that shows disrespect is viewed as a protection against something that is inherently bad, independently of its effects on anybody. Even if the person one proposes to treat disrespectfully would be oblivious of this fact, and even if one could predict this in advance, this would not alter the inherently disrespectful quality of one's act. We thus have two separate objections to consider.

The imperative not to treat people disrespectfully might be simply a way of signaling adherence to a deontological morality, according to which morality commands that one should not do acts that satisfy certain descriptions, whatever the consequences of doing so (at least up to some threshold beyond which consequences are too great to be ignored). This raises an issue beyond the scope of this essay. My aim has been to indicate the plausibility and attractiveness of a form of consequentialism—responsibility-catering prioritarianism—not to defend consequentialism per se against nonconsequentialist ethics.

But one might interpret the objection more narrowly. One might think that disrespectful treatment of another human is an identifiable type of conduct that morality bids one always to avoid. Wolff notes that a consequentialist egalitarianism might regard treating someone disrespectfully as prima facie wrongful but must suppose that the wrong of disrespect can in principle be offset or compensated for by other benefits.[32] This he regards as perverse, a way of not recognizing the inherent wrongfulness of disrespect. I am willing to concede that one should never treat another

---

[31] Wolff alternates between these phrasings in "Fairness, Respect, and the Egalitarian Ethos," 107.
[32] Ibid.

person disrespectfully, but I am inclined to interpret this requirement as satisfied whenever one behaves toward others in accordance with principles that as rational agents they could accept, that is, one acts from principles that are in fact best supported by reason. If you come after me with a pitchfork or invade my privacy, assessing whether these acts fail to treat me with the respect that is owed to persons requires consideration of whether or not these acts are morally justifiable. If this is correct, then it is a mistake to appeal to the rule against disrespect in order to argue that the acts are not justifiable. That just begs the question.

I turn now to the second thought, that if treating someone in a certain way undermines her self-respect, the act can never be justified. In effect, this is an assertion of a consequentialist ethic in which self-respect is the top value that trumps all others. Is this lexical priority of self-respect a plausible position? This seems to me the position Wolff is led to, though he retreats from asserting it for a reason that I do not understand. He says that giving lexical priority to self-respect might be self-defeating, leading to a situation in which self-respect is undermined. But this just means that self-respect is in fact the moral value that has lexical priority, but that it does not follow from this that embedding this priority into institutional rules or employing it in our practical deliberation is justified, because there is at least a logical possibility that these acts might reduce self-respect.

The plausibility of the position that the value of self-respect is lexically prior to all other values depends on how we are to understand self-respect, but I submit that on any remotely plausible interpretation of that phrase, it should not be accorded a supreme position in morality. If self-respect had lexical priority, we would have to rank the scenario in which one has self-respect to a high degree as superior to any alternative position in which one has slightly less self-respect, no matter what one's life is otherwise like. At the risk of making light of self-respect, I confess that I would prefer to have less of it and not slowly be tortured to death over the entire course of my life than to have more self-respect during a lifetime consisting of torture. Self-respect is a constituent of well-being, not something that plausibly outweighs it. Invasions of privacy that bring about net losses of individual self-respect but overall gains in weighted well-being strike me as morally acceptable, not as violations of some absolute moral command. For example, it may be that firmly believing that I am a human and fundamentally as worthy as any other (to insert one possible interpretation of self-respect) requires that some act that I did and now regard as shameful not be exposed to full view either in my own mind or in the public eye. If my privacy in this regard is violated, I inevitably come to think of myself as not fully human. Let us suppose that this is a situation in which my self-respect is on the line and no one else's (so that respecting my privacy does not entail any cost to anyone else's self-respect) and, furthermore, that eschewing the act that reduces my self-respect necessarily imposes large costs on the lives of others and, perhaps, on my own life as well. In this case (and no doubt others) self-respect should give way.

It is fully compatible with this argument to assert that being treated with the honor and equal respect that any human is due is a very significant component of anyone's good. I take no position on the weight that should be accorded self-respect. My claim is that whatever weight the best theory of well-being accords it is the weight that it should get, and this weight will not be infinite, so lexical priority is out. I also take no stand on the degree to which respecting all humans as equals in one's conduct in practice ever comes in conflict with the pursuit of other constituents of human well-being. That there are conflicts and hard tradeoffs here is suggested by this remark by Lieutenant Steve Laguere, head of the Meridien, Connecticut police SWAT unit: "And we don't care if we're dealing with the lowest vermin in the street, it's 'yes sir, no sir.' We never dehumanize these people."[33]

VI. Conclusion

The utilitarian egalitarianism whose praises I have been singing may in the end seem a dreary and uninspiring doctrine. Its romance is bureaucracy. In *Homage to Catalonia*, Orwell observed that a "fat man eating quails while children are begging for bread is a disgusting sight."[34] The doctrine I espouse, taking men as they are and laws as they might be made, cautions that before arriving at a final assessment, we must determine whether subtracting from the fat man's quails will do anything to increase the children's (or anyone else's) bread consumption, and exactly what losses the fat man must sustain to get exactly what benefits for the children. In the same book, Orwell declared that "the thing that attracts ordinary men to socialism and makes them willing to risk their skins for it . . . is the idea of equality," which he associated with a community where "no one was on the make . . . [and there was] no privilege and no boot-licking."[35] In contrast, prioritarianism recommends that we calculate the optimal degree of inequality, the optimal degree of social hierarchy, and, for that matter, the optimal degree of invasion of individual privacy.[36] I applaud the idea that a just society is constituted by human

---

[33] Quoted in Timothy Egan, "Soldiers of the Drug War Remain on Duty," *New York Times*, March 1, 1999, A16.

[34] George Orwell, *Homage to Catalonia* (1938; reprint, New York: Harcourt, Brace, and World, 1952), 115.

[35] Ibid., 105.

[36] Of course, this is misleading in a way, because if the dreariness of prioritarianism muffles allegiance to it, then this very doctrine recommends that inspiring mid-level principles be devised that can elicit people's loyalty in ways that will better achieve prioritarian ends.

relationships as well as by the pattern of the distribution of goods, but both of these factors must ultimately be assessed by their impact on the quality of the individual lives that better-off and worse-off people are enabled to lead. To neglect this bottom line is bad romanticism, not good ethics.

Philosophy, University of California, San Diego

PRIVACY AND LIMITED DEMOCRACY: THE MORAL CENTRALITY OF PERSONS

By H. Tristram Engelhardt, Jr.

I. Introduction

Of all the moral concerns regarding privacy in its various meanings, this essay selects only one: the right to be left alone by others, in particular, by government. Because moral controversies in pluralist societies tend to be interminable, and surely controversies regarding privacy are no exception, I approach the right to privacy in terms of the centrality of persons. When there are foundational disputes about which content-full moral view should govern, it is not possible to resolve such controversies without begging the question or conceding at the outset crucial moral premises. This observation is not to affirm a moral skepticism or relativism. At worst, it involves an epistemic skepticism, a skepticism about the possibility of resolving controversies by sound rational argument without begging the question or engaging in an infinite regress.

When stakeholders in a moral controversy do not share the same foundational moral understandings, but yet wish to collaborate, the only common basis for their morally authoritative collaboration will be their consent, their mutual authorization of what they do together, not a common understanding of the good and the right. What makes their actions right is only one factor: that they act with the consent of those who agree. This grounding of moral authority in the permission of persons gives central moral standing to certain practices, such as making contracts, engaging in the market, and establishing limited democracies. In each of these cases, persons are at liberty to do with themselves and their consenting others as they wish, as long as they have not previously ceded this authority to others. It is out of this grounding in persons and their residual rights over themselves that rights to privacy in the sense of rights to be left alone have a cardinal and original standing.[1] This paper explores rights to privacy in the light of this foundation.

II. The Right to Privacy: Some Ambiguities

Privacy is ambiguous. There are many ways to seek to be left alone, and many reasons to want to be left alone, and many fashions in which such

---

[1] I have developed at some length the arguments regarding this grounding in consent of a morality that can be shared with moral strangers; see my *The Foundations of Bioethics*, 2d ed. (New York: Oxford University Press, 1996).

wants can be advanced as rights, especially in a time in which the fulfillment of almost every desire is advanced as a right. There is ambiguity in rights claims themselves. Rights to privacy are advanced by people as claims to be left alone by government, by corporations, and by the simply curious and intrusive. People claim privacy rights against being observed without their permission, against personal information being transmitted without their leave, and against governments' regulating their private activities with consenting others. No doubt, much about the character of rights claims is shaped by who makes the claim, against whom the claim is made, and the subject matter of the claim. A phenomenology of privacy would likely reveal important differences in the ways in which the various privacies sought are experienced and constituted.[2] At best, there may only be a family resemblance among the many ways in which privacy is invoked to erect claims against the intrusions of others.

In English the cluster of meanings is complex. The English word privacy, derived from the Latin, indicates abstraction from a more general and substantive moral context. At least in some usages, privacy possesses a negative connotation. The etymological roots from the Latin *privo*, *privare*, *privatum* suggest a deficient state, one characterized by privation. After all, the first meaning of *privo* is to bereave, deprive, rob, or strip of something. The second meaning is to be free, released, or delivered of something. The adjective *privatus* derived from this verb has its first meaning: "apart from the State, peculiar to one's self, of or belonging to an individual, private."[3] The sense of being a private person not engaged in public or official life is derived from this adjective. The private was contrasted with public service, which served as a primary moral focus. The private is the sphere of life that excludes the civic. The substantive *privatus*, for example, indicates "a man in private life." More particularly, in the Roman Empire, private identified "not belonging to the emperor or to the imperial family." As this etymology conveys, the private did not possess a standing on its own. It was not defined in its own terms but as a sphere into which the demands of the state did not fully enter.

The first meaning of the English noun 'privacy' is similar to the Latin. "the state or condition of being withdrawn from the society of others, or from public interest; seclusion."[4] The second and third meanings indicate separateness from others: "private or retired places; private apartments; places of retreat"; "absence or avoidance of publicity or display; a condition approaching to secrecy or concealment." The third meaning of the adjective 'private' concerns genitalia, as in one's "*private parts*, the external organs of sex, the pudenda," thus connecting the private with that

---

[2] A phenomenology of privacy would offer a presentation of the lived experience of the importance of various forms of privacy.

[3] Charlton T. Lewis and Charles Short, *A Latin Dictionary* (Oxford: Clarendon Press, 1980), 1447.

[4] *Oxford English Dictionary*, s.v. "privacy."

about which one should be ashamed, drawing on the Latin *pudendum* (i.e., that about which one should show modesty). As an adjective, 'private' also compasses *"private soldier*: an ordinary soldier without rank or distinction of any kind," thus indicating that what is private lacks a certain excellence. Yet, the adjective 'private' also has the meaning "not open to the public; restricted or intended only for the use or enjoyment of particular and privileged persons" as well as "of, or pertaining or related to, or affecting a person, or a small intimate body or group of persons apart from the general community; individual, personal."[5]

The salience of concerns regarding privacy is in part technologically driven. At the beginning of the third millennium A.D., we confront an intrusive cluster of technologies for the observation, interpretation, and storage of data. Spy satellites[6] may photograph naked sunbathers in the middle of a nine-section ranch;[7] special microphones can be directed at houses to pick up conversations through closed windows and glass doors; an immense amount of data can be electronically assembled to provide psychologically interpretable profiles of behavior;[8] and genetics can offer the acquisition and disclosure of unanticipated information.[9] Our concerns regarding privacy have deeper roots than these recent technological developments, stretching back to English legal notions of the rights of persons against their sovereign that themselves were influenced by even older pagan customs.[10] Through these traditions, the West has come to

---

[5] Ibid.

[6] Satellites can not only photograph activities on private property that one might take to be unseen, but can also, by mapping, create a universal set of identifiers. See, for example, Michael R. Curry, "Digital People, Digital Places: Rethinking Privacy in a World of Information," *Ethics Behavior* 7, no. 3 (April 1997): 253–63.

[7] The ordinary and customary measurement for ranchland in Texas and other civilized regions is in sections; a section contains one square mile, a mile being eight furlongs long. It is because a furlong is ten chains long and a chain 66 feet that a mile is 5,280 feet long. A decent ranch would comprise nine sections, because a league is three miles and Spanish land grants were for a square league of land.

[8] See, for example, Timothy H. Engstrom, "Corporate Appropriation of Privacy: The Transformation of the Personal and Public," *Ethics Behavior* 7, no. 3 (April 1997): 239–52; and M. Gregg Bloche, "Managed Care, Medical Privacy, and the Paradigm of Consent," *Kennedy Institute of Ethics Journal* 7, no. 4 (December 1997): 381–86.

[9] The mere comparison of blood types within a family often reveals that the wife's husband, whose role as the father of the children had been taken for granted, cannot be the biological father. Genetic science threatens the disclosure of an immense amount of further information with significant social and economic implications. See, for example, Patrick L. Brockett and E. Susan Tankersley, "The Genetics Revolution: Economics, Ethics and Insurance," *Journal of Business Ethics* 16, no. 15 (November 1997): 1661–76.

[10] Rights to privacy have roots in the vaunted rights of Englishmen, which draw on ancient pagan moral, political, and legal understandings that recognized the individual as having inherent and robust rights against the sovereign. See, for example, Henry Charles Lea, *Torture* (1866; reprint, Philadelphia: University of Pennsylvania Press, 1973), 24–25; and the reports of Tacitus in his *Germania*. Albeit transformed by later influences, these understandings persisted in English law and framed the pagan Icelandic and Viking attitudes toward morals and polity. See Peter Foote and Davis M. Wilson, *The Viking Achievement*

assume that persons have prima facie rights to be unobserved and unmonitored.

Three different senses of privacy as the right to be left alone by others must be distinguished at the outset: (1) freedom from unwanted observation or collection of information, (2) freedom from the disclosure of personal information without one's consent, and (3) freedom from unwarranted government intrusion. The first sense of privacy includes hiding from others parts of one's body, elements of one's life, as well as one's thoughts and opinions. In this first sense, rights to privacy focus on protecting oneself from the gaze, observation, or study of others and from intrusions into one's seclusion, solitude, or private affairs. The second sense of privacy involves protecting what others have observed about oneself from further disclosure. It involves a claim of an embargo right against the further distribution of personal information. This concern, for example, is reflected in three clusters of torts, associated with invasions of privacy, which also receive some statutory legal protection: (1) public disclosures of embarrassing facts, (2) public presentations of an individual in a false fashion, and (3) use without permission of an individual's name or likeness.[11] These concerns for privacy have, as well, a special salience with respect to medical information, especially genetic information. Privacy rights in the first two senses do not possess quite the salience of what in twentieth-century America became enshrined as constitutionally protected spheres of privacy: rights to be left alone by the government. It is this last sense of rights to privacy—fundamental limits on the authority of the government—that will be the focus of this essay.

Our limited secular moral knowledge has implications for government's claim of authority to intrude on our consensual acts and to observe and monitor these acts without our consent. After some two-and-a-half millennia of moral philosophy, we have failed to establish criteria for discerning when someone truly possesses knowledge of the good, the right, the just, and the virtuous.[12] It is not just that the world de facto lacks

---

(London: Sidgwick & Jackson, 1980). Among the Vikings in particular, there was a well-developed view of the limits of sovereignty. Foote and Wilson provide one example of this by drawing on the *Chronicle* of Dido of St. Quentin (ca. 970–1043). Dido reported that Rollo of Normandy, when asked to kiss the foot of King Charles the Simple (the ruler of France [898–929]), responded by lifting the king's foot to his mouth, thus upending the king flat on his back (Foote and Wilson, *The Viking Experience*, 79).

[11] Edward J. Bloustein, "Privacy as an Aspect of Human Dignity," in Ferdinand David Schoeman, ed., *Philosophical Dimensions of Privacy: An Anthology* (Cambridge: Cambridge University Press, 1984), 158. The language of rights to privacy was influenced by Samuel D. Warren and Louis D. Brandeis; see their "The Right to Privacy," *Harvard Law Review* 4, no. 5 (December 1890): 193–220.

[12] The challenge is not simply to know truly what is right, good, just, and virtuous, but also to know truly when we know this.

a universal, canonical moral narrative;[13] there are in addition good reasons to hold that such a narrative can never be established in general secular terms. As a result of this predicament, our only generally definable option is to ground the moral authority of states on the consent of the governed, rather than in arguments on behalf of a particular canonical, content-rich moral vision. Governments, then, lack the moral authority to intrude upon or govern individuals absent their consent. Thus, rights to privacy can sustain spheres of privacy within which consenting individuals may pursue views of the right, the good, the just, and the virtuous in ways that are at odds with the understanding of the larger society. Rights to privacy lie at the root of democracies limited by the consent of the governed.

Put succinctly, my point is this: if we do not all hear God univocally, and if there is no single, canonical, content-full view of the good, the right, the just, and the virtuous, then the moral fabric of society and the authority of the state must be drawn from the agreement of persons. Thus, consent forms the authority for government, not divine will or moral rationality, since both are precluded by competing views of God and moral rationality. Authority only comes from the permission of those who collaborate. In such circumstances, rights to privacy announce the plausible limits of the authority of others and of the state over the individual by disclosing the boundaries of consent. Or to put matters more positively, rights to privacy mark where individuals continue to maintain authority over themselves.

If moral authority is derived not from an antecedent view of the good, the right, the just, and the virtuous, but from the agreement of those who collaborate, then the moral burden of proof falls on those who intrude on individuals in the use of their own private property or their endeavors with consenting others. If permission is the source of moral authority, then the paradigm place for the construction of societal morality or governmental authority is not in a communal Socratic dialogue or deliberative discourse, which aims at establishing an authoritative moral vision

---

[13] Here I borrow an image from Jean-François Lyotard. "In contemporary society and culture—postindustrial society, postmodern culture—the question of the legitimization of knowledge is formulated in different terms. The grand narrative has lost its credibility, regardless of what mode of unification it uses, regardless of whether it is a speculative narrative or a narrative of emancipation" (Jean-François Lyotard, *The Postmodern Condition*, trans. G. Bennington and B. Massumi [Manchester: Manchester University Press, 1984], 37). It is not simply that a universal moral narrative has de facto lost its credibility. More importantly, its credibility cannot be restored in a principled fashion. The moral diversity of postmodernity is not just a socio-moral fact of the matter, but a condition expressing the limits of secular moral knowledge. This recognition, it should be noted, involves a certain epistemological skepticism, but not a metaphysical skepticism. It is not a denial of an ultimate moral truth that should command the assent of all. It involves only a recognition that this truth cannot be conclusively established by sound rational argument.

by sound rational argument, but rather in a marketplace, where bargaining prevails and all agreements are by mutual consent.

In the face of intractable moral disagreement and in the absence of a principled basis for resolving such disagreement, it is consent, contract, and the market that can provide moral authority. These practices do not require agreement about moral probity or justice, only limited agreement about what one will do with others in particular circumstances. Likewise, limited democracies, limited in part by robust areas of privacy, have a prima facie plausibility in a world marked by profound moral disagreements, insofar as they draw their authority from consent. The authority of limited democracies need not be grounded in some view of their divine anointment, or from an affirmation of the good that they might achieve. Limited democracy can be recognized as a default strategy, a way of deriving authority for common action when there is deep disagreement about the demands of both God and reason. In such circumstances, moral authority must come from the bottom up. Moral authority, to be secure and unambiguous, must come from the agreement of actual individuals, for there cannot be another generally justifiable option. Matters become more obscure as one inquires after the authority of large-scale governments. Especially in governments claiming greater scope, however, our epistemological moral predicament and the diversity of our moral visions give spheres of privacy originary and prima facie standing. Privacy and rights to privacy provide a reminder to more ambitious governments that their authority and its limits are derived from the consent of individuals.

The preferred image, though, is of limited governments whose authority is grounded upon the consent of the governed. As such, they can encompass diverse enclaves within which people are at secular moral liberty, by themselves or with consenting others, to exercise their right to act on their own understandings of human flourishing.[14] This right represents the limit of their consent to be controlled by the government. Governments must respect these choices because it cannot plausibly be presumed that individuals would have expressly or tacitly ceded this right. This view makes space for enclaves within which claims of justice and fairness that are generally accepted in the larger society do not prevail. Religious and ideological communities offer prime examples of enclaves in which private morality and free association flourish. These communities possess comprehensive accounts of moral probity, human flourishing, and even justice that may be contrary to the claims of the larger community.

Unlike limited democracies, social democratic polities will not make space for dissenting enclaves and will even wish to disbar from the public

---

[14] The qualification "secular" is attached to "moral" in order to indicate that there are religious moral insights unavailable to general moral reflection. The author of this essay is, after all, an Orthodox Christian.

forum types of moral rationality that are not reasonable in social democratic terms. This may lead to conflicts with particular enclaves that have
not incorporated the larger community's view of fairness and justice.
Consider a few examples. Moslems, who live in the West but do not
oppose polygamy on principle, may not want to have their children
exposed to civics lessons that undermine Moslem beliefs on family relationships and justice.[15] The Amish will have no truck with feminism.
Libertarians will abhor state-imposed affirmative action, especially within
their own communities. Spheres of privacy for such believers should have
a moral legitimacy by default, because they exist as a result of the limits
of secular moral knowledge and the ensuing plurality of moral visions.
Social democracies cannot accommodate these enclaves of dissent; therefore, limited government is a more attractive vision because it allows for
the coexistence of competing paradigms of human flourishing while min-
imizing conflicts.

III. Reason, Rights to Privacy, and the Postmodern World

Robust rights to privacy, in the sense of enclaves free of the intrusion of
the government on the actions of consenting individuals, may appear
implausible because of the West's religious history. In the presence of
God, there is no room for privacy. There is no space to establish one's own
view of the good, the right, the just, and the virtuous against His. In
relationship to an omniscient, omnipotent God, all of being is translucent
and any attempt to wall oneself off in a sphere of privacy is a rejection of
the core of being, a Luciferian sin, a project reminiscent of the devil's in
Milton's *Paradise Lost*. Where God is the ultimate and complete ground of
moral and political authority, there is no room for enclaves with competing visions protected by spheres of privacy. Divine command holds unassailable authority. Because God provides the genesis, justification, and
motivation for morality, the search for a sphere of privacy justifiable in its
own right—where one can establish one's own ranking of the good, one's

---

[15] There is a genre of liberalism that, by affirming a very particular understanding of
liberty, does not allow persons consensually to choose their own understandings of how
freely to relate to each other. For example, John Rawls argues that children should be
required to have knowledge of their constitutional and civic rights and that "their education
should also prepare them to be fully cooperating members of society and enable them to be
self-supporting; it should also encourage the political virtues so that they want to honor the
fair terms of social cooperation in their relations with the rest of society" (Rawls, *Political
Liberalism* [New York: Columbia University Press, 1993], 199). Unlike libertarian liberals,
cosmopolitan liberals or social democrats in fact affirm a "thick" understanding of community as the foundation of societal relationships. While affirming liberty, they give it a
"thick" content which amounts to requiring a particular form of communal life. It is with
regard to education or indoctrination about particular understandings of virtues and vices
that the most significant conflicts may arise. I have examined the development of the liberal
cosmopolitan ethos and its antilibertarian character in my *The Foundations of Bioethics*, chap. 3.

own ordering of right-making principles, and one's own conception of flourishing—is a fundamentally misguided and mistaken quest. It would be viewed as a rejection of the metaphysically correct understanding of the good, the right, the just, and the virtuous, as a project that must fail.

When secular philosophy invokes reason to play a role similar to God's in justifying a universal, content-full morality, a similar judgment seems plausible. If moral reason is univocal, rights and spheres of privacy (in the strong sense of domains in which one is at liberty to pursue one's own view of the right, the good, the just, and the virtuous) represent at best areas of deviation from what true moral rationality requires. In some circumstances, spheres of privacy may be tolerated as compromises, given insuperable ignorance, ambiguity, or other constraints. That is, in the face of a univocal, canonical morality, rights or spheres of privacy may be allowed by default because of the moral and other costs of:

1. forcefully overcoming ignorance of or false consciousness regarding the right, the good, the just, and/or the virtuous
2. overcoming the irresolvably ambiguous character of the right, the good, the just, and the virtuous
3. the direct pursuit of the right, the good, the just, and/or the virtuous when that direct pursuit would undermine the goal itself, thus necessitating a toleration for expediency's sake of enclaves that diverge from the ideal

If morality and political authority are grounded in reason—in a univocal, rational account of a common, content-full morality that should bind all—there will be no space, save by default, for spheres of privacy within which divergent understandings of the good, the right, the just, and the virtuous can by their own right be pursued with consenting others. That is, rights and spheres of privacy will have no special good or right-making character of their own to offer. They will, rather, arise out of compromises with ignorance, ambiguity, and special considerations of expediency. After all, the good, the right, the just, and the virtuous, if rationally justifiable, should as far as possible transform all of society and everyone in it, breaking down boundaries of ignorance and prejudice, walling off spheres of morally deviant private choice.

For social democrats and others in service to a content-rich view of the right, the good, the just, and the virtuous, the appeal to reason as the ground of governmental authority and general secular moral rationality is pronounced. Reason appears to offer the promise of establishing a particular moral understanding by appeal to the most general of moral considerations. If the Enlightenment hope from moral rationality could have been secured, then, despite willful capriciousness and claims of robust spheres of privacy, all people would belong to one moral community, bound by one morality, protests to the contrary notwithstanding. Such protests could be dismissed with good warrant and, all else being equal, spheres of privacy could be invaded as ultimately irrational. State coercion could be employed to bring deviants in line with rationally justified morality, and canons of justice could be imposed upon them for their own good, that is, as congenial to their moral autonomy rightly understood. Enclaves whose moral vision failed fully to accord with this canonical view, despite their claims of rights to privacy, would be understood as deficient and in need of re-education and reformation. Between the individual, particular moral enclaves, and the larger community, there would be no principled space for discordant moral understandings: society as a whole would be properly regarded as one community in which there are no robust rights to privacy against the all-encompassing community and its morality.[16]

IV. RAWLS AND PSEUDO-SPHERES OF PRIVACY

Social democratic approaches may, nevertheless, appear to offer space for spheres of privacy and moral diversity. Rawls, for example, offers an account of a well-ordered, constitutional, democratic society that appears to affirm moral pluralism, though only within the bounds of a social democratic vision of political community.[17] Pluralism is domesticated by a particular, rather content-rich notion of the reasonable. Reasonable pluralism spans enclaves, each with its own comprehensive doctrine,[18] that may participate in the dialogue of public reason, as long as they give "properly public reasons,"[19] that is, reasons "we also reasonably think that other citizens might reasonably accept."[20] In the public forum, it will not do for Amish or Moslems to speak of divine commands, or for libertarians to advance arguments to show the immorality of "ownership of the people, by the people, and for the people,"[21] and, hence, the foun-

---

[16] In two articles bearing on issues of privacy, Thomas Nagel warns against the communitarian identification of community and society with a "thick" view of human virtue: "The radical communitarian view that nothing in personal life is beyond the legitimate control of the community if its dominant values are at stake is the main contemporary threat to human rights" (Nagel, "Personal Rights and Public Space," *Philosophy and Public Affairs* 24, no. 2 [Spring 1995]: 106); "Communitarianism—the ambition of collective self-realization—is one of the most persistent threats to the human spirit" (Nagel, "Concealment and Exposure," *Philosophy and Public Affairs* 27, no. 1 [Winter 1998]: 29).

[17] It turns out, *mirabile factu*, that only that pluralism that is reasonable in social democratic terms is accepted as compatible with a social democratic polity. See, for example, Rawls, *Political Liberalism*, 36ff.

[18] "A doctrine is fully comprehensive if it covers all recognized values and virtues within one rather precisely articulated system. . . ." (ibid., 152).

[19] John Rawls, "The Idea of Public Reason Revisited," *University of Chicago Law Review* 64, no. 3 (Summer 1997): 776.

[20] Ibid., 771.

[21] Robert Nozick, *Anarchy, State, and Utopia* (New York: Basic Books, 1974), 290.

dational immorality of the progressive income tax and affirmative action. Rawls ties his account of justice and proposed limits to spheres of privacy to a "thick" understanding of social democracy that in turn defines the limitations of public reason. Additionally, for Rawls, neither religion nor libertarian political theory is a permissible source of foundational claims that can bring into question the claims of social democratic justice, society, or public reason.[22] Indeed, religious or philosophical commitments should not be introduced into the public forum, if they cannot be recast in terms of social democratic reason-giving. Social democratic reason is the foundation for appropriate civil discourse. It is in this sense that "adult members of families and other associations are equal citizens first: that is their basic position."[23] Because religious believers are equal citizens before they are members of a family, community, or religion, their citizenship in a social democracy has moral-and-social ontological priority over their religious beliefs. Public secular reason provides the canonical point of justification for justice, morality, and civil society.

Because Rawls assigns centrality to the justifications of social democratic public reason and to the ontology of its civil society, religious groups are set within strong political constraints. They are preemptively defined in terms of public reason and demands of justice. For Rawls, "[n]o institution or association [including churches] in which [persons] are involved can violate their rights as citizens."[24] This brings into question spheres of life and education where views on human reproduction, relationships, suffering, and death do not conform to prevailing social democratic views. Rawls makes this clear: "If the so-called private sphere is alleged to be a

---

[22] The notion of social democratic reason is introduced in order to establish the bar that Rawls wishes to erect against those, such as libertarians, who may have philosophical accounts denying the moral legitimacy of a social democratic state and who will cooperate with a social democratic state only as a modus vivendi. Rawls, for example, holds that, "[t]o be reasonable, political conceptions must justify only constitutions that satisfy this principle" (Rawls, "The Idea of Public Reason Revisited," 771). That is, political conceptions must involve an understanding of political justice that affirms a social democracy as more than a modus vivendi. Therefore, Rawls holds that "comprehensive doctrines that cannot support such a democratic society are not reasonable" (ibid., 801). The principle that Rawls has in mind is: "Our exercise of political power is proper only when we sincerely believe that the reasons we would offer for our political actions—were we to state them as government officials—are sufficient, and we also reasonably think that other citizens might also reasonably accept those reasons" (ibid., 771). Thus, one would be disbarred from arguing that there are unavoidable limits on the authority of citizens to impose constraints on consensual actions, not to mention limits on the imposition of many forms of taxation. If it were the fact of the matter that most citizens accepted social democratic premises—thus, by consent, licensing interferences with consensual actions—then for Rawls an appeal to step back from such commitments would be illegitimate, even if well-founded in libertarian terms. Libertarians may not "accept a democratic government merely as a modus vivendi" (ibid., 780) with the hope that in the future they will be able to persuade enough citizens to amend the constitution in order to erect libertarian constraints on the actions of the majority.

[23] Ibid., 791.
[24] Ibid.

space exempt from justice, then there is no such thing."[25] In the light of this claim, the force of Rawls's phrase "citizens of faith" becomes clear. One is first and foremost a citizen of a social democratic polity, and only secondarily a person of faith or a libertarian. After all, for Rawls, "citizens of faith" must be "wholehearted members of a democratic society who endorse society's political ideals and values and do not simply acquiesce in the balance of political and social forces."[26] Given these considerations, Rawls defines 'fundamentalism' by reference to views that "assert that the religiously true, or the philosophically true, overrides the politically reasonable."[27] The "politically reasonable," for Rawls, is set by social democratic assumptions. If a religious or philosophical view claims priority in knowledge or moral authority over the social democratic polity, in order to criticize the polity in terms not compatible with its basic assumptions, then it is by definition 'fundamentalist'.

One might still attempt to interpret Rawls's account as making only weak demands: as requiring only that one peaceably abide by the constraints of a tolerant, democratic society. But Rawls demands more, including that one not amend the basic political framework for one's own view of proper governance, should one's religious or ideological group command a constitutional majority. In addition, Rawls's proviso requires that one participate in the societal framework for the correct reasons:

> [R]easonable comprehensive doctrines, religious or nonreligious, may be introduced in public political discussion at any time, provided that in due course proper political reasons—and not reasons given solely by comprehensive doctrines—are presented that are sufficient to support whatever the comprehensive doctrines introduced are said to support. This injunction to present proper political reasons I refer to as *the proviso*, and it specifies public political culture as distinct from the background culture.[28]

By this proviso, Rawls does not simply distinguish the political culture from the background culture. He also affirms that the political culture is the point of view from which one should criticize, revise, and reform the background culture. The ties of "civil friendship" require an endorsement of public reason. Citizens must converse as people committed to the moral unity of a social democratic polity, and they must mutually recognize each other as first and foremost citizens in a social democracy.

[25] Ibid.
[26] Ibid., 781.
[27] Ibid., 806.
[28] Ibid., 783–84.

Thus, Rawls recasts spheres of life that are typically held to be robustly private, in the sense of being exempt from the requirements of justice. Private spheres of association do remain partially exempted from the full governance of civic norms, public reason, and the demands of justice, but only at the price of being tolerated as in some sense deficient. A true sphere of privacy would be an area of moral privation for Rawls. This is because reason is public—the reason of free and equal citizens, addressing the public good of constitutional essentials and matters of basic justice—as well as binding, due to the very nature and content of public justice.[29] For Rawls, any sphere of privacy, in the sense of an area not fully translucent to the concerns of public reason, exists only insofar as room is needed for "a free and flourishing internal life appropriate to the association in question."[30] This obtains only when political principles of justice do not clearly indicate how to govern such associations, thus allowing the political principles of justice to apply indirectly rather than directly to them.

Rawls's point is that churches, families, and other associations do not exist as enclaves free from the intrusion of the general political conception of justice.

> A domain so-called, or a sphere of life, is not, then, something already given apart from political conceptions of justice. A domain is not a kind of space, or place, but rather is simply the result, or upshot, of how the principles of political justice are applied, directly to the basic structure and indirectly to the associations within it.[31]

Rawls's account of spheres of private life fundamentally contrasts with how such spheres appear if one recognizes the authority of the state as derivative from the consent of individuals. On the latter view, individuals only partially transform themselves into citizens, and they retain authority over themselves to join with consenting others in familial and religious associations. Such a limited democracy conflicts with Rawls's account of justice in which persons are understood as citizens first, and only secondarily as having other commitments. For example, Rawls's feminist and democratic concerns about the family (drawing on John Stuart Mill[32]) lead him to conclude that the principles of justice may require that "a reasonable constitutional democratic society can plainly be invoked to reform the family."[33]

---

[29] Ibid., 767.
[30] Ibid., 790.
[31] Ibid., 791.
[32] Rawls, for example, cites John Stuart Mill, *Subjection of Women*, chap. 2.
[33] Rawls, "The Idea of Public Reason Revisited," 791.

For Rawls, the cement of society is found in the possibility of reciprocal reason-giving, which defines an idea of public reason within which claims of justice are grounded.

> A basic feature of democracy is the fact of reasonable pluralism—the fact that a plurality of conflicting reasonable comprehensive doctrines, religious, philosophical, and moral, is the normal result of its culture of free institutions. Citizens realize that they cannot reach agreement or even approach mutual understanding on the basis of their irreconcilable comprehensive doctrines. In view of this, they need to consider what kinds of reasons they may reasonably give one another when fundamental political questions are at stake. I propose that in public reason comprehensive doctrines of truth or right be replaced by an idea of the politically reasonable addressed to citizens as citizens.[34]

Comprehensive doctrines of the true or right are reasonable only insofar as they are compatible with this ideal of public reason-giving, that is, the public reason-giving of a social democracy. All comprehensive doctrines must be domesticated in terms of this social democratic ideal of public reason.

V. After Rawls, After the Enlightenment

The difficulty for all social democratic approaches—even ones as heavily qualified as that of the later Rawls—is that they carry with them presumptions of a common understanding of moral rationality or of public reason. Fundamentally, social democrats view the interaction of citizens not in bargaining terms but as occasions for reason-giving, deliberative discourse. Rather than envisaging the public space as preeminently that of the market, of agreement, they see the public space on the model of a philosophy graduate school seminar, whose members all just happen to be social democrats. Social democrats, like the graduate students, assume that the objective is to reason toward a common understanding of the good, the right, the just, and the virtuous, *within* prior constraints about the nature of the good, the right, the just, and the virtuous. Neither see their mission as one of forging agreements about how people will interact in the face of *divergent* understandings of the good, the right, the just, and the virtuous. Both share the Enlightenment assumption that public space should be defined in terms of an encounter between reason-giving philosophers bound together in a common, content-rich understanding of morality. Neither views public space as the venue for a robust, morally

---

[34] Ibid., 765–66.

diverse bargaining among market participants. Social democrats, including Rawls, ground authority in reason, while marketeers ground authority in permission. The former embed secular morality in game-theoretical rationality, while the latter delivers moral authority from consent.

The image of the agora, the marketplace, as the root metaphor of public space becomes unavoidable if one recognizes that a common, canonical, content-full understanding of the good, the right, the just, and the virtuous cannot be established through sound rational argument without begging the question, engaging in a circular argument, or succumbing to an infinite regress. The social democrat can only use rational arguments to arrive at a content-full understanding of a common morality by granting foundational moral premises before the discussion begins. In order for sound rational argument to establish a content-full understanding of morality, one must already have in hand an understanding of how to rank consequences and/or right-making principles. In the absence of such foundational premises, the specification of the right and the good, as well as of the just and the virtuous, will remain crucially underdetermined. This will allow for different views of the right, the good, the just, and the virtuous by default, such that no canonical moral vision can be established to supply the moral authority for imposing one understanding uniformly on the larger community, or for providing the basis for a global ethics. By default, rights to privacy emerge because of the irremedial inability of sound rational argument to establish a canonical moral vision.

To put matters briefly:[35] if one attempts to establish canonical, content-full principles of morality by an appeal to intuitions, any particular appeal can be countered by contrary intuitions. Nor will an appeal to an equilibrium between competing intuitions and competing principles help, until it can be decided which principles and intuitions should have salience, as well as which intuitions should provide guidance in fashioning an equilibrium. This difficulty cannot be remedied by appeals to cases or casuistry, for the selection of cases as morally significant, as well as the inferences needed to reason from one case to another, already presupposes a background moral framework. Nor is it feasible to engage in the balancing of different moral principles, unless one already has a higher-order, canonical moral perspective to direct the balancing of such considerations. If one attempts to appeal to consequences, one must already have a normative principle on the basis of which to rank consequences. Otherwise, a calculation to compare outcomes cannot be made. Even

---

[35] For a more extensive development of this argument, see Engelhardt, *The Foundations of Bioethics*, chaps. 2, 3, and 4; see also H. Tristram Engelhardt, Jr., *Bioethics and Secular Humanism* (Philadelphia: Trinity Press International, 1991), chap. 5. For an introduction to the issues associated with resolving moral controversies by sound rational argument, see H. Tristram Engelhardt, Jr., and Arthur Caplan, *Scientific Controversies* (New York: Cambridge University Press, 1987).

utilitarians who focus simply on the satisfaction of preferences must be able to compare impassioned with reasoned preferences, in addition to knowing God's discount rate for the realization of preferences over time. Also, the correction of preferences requires that one already possess a moral vision antecedent to the preferences themselves. Any appeal to a hypothetical decision-maker or a group of hypothetical decision-makers (i.e., a hypothetical contract theory) requires fitting out the decision-makers or contractors with at least a particular "thin" theory of the good. In the absence of an antecedent "thin" theory of the good, hypothetical decision-makers will not have a principled basis from which to endorse as canonical particular structures of morality and justice. To choose the correct "thin" theory of the good, one must have a higher-order account, and so the matter goes in a circle or forever.

Nor will one be able to identify the correct canonical account of moral rationality in order to deliver the appropriate ordering of right-making conditions without already having a higher-level perspective from which to make such choices. But that higher-level perspective itself requires normative guidance. This difficulty cannot be escaped by game-theoretic expedients. As soon as someone gives an overriding value to any particular outcome, a commonly acceptable resolution cannot be delivered. Similarly, when in a prisoner's dilemma with a person hoping to be a martyr, one cannot win unless one shares the would-be martyr's faith.[36] As always, one must have a normative perspective from which to make foundational moral choices. Whether in natural law accounts or in appeals to moral rationality, one must have a way to sort out what is morally normative, and to rank those principles. Nor will an appeal to rational discourse or public reason resolve controversies: there are different ways in which rational discourse and public reason can be understood.

Of course, one can abandon all foundationalist projects and presuppose that a taken-for-granted, contingent moral framework will be sufficient, á la philosopher Richard Rorty. One can attempt to canonize a happenstance of history and accept as canonical the moral and political vision that "'we twentieth-century liberals' or 'we heirs to the historical contin-

[36] In a prisoner's dilemma, cooperation or coordination allows cooperating individuals to improve their outcome over what they would have obtained had they acted independently. Suppose Bubba and J. R. fall upon the Houston branch of the Yankee Bank of Commerce and are arrested by the police with only circumstantial evidence against them. If both of them hold to their story denying their involvement, they will both go free. However, if the police can get one of the pair to confess in exchange for a reduced sentence, the one who first cooperates still receives a sentence (and the other receives a longer sentence), so both will be worse off. However, if J. R. (but not Bubba) has engaged in the robbery on behalf of the Texas National Liberation Front, J. R. may in fact wish to confess so he can be tried as a martyr. Thus, in this situation, Bubba has no possibility of a successful outcome because whatever choice he makes—silence or confession—he cannot win. In other words, Bubba has no winning strategy. Coordination or cooperation only works when the participants share the same values.

gencies which have created more and more cosmopolitan, more and more democratic political institutions'" have inherited.[37] However, no cluster of intuitions or prejudices, no matter how firmly held, has necessary moral standing. Moreover, the world is inhabited not just by convinced social democrats who view Sweden as the ideal polity, but also by those who idealize quasi-authoritarian capitalist polities such as Singapore, quasi-theocracies such as Saudi Arabia and Iran, and even those who fantasize about the restoration of the Hapsburg Empire. In addition, *pace* Rorty and Rawls, there are those who idealize a libertarian, limited democracy, not a social democracy. It is because of the inability to resolve such disputes by appeals to God or reason that, by default, individuals and their consent become imperative to the only generally justifiable account of moral and political authority. What we are left with is a strategy of last resort that draws moral authority from the consent of individuals.

Rights to privacy have a primacy because one cannot appeal to a canonical moral vision or a divine authority to establish an encompassing canonical, secular moral understanding. In the absence of a universal, canonical moral narrative or account, moral authority cannot be derived from a content-rich, philosophical moral vision. General secular moral authority must by default be derived from the consent of those who agree to collaborate. In the face of moral pluralism as well as the limits of secular moral rationality, one must by default ground the moral authority of social interaction and of governments in the consent of those who authorize them. As a result of this unavoidable grounding on individual consent, the burden is placed on the state to justify its interventions in the peaceable, consensual activities of individuals. Once individual permission or authorization becomes recognized as the source of secular governmental moral authority, spheres of privacy can be seen in a positive light, representing areas where an explicit agreement or a tacit authorization for others to intrude is implausible. Privacy in this sense only secondarily announces limits to the authority of the state. Primarily, privacy identifies where the moral authority for action and governance has its roots in the authority of persons. Rights to privacy are advanced, not as a good, or as a condition for human flourishing, but as a right-making condition tied to the origin of general secular moral authority: individual permission.

VI. Limited Democracy and Rights to Privacy

The view of the possibility of spheres of privacy that I am developing is intimately tied to a notion of limited democracy. This notion contrasts

---

[37] Richard Rorty, *Contingency, Irony, and Solidarity* (Cambridge: Cambridge University Press, 1989), 196.

with the ideals of social democratic societies that embrace a canonical, content-rich understanding of moral reasonableness and justice, thus setting limits to freedom of association, on behalf of "thick" views of fairness and welfare rights, that is, on behalf of a "thick understanding" of cosmopolitan liberalism (see footnote 16). The contrast is rooted in the difference between grounding the legitimacy of government in the consent of citizens or in a notion of the morally reasonable. In the first sense, legitimacy is drawn from consent and governs the fabric of a society prior to and independently of any content-rich understandings of moral rationality, justice, and human flourishing that might aspire to universal governance. In the second sense, legitimacy is drawn from rationally established, content-full moral norms that govern prior to and independently of the consent of those governed. In the first sense, freedom becomes central because of epistemic moral limits that preclude establishing a particular content-rich vision of moral rationality. Consent becomes the cardinal right-making condition for the use of persons, and rights to privacy become understood as cardinal forbearance rights that establish spheres of self-sovereignty. In the second case, an account of moral rationality sets limits to freedom.

Claims of privacy as self-sovereignty have at law been primarily understood as claims against other persons, not against the government (although there are important exceptions in English and Icelandic law). Samuel Warren and Louis Brandeis noted, in their influential article on privacy published in 1890, just how long-standing the recognition of self-sovereignty is in Anglo-American law: "That the individual shall have full protection in person and in property is a principle as old as the common law...."[38] Later, Brandeis, as a Supreme Court justice, transformed these centuries-old claims to protection in person and property into the beginnings of a constitutional principle of a robust privacy right.

The makers of our Constitution undertook to secure conditions favorable to the pursuit of happiness. They recognized the significance of man's spiritual nature, of his feelings and of his intellect. They knew that only a part of the pain, pleasure, and satisfactions of life are to be found in material things. They sought to protect Americans in their beliefs, their thoughts, their emotions and their sensations.

---

[38] Warren and Brandeis, "The Right to Privacy," 193. Rights to privacy in English law have roots in ancient Germanic proscriptions of battery and their robust recognition of forbearance rights. See, for example, Katherine Fischer Drew, trans., *The Lombard Laws* (Philadelphia: University of Pennsylvania Press, 1973); and Katherine Fischer Drew, trans., *The Burgundian Code* (Philadelphia: University of Pennsylvania Press, 1972). As already noted, in ancient pagan Germany, legal protections were nested within a general notion of a limited government. See, for example, Lea, *Torture*, 24–25. These protections have a resonance in the Magna Carta (A.D. 1215), especially in sec. 39. All of this underlies a background of concerns that culminate in claims to rights to privacy.

They conferred, as against the government, the right to be let alone—the most comprehensive of rights and the right most valued by civilized men.[39]

Brandeis's position was penned in a dissenting opinion written in 1928. Years later it was taken up in another dissenting opinion by Judge Warren Burger when he served on the Court of Appeals for the District of Columbia, before his appointment as chief justice of the U.S. Supreme Court:

Nothing in this utterance suggests that Justice Brandeis thought an individual possessed these rights only as to *sensible* beliefs, *valid* thoughts, *reasonable* emotions, or *well-founded* sensations. I suggest he intended to include a great many foolish, unreasonable and even absurd ideas which do not conform, such as refusing medical treatment even at great risk.[40]

The constitutional roots for this understanding of a right to privacy as a limit on governmental intrusions have been sought in the First,[41] Fourth,[42] and especially Ninth[43] Amendments to the U.S. Constitution,[44] which, respectively, recognize freedom of religion, speech, press, assembly, and petition; freedom from unreasonable search and seizure; and the retention by the people of all rights not explicitly delegated to the government. It is within this constitutional space that a right to privacy broad enough to encompass the contemporary American, secular sexual morality on the use of contraception and the permissibility of abortion received constitutional protection.[45]

[39] *Olmstead v. United States,* 277 U.S. 438, 478 (1928) (Brandeis, J., dissenting).

[40] *In re President and Directors of Georgetown College, Inc.,* 331 F.2d 1000, 1017 (D.C. Cir.) *cert. denied,* 337 U.S. 978 (1964) (Burger, J., dissenting) (emphasis in original).

[41] The First Amendment states: "Congress shall make no law respecting an establishment of religion, or prohibiting the free exercise thereof; or abridging the freedom of speech, or of the press; or the right of the people peaceably to assemble, and to petition the government for a redress of grievances."

[42] The Fourth Amendment states: "The right of the people to be secure in their persons, houses, papers, and effects, against unreasonable searches and seizures, shall not be violated, and no warrants shall issue, but upon probable cause, supported by oath or affirmation, and particularly describing the place to be searched, and the persons or things to be seized."

[43] The Ninth Amendment states: "The enumeration in the Constitution of certain rights shall not be construed to deny or disparage others retained by the people."

[44] John E. Nowak, Ronald D. Rotunda, and J. Nelson Young, *Constitutional Law,* 2d ed. (St. Paul, MN: West, 1983), 1412–14. For an exploration of the development of legal concepts of privacy, see Tom Gerety, "Redefining Privacy," *Harvard Civil Rights-Civil Liberties Law Review* 12, no. 2 (Spring 1977): 233–96. See also David M. O'Brien, *Privacy, Law, and Public Policy* (New York: Praeger, 1979), esp. 177–99.

[45] For example, see *Griswold v. Connecticut,* 381 U.S. 479 (1965) (establishing a constitutional right of married couples to use contraception); *Eisenstadt v. Baird,* 405 U.S. 438 (1972)

Although the Court seems to be retreating from the constitutional recognition of a right to privacy under that explicit term, at least aspects of
its privacy jurisprudence have been recast as liberty interests.[46] Rights to
privacy should be read, I maintain, as a fundamental limit on governmental moral authority, as well as a bulwark for limited democracy. The
Ninth Amendment, for example, has language indicating the priority of
the rights of individuals over the claims of government and publicly
established morality. "The enumeration in the Constitution of certain
rights shall not be construed to deny or disparage others retained by the
people."[47] It is for this reason that Justice Arthur Goldberg (in his 1965
opinion in *Griswold v. Connecticut*, which established the right of married
couples to have access to contraception) drew on the Ninth Amendment
in defending his view of rights to privacy

> as almost entirely the work of James Madison. It was introduced in
> Congress by him and passed the House and Senate with little or no
> debate and virtually no change in language. It was proffered to quiet
> expressed fears that a bill of specifically enumerated rights could not
> be sufficiently broad to cover all essential rights and that the specific
> mention of certain rights would be interpreted as a denial that others
> were protected.[48]

The Ninth Amendment indicates not just a constitutional, prima facie
right to act on one's own moral and religious commitments in areas over
which individuals have not ceded authority to the government; it also
establishes a view of democracy as essentially limited.

The moral force of the Ninth Amendment's acknowledgment that individuals have moral authority over themselves, comes from its retained-
rights language. This wording roots the authority of government not in a
moral ideal or in claims of justice, but in the consent of individuals. As
Bennett Patterson has argued:

> There is no clause in the Constitution, except the Ninth Amendment,
> which makes a declaration of the sovereignty and dignity of the
> individual. . . .
>
> The Ninth Amendment announces and acknowledges in a single
> sentence that (1) the individual, and not the State, is the source and
> basis of our social compact and that sovereignty now resides and has
> always resided in the individual; (2) that our Government exists

---

(establishing the right of unmarried individuals to acquire contraceptives); and *Roe v. Wade*,
410 U.S. 113 (1973) (establishing a constitutional right to access to abortion).

[46] *In re Cruzan*, 58 LW 4916 (1990).

[47] U.S. Constitution, amend. 9.

[48] *Griswold*, 381 U.S. at 488.

through the surrender by the individual of a portion of his naturally endowed and inherent rights; (3) that everyone of the people of the United States owns a residue of individual rights and liberties which have never been, and which are never to be surrendered to the State, but which are still to be recognized, protected and secured; and (4) that individual liberty and rights are inherent, and that such rights are not derived from the Constitution, but belong to the individual by natural endowment.[49]

This is a recognition that political authority is drawn from individual consent. This origin of political authority establishes rights to privacy as the logical limit of that consent.

Rights to privacy in this sense represent more than individual interests in seclusion from observation or in restricting access to personal data. At stake are the limits of public moral authority to interfere in private consensual choices and associations. Because this last sense of rights to privacy is rooted in individual consent, it sets moral limits to governmental intrusion on the acts of individuals and their consensual associations. Large-scale, modern societies are not united in a common, content-full, morally canonical, authoritative view of human fairness or flourishing. In them, therefore, fairness and flourishing must be realized indirectly, through the peaceable interchange between competing and incompatible understandings of justice, moral rationality, community, and human excellence.

VII. Conclusion

Once persons and their consent are recognized as central to general secular morality and political authority, the space of civil society should make room not just for individual choice unregulated by government, but for enclaves within which individuals can share with like-minded others their common understandings of the good, the right, the just, and the virtuous. These enclaves might hold views that are radically at odds with views held in other enclaves, and indeed with most others in the larger society. The conditions that need to be met in each enclave are those that accord with the foundation and source of secular authority: consent. Enclaves must derive their legitimacy from the explicit consent of those who participate.[50] There is much more that would need to be said to give flesh to this vision. One would need to explore the boundaries of competence

---

[49] Bennett B. Patterson, *The Forgotten Ninth Amendment: A Call for Legislative and Judicial Recognition of Rights Under Social Conditions of Today* (Indianapolis, IN: Bobbs-Merrill, 1955), 1–2.

[50] In exploring the lineage of legitimacy, the focus must be on bare consent or permission in order to avoid value-laden construals of legitimacy that seek to disclose unfair imbalances of power or the marks of false consciousness. In the absence of a canonical, content-full moral vision, bare procedure must be central.

and the character of consent. One would need, also, to address the ways in which understandings of honesty, dishonesty, and compliance can, in particular markets or areas of life, arise spontaneously through innumerable, seemingly inconsequential decisions by individuals over time. At this juncture, it is enough to indicate once more that the guiding image of a liberal democracy is not that of a Socratic discourse, or of Rawlsian public reason. Instead, the cardinal image is that of bargaining. Within this bargaining paradigm, persons and spheres of privacy are not deficient, secondary, or less morally legitimate than the general political, civic, or moral fabric that binds society. Rights to privacy are not merely privileges dispensed by governments. They are spheres of authority maintained by individuals and not ceded to society or government. Hence, the burden of proof falls on government when it claims the right to intrude on the sphere of privacy.

The claim of a right to privacy is, thus, not to be regarded as requiring a justification for an exemption from the constraints of good public morals, fairness, and justice that provide the structure for the general society. The moral burden of proof lies on those who would interfere in spheres of privacy by imposing a particular morality, view of human flourishing, or conception of fairness. Spheres of privacy, rather than being a negation of public morality, are a positive value, a domain in which there is prima facie moral authority for individuals to act peaceably for themselves, to use their property, and to cooperate with others. As such, spheres of privacy are integral to limited government, which derives its legitimacy from the only secularly viable source: the consent of the governed.

Medicine and Philosophy, Baylor College of Medicine and Rice University

LEGAL CONVENTIONALISM IN THE U.S. CONSTITUTIONAL LAW OF PRIVACY*

By Mark Tushnet

I. Introduction: Why Privacy Is a Legal Conventional Concept

Drawing on themes important in moral and political philosophy, much of the scholarship on the constitutional law of privacy in the United States distinguishes between privacy understood as a person's control over information and privacy understood as a person's ability to make autonomous decisions.[1] For example, *Katz v. United States* (1967) established the framework for analyzing whether police activity constituted a "search" subject to the Fourth Amendment's requirement that the police either obtain a warrant before conducting a search or otherwise act reasonably.[2] The defendant was a professional gambler who knew enough about police techniques to use a public telephone to make his business calls. Police agents attached a listening device to the outside of the phone booth, and sought to use the recordings against the defendant. The Supreme Court agreed with the defendant that the Fourth Amendment had been violated. Justice John Marshall Harlan's influential concurring opinion asserted that a person's privacy, in the sense of control over information, depended on two factors: "that a person have exhibited an actual (subjective) expectation of privacy and, second, that the expectation be one that society is prepared to recognize as 'reasonable.'"[3] Fourth Amendment cases like *Katz* involve informational control; they define the circumstances under which the government may acquire information from

---

* As usual, I am indebted to L. Michael Seidman for insights that I have drawn on in this essay.

[1] These concepts may be connected: control over information shields decisions from public scrutiny, and thereby enables truly autonomous decision-making.

[2] *Katz v. United States*, 389 U.S. 347 (1967). The text's statement of the Fourth Amendment's requirements is a gross oversimplification; for example, it elides a significant controversy over whether the probable cause requirement applies to searches conducted without a warrant. The Fourth Amendment states: "The right of the people to be secure in their persons, houses, papers, and effects against unreasonable searches and seizures, shall not be violated. . . ."

[3] Ibid., at 360 (Harlan, J., concurring).

or about a person without first obtaining the person's agreement.[4] In contrast, cases like *Griswold v. Connecticut* (1965),[5] which barred the state from making it a criminal offense to use contraceptives, and *Roe v. Wade* (1973),[6] which restricted the state's power to prohibit or regulate abortions, used the language of privacy rights to protect a much broader interest in autonomous decision-making.[7] Seeing these cases and related ones through lenses provided by moral and political philosophy, scholars have attempted to describe what a morally sound constitutional law of privacy would be, and the extent to which a well-regulated liberal state would respect informational privacy and decision-making autonomy.[8] These efforts are, in the broadest sense, Dworkinian. That is, they seek to provide an account of privacy with two characteristics: it is broadly consistent with the relevant constitutional decisions, and it is the most morally attractive account possible that satisfies the requirement of consistency with the decisions.[9]

Here I develop a non-Dworkinian approach to the concept of privacy in U.S. constitutional law. I argue that the constitutional right of privacy is fundamentally a *legal* concept, rather than one derived from moral or political philosophy. The legal idea of privacy, as constructed by the Supreme Court, draws primarily on what the Court has taken to be settled

[4] In this essay I consider the main lines of discussion of the relevant constitutional doctrines. William Stuntz and L. Michael Seidman have offered alternative accounts of the Fourth Amendment's normative basis. Stuntz stresses the inadequacy of doctrine focused on privacy-as-information-control in a world where the government's substantive regulatory power is unchecked; Seidman stresses the role of privacy in protecting against embarrassment and shame (as distinct from the more antiseptic release of information), and in ensuring that government investigative techniques intrude as little as possible and cause no collateral damage. See William J. Stuntz, "Privacy's Problem and the Law of Criminal Procedure," *Michigan Law Review* 93, no. 5 (March 1995): 1016–78; and Louis Michael Seidman, "The Problems with Privacy's Problem," *Michigan Law Review* 93, no. 5 (March 1995): 1079–101.

[5] *Griswold v. Connecticut*, 381 U.S. 479 (1965).

[6] *Roe v. Wade*, 410 U.S. 113 (1973).

[7] Constitutional questions regarding privacy can arise in other settings, which I do not examine here. For example, there may be questions about the constitutionality of legislation authorizing private entities to inquire into, or make use of, certain types of personal information. As a general matter, these questions would face the initial hurdle of showing that the legislation made the inquiries subject to constitutional restriction. Ordinarily the constitutional challenge would not get over that hurdle because of the "state-action" doctrine, according to which constitutional restrictions apply only to actions taken by the government. The *legislation* at issue would be subject to constitutional restriction, but the *inquiries* themselves would not. Ordinarily the inquiries would be exercises of nongovernmental power, derived from the private entity's general property rights, and typically, the fact that a private party derives its power from the general law of property is insufficient to trigger constitutional scrutiny of its actions. (The foregoing brutally simplifies the state-action doctrine, but for the present inquiry, the benefits of a more extensive explanation would be too small to be justifiable.)

[8] For examples of works using Supreme Court cases and other cases to illustrate moral theories of privacy, see Anita L. Allen, *Uneasy Access: Privacy for Women in a Free Society* (Totowa, NJ: Rowman & Littlefield, 1987); and Judith Wagner DeCew, *In Pursuit of Privacy: Law, Ethics, and the Rise of Technology* (Ithaca, NY: Cornell University Press, 1997).

[9] For Dworkin's general account, see Ronald Dworkin, *Law's Empire* (Cambridge, MA: Harvard University Press, 1986).

understandings of the American people.[10] It is therefore a conventionalist concept, but it would be wrong to think that the Court's construction somehow depends on the validity of conventionalism as a moral theory. Instead, the Court's conventionalism rests upon the proposition that constitutional concepts are appropriately developed on the basis of the American people's conventions without being committed to a metaethical theory that the Constitution's concepts, even those using moral-sounding terms, are made true by convention alone.[11] The Court's legal conventionalism holds that constitutional rules can properly rest on what the Court describes as the normative understandings of the American people about some practice.[12] My account of legal conventionalism is descriptive: The Court in its privacy decisions in fact takes its task to be enforcing the people's normative understandings rather than, for example, enforcing either the justices' normative understandings or (if this is different) the morally correct understandings.[13]

Two preliminary and related observations are appropriate before I begin to develop the argument. First, my argument is non-Dworkinian but not anti-Dworkinian. In particular, it might be seen as an argument that elevates the dimension of fit—here, between these constitutional rules and the conventions of the American people as expressed periodically through their law—over the dimension of moral rightness that has been Dworkin's primary concern. Second, my argument's conventionalism necessarily implies that the concept of privacy in U.S. constitutional law need have no general force beyond the community whose conventions it elaborates. It might be, of course, that the conventions of communities other than the American people are the same as those of the American people, or even that the American people are a subset of a broader community whose conventions happen to be accurately described by examining only

---

[10] As I discuss below, determining what these settled understandings are is itself an interpretive task, the performance of which may require some nonconventionalist resources.

[11] The argument I develop was first made, I believe, by Philip Bobbitt, in *Constitutional Fate* (New York: Oxford University Press, 1982), esp. at 169–75. Bobbitt called the kind of argument that he and I describe *ethical*, a somewhat misleading term to the extent that it evokes ideas connected to moral philosophy. Bobbitt defined *ethical argument* as follows: "constitutional argument whose force relies on a characterization of American institutions and the role within them of the American people. It is the character, or *ethos*, of the American polity that is advanced in ethical argument as the source from which particular decisions derive" (ibid., 94).

[12] In this essay I apply legal conventionalism to the constitutional issue of privacy to identify some characteristics of, and difficulties associated with, the general idea of legal conventionalism. In doing so I necessarily confine the argument to the kinds of conventions associated with privacy—roughly, social conventions about a person's material being in the world. Applying legal conventionalism to conventions about morality itself might raise different issues, although my intuition is that it does not. I do not defend that intuition here, however.

[13] In the end, it might be possible to develop a normative defense of legal conventionalism, but I do not attempt to do so here. As noted immediately in the text, such a normative defense would have to confront a large number of issues—for example, questions about moral relativism—about which I can claim no particular insight.

the conventions of the American people.[14] But both of these propositions could be false and yet the argument about *American* conventionalism could nonetheless be true.

Two major problems make it difficult to understand the U.S. constitutional law of privacy in terms drawn directly from moral or political philosophy. (1) With respect to privacy understood as control over information, the immediate difficulty is that U.S. constitutional law does *not* respect privacy-as-information-control. The primary issue concerning the Fourth Amendment is whether the conditions for securing information without a person's consent have been met. The constitutional analysis raises two questions in sequence: First, does the information the government seeks to obtain fall in a domain within which a person's control over information is presumptively protected by the Constitution? Second, if the information does, has the government overcome the presumptive protection?

It might seem that moral philosophy might answer the first question, and political philosophy the second. That is, there might be ideas associated with the concept of personhood or with other moral concepts that identify a domain of presumptive informational control: One might not truly be a person if each of one's actions were exposed to anyone who asked, but perhaps personhood *would* be respected if others could obtain information about a person only under specified conditions. Once this was established, political theory could then be used to define the circumstances under which a politically organized society could obtain information.

The difficulty is that this combination of answers does not track U.S. constitutional law. The basic point here is that the government may learn anything it wants about a person without the person's consent, if it demonstrates that it has a factual basis for seeking the information, unless the information is irrelevant to any proper governmental purpose. However, identifying whether the information is indeed irrelevant in that sense turns on analyzing privacy-as-decisional-autonomy rather than privacy-as-information-control.

For example, suppose that being able to control information about one's private sexual practices is at the heart of the moral theory of privacy. U.S. constitutional law does not protect the ability to control such information if concerns about decisional autonomy do not rule out government inquiries into such practices. The government may obtain the information in various ways, again on the assumption that it is unconstrained by decisional-autonomy concerns. It may compel a person to reveal the information directly, but it must guarantee that neither the information nor any other information derived from it will be used against the person in

---

[14] My thought here is that the U.S. constitutional concept of privacy may be an aspect of the conventions of Western liberal democracies.

a criminal prosecution.[15] Alternatively, it may obtain the information itself, by demonstrating to a judge that there is probable cause to believe that physical evidence of the person's sexual practices can be found at a particular place. As a matter of U.S. constitutional law, then, there is no domain of privacy-as-information-control when we put decisional-autonomy concerns aside. Whatever moral theory might say, U.S. constitutional law does not track it in any way. And, because moral theory does not provide an answer (relevant to U.S. constitutional law) to the first question mentioned earlier, political theory cannot provide an answer to the second.[16]

(2) The second major problem with attempting to understand the U.S. constitutional law of privacy in terms drawn directly from moral or political philosophy involves privacy-as-decisional-autonomy. The problem is straightforward: U.S. constitutional law simply does not have a coherent theory of protecting privacy in that sense. A large swathe of activity guided by autonomous decision-making is subject to a wide range of regulations, as any libertarian would point out. Aligning U.S. constitutional law with a moral or political theory describing the limits of public regulation of autonomous decision-making requires a far more robust account of these limits than seems presently available from within such theories. Sexual practices and business practices are both ways in which different autonomous decision-makers decide to invest their time, but in the United States, governments are barred from regulating (some) sexual practices, but not from regulating many business practices. Moral and political philosophers have offered a range of theories explaining the significance of the differences between sexual and business practices, and perhaps some of those theories will provide a robust account of what governments may and may not do.[17] However, as Roberto Unger ob-

---

[15] *Kastigar v. United States*, 406 U.S. 441 (1972).

[16] A minor problem in attempting to link moral and political theories of privacy and its regulation to U.S. constitutional law is that privacy-as-information-control and privacy-as-decisional-autonomy might sometimes be connected, but U.S. constitutional law does not recognize the connection. Suppose that moral and political philosophy establish that governments may not bar women from obtaining abortions for certain reasons (the list of which may be quite long), but may do so when women seek abortions for other reasons. (The example usually given is abortion for sex-selection reasons.) Determining whether a woman had a morally permissible or a morally improper reason for obtaining an abortion would intrude on her privacy-as-information-control. U.S. constitutional law does not, however, acknowledge that the government may bar abortions when they are sought for specific reasons. Perhaps the U.S. approach may be understood as a way of protecting privacy-as-information-control: The only way to do so is to bar inquiries into reasons for obtaining an abortion, and the only way to do that is to allow women to obtain abortions without regard to their reasons.

[17] I must confess, however, a lurking suspicion that any moral theory that does distinguish between sexual practices and business practices will not, ultimately, respect the autonomous decision-making of the person who happens to care much more about the analytically disfavored practices than the analytically favored ones. Consider, for example, how a person whose entire self-conception rests on success at business will fare under theories that make sexuality, but not business, central to their accounts of human flourishing or whatever they take to be morally significant.

served in a related context, it would be a miracle if existing U.S. constitutional law had much in common with the hypothesized theory or theories.[18]

Dworkin would have judges resolve these difficulties by seeking or developing and then applying the best moral/political theory of privacy. Of course, he does not contend that U.S. judges actually proceed self-consciously in that manner.[19] Explicit references to moral or political theory are essentially nonexistent in judicial decisions dealing with privacy. Sometimes an astute reader can reconstruct a moral or political theory that, the reader contends, lies beneath what an opinion says. Unusual exceptions aside, the opinions themselves explicitly invoke only law. I therefore turn to the role the Supreme Court has played in constructing the constitutional law of privacy in the United States.

II. Constructing a Legal Conventionalist Right to Privacy

The Supreme Court first articulated a constitutional right to privacy in 1965, when it decided *Griswold*, which involved a criminal prosecution for aiding and abetting the use of contraceptives by married people.[20] To determine whether the defendants could be convicted of aiding and abetting, the Court concluded that it had to decide whether the state could make the underlying activity—the use of contraceptives—illegal. The Court said that the state could not do so, because the prohibition violated the constitutional right to privacy.

Justice William O. Douglas's opinion for the Court used a metaphor to describe the source of that right: "[S]pecific guarantees in the Bill of Rights have penumbras, formed by emanations from those guarantees that help give them life and substance."[21] The metaphor has been subjected to ridicule,[22] but Douglas's idea was simple enough. He began by describing several cases in which the Supreme Court had directly protected what we can call *core* constitutional rights, such as freedom of expression. He then noted several cases that indirectly protected such

---

[18] Roberto Mangabeira Unger, *The Critical Legal Studies Movement* (Cambridge, MA: Harvard University Press, 1986), 3.

[19] Dworkin does require that his account of adjudication fit existing practice. However, his characterization of that practice is interpretively constructed in light of his moral requirements, and so his account need not require that judges self-consciously apply moral/political theories.

[20] The case was the last phase in a long effort by Connecticut's Planned Parenthood organization to invalidate Connecticut's statutory ban on using contraceptives. After failing to obtain a judicial ruling in the early 1940s and early in the 1960s without violating the statute, the organization opened a clinic and invited the prosecution.

[21] *Griswold*, 381 U.S. at 484.

[22] For a discussion of the metaphor's origins, and a brief criticism of its use, see Henry T. Greely, "A Footnote to 'Penumbra' in *Griswold v. Connecticut*," *Constitutional Commentary* 6, no. 2 (Summer 1989): 251–65.

rights by protecting other *peripheral* rights not specifically mentioned in the Constitution. For example, the Constitution does not expressly guarantee a right to an education, or even a parent's right to control a child's education, and yet the Court invalidated a statute barring parents from sending their children to nonpublic schools.[23] As Douglas described the case, protecting the parents' rights was essential to securing the protection of rights that *were* enumerated in the Constitution, such as the right of free expression.

Douglas then examined the different ways in which core and peripheral constitutional rights are protected. As he read the cases, core constitutional rights receive near-absolute protection (in the sense that only government interests of the highest order can justify their infringement) or even absolute protection (meaning that there are no circumstances under which core constitutional rights could be justifiably overridden). In contrast, peripheral rights receive less stringent protection; intrusions on these rights are balanced against government interests. Douglas's strongest examples of this distinction came from the law of free expression and association. Expression received absolute or near-absolute protection. The Supreme Court also protected freedom of association, because many forms of expression could not be effectively exercised if the government had unrestricted power to regulate associations.[24] According to Justice Douglas's analysis, government interests that would not justify restricting expression might justify restricting association.[25]

The cases established, then, that rights in the penumbras received some protection, but less protection than was accorded to core rights. Douglas next pointed out that explicitly protected constitutional rights dealt with discrete but not entirely unrelated topics. For example, the Fourth and Fifth Amendments each have something to do with different forms of informational privacy. The Fourth Amendment protects "[t]he right of the people to be secure in their persons, houses, papers, and effects," by banning unreasonable searches and imposing some procedural requirements on permissible searches. The Fifth Amendment's ban on compulsory self-incrimination protects an aspect of decisional autonomy. These provisions clearly deal with different subjects, and their coverage might

---

[23] *Pierce v. Society of Sisters*, 268 U.S. 510 (1925).

[24] The First Amendment does explicitly protect association for a particular purpose when it protects the freedom of assembly for the purposes of petitioning the government for a redress of grievances. However, the amendment does not protect associations—even political associations—that take other forms.

[25] This is Justice Douglas's analysis of *NAACP v. Alabama*, 357 U.S. 449 (1958). I should note that the approach I am imputing to Justice Douglas, while clearly grounded in *Griswold*, may also represent his effort to work around an approach to constitutional interpretation, the balancing of competing interests, with which he was fundamentally unsympathetic. In this connection it may not be irrelevant that the decision in *NAACP v. Alabama* was written by Justice Harlan, the Supreme Court's leading proponent of balancing.

not overlap. However, the peripheral rights surrounding the amendments might.[26]

Douglas argued that two consequences followed when such peripheral rights overlapped. First, whatever fell within the area of overlap was protected to the same extent that core constitutional rights were. As Douglas presented it, the lesser protections afforded in the periphery of each core right added up to produce the full protection available in the core. Second, the peripheral (or penumbral) rights were free-standing. Having identified a penumbral right, the Court could then analyze what *it* protected—what privacy protected, for example—rather than what each of the core rights protected. It no longer mattered that the activity at issue in *Griswold*—the use of contraceptives—had no obvious connection to political expression, even though Douglas constructed the right to privacy in part on the ground that some forms of privacy fell within the First Amendment's penumbra.

Justice Douglas's analysis is ingenious and, I believe, clearly defensible. It does, however, leave several important questions open. How do we know, for example, that penumbral rights actually overlap in the way necessary for Justice Douglas's construction to work? Even if the penumbral rights overlap, what falls within the area of overlap? Conceding that the rights identified in the area of overlap are free-standing, how can we best characterize them? A standard Dworkinian approach offers clear answers to these questions. According to such an approach, Douglas's construction establishes that the Constitution can properly be interpreted to protect something *like* a free-standing right of privacy. Moral and political theory identify the best concept of privacy, which the courts then enforce.[27]

That is not how Justice Douglas proceeded. After showing to his satisfaction that there was a penumbral constitutional right to privacy, Justice Douglas concluded his argument with a question: "Would we allow the police to search the sacred precincts of marital bedrooms for telltale signs of the use of contraceptives? The very idea is repulsive to the notions of privacy surrounding the marriage relationship."[28] Perhaps this answer can be read in Dworkinian terms: The "notions of privacy surrounding the marriage relationship" would then be connected to some systematic account of marriage. This seems to me unpromising. While there may be moral/philosophical concepts of privacy and the like, I

---

[26] For a pictorial presentation of this point, see Mark Tushnet, "Two Notes on the Jurisprudence of Privacy," *Constitutional Commentary* 8, no. 1 (Winter 1991): 77.

[27] Fit between prior decided cases and the concept of privacy is guaranteed by Justice Douglas's construction.

[28] *Griswold*, 381 U.S. at 485–86. Note that Justice Douglas's question rests on the proposition that the Constitution does not protect privacy-as-information-control as such. If the state could make it a criminal offense to use contraceptives, the Fourth Amendment would allow a search to discover evidence of the offense upon a proper showing, either of reasonableness or of probable cause.

doubt that there is an equivalent concept of marriage, a social institution so variable that it is doubtful whether the concept is subject to Dworkinian analysis.[29]

Justice Douglas's argument is more easily understood as conventionalist: the notions of privacy held by the American people rule out the possibility of a police search of bedrooms for evidence of contraceptive use. The Court's next forays into the area of sexual privacy confirm the constitutional concept's conventionalist nature. *Eisenstadt v. Baird* (1972) invalidated a Massachusetts statute making it an offense to distribute contraceptives to *unmarried* people.[30] Doctrinally, *Eisenstadt* relied on the Fourteenth Amendment's equal protection clause. According to the Supreme Court, the statute was unconstitutional because there was no acceptable reason for banning distribution of contraceptives to unmarried people while allowing it to married ones. The state defended the statute as a means of prohibiting contraception. The Court replied that "[i]f the right of privacy means anything, it is the right of the *individual*, married or single, to be free from unwarranted governmental intrusion into matters so fundamentally affecting a person as the decision whether to bear or beget a child."[31] *Eisenstadt* disconnected the right of privacy from the marital context. According to the Court in *Eisenstadt*, marriages were not "independent entit[ies]" but were, rather, "association[s] of two individuals each with a separate intellectual and emotional makeup."[32] The final step was taken in *Roe v. Wade*, which confirmed that the right of privacy was free-standing in the sense needed to describe Justice Douglas's construction in *Griswold*. *Roe*'s central analytic proposition, largely undefended in the opinion, was the assertion that the right of privacy was "broad enough to encompass a woman's decision whether or not to terminate her pregnancy."[33] The term "broad" in this statement works well in conjunction with the idea of overlapping penumbras that is drawn from *Griswold*.

Although they can be given Dworkinian readings, the Supreme Court's constitutional privacy cases are best understood as conventionalist, relying on notions of privacy that the Court attributes to the American people. I defer the obvious question—how can a conventionalist account lead to the invalidation of statutes on the books in a substantial majority of states?—until we have examined the Court's Fourth Amendment cases that bear on my argument.

In asserting that "the Fourth Amendment protects people, not places,"[34] *Katz v. United States* directed attention away from the question of whether

---

[29] I acknowledge, however, the Catholic natural law tradition that does give marriage a specific and rather detailed content.

[30] *Eisenstadt v. Baird*, 405 U.S. 438 (1972).

[31] Ibid., at 453.

[32] Ibid.

[33] *Roe*, 410 U.S. at 153.

[34] *Katz*, 389 U.S. at 351.

a search invaded some traditionally protected property interest. Instead, as noted earlier, courts were to ask whether police activity intruded on privacy interests that people subjectively held and that "society was prepared to recognize as 'reasonable.'" *Katz* itself concluded that people did have, and that society was prepared to recognize, privacy interests in conversations conducted from public telephone booths. Wiretapping such a conversation could be justified only if the Fourth Amendment's various requirements were satisfied, because such wiretapping would be a search.

As is widely recognized, *Katz* shifted the Court's analytic focus because it presented the Court with a case involving what the justices saw as a novel investigative technique. Subsequent cases presented the Court with additional novelties. The Court's conventionalism in these cases is apparent. Furthermore, it is unsurprising that the Court's decisions regularly (though not uniformly) uphold the techniques in question, precisely because society is unlikely to have settled expectations with respect to novel investigative techniques.

One important set of cases involves investigative techniques that allow the police to supplement their unaided senses of sight and smell. The Court began by acknowledging that people had no reasonable expectation that the police could not examine "what a person knowingly exposes to the public."[35] No Fourth Amendment question arises if a police officer observes a drug transaction on a public street. Nor do "traditional" methods of vision-enhancement raise questions: a police officer on a stakeout can use binoculars to observe a transaction that would not be clearly observable if the officer were to look with unaided eyes.

Problems do arise when police use less traditional methods of enhancing their senses. The Court approved the use of high-resolution photography to investigate an industrial site, although the opinion suggested that the outcome might be different if the photographs were good enough to reveal personal information about people on the site.[36] Also, international travelers are familiar with the use of drug-sniffing dogs who are more sensitive to smell than are humans.[37]

Various forms of tracking devices intrude on privacy-as-information-control, except for the fact that the person being tracked leaves a trail that is available to anyone who looks, albeit with enhanced senses. The Supreme Court's cases in this area involve tracking devices such as "beepers," which emit a signal that can be detected with electronic equipment. If a beeper is put in a container of chemicals used in making illegal drugs, the police can find out where a drug factory is. Beepers are simply methods of enhancing the senses. The police could keep the container under visual observation from the moment it is picked up until it is delivered to

---

[35] Ibid.
[36] *Dow Chemical Co. v. United States*, 476 U.S. 227 (1986).
[37] *United States v. Place*, 462 U.S. 696 (1983).

the drug factory; the beeper simply makes the task easier and safer. The Supreme Court, accordingly, held that neither installing a beeper nor tracking its movement was a search.[38] The reason for the latter holding was that "[a] person travelling in an automobile on public thoroughfares has no reasonable expectation of privacy in his movements from one place to another."[39] The beeper did not disclose anything more than an officer following the subject in a marked police car could have learned.

One can imagine increasingly exotic technologies that can fairly be characterized as nothing more than novel and complex methods of enhancing the senses. For example, eavesdropping equipment that translates the vibrations that voices inside a room make on the room's windows can be described as simply detecting what a person with extraordinarily good hearing would pick up when walking past the windows. As the Court put it in one of the beeper cases, "Nothing in the Fourth Amendment prohibit[s] the police from augmenting the sensory faculties bestowed upon them at birth with such enhancement as science and technology afforded them in this case."[40] The last three words hint, however, that using some technological enhancements, perhaps ones that the Court considers more exotic than beepers, might violate the Fourth Amendment. The words suggest an inchoate sense on the Court's part that some technologies are too intrusive, or perhaps too novel, for comfort. Yet as we will see, that sense may be in some tension with the Court's conventionalism once we understand that social understandings of the intrusiveness and novelty of technologies are themselves shaped in part by the Court's decisions.

"Public data harvesting" offers an interesting variant of the idea of sensory enhancement, where the technology of high-power computers is the means of sense-enhancement.[41] Harvesting occurs when investigators search through databases that are open to public examination, then combine the information from these databases to produce a detailed portrait of a person's activities—a portrait that would not be available without the harvesting. Public data harvesting is a close analogue to sense-enhancement. The information in any particular database is available to anyone who looks, as with the drug transaction on the public street. However, assembling all this publicly available information without assistance is extremely time-consuming and costly. Technology, in the form of computer assistance, reduces the cost and time to the point where public data harvesting can be a routine investigative technique. In an

---

[38] *United States v. Knotts*, 460 U.S. 276 (1983); *United States v. Karo*, 468 U.S. 705 (1984). *Karo* holds in addition that police need a warrant if they use a beeper to determine that the article containing the beeper remains at the place to which it was delivered.

[39] *Knotts*, 460 U.S. at 281.

[40] Ibid., at 282.

[41] For a discussion, see Helen Nissenbaum, "Protecting Privacy in an Information Age: The Problem of Privacy in Public," *Law and Philosophy* 17, nos. 5 and 6 (November 1998): 559–96.

important sense, however, any person with a really good memory and a lot of time could assemble the information that is made available to many more people through public data harvesting.

It seems unnecessary to provide more examples. As the foregoing discussion indicates, the Supreme Court has generally accepted the investigative techniques that it has considered. The best explanation of this lies in the Court's legal conventionalism, which is revealed in the words that the Court has used to explain why a person's subjective expectation of privacy in some location or activity is or is not, in *Katz*'s terms, one that society is willing to accept as reasonable.

We can begin with *dicta* acknowledging that some expectations are reasonable. In *United States v. Karo* (1984), the Court stated that it is "belaboring the obvious" to point out that "private residences are places in which the individual normally expects privacy . . . , and that expectation is plainly one that society is prepared to recognize as justifiable."[42] Justice Sandra Day O'Connor, in her concurring opinion, described a case she viewed as similarly "easy," when "two persons share identical, overlapping privacy interests in a particular place. . . . Here both share the power to surrender each other's privacy to a third party."[43] What makes these conclusions obvious and easy is that the justices, acting as participants in the nation's culture, are able to discern what society taken in the large regards as reasonable.

The Court's holdings, in contrast to its *dicta*, more often conclude that a person's subjective expectation of privacy, if any, was not a reasonable one. In *California v. Greenwood* (1988), the Court concluded that society is not willing to regard as reasonable a homeowner's expectation that materials he or she wraps up and places in garbage cans for collection will remain immune from police search.[44] Six justices joined Justice Byron White's opinion in the case, which drew its judgment about society's views from two sources. First, Justice White wrote, "It is common knowledge that plastic garbage bags left on or at the side of a public street are readily accessible to animals, children, scavengers, snoops, and other members of the public."[45] No one could reasonably expect that the contents of such bags would actually remain secret, because so many people might have access to these contents. Second, Justice White cited a long list of cases in which other judges had upheld such searches. Responding to the two dissenters, whose views appeared to represent those of a "tiny minority of judges," Justice White was "distinctly unimpressed with the dissent's prediction that 'society will be shocked to learn' of [the Court's] decision."[46] The dissenters themselves assembled some evidence to sup-

---

[42] *Karo*, 468 U.S. at 714.
[43] Ibid., at 726 (O'Connor, J., concurring in the judgment).
[44] *California v. Greenwood*, 486 U.S. 35 (1988).
[45] Ibid., at 40.
[46] Ibid., at 43 n. 5.

port their prediction, citing an incident in which a tabloid reporter examined the trash of former secretary of state Henry Kissinger. The public, they said, "condemn[ed]" the reporter, with some calling the conduct "a disgusting invasion of personal privacy" and "indefensible."[47] Plainly, the justices on both sides are engaged in cultural interpretation: they seek to identify society's understandings about privacy, just as a conventionalist account would suggest.

California v. Ciraolo (1986), one of the Court's cases involving airplane overflight, has the same structure.[48] Police officers received a tip that marijuana was growing in a suspect's yard. They could not observe the yard from the street because the suspect had put up two substantial fences around the yard. One officer flew over the suspect's house in a private plane at an altitude of 1,000 feet, from which he was able to identify marijuana plants in the yard. In an opinion by Chief Justice Warren Burger, the Court held that the overflight did not constitute a search. Accepting, albeit with some skepticism, the claim that the suspect had a subjective expectation of privacy,[49] Chief Justice Burger concluded that society would not recognize that expectation as reasonable. This conclusion rested largely on an enumeration of the facts of the case, accompanied by almost no analysis. "In an age where private and commercial flight in the public airways is routine," he wrote, "it is unreasonable for [the suspect] to expect that his marijuana plants were constitutionally protected from being observed with the naked eye from an altitude of 1,000 feet."[50] Justice Lewis F. Powell, writing for four dissenters, took issue with this observation. As he saw it, "the actual risk to privacy from commercial or pleasure aircraft is virtually nonexistent." People on such planes "normally obtain at most a fleeting, anonymous, and nondiscriminating glimpse of the landscape over which they pass." He noted, "As all of us know from personal experience, at least in passenger aircraft, there rarely—if ever—is an opportunity for practical observation and photographing of unlawful activity. . . ."[51] Again, the invocation of personal experience reveals the conventionalist nature of the Court's analytic structure; Justice Powell's dissent is merely a bit more explicit than the Court's opinion is about the way in which the conventionalist proceeds.[52]

---

[47] Ibid., at 51–52 (Brennan, J., dissenting).

[48] *California v. Ciraolo*, 476 U.S. 207 (1986).

[49] According to the Chief Justice, the fences would not "shield these plants from the eyes of . . . a policeman perched on top of a truck or a two-level bus" (ibid., at 211).

[50] Ibid., at 215.

[51] Ibid., at 223–24 and note 8 (Powell, J., dissenting).

[52] I do not contend, however, that the Court's descriptions of the American people's settled understandings are always correct. Decisions allowing searches of areas around houses—technically, their curtilages—sometimes involve intrusions that I think many people would find to be violations of their sense of privacy. See, e.g., *Oliver v. United States*, 466 U.S. 170 (1984), where the police walked around a locked gate that had a "No Trespassing" sign on it, and *Florida v. Riley*, 488 U.S. 455 (1989), where the police observed property by hovering in a helicopter at four hundred feet above the property.

III. The Contours of the Legal Conventionalist Right of Privacy

One might think that legal conventionalism is inconsistent with the very idea of constitutionalism, if constitutionalism is understood as the effort to impose some constraints on what majorities can do. Properly understood, however, legal conventionalism is a way of respecting some majorities while constraining others. It purports to satisfy the dual demand of democratic constitutionalism by authorizing judges to invalidate some decisions taken by democratic majorities while requiring them to respect majoritarianism in the large. Its difficulty lies in identifying which majorities to respect and which to constrain. The disagreement between Justice White and the dissenters in *Greenwood* illustrates one specific aspect of this difficulty: judges may not be particularly astute observers of social conventions, or at least they may not be uncontroversially accurate when in this role. This section explores some general questions about legal conventionalism.

If the U.S. constitutional law of privacy is conventionalist, the Supreme Court's legal conventionalism nonetheless raises a number of questions: How can a conventionalist court invalidate, as inconsistent with the nation's conventions, practices in which public authorities actually engage? Aren't those authorities better situated to determine the nation's conventions than the justices? How can a conventionalist deal with innovations of the sort presented in the cases involving technological enhancements? How can a conventionalist deal with the apparent fact that court decisions contribute to developing the nation's understandings over time? After examining some aspects of these questions, I will suggest that they all are variants of a single one: what basis does a conventionalist court have for *describing* the conventions it seeks to invoke? The conventionalist needs to establish some space between the practices at issue and the conventions against which the practices are to be measured, but it is unclear that a purely legal conventionalism can create that space. In the end, therefore, the legal conventionalist may be forced into some other conceptual space: moral conventionalism, for example, or some nonconventionalist moral and political philosophy.

The first problem a legal conventionalist confronts is that courts invalidating a practice as inconsistent with the nation's conventions face a simple fact: some other public institution—the legislature or the police, for example—has engaged in the practice. That in itself is some evidence that the practice is not inconsistent with the nation's conventions. This provides another reason, apart from considerations of the reasonableness of subjective privacy expectations, for the Court's pattern of upholding police practices in its Fourth Amendment decisions. Still, the conventionalist does have some resources for separating practices from conventions. He or she might argue, for example, that a particular police practice does not truly have substantial public sentiment behind it. Police officers, Justice Robert Jackson famously pointed out over fifty years ago, are engaged in an enterprise that may distort their judgment.[53] They may think that they are acting in accord with public understandings of privacy, but their interest in detecting crime may lead them to err. One might respond by saying that the police always act under the umbrella of a *general* public authorization for what they do. The conventionalist might require some more specific authority for actions that seem at odds with public understanding, however.[54]

In addition, the legal conventionalist might shift the inquiry from conventions regarding the practices in question to those dealing with the political process itself. For example, a legal conventionalist might invoke John Hart Ely's idea of "representation-reinforcing review" as an account of the American people's understanding about the political process.[55] Legislatures might authorize certain types of searches because the large majority of the public does not see itself as a potential target of the searches. Placed in a conventionalist frame, Ely accounts for judicial review on the ground that the American public understands the courts to be the institution that corrects for defects in the political process. Among those defects are self-interested biases, or, in the present context, the self-interested disregard of the costs that policies impose on those who are not represented in the legislature.[56]

The conventionalist also has room to invalidate *some* statutes. If the Constitution asks the courts to measure legislation against the *nation's* conventions, it is possible that one or a few states might be so out of line that their legislatures do things that are inconsistent with the nation's conventions. Also, statutes may have been enacted when they were consistent with the nation's conventions, yet persist even as the conventions change in such a way that the statutes and conventions become incon-

---

[53] *Johnson v. United States*, 333 U.S. 10, 14 (1948) (referring to the fact that police officers are "engaged in the often competitive enterprise of ferreting out crime").

[54] An interesting case from the Netherlands illustrates the argument. The Netherlands Constitution expressly provides that none of its provisions (other than the one requiring compliance with international agreements) are enforceable in Dutch courts (Netherlands Constitution, art. 120). The Netherlands Supreme Court nonetheless invalidated a practice in which jail authorities placed detainees under continuous television surveillance as an infringement of a constitutionally identified right of privacy. (The decision is described in *Bulletin on Constitutional Case-Law* [Strasbourg] 1996, no. 1 [1996]: 54.) The Court held that police authorities had to have specific authorization for a practice that so seriously intruded on privacy interests. (The British quasi-constitutional law of *ultra vires* operates in much the same way.)

[55] John Hart Ely, *Democracy and Distrust: A Theory of Judicial Review* (Cambridge, MA: Harvard University Press, 1980).

[56] Working out a representation-reinforcing account of the Fourth Amendment is, however, quite difficult. Those adversely affected by a legislatively authorized search policy may be in a minority, but as long as they can vote, they are in a position to participate in a pluralist bargaining process that can be expected to take account of their interests. For a discussion of this difficulty, see Mark Tushnet, *Red, White, and Blue: A Critical Analysis of Constitutional Law* (Cambridge, MA: Harvard University Press, 1988), 96–98.

sistent with each other. A conventionalist court might invalidate these aberrational or out-of-date statutes. *Griswold* itself provides a good example of these phenomena. By 1965 only two states, Connecticut and Massachusetts, had statutes on the books making the use of contraceptives illegal. Furthermore, there was some reason to think that Connecticut's statute was inconsistent even with the values of Connecticut's people, taken as a whole, in 1965; repeal of the anti-contraceptive statute had been blocked by the strategic position that devout Roman Catholics held in the state legislature.[57]

Yet a conventionalist focus on aberrational or out-of-date statutes encounters difficulties suggested by the example of *Griswold*. The United States is a federal nation, which means that the people of one state can have and enforce through law values that are distinct from, and perhaps sharply at odds with, the values of a large majority of those who are equally citizens of the United States but not citizens of that state. Conventionalism at the constitutional level is thus in some tension with federalism. In addition, the conventionalist who is concerned about out-of-date statutes must provide some account of why such statutes remain on the books. Invoking the specifics of Connecticut's political system in 1965 may not be sufficient, because those specific political arrangements were themselves the product of a more generally democratic political order that at least arguably embodied national commitments that were more fundamental than the conventions about privacy and marriage that *Griswold* invoked.[58] Of course, even this line of argument is unavailable with respect to statutes that are in force and actually being implemented in more than a handful of states.

The problem legal conventionalism has with federalism recurs in connection with innovations, both normative and technological. Consider a city that adopts an ordinance severely regulating the right of people to congregate in public places, a right that might be understood as related to the right to make one's own choices about with whom and where to associate. At its inception the ordinance is aberrational, but how can a legal conventionalist tell that the city is not a harbinger of normative changes that will shortly be widely shared? If the legal conventionalist invalidates the ordinance as inconsistent with the values of the nation at large—as it well might be—the nation will be denied the opportunity to develop a new normative order. Alternatively, the legal conventionalist

---

[57] For a description of the political setting in Connecticut, see David J. Garrow, *Liberty and Sexuality: The Right to Privacy and the Making of Roe v. Wade* (New York: Macmillan, 1994), 125–29.

[58] Perhaps the legal conventionalist would shift attention to the Constitution itself, and contend that the conventional understanding of the Constitution is that it identifies the situations in which a national solution is appropriate. Even that move seems unhelpful, however, because we can concede its validity and still wonder whether the practice in question is one of the situations the Constitution, conventionally understood, singles out for national resolution.

might uphold the ordinance precisely because it is so different from established practices that there are no conventions against its use.

Technological changes raise similar problems. There are no conventions applicable to such changes when they are first used; at most there are conventions bearing on the use of roughly similar but more established technologies. When wiretapping was first used we may have had conventions about literal eavesdropping, but we could have had none about wiretapping. As with normative innovations, the legal conventionalist might have allowed government agents to use the technological innovation because there was no convention against its use. Alternatively, the legal conventionalist might have barred use of the innovation on the ground that its use would have resembled practices about which there were conventions. Legal conventionalism itself could not have determined which course to take.

A final problem arises when we recognize that national understandings develop over time, and are influenced to some extent by the courts' willingness to allow or obstruct normative or technological innovations. Perhaps the best example of this is the nation's ready acceptance in the 1990s of the use of screening devices at airports. When the government first required the use of such devices in the late 1960s to reduce the risk of airplane hijacking, some people challenged the practice as inconsistent with established understandings of privacy. Although the courts rejected such challenges,[59] they were not frivolous when made. They would be frivolous today, however, because we have become so used to the devices that no one could reasonably think that they intruded improperly on a right to privacy.[60]

The dynamic effects of court decisions resting on legal conventionalism are two-fold.[61] As I have mentioned, decisions invalidating practices as inconsistent with existing understandings freeze, or at least retard, changes in those understandings. The example of airport screening devices illustrates the other dynamic, which is more interesting. There may be significant controversy over the content of the nation's understandings at the

---

[59] For the most extensive early discussions of the constitutionality of this use of metal detectors, see *United States v. Bell*, 464 F.2d 667 (2d Cir. 1972); *United States v. Davis*, 482 F.2d 893 (9th Cir. 1973); and *United States v. Edwards*, 498 F.2d 496 (2d Cir. 1974).

[60] Suppose a new technology became available which allowed users to detect more details about what a person was carrying, and that the technology was subsequently deployed not just in airports, but in other areas as well. The film *Total Recall* depicts such a technology used at underground transportation systems, such as subways. The conditions under which governments might require using screening devices in subways are not hard to imagine. The privacy-based objection to this use of screening technology would not be frivolous today, though it might be rejected. I note that Justice John Paul Stevens, dissenting in *Michigan Department of Public Safety v. Sitz*, 496 U.S. 444, 473–74 (1990), wrote: "I would suppose that all subway passengers could be required to pass through metal detectors."

[61] I would not of course overestimate the contribution that *court* decisions make to changes in the nation's understandings of privacy. My only claim here is that such decisions have some effect.

moment of decision. A judicial decision resting on legal conventionalism resolves that controversy. Judicial approval of practices as consistent with existing understandings may undermine the seriousness of the challenges offered by those whose arguments the courts reject, even if the courts were correct in identifying the center of gravity of the nation's understandings. We may then become used to practices that we might earlier have seen as raising serious privacy questions. Legal conventionalism may thus have the effect of a one-way ratchet, allowing change in one direction but barring us from changing back to our previous position. The dynamic effects of legal conventionalism introduce circularity: judges act to enforce what they take to be conventional understandings, but the very act of doing so may change those understandings. This circularity can be broken only by moving outside of legal conventionalism.

Some justices have noted the dynamic effects of legal conventionalism. Justices Anthony Kennedy, Sandra Day O'Connor, and David Souter wrote a joint opinion announcing the Court's judgment in *Planned Parenthood of Southeastern Pennsylvania v. Casey* (1992), which reaffirmed what the opinion called the "central holding" of *Roe*.[62] The three justices suggested that they might have doubts about *Roe*'s correctness as an initial matter,[63] but they concluded that strong reasons rooted in *stare decisis* argued in favor of reaffirming *Roe*. Traditionally the Court has said that the fact that people relied on a prior decision was an argument against overruling it, and the three justices in *Casey* also invoked the reliance concern. They put to one side the argument that people who engage in sexual intercourse rely on the availability of abortion because, they said, "[a]bortion is customarily chosen as an unplanned response to the consequence of an unplanned activity."[64] The justices suggested that the prospect that abortions would be unavailable would have little effect in deterring people from engaging in intercourse in the first place. People do not "rely on" the availability of abortion when they engage in intercourse; therefore, overruling *Roe* would not defeat reliance understood in that way.

However, the justices noted a more extended sense of reliance, which they believed would be defeated if *Roe* were overruled. As they put it, "for two decades of economic and social developments, people have organized intimate relationships and made choices that define their views of themselves and their places in society, in reliance on the availability of abortion. . . . The ability of women to participate equally in the economic and social life of the Nation has been facilitated by their ability to control

---

[62] *Planned Parenthood of Southeastern Pennsylvania v. Casey*, 505 U.S. 833 (1992). Two other justices concurred in the judgment; four justices dissented. The opinion discussed in the text is therefore not accurately described as a plurality opinion, a term that, in cases in which there is no majority opinion, refers to the opinion that received the most votes; the standard designation has become *joint opinion*.

[63] See ibid., at 861 (referring to the "personal reluctance any of us may have" in "affirming *Roe*'s central holding"), 836 (referring to *Roe*'s "error, if error there was").

[64] Ibid., at 856.

their reproductive lives."[65] Because people had "ordered their thinking and living around" *Roe*,[66] it could not easily be overruled.

This passage meshes two themes. The claim about "organiz[ing] intimate relationships" in prior decades is a claim about reliance. Knowing that abortions were available, men and women developed ways of relating to each other that were different from those that occurred when abortions were illegal. Though the justices do identify a form of reliance here, it is not obvious that overruling *Roe* would impair that reliance, at least in the long run. Consider a couple initiating a relationship after *Roe* had been overruled. They could have no reliance interests predicated on *Roe*. Even couples who initiated relationships while *Roe* was good law could restructure their relationships in light of the overruling. Such restructurings occur all the time: Consider a couple who develops a relationship based on their expectation that they both would have good jobs in the same city, and then one unexpectedly gets a much more desirable job offer that would require him or her to relocate. The relationship adjusts, even if the job offer is rejected (perhaps, of course, to the point of ending). The expectations about being in the same city generate a certain kind of reliance, just as expectations about *Roe* do, but I believe we would regard the need to restructure the relationship in light of the new job offer as part of the ordinary course of long-term relationships. The joint opinion in *Casey* treats expectations resting on law differently, without explaining why restructuring relationships is a troubling consequence of legal change but an accepted facet of ordinary life.[67]

The second part of the justices' analysis suggests an answer, but one that moves outside the opinion's apparent conventionalism to break the circle in which judicial accounts of conventional understandings themselves influence those understandings. Referring to the way in which women's ability to control their reproductive lives facilitated their equal participation in economic and social life makes a straightforward equality-based argument that would be just as good in supporting *Roe* as an initial matter as it is in explaining why *Roe* should not be overruled.[68] The initial reference to expectations seems simply to describe how people in the United States responded to *Roe*. That kind of description is consistent with a legal conventionalism that makes legal outcomes turn on what

---

[65] Ibid.

[66] Ibid.

[67] To the extent one is concerned about the costs of restructuring, one might phase in the legal change, for example, by invalidating legislation that does not contain a sufficiently long transition period.

[68] It is probably worth noting here that a later section of the joint opinion, which invalidated a provision requiring a married woman to notify her husband before she obtained an abortion, relied heavily on factual findings about the prevalence of domestic violence (*Casey*, 505 U.S. at 887–98). I believe that the joint opinion in *Casey* is the first opinion in any of the Court's abortion decisions to rely explicitly on equality reasons for limiting the government's power to regulate abortion.

people believe. As we have seen, legal conventionalism works reasonably well when its task is to stabilize the status quo. It has difficulty, however, with problems like that in *Casey*, where the question is accounting for changes in expectations. In 1965 people held one set of beliefs, which the Court used to decide *Griswold*. The Court then used *Griswold*'s free-standing notion of privacy in deciding *Roe*. A new set of beliefs developed around *Roe*, and the joint opinion in *Casey* appeared to invoke those beliefs in its analysis of reliance. One might respond that just as new beliefs developed around *Roe*, so could other beliefs develop around its overruling. The joint opinion in *Casey* treated changed expectations as a one-way ratchet without recognizing that the wheel actually can turn in both directions.

IV. Legal Conventionalism and the Judicial Role

Legal conventionalism as I have described it so far cannot account for the treatment of reliance in the *Casey* joint opinion. I suggest that there are two ways of augmenting legal conventionalism. The first is to go outside legal conventionalism, as the joint opinion does in invoking general ideas about gender equality. In pursuing this method, however, the legal conventionalist would abandon one apparently attractive feature of legal conventionalism: its resistance to taking positions on contentious questions about substantive moral or political theory by referring only to the understandings of the nation's people.[69] The second way, which I explore in this section, is to become even more firmly conventionalist, by taking the justices' own conventionalist judgments as *self*-validating.

The difficulty for legal conventionalism occurs most prominently at the point when a legal conventionalist must describe the activity about which common understandings are to be invoked. The contours of this difficulty are revealed in a passage in Justice John Paul Stevens's separate opinion in one of the beeper cases. The defendant had ordered fifty gallons of ether from a government informant. The informant told a law enforcement officer that the defendant planned to use the ether to extract cocaine from clothing that had been brought into the country. The officer then got a court's permission to place a beeper in one of the cans of ether, so that the government could locate the defendant's drug operation. Police agents tailed the defendant after he picked up the ether. They used the beeper to track the passage of the ether from its initial location to first one, then another locker, and then to one, and then another house. Telling a judge that the ether was in this last location, the police obtained a warrant,

[69] Analytically, one could go outside legal conventionalism to something other than moral or political theory. For example, one could rely on original understanding. However, the legal conventionalist relies on the people's understandings precisely in those cases where original understanding and other sources of constitutional decision-making are insufficient for the decision-maker's purposes.

searched the house, and seized the cocaine. The Court held that the agents should have obtained a warrant to monitor the beeper when it arrived at a private residence.[70] Justice Stevens's separate opinion focused on the moment the cans of ether left public view and were moved inside the defendant's house: "This 'search' began at the moment [the defendant] brought the can into his house and hence concealed it from public view. *As a general matter, the private citizen is entitled to assume, and in fact does assume, that his possessions are not infected with concealed electronic devices.*"[71] Perhaps this is true of most people, but why should the relevant universe be one that is law-abiding? I assume that my possessions are not infected, but perhaps drug dealers do—or should—assume that theirs are. Also, the dynamic effects of the Court's conventionalism once again come into play. After the Court's decision, should law-abiding citizens assume that their goods might be infected, or should only drug dealers?

The general problem is that legal conventionalism cannot define the practices about which its rules are to be made, at least not from within legal conventionalism as described so far. The Court has confronted a similar problem with respect to another interpretive approach, and its inability to solve the problem there suggests that it cannot solve it here either. Legal conventionalism looks to the understandings of the American people *today*. Another approach is to look to the traditions of the American people.[72] But the legal traditionalist must identify the traditions he or she seeks to apply, just as the legal conventionalist must describe the practices about which the people are taken to have conventional understandings. These traditions can be described in various ways, some more general than others. Justice Antonin Scalia proposed to choose the appropriate level of generality by identifying the tradition at the most specific level that one could. That proposal has not seemed acceptable to most commentators or to other justices. It assumes that there is a single dimension of abstraction/specificity along which traditions can be measured, but in most cases, traditions can be described as abstract or general with respect to one of their components but specific or particular with respect to another.

The Court's present position is a slight but significant variant on Justice Scalia's approach. The Court confronted the issue in its recent cases involving claims that people had a constitutional right to assistance in committing suicide.[73] Proponents of those claims argued that the right

---

[70] It upheld the search nonetheless, on the ground that the warrant the police obtained was based on adequate information even when one omitted the information the police provided that was based upon the constitutional violation.

[71] *Karo*, 468 U.S. at 735 (Stevens, J., concurring in part and dissenting in part).

[72] The Court remains divided on the question of whether legal conventionalism can appropriately supplement tradition. For an exchange, in which a majority allows supplementation over a vigorous protest by Justice Antonin Scalia, see *County of Sacramento v. Lewis*, 523 U.S. 833 (1998).

[73] *Washington v. Glucksberg*, 117 S.Ct. 2258 (1997); *Vacco v. Quill*, 117 S.Ct. 2293 (1997).

arose out of a general interest in decisional autonomy and a more specific interest in bodily integrity. The proponents sought to root their claims in traditions about privacy in both senses. The Court held in *Washington v. Glucksberg* (1997) that such traditions should be described "carefully."[74] Some have taken this to be equivalent to Justice Scalia's position, by reading "careful description" to mean *narrow description*.[75] Aside from the fact that the Court itself has not treated the positions as equivalent,[76] requiring a narrow description seems unsatisfactory for reasons suggested earlier. Narrow definitions may help the Court identify "outliers" or aberrational statutes, but they cannot have the more general effect that the Court has sought in developing its doctrine. Nor can they produce a free-standing concept, such as privacy, that the courts can then enforce independently of the traditions upon which they are based.

From the perspective of legal conventionalism, we should take the word *careful* seriously. Rather than describing the outcome of a process, as *narrow* does, *careful* describes the process itself. The joint opinion in *Casey* uses a similar locution. It described the Court's role in specifying the content of constitutional rights as the exercise of a capacity that courts have traditionally exercised: "reasoned judgment."[77] This is a capacity, not a conclusion, and, according to the joint opinion, "[i]ts boundaries are not susceptible of expression as a simple rule."[78] By focusing on capacities and processes, the legal conventionalist hopes to defuse the problems that arise when we seek to solve problems like that of the level of generality. Judges need not have analytic tools that lead them to the right solutions; they simply must have the appropriate capacities.

What are those capacities? Consider the implicit contrasts between careful description and careless description, and between reasoned judgment and either unreasoned judgment or sheer willfulness. These contrasts suggest that people with the appropriate capacities are those who take their jobs seriously. We know that judges have chosen the right level of generality when they demonstrate the seriousness with which they take their jobs. The suggestion, then, is to shift conventionalism to a higher level. Judges *do* seek to identify the commonly shared understandings of the American people. They do so because the American people understand this to be the job that judges are called upon to perform. A properly conducted inquiry, not any specific answers, is all that the American people demand.

The remaining question, perhaps, is whether the legal conventionalist's description of understandings about judging is accurate. Dissenting in

---

[74] *Glucksberg*, 117 S.Ct. at 2268.
[75] See, e.g., Michael McConnell, "The Right to Die and the Jurisprudence of Tradition," *Utah Law Review* 1997, no. 3 (1997): 665–708.
[76] See *Lewis*.
[77] *Casey*, 505 U.S. at 849.
[78] Ibid.

Casey, Justice Scalia thought it surely was not. For him, the judge's job is to interpret the Constitution by examining its text, the nation's traditions, and the Court's precedents, all in light of a general account of democratic self-rule that cautions judges against displacing legislative judgments without the clearest justification. His point can be made within conventionalism itself: does conventionalism satisfy the demands of conventionalism? That is, do the American people understand the role of courts to be identifying the understandings of the American people? Scalia would answer no: the people understand the role of judges to be the one that he describes.

What is striking is that the joint opinion simply does not engage with Scalia's criticism. One reason for this, I believe, is that the authors of the joint opinion may think that Scalia is asking a question that no longer matters. He is concerned with defining a limited role for judges, one in which they have the authority to overturn some decisions taken by democratic majorities, but only under well-defined conditions. That concern was at the heart of U.S. constitutional thought in the legal academy from the era of the New Deal through the late 1980s. Throughout this period, academics struggled to identify the conditions that might justify activist Warren Court decisions—whose results they generally admired but whose constitutional theory was at best underdeveloped—without simultaneously justifying the decisions made by the pre-New Deal Court, which overruled many legislative attempts to regulate the economy.

Perhaps the joint opinion in *Casey*, and its version of legal conventionalism, expresses the concerns associated with a new constitutional order.[79] Perhaps the issue of a limited judicial role is not important in that new order. The lack of engagement between Scalia and the authors of the joint opinion points to a final difficulty with legal conventionalism. We know that conventions change, albeit gradually. What is a conventionalist to do in an era of change? More particularly, what is a conventionalist to do when conventions about the proper judicial role are themselves changing?

V. Conclusion

I have argued that the U.S. Supreme Court's constitutional decisions dealing with privacy are best understood as resting on legal conventionalism. But legal conventionalism raises a number of puzzles. For example, is legal conventionalism consistent with constitutionalism and its aspiration to *limit* what majorities can do? Legal conventionalism answers that it is, by noting, first, that legal conventionalism can distinguish between those majorities whose conventions it enforces and those whose decisions

---

[79] I explore this suggestion in "The New Constitutional Order and the Chastening of Constitutional Aspiration," *Harvard Law Review* 113, no. 1 (November 1999): 29–109.

it overturns, and by noting, second, that legal conventionalism is an account of judicial review, which must be somehow limited in a system of democratic constitutionalism. The same kind of distinction reconciles legal conventionalism with majoritarianism broadly understood. Legal conventionalism serves some majorities even as it restricts others. Yet the deepest problems with legal conventionalism remain. The most fundamental problem, I believe, arises from what I have called the dynamic effects of judicial decisions invoking, and thereby helping to shape, social conventions. As judges confront these dynamic effects, they are forced to look elsewhere for answers—perhaps to the moral or political theories that it was legal conventionalism's hope to avoid.

Law, Georgetown University

PRIVACY AND CONSTITUTIONAL THEORY*

By Scott D. Gerber

I. Introduction

There has been a flood of scholarship over the years on whether there is a "right to privacy" in the Constitution of the United States. *Griswold v. Connecticut* (1965) was, of course, the Supreme Court decision that opened the floodgates to this river of commentary.[1] A subject search for "privacy, right of" in the College of William and Mary's on-line library catalog located 360 book titles. A perusal of the leading law review bibliographic indices turned up still more. Whether the Constitution contains some sort of "right to be let alone" is plainly one of the central questions of contemporary constitutional discourse.

Modern privacy scholars have identified four main types of privacy: physical, decisional, informational, and formational.[2] I will focus on decisional privacy—autonomy—because that is the type of privacy that *Griswold* was chiefly about and because *Griswold* is the case on which constitutional theorists have concentrated.

At the heart of virtually all of the specific discussions about the right of privacy is the more general question of constitutional theory. In fact, Charles L. Black, Jr., one of the leading constitutional theorists of the previous generation—the generation in which *Griswold* was decided— stated that the Connecticut birth control case "created what many thought to be a methodological crisis in constitutional law."[3]

* I would like to thank Mark D. Hall for his helpful comments on a draft of this essay, the contributors to this volume for their keen insights, and Ellen Frankel Paul for her superb editorial suggestions.

[1] *Griswold v. Connecticut*, 381 U.S. 479 (1965). The initial analysis in the scholarly literature of the concept of privacy—albeit one undertaken in the context of tort law—was by Samuel D. Warren and Louis D. Brandeis; see their "The Right of Privacy," *Harvard Law Review* 4, no. 5 (December 1890): 193-220. See also Thomas MacIntyre Cooley, *A Treatise on the Law of Torts, or, the Wrongs Which Arise Independent of Contract*, 2d ed. (Chicago: Callaghan and Company, 1888), 91 (noting a "right to be let alone").

[2] See, for example, Stefano Scoglio, *Transforming Privacy: A Transpersonal Philosophy of Rights* (Westport, CT: Praeger, 1998), 1-2. "Physical" privacy is a property concept (e.g., "a man's home is his castle"). "Decisional" privacy concerns a person's decisions and choices about his or her private actions. "Informational" privacy speaks to the control of information about oneself. "Formational" privacy refers to privacy as interiority.

[3] Charles L. Black, Jr., "The Unfinished Business of the Warren Court," *Washington Law Review* 46, no. 1 (October 1970): 32.

This essay is an exercise in methodological self-consciousness.[4] More specifically, I will apply the six prevailing methods of constitutional interpretation—textual, historical, structural, doctrinal, prudential, and ethical—in an effort to discern whether there is a right of privacy in the Constitution.[5] In so doing, I hope to say something useful about not only the right of privacy, but about constitutional theory itself. I should note at the outset that space constraints permit me to present only a sketch of my argument. However, I almost certainly would have expressed the same thoughts on the subject of privacy and constitutional theory had I been able to paint a more complete portrait.

II. TEXT

William J. Brennan, Jr., one of the most significant liberal voices on the Supreme Court in the twentieth century, once stated that he was a "conservative": He was endeavoring to "conserve" the Bill of Rights against the tyranny of the majority.[6] Linguistic gymnastics such as Justice Brennan's are par for the course in the debate over constitutional interpretation. Indeed, attempting to navigate through the minefield of "textualism" scholarship with the hope of deriving a workable definition of that particular approach to reading the Constitution illustrates well both the perils of attempting constitutional theory in general, and of trying to decide whether the Constitution contains a right of privacy in particular.

Textualism focuses on the language of the Constitution. However, the spectrum of approaches to textualism runs from the "nihilism" of contemporary legal scholars such as Sanford Levinson to the "literalism" of Justice Hugo L. Black, a titan of the New Deal and Warren Courts who was famous for referring to a small pamphlet version of the Constitution that he carried in his pocket when deciding questions of constitutional law.[7]

---

[4] See, for example, Scott Douglas Gerber, ed., *Seriatim: The Supreme Court before John Marshall* (New York: New York University Press, 1998) (arguing for methodological self-consciousness when examining specific questions of public law).

[5] The taxonomy is from Philip Bobbitt, *Constitutional Fate: Theory of the Constitution* (New York: Oxford University Press, 1982). See also Bobbitt, *Constitutional Interpretation* (Oxford, UK: Blackwell, 1991). Bobbitt's taxonomy is the standard one. See, for example, Michael J. Gerhardt and Thomas D. Rowe, Jr., eds., *Constitutional Theory: Arguments and Perspectives* (Charlottesville, VA: Michie, 1993); and also Mark V. Tushnet, *Red, White, and Blue: A Critical Analysis of Constitutional Law* (Cambridge, MA: Harvard University Press, 1988).

[6] *In Search of the Constitution*, vol. 4, "Mr. Justice Brennan" (Chicago: Films Incorporated, 1987), videotape.

[7] There are many interesting approaches to textualism, but space constraints require me to discuss only a few. For another interesting approach, see Frederick Schauer, "Easy Cases," *Southern California Law Review* 58, no. 2 (January 1985): 399–440.

Levinson, a respected law professor at the University of Texas, is one of the leading proponents of approaching legal texts through hermeneutics.[8] Levinson's position is essentially this: Meaning cannot be extracted from legal texts, but only can be put into them—in other words, legal texts such as the Constitution mean nothing and mean anything.

Does this type of approach to constitutional interpretation recognize a right of privacy? The answer is: yes and no. Yes, if the interpreter wants there to be such a right; no, if she or he does not. It is no more complicated—as well as no *less* complicated—than that. (Levinson himself has argued that there is a right of privacy in the Constitution.)[9]

"Law and literature," as Levinson's particular school of textualism is called, was all the rage in the 1980s. The 1980s was, of course, the decade in which left-leaning academics searched for ways to win the debate over "original intent" (see the next section).[10] Unfortunately, although theories such as Levinson's are entertaining to read, they ultimately are unconvincing. In my judgment, Richard A. Posner's contention—that literary techniques have little relevance for interpreting legal texts because of the profound differences between literature and law in character, origin, and, most importantly, social function—is correct.[11]

The debate over original intent reached a fever pitch during the 1987 Senate confirmation hearings on Robert H. Bork's nomination to the Supreme Court. The Bork hearings were a long time ago, and legal scholars, being impatient souls, have moved on to new interpretive challenges. At this writing, the debate over constitutional interpretation is being shaped by Justice Antonin Scalia's book on textualism, *A Matter of Interpretation: Federal Courts and the Law* (1997).[12] Scalia's book is actually a collection of essays, edited by the political philosopher Amy Gutmann, that includes a long opening essay by the justice and comments upon the essay by historian Gordon S. Wood and legal scholars Laurence H. Tribe, Mary Ann Glendon, and Ronald Dworkin.

Justice Scalia's approach to textualism falls somewhere between the abstrusity of Levinson's hermeneutics on one end of the spectrum and the

[8] See, for example, Sanford Levinson and Steven Mailloux, eds., *Interpreting Law and Literature: A Hermeneutic Reader* (Evanston, IL: Northwestern University Press, 1988). "Hermeneutics" is the study of the methodological principles of interpretation and explanation.

[9] See, for example, Sanford Levinson, "Privacy," in Kermit L. Hall, ed., *The Oxford Companion to the Supreme Court of the United States* (New York: Oxford University Press, 1992), 71–76.

[10] See, for example, Jack N. Rakove, ed., *Interpreting the Constitution: The Debate over Original Intent* (Boston: Northeastern University Press, 1990).

[11] Richard A. Posner, *Law and Literature: A Misunderstood Relation* (Cambridge, MA: Harvard University Press, 1988), 209–68. There are, of course, variations—and often disagreements—within the law and literature movement itself. I have discussed Levinson's approach because it is among the most extreme articulated to date.

[12] Antonin Scalia, *A Matter of Interpretation: Federal Courts and the Law*, ed. Amy Gutmann (Princeton, NJ: Princeton University Press, 1997).

simplicity of Justice Black's literalism on the other. (Black's position is discussed below.) Scalia's thesis is that interpretation must be based on the constitutional (or statutory) text, that words have discernable meaning, and that a judiciary that "invents" law rather than "applies" it threatens democratic governance.[13] The conservative jurist distinguishes textualism as he defines it from both the free-wheeling notion of a "living Constitution" that Justice Brennan made famous and the rigid literalism of Justice Black. A legal text such as the Constitution, Justice Scalia maintains, should be construed neither "strictly" nor "leniently," but "reasonably."[14] If the written text fails to supply the answer to the question at bar, he continues, the structure of the legal document and prevailing historical traditions are useful and legitimate sources to consult. Moreover, case precedents are appropriate supplements as well. Ultimately, then, Justice Scalia concludes that textualism's principal virtue lies in safeguarding against *new* judicial lawmaking.

Frankly, it is difficult to know what to make of Justice Scalia's textualism.[15] It is not *really* textualism. It is more of a hodgepodge of interpretive approaches—originalism, structuralism, doctrinalism—all rolled up into a long polemic against Warren Court liberalism. Indeed, it is difficult to know whether Justice Scalia *himself* believes that he is a textualist. After all, it was not that long ago when he proclaimed that he was an "originalist"—or at least a "feint-hearted" originalist[16]—and he also has employed a sort of Burkean conventionalism in several of his recent Supreme Court opinions.[17] One thing *is* for sure, though: Justice Scalia the "textualist," like Justice Scalia the "originalist" and Justice Scalia the "conventionalist," rejects the idea that the Constitution contains a right of privacy. His ferocious dissents in *Romer v. Evans* (1996)[18] (the case in which the Supreme Court declared that the voters of Colorado could not

---

[13] Antonin Scalia, "Common-Law Courts in a Civil-Law System: The Role of the United States Federal Courts in Interpreting the Constitution and Laws," in Scalia, *A Matter of Interpretation*, 3–47.

[14] Ibid., 23.

[15] The other contributors to the Scalia book do not appear to know what to make of Justice Scalia's textualism either. For example, Tribe and Dworkin—two of the most egalitarian constitutional theorists writing today—both profess an unflinching commitment to textualism. Tribe claims to "share with Justice Scalia the belief that the Constitution's written text has primacy and must be deemed the ultimate point of departure," while Dworkin calls the idea of a nontextualist approach to interpreting the Constitution "hardly even intelligible" (Laurence H. Tribe, "Comment," in Scalia, *A Matter of Interpretation*, 77; and Ronald Dworkin, "Comment," in ibid., 122).

[16] See Antonin Scalia, "Originalism: The Lesser Evil," *University of Cincinnati Law Review* 57, no. 3 (1989): 849–65.

[17] See, for example, *McIntyre v. Ohio Elections Commission*, 514 U.S. 334, 371–85 (1995) (Scalia, J., dissenting). Justice Scalia attempts to avoid appearing methodologically inconsistent by redefining terms of art. For example, he sometimes calls "textualism" "originalism." They are, of course, not the same (see the next section).

[18] *Romer v. Evans*, 116 S.Ct. 1620, 1629–37 (1996) (Scalia, J., dissenting).

bar the enactment of special civil rights protections for homosexuals) and *Planned Parenthood of Southeastern Pennsylvania v. Casey* (1992)[19] (the decision in which the Court refused—seemingly once and for all—to overrule *Roe v. Wade* [1973] and a woman's right to an abortion[20]) leave no room for doubt on this score.[21]

The most restrained—Justice Scalia calls it the most "degraded"[22]—approach to textualism is "literalism." (Scalia does not discuss hermeneutics in his essay on textualism. God only knows how the sharp-penned jurist would have referred to that approach!) Literalists defer to the *written* words of the Constitution. If a certain right or power is enumerated there, it exists. If it is not, it does not. In short, literalism is the mirror image of Levinson's nihilism, and offers welcome relief from Justice Scalia's methodological mood swings.

Literalism is, in fact, the approach most closely identified with textualism[23]—and with the debate over *Griswold* and the right of privacy itself. *Griswold* involved a Connecticut statute that made the use of contraceptive devices—as well as counseling, aiding, or abetting such use—a criminal offense. The executive director of the Planned Parenthood League of Connecticut and a physician teaching at the Yale Medical School were convicted in a state court for giving birth control information to a married couple. The U.S. Supreme Court, in a 7–2 vote, declared the statute an unconstitutional infringement on marital privacy and overturned the convictions. Writing for the majority, Justice William O. Douglas argued that while there is no "right of privacy" mentioned in the Constitution, such a right can be inferred from the existence of "penumbras" that are formed by "emanations" from provisions of the Bill of Rights that recognize "zones of privacy."[24] Justice Black, constitutional law's most famous literalist, dissented vigorously from the Court's decision. He wrote:

> The Court talks about a constitutional "right of privacy" as though there is some constitutional provision or provisions forbidding any law ever to be passed which might abridge the "privacy" of individuals. But there is not. . . . I like my privacy as well as the next one, but I am nevertheless compelled to admit that the government has a

---

[19] *Planned Parenthood of Southeastern Pennsylvania v. Casey*, 505 U.S. 833, 979–1002 (1992) (Scalia, J., concurring in the judgment in part and dissenting in part).

[20] *Roe v. Wade*, 410 U.S. 113 (1973).

[21] See also Scalia, "Common-Law Courts in a Civil-Law System," 13 (criticizing the judicial creation of a right of privacy).

[22] Ibid., 23.

[23] Bobbitt discusses Justice Black as the prime champion of textualism. See Bobbitt, *Constitutional Fate*, 26–38.

[24] *Griswold*, 381 U.S. at 484. Justice Douglas alluded to the First, Third, Fourth, Fifth, and Ninth Amendments.

right to invade it unless prohibited by some specific constitutional provision.[25]

III. History

Justice Black was not the only student of the Constitution who was upset by the Court's decision in *Griswold*. In fact, almost every conservative commentator was apoplectic about it. Robert Bork, to name the most well-known of these commentators, wrote that "the protection of marriage was not the point of *Griswold*. The creation of a new device for judicial power to remake the Constitution was the point."[26] Indeed, the Court's decision in *Griswold* that there is a right of privacy in the Constitution was a principal cause of the call, by Bork and other conservatives, for a "jurisprudence of original intention."[27]

"Originalism," as it has come to be known in the literature, is another name for the second method by which the Constitution typically is interpreted: the historical method. It is probably safe to say that the historical method of constitutional interpretation is the method with which nonlawyers are most familiar. The Bork confirmation hearings are primarily responsible for the prominent place originalism occupies in the popular consciousness. However, as seems inevitably to occur in any debate over constitutional interpretation in which academics are involved—note also the debate over textualism, for example—originalism has taken on a life of its own in the scholarly discourse. In fact, one prominent law professor, Michael J. Perry, has gone so far as to say that Justice Brennan was an originalist![28] Justice Brennan was, of course, the most vigorous *opponent* of originalism.[29]

The essence of originalism—at least as practiced by conservatives[30]—is that judges should interpret the Constitution as the Framers themselves

[25] Ibid., at 508, 510 (Black, J., dissenting). See also Hugo L. Black, *A Constitutional Faith* (New York: Alfred A. Knopf, 1968), 9.

[26] Robert H. Bork, *The Tempting of America: The Political Seduction of the Law* (New York: Free Press, 1990), 99.

[27] See, for example, Edwin Meese III, "Address before the American Bar Association," reprinted in *The Great Debate: Interpreting Our Written Constitution* (Washington, DC: The Federalist Society, 1986), 1–10.

[28] See Michael J. Perry, *The Constitution in the Courts: Law or Politics?* (New York: Oxford University Press, 1994), 215 n. 15 (arguing that the "activist" Brennan was committed to enforcing the "aspirational" principles of the Constitution's text).

[29] See, for example, William J. Brennan, Jr., "The Constitution of the United States: Contemporary Ratification," reprinted in Steven Anzovin and Janet Podell, eds., *The U.S. Constitution and the Supreme Court* (New York: H. W. Wilson, 1988), 166–79.

[30] I argue elsewhere for what I call "liberal originalism." See Scott Douglas Gerber, *To Secure These Rights: The Declaration of Independence and Constitutional Interpretation* (New York: New York University Press, 1995). Liberal originalism maintains that the Constitution should be interpreted in light of the political philosophy of the Declaration of Independence.

would have interpreted it.[31] Conservative originalists regard originalism as the only legitimate approach to constitutional interpretation, because only that "can give us law that is something other than, and superior to, the judge's will,"[32] and only that will eliminate the "anomaly of judicial supremacy in democratic society."[33] Critics of originalism, most of whom are political liberals, regard originalism as methodologically impossible (for example, which Framer are originalists talking about?) and substantively unattractive (for example, most of the Framers would be considered racists and sexists by today's standards).[34]

With respect to the right of privacy itself, the Ninth Amendment is the provision of the Constitution that has received the most attention from proponents of the historical method.[35] Justice Arthur Goldberg, for one, invoked the Ninth Amendment in his famous concurring opinion in *Griswold*. He contended that the language and history of the amendment reveal that "the Framers believed that there are additional fundamental rights, protected from governmental infringement, which exist alongside those fundamental rights specifically mentioned in the first eight amendments."[36] And while Bork dismisses the Ninth Amendment out of hand—he maintains that it should be ignored as an "inkblot"[37]—other scholarly proponents of the historical method have delved more deeply into the record. Perhaps not surprisingly, they have come to opposing conclusions about its meaning.

The Ninth Amendment provides: "The enumeration in the Constitution, of certain rights, shall not be construed to deny or disparage others retained by the people."[38] That the Ninth Amendment was intended to protect unenumerated rights seems clear from its text, but we are concerned with the historical method in this section. James Madison, who

---

[31] See, for example, Bork, *The Tempting of America*. This interpretive approach did not originate (no pun intended) with modern-day conservatives such as Bork. As early as 1838, for example, the Supreme Court declared that interpretation of the Constitution must rely on "the meaning and intention of the convention which framed and proposed it for adoption and ratification" (*Rhode Island v. Massachusetts*, 37 U.S. [12 Pet.] 657, 721 [1838]).

[32] Robert H. Bork, "Original Intent and the Constitution," *Humanities* 7, no. 1 (January/February 1986): 26.

[33] Robert H. Bork, "Neutral Principles and Some First Amendment Problems," *Indiana Law Journal* 47, no. 1 (Fall 1971): 2.

[34] See, for example, Leonard W. Levy, *Original Intent and the Framers' Constitution* (New York: Macmillan, 1988).

[35] See, for example, Paul L. Murphy, ed., *The Right to Privacy and the Ninth Amendment*, 2 vols. (New York: Garland, 1990).

[36] *Griswold*, 381 U.S. at 488 (Goldberg, J., concurring).

[37] Testimony of Robert H. Bork, as quoted in *Wall Street Journal*, October 5, 1987, A22. Ironically, Goldberg, a liberal justice, employed conservative originalism in *Griswold* and reached a liberal result. This might explain why Bork wishes to ignore the Ninth Amendment. For a more recent example of a liberal justice employing conservative originalism and reaching a liberal result, see Justice John Paul Stevens's opinion for the Court in *U.S. Term Limits, Inc. v. Thornton*, 115 S.Ct. 1842 (1995).

[38] U.S. Constitution, amend. 9.

was the chief architect of the Ninth Amendment (as well as of the other provisions of the Bill of Rights and of the Constitution itself), said the following about the amendment in his widely cited June 8, 1789 speech to the U.S. House of Representatives advocating the adoption of the Bill of Rights:

> It has been objected also against a bill of rights, that, by enumerating particular exceptions to the grant of power, it would disparage those rights which were not placed in that enumeration; and it might follow by implication, that those rights which are not singled out, were intended to be assigned into the hands of the General Government, and were consequently insecure. This is one of the most plausible arguments I have ever heard against the admission of a bill of rights into this system; but, I conceive, that it may be guarded against. I have attempted it, as gentlemen may see by turning to the last clause of the fourth resolution [the Ninth Amendment].[39]

In a well-known argument, Raoul Berger (an originalist before originalism became fashionable[40]), among other conservative legal scholars,[41] interprets Madison's remarks to mean that the Ninth Amendment was designed to ensure that rights already held by the people under state law would remain with the people and that the enumeration of rights in the federal Constitution did not change this fact.[42] In other words, the Ninth Amendment, like the Tenth—which reads "The powers not delegated to the United States by the Constitution, nor prohibited by it to the States, are reserved to the States respectively, or to the people"[43]—was a reification of the Framers' commitment to a national government of limited powers.

However, in the most famous exegesis on the Ninth Amendment to date, attorney Bennett B. Patterson emphasizes *rights* rather than *powers*. More specifically, Patterson reads the historical record surrounding the Ninth Amendment as a general recognition of the natural rights of the individual—including the right of privacy.[44] As he puts it in his 1955 book

---

[39] As reprinted in Marvin Meyers, ed., *The Mind of the Founder: Sources of the Political Thought of James Madison*, rev. ed. (Hanover, NH: University Press of New England, 1981), 171.

[40] See, for example, Raoul Berger, *Government by Judiciary: The Transformation of the Fourteenth Amendment* (Cambridge, MA: Harvard University Press, 1977).

[41] See, for example, Russell L. Caplan, "The History and Meaning of the Ninth Amendment," *Virginia Law Review* 69, no. 2 (March 1983): 223–68; and Charles J. Cooper, "Limited Government and Individual Liberty: The Ninth Amendment's Forgotten Lessons," *Journal of Law and Politics* 4, no. 1 (Summer 1987): 63–80.

[42] Raoul Berger, "The Ninth Amendment," *Cornell Law Review* 66, no. 1 (November 1980): 8.

[43] U.S. Constitution, amend. 10.

[44] Bennett B. Patterson, *The Forgotten Ninth Amendment: A Call for Legislative and Judicial Recognition of Rights Under Social Conditions of Today* (Indianapolis, IN: Bobbs-Merrill, 1955), 55.

The Forgotten Ninth Amendment: A Call for Legislative and Judicial Recognition of Rights Under Social Conditions of Today:

> The concept of individual sovereignty, and supremacy in the realm of natural and inherent rights and liberties was not a creature of the Constitution of the United States. This basic concept of individual liberty was absolute in the theory of American Government from the very beginning of American Government. This theory was carried over from the English Constitution . . . [T]he framers of the Constitution and the signers of the Declaration of Independence were Englishmen by blood, tradition, and citizenship until the signing of the Declaration of Independence. Therefore, the framers of the Constitution and the Bill of Rights carried with them into their work the English concept of individual liberties, as being inherent in the individual irrespective of the form of government.[45]

My own research on Roger Sherman's contributions to the Bill of Rights supports Patterson's position. Sherman was the only Founder to have signed all the basic American documents: the Articles of Association (1774), the Declaration of Independence (1776), the Articles of Confederation (1777), and the U.S. Constitution (1787). The draft Bill of Rights written in his handwriting states that "[t]he people have certain natural rights which are retained by them when they enter into society." In my view, this language makes explicit what the Ninth Amendment leaves implicit about the natural-rights content of the Bill of Rights.[46] Other scholars who have written on the subject have reached the opposite conclusion, however—including several with more formal training in history than I.[47] At bottom, then, a historical investigation into whether the Ninth Amendment guarantees a natural right of privacy seems to suffer from the same shortcoming as does conservative originalism itself: the ambiguity of the historical record.[48]

IV. STRUCTURE

In his classic monograph on "structural" reasoning, *Structure and Relationship in Constitutional Law* (1969), Charles Black characterized it as a

---

[45] Ibid., 19.

[46] See Scott D. Gerber, "Roger Sherman and the Bill of Rights," *Polity* 28, no. 4 (Summer 1996): 521–40, esp. 530–31. See generally Gerber, *To Secure These Rights*.

[47] See, for example, James H. Hutson, "The Bill of Rights and the American Revolutionary Experience," in Michael J. Lacey and Knud Haakonssen, eds., *A Culture of Rights: The Bill of Rights in Philosophy, Politics, and Law—1791 and 1991* (New York: Cambridge University Press, 1991), 71.

[48] Randy E. Barnett, ed., *The Rights Retained by the People: The History and Meaning of the Ninth Amendment* (Fairfax, VA: George Mason University Press, 1989), demonstrates how a host of thoughtful scholars can disagree about the meaning of the same historical record. I argue elsewhere that the historical record is clear on the *principles* to which the Framers dedicated the regime. See Gerber, *To Secure These Rights* (arguing for "liberal originalism").

"method of inference from the structures and relationships created by the constitution in all its parts or in some principal part."[49] Black did not claim to be creating a new type of approach to constitutional interpretation. Rather, he hoped to bring more attention to an existing type—the structural type—that had served constitutional law well in the past. In fact, Black correctly noted that Chief Justice John Marshall's landmark opinion in *McCulloch v. Maryland* (1819) relied heavily upon structural reasoning.[50]

Some of the most significant works in American constitutional theory have employed structural reasoning. John Hart Ely's *Democracy and Distrust: A Theory of Judicial Review* (1980) is arguably the most well known.[51] Ely's book, like the vast majority of structurally based exegeses on constitutional law, identifies majority-rule democracy as the central imperative of the Constitution. (Ely, also like most other structurally oriented theorists, was attempting in his book to reconcile judicial review with democracy.[52]) However, a strong argument can be made that structural theorists such as Ely mischaracterize the Constitution's overarching structure. In other words, it is not unreasonable to suggest that the Constitution does *not* establish a majority-rule democracy. Indeed, "the framers openly and explicitly distrusted majority rule; virtually every government institution they created had strong anti-majoritarian features."[53] For example, the president is elected by the electoral college, not directly by the people, and he can veto measures passed by the popularly elected Congress; many executive officials are not electorally accountable; the Senate was originally appointed by the state legislatures, and a minority of senators still can block the ratification of treaties; and the judiciary is nominated by the president, confirmed by the Senate, and given life

[49] Charles L. Black, Jr., *Structure and Relationship in Constitutional Law* (Baton Rouge, LA: Louisiana State University Press, 1969), 7.

[50] *McCulloch v. Maryland*, 17 U.S. (4 Wheat.) 316 (1819). *McCulloch*, which advanced a broad reading of congressional power in general and of the Bank of the United States in particular, remains the Supreme Court's most important statement on the relationship between the national government and the state governments. In that case, Chief Justice Marshall articulated what has come to be known as the "national theory" of federalism. See generally Samuel H. Beer, *To Make a Nation: The Rediscovery of American Federalism* (Cambridge, MA: Harvard University Press, 1993). The "national theory" identifies the people of the United States, collectively, as the source of the legitimate powers of any and all governments in the republic. The "compact theory," by contrast, posits that the national government was brought into existence by a compact among sovereign states.

[51] John Hart Ely, *Democracy and Distrust: A Theory of Judicial Review* (Cambridge, MA: Harvard University Press, 1980). See generally a symposium on Ely's work in "*Democracy and Distrust*: Ten Years Later," *Virginia Law Review* 77, no. 4 (May 1991).

[52] See, for example, John Agresto, *The Supreme Court and Constitutional Democracy* (Ithaca, NY: Cornell University Press, 1984); Alexander M. Bickel, *The Least Dangerous Branch: The Supreme Court at the Bar of Politics* (Indianapolis, IN: Bobbs-Merrill, 1962); and Jesse H. Choper, *Judicial Review and the National Political Process: A Functional Reconsideration of the Role of the Supreme Court* (Chicago: University of Chicago Press, 1980).

[53] Erwin Chemerinsky, "Foreword: The Vanishing Constitution," *Harvard Law Review* 103, no. 1 (November 1989): 74–75.

tenure. And, of course, there is the Bill of Rights. As Justice Robert Jackson reminded the nation in 1943:

> The very purpose of a Bill of Rights was to withdraw certain subjects from the vicissitudes of political controversy, to place them beyond the reach of majorities and officials and to establish them as legal principles to be applied by the courts. One's right to life, liberty, and property, to free speech, a free press, freedom of worship and assembly, and other fundamental rights may not be submitted to vote: they depend on the outcome of no elections.[54]

Because of the Framers' desire to avoid what Elbridge Gerry, a Massachusetts delegate to the Constitutional Convention, called the "excess of democracy,"[55] they can be said to have created a "republican" form of government, not a majority-rule democracy.[56]

It matters a great deal as far as the right of privacy is concerned whether the Constitution is said to create a democratic structure or a republican structure. Nowhere was this more in evidence than in "A Debate on Judicial Activism" held at the Cato Institute on November 20, 1986 between libertarian political theorist Stephen Macedo and conservative constitutional scholar Gary L. McDowell. The debate was reprinted as a postscript in the 1987 revised edition of Macedo's broadside against what he saw as the untrammeled majoritarianism of the so-called "New Right's" originalism.[57] Macedo's position on the structure of the Constitution is nicely captured by his remark—which, revealingly, is located in a chapter titled "The Majoritarian Myth"—that "[w]hen conservatives like Bork treat rights as islands surrounded by a sea of government powers, they precisely reverse the view of the Founders as enshrined in the Constitution, wherein government powers are limited and specified and rendered as islands surrounded by a sea of individual rights."[58] Macedo is particularly troubled by the New Right's treatment of *Griswold*. He states:

> [I]n condemning the interpretive style of *Griswold v. Connecticut*, it seems to me that Gary [McDowell] must rely upon the sorts of claims

---

[54] *West Virginia Board of Education v. Barnette*, 319 U.S. 624, 638 (1943).

[55] As quoted in Max Farrand, ed., *The Records of the Federal Convention of 1787* (New Haven, CT: Yale University Press, 1911), 1:48 (remarks of Elbridge Gerry). See generally George Athan Billias, *Elbridge Gerry: Founding Father and Republican Statesman* (New York: McGraw Hill, 1976), 160 (explaining that "[w]hat Gerry meant by 'an excess of democracy' was that the mixed constitution, at the time, was weighted too much in favor of the democratic branch of government").

[56] Clinton Rossiter, ed., *The Federalist Papers* (New York: New American Library, 1961), no. 10, p. 82 (Madison). See also ibid., no. 39, p. 241 (Madison).

[57] See Stephen Macedo, *The New Right v. the Constitution*, rev. ed. (Washington, DC: Cato Institute, 1987), 97–115.

[58] Ibid., 32.

he says he wants to eschew. Any conscientious constitutionalist must be prepared to allow the judicial protection of rights not explicitly stated in the founding document, and that is because the founding document itself tells us, in the Ninth Amendment, that we have such rights.[59]

McDowell, who wrote many of the speeches that then-Attorney General Edwin Meese III delivered calling for a jurisprudence of original intention,[60] could not disagree more with Macedo's reading of the structure of the Constitution. He declares:

> Mr. Macedo's logic is guided by reference to two of constitutional decisional law's strangest polestars—*Lochner v. New York* (1905) and *Griswold v. Connecticut* (1965). . . . The liberty of contract doctrine of *Lochner* and the right to privacy doctrine of *Griswold* are ultimately rooted in the same shallow soil, that of personal predilection and political preference. They are juridical contrivances at war with the Constitution, at war with the idea of limited government, and at war with the basic principles of democratic government upon which our entire political system and legal traditions rest.[61]

What, then, does structural reasoning have to say about whether there is a right of privacy in the Constitution? It is difficult to tell. Indeed, when Charles Black finally addressed *Griswold* in a 1970 law review article— he had failed to mention the case in his earlier monograph on structuralism—he appeared to analyze it through civil-law analogical reasoning rather than structuralism.[62] Moreover, although I personally believe that Macedo has the better argument when he maintains that the American constitutional order is *anti*majoritarian and that, as a consequence, the right of privacy is *central* to American constitutionalism,[63] most structural theorists tend to favor arguments, such as that advanced by McDowell, that the Constitution creates a democratic structure. These theorists are not all conservatives.[64]

---

[59] Ibid., 112.

[60] McDowell's use of both historical and structural arguments demonstrates well how the various approaches to constitutional interpretation sometimes overlap. See, for example, Bobbitt, *Constitutional Fate*, 7.

[61] As quoted in Macedo, *The New Right v. the Constitution*, 108–9. See generally Gary L. McDowell, *Curbing the Courts: The Constitution and the Limits of Judicial Power* (Baton Rouge, LA: Louisiana State University Press, 1988).

[62] See Black, "The Unfinished Business of the Warren Court," 44–45 ("our polity has bound itself to respect all those rights which can be thought to stand in sound analogy to the rights named in the Constitution, as these may be read and reasoned from in the light of our concept of ordered liberty").

[63] See, for example, Gerber, *To Secure These Rights*, 70–74, 187–88.

[64] See, for example, Ely, *Democracy and Distrust*. Interestingly, Ely does claim that there is some sort of right of privacy in the Constitution, albeit not one that can be extended to

V. Doctrine

Law professor Vincent Blasi maintains in a review of Charles Black's monograph on structuralism that Justice Douglas employed structural reasoning in his majority opinion in *Griswold*.[65] Law professor Philip Bobbitt claims that Douglas utilized prudential reasoning (i.e., a balancing test).[66] The fact that constitutional theorists as capable as Blasi and Bobbitt read Douglas's argument in such different ways speaks volumes about the awkwardness of Douglas's opinion. Indeed, at times Justice Douglas used doctrinal reasoning in *Griswold*.[67] Doctrinal analysis—principally, analysis based upon the application of precedent—is, of course, the type of analysis with which lawyers and judges are most familiar.

The reasons that doctrinal analysis occupies a prominent place in the legal landscape are many.[68] The most important is probably the need for stability in the law.[69] What, though, does doctrinal analysis have to say about whether there is a right of privacy in the Constitution? As noted above, as schizophrenic as Justice Douglas's opinion for the Court in *Griswold* was, he claimed to be relying, at least in part, on precedent.[70] However, law professor David P. Currie, the author of a widely acclaimed two-volume opus on constitutional doctrine, calls Douglas's *Griswold* opinion, essentially, a joke. Currie writes: "Despite Douglas's mystical references to 'penumbras' and 'emanations,' it is difficult to take seriously his suggestion that the use of contraceptives had anything to do with freedom of expression, unreasonable searches, self-incrimination, or the quartering of troops."[71]

---

legitimate *Roe v. Wade*. See John Hart Ely, "The Wages of Crying Wolf: A Comment on *Roe v. Wade*," *Yale Law Journal* 82, no. 5 (April 1973): 928–33. Ely served as a law clerk to Chief Justice Earl Warren when *Griswold* was decided. In a bench memorandum on the case, he argued *against* there being a constitutional right of privacy. See David J. Garrow, *Liberty and Sexuality: The Right to Privacy and the Making of Roe v. Wade* (New York: Macmillan, 1994), 236–37.

[65] See Vincent Blasi, "Creativity and Legitimacy in Constitutional Law," review of *Structure and Relationship in Constitutional Law*, by Charles L. Black, Jr., *Yale Law Journal* 80, no. 1 (November 1970): 182.

[66] See Bobbitt, *Constitutional Fate*, 170–71.

[67] Justice Douglas contended that *Pierce v. Society of Sisters*, 268 U.S. 510 (1925), and *Meyer v. Nebraska*, 262 U.S. 390 (1923), stood for the proposition that "the State may not, consistently with the spirit of the First Amendment, contract the spectrum of available knowledge" (*Griswold*, 381 U.S. at 482). The "available knowledge" in question in *Griswold* was information about birth control for married persons.

[68] See generally Geoffrey R. Stone, "Precedent, the Amendment Process, and Evolution of Constitutional Doctrine," *Harvard Journal of Law and Public Policy* 11, no. 1 (Winter 1988): 70 (discussing the reasons).

[69] See, for example, Henry J. Abraham, *The Judicial Process: An Introductory Analysis of the Courts of the United States, England, and France*, 7th ed. (New York: Oxford University Press, 1998), 360.

[70] Justice Brennan had a large hand in the formulation of Justice Douglas's opinion. See Garrow, *Liberty and Sexuality*, 246–48.

[71] David P. Currie, *The Constitution in the Supreme Court: The Second Century, 1888–1986* (Chicago: University of Chicago Press, 1990), 458 (citations omitted).

Law professor Paul G. Kauper echoed—antedated, to be precise—Currie's criticism of Justice Douglas's opinion in an article that appeared in the *Michigan Law Review* shortly after *Griswold* was decided.[72] However, Kauper maintained that the result reached in *Griswold*—that there is a right of privacy in the Constitution—was, in fact, consistent with previous Supreme Court doctrine: specifically, with the Court's myriad of substantive due process decisions.[73] ("Substantive due process" is the interpretation of the Constitution's due process clauses to extend protection to substantive rights and liberties, and not simply to guarantee procedural safeguards.) Kauper emphasized *Meyer v. Nebraska* (1923), which invalidated a Nebraska statute that forbade the use of foreign languages in teaching public school classes, and *Pierce v. Society of Sisters* (1925), which struck down an Oregon statute that required parents to send their children to public schools. He wrote: "As was made clear in the concurring opinions [in *Griswold*], the past decisions of the Court, notably the *Meyer* and *Pierce* cases, offered an immediate opening for finding that marital privacy, as a facet of the freedom of family life, was a fundamental right."[74]

For the reasons that others have explained at length elsewhere—most notably, that one can find a precedent to support or oppose almost any proposition[75]—I am no great fan of doctrinal reasoning. This said, I agree with Kauper that a doctrinal argument can be made to support the right of privacy announced in *Griswold*.[76] However, the precedent on which I would rely most is *Boyd v. United States* (1886), the case in which the Supreme Court first recognized privacy interests in the Constitution. In that case, the Court declared unconstitutional a statute that allowed the government to order individuals to produce private papers and invoices as evidence of illegally imported goods. The Court emphasized the privacy interests involved and held that the Fourth[77] and Fifth[78] Amendments apply

---

[72] See Paul G. Kauper, "Penumbras, Peripheries, Emanations, Things Fundamental and Things Forgotten: The *Griswold* Case," *Michigan Law Review* 64, no. 2 (December 1965): 235–58.

[73] Ibid. Not surprisingly, Kauper gave high marks to the concurring opinions of Justices John Marshall Harlan II and Byron R. White for relying upon substantive due process analysis. See generally *Griswold*, 381 U.S. at 499–502 (Harlan, J., concurring in the judgment), 502–7 (White, J., concurring in the judgment).

[74] Kauper, "Penumbras, Peripheries, Emanations, Things Fundamental and Things Forgotten," 253.

[75] See, for example, Joseph C. Hutcheson, Jr., "The Judgment Intuitive," *Cornell Law Quarterly* 14, no. 3 (April 1929): 274–88.

[76] Historian David J. Garrow argues that Justice Douglas's *own* prior doctrinal pronouncements provided ample support for declaring that there is a right of privacy in the Constitution—pronouncements that Douglas inexplicably failed to mention in his *Griswold* opinion. See Garrow, *Liberty and Sexuality*, 260–63.

[77] The Fourth Amendment reads: "The right of the people to be secure in their persons, houses, papers, and effects, against unreasonable searches and seizures, shall not be violated, and no Warrants shall issue, but upon probable cause, supported by Oath or affirmation, and particularly describing the place to be searched, and the persons or things to be seized."

[78] The Fifth Amendment states: "No person shall be held to answer for a capital, or otherwise infamous crime, unless on a presentment or indictment of a Grand Jury, except in

to all invasions on the part of the government and its employees of the sanctity of a man's home and privacies of life. It is not the breaking of his doors, and the rummaging of his drawers, that constitutes the essence of the offense; but it is the invasion of his indefeasible right of personal security, personal liberty and private property.[79]

Although *Boyd* was a search and seizure/self-incrimination case, and not a *Griswold*-like intimate relations case, it is important to remember that both cases were *criminal* cases and that both were ultimately about the "privacies of life."[80] Both cases, in other words, were about the right to be let alone.

VI. Prudence

Prudential arguments are arguments that balance the interests and values surrounding a case.[81] The Supreme Court is notorious for its balancing tests. In arguably the most comprehensive examination of the subject to date, T. Alexander Aleinikoff of the University of Michigan Law School maintains that constitutional adjudication largely consists of two kinds of balancing.[82] First, he identifies the method by which "the Court talks about one interest outweighing another. Under this view, the Court places the interests on a set of scales and rules the way the scales tip."[83] Second, he identifies a form of balancing under which the Court "speaks of 'striking a balance' between or among competing interests. The image is one of balanced scales with constitutional doctrine calibrated according to the relative weights of the interests."[84]

Surprisingly—given the Court's near obsession with balancing tests—only Justice Byron White appeared to employ balancing in *Griswold* (with

---

cases arising in the land or naval forces, or in the Militia, when in actual service in time of War or public danger; nor shall any person be subject for the same offence to be twice put in jeopardy of life or limb, nor shall be compelled in any criminal case to be a witness against himself, nor be deprived of life, liberty, or property, without due process of law; nor shall private property be taken for public use, without just compensation."

[79] *Boyd v. United States*, 116 U.S. 616, 630 (1886).

[80] Justice Douglas did quote this language from *Boyd*. However, the doctrinal portion of his opinion was limited to a brief discussion of *Meyer* and *Pierce*.

[81] See Bobbitt, *Constitutional Fate*, 61.

[82] See T. Alexander Aleinikoff, "Constitutional Law in the Age of Balancing," *Yale Law Journal* 96, no. 5 (April 1987): 943–1005.

[83] Ibid., 946. Aleinikoff cites *New York v. Ferber*, 458 U.S. 747 (1982), as an example of this type of balancing. In that case the Court upheld a statute criminalizing the distribution of child pornography because "the evil . . . restricted [by the statute] so overwhelmingly outweighs the expressive interests, if any, at stake" (*Ferber*, 458 U.S. at 763–64).

[84] Aleinikoff, "Constitutional Law in the Age of Balancing," 946. Aleinikoff cites as an example of this type of balancing *Tennessee v. Garner*, 471 U.S. 1 (1986), in which the Court did not recognize as paramount either the state's interest in preventing the escape of criminals or an individual's interest in life, but rather held that a police officer may not use deadly force unless such force is necessary to prevent escape and the officer had probable cause to believe that the suspect poses a threat of serious physical harm.

a healthy dose of substantive due process thrown in for good measure). He invoked the following calculus when voting to strike down the Connecticut birth control statute:

> There is no serious contention that Connecticut thinks the use of artificial or external methods of contraception immoral or unwise in itself, or that the anti-use statute is founded upon any policy of promoting population expansion. Rather, the statute is said to serve the State's policy against all forms of promiscuous or illicit sexual relationships, be they premarital or extramarital, concededly a permissible and legitimate legislative goal. Without taking issue with the premise that the fear of conception operates as a deterrent to such relationships in addition to the criminal proscriptions Connecticut has against such conduct, I wholly fail to see how the ban on the use of contraceptives by married couples in any way reinforces the State's ban on illicit sexual relationships. . . . At most the broad ban is of marginal utility to the declared objective. A statute limiting its prohibition on use to persons engaging in the prohibited relationship would serve the end posited by Connecticut in the same way, and with the same effectiveness, or ineffectiveness, as the broad anti-use statute under attack in this case. I find nothing in this record justifying the sweeping scope of this statute, with its telling effect on the freedoms of married persons, and therefore conclude that it deprives such persons of liberty without due process of law.[85]

Put more succinctly, Justice White found the state's interest in discouraging sex outside of marriage to be outweighed by the interest of married persons to practice what we today call "safe sex."

Perhaps because of their well-documented preference for "grand theory,"[86] few constitutional scholars have addressed the right of privacy in the prudential terms of a Justice White. Indeed, arguably the two most prominent prudentialists of the modern era—the late Alexander M. Bickel of the Yale Law School and Richard A. Posner of the U.S. Court of Appeals for the Seventh Circuit—have had little, if anything, to say about *Griswold* as a matter of prudentialism. Bickel's analysis of the case was limited to a throwaway line criticizing it as the second coming of *Lochner*—long among the favorite targets of critics of judicial activism[87]—while Posner's

---

[85] *Griswold*, 381 U.S. at 505–7 (White, J., concurring in the judgment).

[86] Tushnet, *Red, White, and Blue*, 1.

[87] Alexander M. Bickel, *The Supreme Court and the Idea of Progress* (New Haven, CT: Yale University Press, 1978), 41. See generally *Lochner v. New York*, 198 U.S. 45 (1905). In *Lochner*, a bare majority of the Court struck down New York's labor law limiting the number of hours bakers could work as an interference with their "liberty of contract." And in one of the most famous dissenting opinions in the history of the Court, Justice Oliver Wendell Holmes, Jr., sharply criticized his brethren for reading their own economic philosophy into the Constitution.

tack was to mock *Griswold* as a manifestation of "doing your own thing" and "letting it all hang out" sixties' radicalism.[88] (Obviously, both Bickel and Posner believed that *Griswold* was wrongly decided.)

One scholar who does take a sustained prudential approach to the right of privacy is political scientist Philippa Strum of the City University of New York. Strum, who addresses all aspects of privacy in her excellent book on the subject, *Privacy: The Debate in the United States Since 1945* (1998), is particularly adept at explicating the need to balance both communitarian and individualistic concerns when determining whether there is a right of privacy in the Constitution. Her argument for why she believes there is such a right is worth quoting at length:

> Privacy and community are complementary. Both are necessary for a fulfilled human life and for the kind of political system known as democracy. The community provides the individual not only with physical safety but, more importantly in this context, the opportunity to interact with others, to hear others' ideas and try out one's own, to enjoy activities with others, to forge the human relationships that are necessary to a rich life and that help the individual to develop.
>
> Privacy is equally necessary. . . . Human beings need a community in which to develop, but human development cannot take place in the absence of privacy. Community without privacy implies not individual growth but social control and conformity. Privacy deprives the community of its major and easiest method of social control: public exposure as a means of controlling individual behavior. But a society that must rely upon exposure rather than persuasion for social control is neither democratic nor best suited to create the strong individuals that enable a society to thrive. Any community would be poorer without individuals as developed and fulfilled as they can be; no true democracy can exist unless part of that development is political and results in citizen participation. But the political development of the individual, as with all other aspects of individual growth, requires privacy.[89]

Personally, I dislike balancing approaches almost as much as I dislike doctrinal approaches.[90] First, they are inherently awkward. For example, for years the Court has been employing a clumsy multitier approach to questions of equality, wherein some classifications (e.g., race) are handled in one way ("strict scrutiny" review), others (e.g., sex) in another way ("strict rationality" review), and still others (e.g., indigency) in yet a third

[88] Richard A. Posner, *The Economics of Justice* (Cambridge, MA: Harvard University Press, 1981), 345.

[89] Philippa Strum, *Privacy: The Debate in the United States Since 1945* (Fort Worth, TX: Harcourt Brace College Publishers, 1998), 202–3.

[90] See Gerber, *To Secure These Rights*, 175.

way ("rational basis" review).[91] Second, there is the underlying problem of deciding how to give one interest or value more weight than a competing interest or value. Indeed, as eloquent as Strum's analysis is, it still turns—as it must—on constitutional ethics: in Strum's case, on the relative places of community and individualism in the American constitutional order. It is to the question of constitutional ethics that the next section in this essay now turns.

VII. ETHICS

Ethical arguments are based upon the *ethos* of the Constitution.[92] They are a relatively recent phenomenon in the annals of American law.[93] The leading lights of prior generations of the legal professoriate tended to focus their attention on private law subjects; Arthur L. Corbin's work on contracts comes quickly to mind, for example.[94] However, today's "who's who" in the legal academy is dominated by scholars at first-tier law schools such as Yale, New York University, and the University of Chicago who write articles and books about constitutional ethics. Bruce A. Ackerman, Ronald Dworkin, and Cass R. Sunstein lead an impressive list of scholars of this type.[95]

What scholars who write in the ethical tradition tend to do in their work is attempt to explain what the Constitution "really" means, and why the other major scholars who wrote in the prior year or two were wrong about what *they* said it means. Leading Supreme Court cases (e.g., *Brown v. Board of Education* [1954], which declared segregated public schools unconstitutional) and/or areas of Supreme Court doctrine (e.g., free speech) invariably serve as vehicles by which the *ethos* of the Constitution is lifted from the level of abstraction that constitutional ethicists appear to believe constitutional theorizing requires.

[91] Under "strict scrutiny" review—the Court's most exacting standard of review—the Court endeavors to determine, in the language of the test, whether there is a "compelling state interest" in the legislative classification in dispute; under "strict rationality" review—the intermediate test—the Court attempts to decide whether there is a "substantial relationship" in fact between the means and ends of the legislation at issue; and under "rational basis" review—the most lenient of the three levels—the Court assesses whether there is a "reasonable basis" for the legislation in question.

[92] See, for example, Bobbitt, *Constitutional Fate*, 94.

[93] See Tushnet, *Red, White, and Blue*, vii–viii (describing the rise of ethical arguments in constitutional law as a liberal reaction to conservative attacks on the decisions of the Warren Court).

[94] Corbin (1874–1967) taught for decades at Yale Law School, was a leading figure in the drafting of the *Restatement of Contracts*, and his 1950 treatise on contract law was called, by no less a figure than the late Grant Gilmore of *The Death of Contract* (1974) fame, "the greatest book ever written." See generally Arthur L. Corbin, *Corbin on Contracts: A Comprehensive Treatise on the Rules of Contract Law*, 8 vols. (St. Paul, MN: West, 1950); and Grant Gilmore, *The Death of Contract* (Columbus, OH: Ohio State University Press, 1974).

[95] See, for example, Bruce A. Ackerman, *We the People: Foundations* (Cambridge, MA: Harvard University Press, 1991); Ronald Dworkin, *Law's Empire* (Cambridge, MA: Harvard University Press, 1986); and Cass R. Sunstein, *The Partial Constitution* (Cambridge, MA: Harvard University Press, 1993).

Not surprisingly, the right of privacy has received considerable attention in the literature of constitutional ethics. In fact, two leading legal scholars make privacy one of the centerpieces of their work. These scholars are David A. J. Richards of New York University School of Law and Catharine A. MacKinnon of the University of Michigan Law School.

As the title to his book *Toleration and the Constitution* (1986) makes plain, Richards argues that toleration, or equal respect for conscience, is the "central constitutional ideal."[96] At the heart of this ideal, Richards maintains, is the right of privacy. He writes:

> Contractarian political theory justifies a right of private life, the control a free person enjoys over personal relationships essential to personal and moral identity. That right is grounded in the same background right of moral independence which actuates the constitutional protections of the religion clauses: equal respect for the moral powers of human personality. The internal ideals of equal respect of the contractarian political theory of American constitutional law thus interpretively explain and validate [a broad right of privacy] . . . as a fundamental unenumerated right textually protected by the Constitution.[97]

Richards is plainly a huge fan of privacy. MacKinnon, the leading feminist legal theorist in the nation, loathes it. According to MacKinnon, the law is used by men to "dominate" women—especially for sexual purposes. Indeed, MacKinnon goes so far as to claim that all sex is rape.[98] Her position on the specific issue of privacy is consistent with her more general views on law and sex. MacKinnon writes:

> It is probably not a coincidence that the very things feminism regards as central to the subjection of women—the very place, the body; the very relations, heterosexual; the very activities, intercourse and reproduction; and the very feelings, intimate—form the core of privacy doctrine's coverage. Privacy law assumes women are equal to men in [the home]. Through this perspective, the legal concept of privacy can and has shielded the place of battery, marital rape, and women's exploited domestic labor. . . . Just as pornography is legally protected as individual freedom of expression—without any questions about whose freedom and whose expression and at whose expense— abstract privacy protects autonomy, without inquiring into whose freedom of action is being sanctioned, at whose expense. . . . Th[e]

---

[96] David A. J. Richards, *Toleration and the Constitution* (New York: Oxford University Press, 1986), x.

[97] Ibid., 252.

[98] See, for example, Catharine A. MacKinnon, *Feminism Unmodified: Discourses on Life and Law* (Cambridge, MA: Harvard University Press, 1987), 87–89.

right of privacy is a right of men "to be let alone" to oppress women one at a time.[99]

Consequently, whereas Richards seeks to expand the right of privacy in American constitutional law—for example, he believes that the Supreme Court was wrong to hold that the Constitution does not protect the right to engage in private, consensual homosexual activities[100]—MacKinnon aspires to replace the right of privacy with a more gender-sensitive approach to questions of equal protection.[101] To make the point somewhat differently, Richards believes that the right to be let alone is at the heart of *our* constitutional *ethos*, while MacKinnon believes that only *men* feel this way.

VIII. CONCLUSION

I opened this essay by stating that I hoped that by applying the six prevailing approaches to constitutional interpretation to the subject of this volume—the right of privacy—I would be able to say something useful about both privacy and constitutional theory itself. I close by stating that, unfortunately, I have nothing useful to say about privacy but that, I believe, I do have something useful to say about constitutional theory.

With respect to privacy, all of the prevailing approaches to constitutional interpretation—textual, historical, structural, doctrinal, prudential, and ethical—were shown to recognize a right of privacy, and all were shown to deny it. Obviously, this conclusion does not tell us much about the right of privacy.

Of course one might be tempted to say that simply because scholars can argue for privacy and against it based on each of the six methods, that does not mean that each side of the argument in each of the six methods is equally valid. For example, I *personally* believe, as I suggest at several points in the essay (as well as in my prior writings), that the better reading of constitutional history, structure, and doctrine supports a broad right of privacy. However, as I also suggest in this essay, some distinguished constitutional scholars—Berger, McDowell, and Currie—offer powerful arguments to the contrary.

The real question, then, is this: What does an examination of the right of privacy tell us about constitutional theory itself? After all, when *all* of the major approaches to constitutional interpretation can be shown to

---

[99] Catharine A. MacKinnon, *Toward a Feminist Theory of the State* (Cambridge, MA: Harvard University Press, 1989), 193–94.

[100] See, for example, David A. J. Richards, *Women, Gays, and the Constitution: The Grounds for Feminism and Gay Rights in Culture and Law* (Chicago: University of Chicago Press, 1998), 362–65. See generally *Bowers v. Hardwick*, 478 U.S. 186 (1986).

[101] See, for example, MacKinnon, *Feminism Unmodified*, 93–102. MacKinnon's solution, concisely stated, is to give women more power in political and social life.

both support and oppose a right as significant as privacy, constitutional theorists have some explaining to do. Does the explanation lie in the fact that privacy—like most of the issues that constitutional theorists tend to examine (e.g., affirmative action, prayer in the public schools)—is so politically charged that it is impossible for the constitutional theorists in question to apply a particular method in an impartial fashion? Or is privacy the ideal vehicle for illustrating a more systematic problem with constitutional theory: that the existing methods of constitutional interpretation are unworkable and, as a consequence, constitutional theorists need to search for new decisional approaches?

To put the issue directly, does an examination of the right of privacy establish that the prevailing interpretive methods are impotent, or does it suggest that possibly valid methods are being misused for ideological reasons? In my judgment—and I can do no more than *state* my judgment here—the prevailing approaches *can* work, but scholars and Supreme Court justices alike appear unwilling to *allow* them to do so. Constitutional *theory* has, I am sorry to report, become corrupted by the *practice* of constitutional politics.[102]

Law and Politics, Social Philosophy and Policy Center

---

[102] For more on this theme, see Scott Douglas Gerber, *First Principles: The Jurisprudence of Clarence Thomas* (New York: New York University Press, 1999).

PRIVACY AND TECHNOLOGY

By David Friedman

I. Introduction

Privacy: 1. state of being apart from the company or observation of others. . .[1]

The definition above nicely encapsulates two of the intertwined meanings of 'privacy'. In the first sense—*physical seclusion*—the level of privacy in modern developed societies is extraordinarily high by historical standards. We take it for granted that a bed in a hotel will be occupied by either one person or a couple—not by several strangers. At home, few of us expect to share either bed or bedroom with our children. In these and a variety of other ways, increased physical privacy has come as a by-product of increased wealth.[2]

The situation with regard to the second sense—*informational privacy*—is less clear. While the ability of other people to see with their own eyes what we are doing has decreased as a result of increased physical privacy, their ability to observe us indirectly has increased for two quite different reasons.

One reason is the development of increasingly sophisticated technologies for transmitting and intercepting messages. Eavesdropping requires that the eavesdropper be physically close to his victim; wiretapping does not. Current satellite observation technology may not quite make it possible to read lips from orbit, but it is getting close.

The other reason that indirect observation has become easier is the development of greatly improved technologies for storing and manipulating information. What matters to me is not whether information about me exists, but whether other people can find it. Even if all of the information I wish to keep private—say, my marital history or criminal record—exists in publicly accessible archives, it remains, for all practical purposes, private so long as the people I am interacting with do not know that it exists nor where to look for it. Modern information processing has at least the potential to drastically reduce this sort of privacy. The same search engines and collections of information that provide the ideal tools for the researcher who dives into the World Wide Web in the hope of emerging

---

[1] *Webster's International Dictionary*, 2d ed., s.v. "privacy."

[2] See the references in Richard Posner, "The Right of Privacy," *Georgia Law Review* 12, no. 3 (Spring 1978): 393–428, to the anthropological literature on the lack of privacy in primitive societies.

with a fact in his teeth work equally well whether the fact is historical or personal. Privacy through obscurity is not, or at least soon will not be, a practical option.

The two sorts of privacy—physical and informational—are connected. Physical privacy is a means, although a decreasingly effective means, to informational privacy. And lack of informational privacy—in the limiting case, a world where anyone could know everything about you at every instant—feels like a lack of physical privacy, a sort of virtual crowding.

Physical privacy can be a means to informational privacy, but so can the lack of physical privacy; the individual in the crowded city is more anonymous, and has more informational privacy, than an individual in the less-crowded village. But the reason for that is that his privacy is protected by the difficulty of sorting through such a vast amount of data in order to find the particular facts relevant to him. That form of protection cannot survive modern information technology. Hence the connection between physical and informational privacy may become stronger, not weaker, over the course of the next few decades.

There is a third sort of privacy not captured by the definition with which I began this essay—*attentional privacy*. It is the privacy that is violated by unsolicited e-mail or telephone calls from people trying to sell you things that you do not want to buy. Modern technology's impact on this type of privacy has been mixed; the technology makes sending messages less expensive, facilitating bulk e-mail and telemarketing calls, but also makes filtering out messages without human intervention easier, thus lowering the cost of dealing with unwanted messages.

In this essay I will be focusing on issues of informational privacy. As we will see, however, the technology of protecting informational privacy may depend in part on the existence of physical privacy. One interesting question for the future will be whether it is possible to develop technologies that break that link by making it practical to engage in informational transactions without taking any physical actions that can be observed and understood by an outside observer.

Section II of this essay explores the questions of what informational privacy is, why and whether it is a good thing, and why it is widely regarded as a good thing. Section III surveys new technologies that are useful for either protecting or violating an individual's control over information about himself. The final section summarizes my conclusions.

In the course of my discussion, I will be using the term 'privacy rights' in a sense that some readers may find confusing. What I mean by a privacy right is neither a legal nor a moral right, but a *positive* right—a description of an individual's ability to control something. I have strong informational privacy rights if I can easily and inexpensively control other people's access to information about me. If I have a legal right not to have you tap my phone, but it is impractical to enforce that right—the situation at present for those using cordless phones without encryption—

then I have only a very weak right, in the sense that I am using here, to that particular form of privacy. In contrast, I have substantial rights to privacy with regard to my own thoughts, even though it is perfectly legal for other people to use the available technologies—listening to my voice and watching my facial expressions—to try to figure out what I am thinking. I have strong privacy rights over my thoughts because those technologies are not adequate to read my mind.[3]

One source of strong positive rights might be strong legal rights—provided that the legal rights are readily enforceable. Another source might be widely held beliefs about moral rights; it is easier to keep personal matters secret in a society where violating other people's privacy is considered wicked. Positive rights can also be affected by things unrelated to legal or moral rights, such as technological changes. If, for example, someone invented an easy and accurate way of reading minds, positive privacy rights would be radically reduced, even if there were no change in legal or moral privacy rights.

There are two reasons why I define rights in this way. The first is that I am interested in the consequences of privacy rights, that is, in the ways in which my ability to control information about me benefits or harms myself and others—whatever the source of that ability may be. The second is that I am interested in the ways in which technology is likely to change the ability of an individual to control information about himself—hence in changes in positive rights that are due to sources other than changes in legal or moral rights.

II. What Is Informational Privacy and Why Does It Matter?

If all information about you is readily available to anyone who wants it, you have no informational privacy. If nobody else knows anything about you, you have perfect informational privacy. All of us live between those two extremes.

Informational privacy is not always desirable. Film stars and politicians pay to have their privacy reduced by getting (some) information about themselves widely distributed by professional public relations firms. Many other people, however, bear costs in order to reduce the amount that other people know about them, demonstrating that, to them, privacy has positive value. Many people also bear costs to learn about others, demonstrating that to them the privacy of those other people has negative value. At the same time, most people regard privacy in the abstract as a good thing. It is common to see some new product, technology, or legal rule

---

[3] For a more general discussion of rights from a related perspective, see David Friedman, "A Positive Account of Property Rights," *Social Philosophy and Policy* 11, no. 2 (Summer 1994): 1–16.

attacked as reducing privacy, rare to see anything attacked as increasing privacy.

This raises two related questions. The first is why individuals (sometimes) value their own privacy, and so are willing to take actions to protect it. The second is why many individuals speak and act as though the cost to them of a reduction in their privacy is larger than the benefit to them of a similar reduction in other people's privacy, making privacy in general, not merely privacy for themselves, a good.

The answer to the first question is fairly straightforward. Information about me in the hands of other people sometimes permits them to gain at my expense. They may do so by stealing my property—if, for example, they know when I will or will not be home. They may do so by getting more favorable terms in a voluntary transaction—if, for example, they know just how much I am willing to pay for what they are selling.[4] They may do so by preventing me from stealing their property—by, for example, not hiring me as company treasurer after discovering that I am a convicted embezzler, or by not lending me money after discovering that I have repeatedly declared bankruptcy.

Information about me in other people's hands may also sometimes make me better off—for example, the information that I am an honest and competent attorney. But privacy rights do not prevent people from giving out information about themselves; they merely prevent people from obtaining information about others without their consent. If I have control over information about myself, I can release it when doing so benefits me and keep it private when releasing it would make me worse off.[5] Hence it is not surprising that people value having such control.

This does not, however, answer the second question. To the extent that my control over information about me makes me better off at the expense of other people, and their control over information about them makes them better off at my expense, it is not clear why I should regard privacy rights as on net a good thing. The examples I offered above included one

---

[4] One example of this occurs in the context of a takeover bid. In order for the market for corporate control to discipline corporate managers, it must be in the interest of someone to identify badly managed corporations and take them over. Doing this requires that a takeover bid can remain secret long enough for the person responsible to accumulate a substantial ownership in a corporation at the pre-takeover price. In a very public world, this is hard to do. Currently it is also hard to do in the United States because of legal rules deliberately designed to limit the secrecy of takeover bids. The result is not, of course, to eliminate all takeover bids or all market discipline over corporate managers, but merely to reduce both below what they would be in a more private and less regulated market.

[5] An exception is the case where the relevant information is negative. If I have control over information about me, potential lenders have no way of knowing whether the reason they have seen no reports of my having ever declared bankruptcy is that I have not done so, or that I have done so and have suppressed the information. Thus, borrowers who have not declared bankruptcy in the past will be better off in a world where privacy rights with regard to such information are weak. The problem disappears if a borrower can take an observable action—such as signing a legally enforceable waiver of the relevant legal privacy rights—which demonstrates that the information is not being suppressed.

case in which my privacy protected me from burglary; in this case, privacy produced a net benefit, since the gain that a burglar receives from a theft is normally less than the loss suffered by his victim. They included one case in which my privacy permitted me to steal from or defraud others; in this case, privacy produced a net loss, for similar reasons. And they included one case—bargaining—in which the net effect appears to be a wash.[6]

The bargaining case is worth a little more attention. Suppose you have something to sell—say an apple. I am the only buyer. The apple is worth one dollar to you and two to me. We are engaged in the game known as *bilateral monopoly.*[7] At any price between one dollar and two, both of us benefit from the transaction, but as the price increases within that range, the amount of the benefit that you get rises and the amount of the benefit that I get falls.

I can try to get you to sell at a lower price by persuading you that the apple is worth less to me than it really is, and hence that if you insist on a high price there will be no sale. You can try to get a higher price by persuading me that the apple is worth more to you than it really is, so that if I do not agree to a higher price there will be no sale. One risk with both tactics is that they may succeed too well. If you persuade me that the apple is worth more than two dollars to you, or if I persuade you that it is worth less than one dollar to me, the deal will fall through.

Suppose I get accurate information on the value of the apple to you. One result of this is that your persuasion no longer works, making it more likely that I will get the apple at a low price. That is merely a transfer from you to me, involving no change in the net benefit of the transaction. A second result is to make bargaining breakdown less likely. I will still try to persuade you that the apple is worth less than two dollars to me, but I will not try to persuade you that it is worth less than one dollar, because I now know that doing so is against my interest. This second result produces a net benefit, since it increases the chance that you will end up selling me the apple instead of keeping it yourself (leading to a net gain of one dollar, since the apple is worth a dollar more to me than it is to you).

Generalizing the argument, it looks as though privacy produces, on average, a net loss in situations, such as the one just discussed, where

---

[6] Many of the points made in this section of the essay can be found, in somewhat different form, in Posner, "The Right of Privacy," and Posner, "An Economic Theory of Privacy," *Regulation* 2, no. 3 (May/June 1978): 19. He finds the case for the general desirability of privacy to be weak.

[7] It is called bilateral monopoly because it corresponds to a situation in which there is both a monopoly seller and a monopoly (strictly speaking, monopsony) buyer. Discussions of bilateral monopoly can be found in David Friedman, *Hidden Order: The Economics of Everyday Life* (New York: HarperBusiness, 1996), chap. 11; and in David Friedman, *Law's Order: What Economics Has to Do with Law and Why It Matters* (Princeton, NJ: Princeton University Press, forthcoming), chap. 8. *Law's Order* is also available on the World Wide Web at http://www.best.com/~ddfr/Laws_Order/laws_order_ToC.htm.

parties are seeking information about each other in order to improve the terms of a voluntary transaction. This is because privacy, in these situations, increases the risk of bargaining breakdown, when one party's ignorance leads to an incorrect estimate of the terms that the other will accept.[8] In situations involving involuntary transactions, privacy produces a net gain if it is being used to protect other rights (the burglary example), and a net loss if it is being used to violate other rights (the embezzler and fraudulent loan examples). (In both sets of examples, I assume that those rights have been defined in a way that makes their protection efficient.) There is no obvious reason why the former situation should be more common than the latter. So it remains puzzling why people in general support privacy rights—why they think it is, on the whole, a good thing for people to be able to control information about themselves.

A. Privacy rights and rent seeking

One possible approach to this puzzle starts by viewing privacy rights as a mechanism for reducing costs associated with *rent seeking*, that is, expenditures by one person that are designed to benefit him at the cost of another. Consider again our bilateral-monopoly bargaining game. Assume this time that each player can, at some cost, obtain information about the value of the apple to the other player. For example, suppose that I can plant listening devices or miniature video cameras about your home in the hope of seeing or hearing something that will tell me just how much you value the apple; suppose also that you can take similar actions with regard to me. Such activities may produce a benefit by reducing the risk of bargaining breakdown, but there is no guarantee that that benefit will be larger than the cost of the spying. Even if it is not, my spying may still be in my interest, since it is a way of getting better terms and thus gaining at your expense.

The rent seeking becomes clearer if we include not only your efforts to learn things about me but also my efforts to prevent you from doing so. Suppose, for example, that I have a taste for watching pornographic videos, and that my boss is a puritan who does not wish to employ people who enjoy pornography. We consider two possible situations—one in which my boss is able to keep track of what I am renting from the local video store, and another in which he is not.

---

[8] This might not be the case if we are frequently faced with situations in which my prospective gains from the bargain provide the incentive for me to generate information that is of value to other people as well. There is little point to spending time and money predicting a rise in wheat prices if everything you discover is revealed to potential sellers before you have a chance to buy from them. See Jack Hirschleifer, "The Private and Social Value of Information and the Reward to Inventive Activity," *American Economic Review* 61, no. 3 (September 1971): 561–74.

If I know the boss may be monitoring my rentals from that store, I respond by renting videos from a more distant and less convenient outlet. My boss is no better off as a result of the reduction in my privacy; I am still viewing pornography, and he is still ignorant of the fact. I am worse off as a result of the additional driving time required to visit the more distant store.

Generalizing the argument, we consider a situation where I have information about myself and can, at some cost, prevent other people from having that information. Under one legal (or technological) regime, the cost of doing so is low, under another, it is high. Under both regimes, however, the cost is low enough that I am willing to pay it. The former regime is then superior, not because I end up with more privacy, but because I end up getting it at a lower cost. Therefore, laws, norms, or technologies that lower the cost of protecting privacy may produce net benefits.[9]

I say "may" because the conclusion depends on assuming that it will, in either case, be worth the cost to me to protect my privacy.[10] If we assume instead that under the second regime protecting my privacy is prohibitively expensive, and if we are considering situations where the loss of privacy produces a transfer from me to someone else but no net cost (or, a fortiori, if it produces a net benefit), we get the opposite result. If privacy is cheap, I buy it and, even though it is cheap, it still costs something and produces no net benefit. If privacy is expensive, I do not buy it and, while I am then worse off for not having it, my loss is balanced by someone else's gain, so on net we are better off by the amount saved through not bearing the cost of protecting my privacy.

Viewing privacy as a way of reducing rent seeking provides a possible explanation for why circumstances that make privacy easier to obtain might be desirable, but it is an explanation very much dependent on assumptions about the technology of getting and concealing information. In a world where concealing information is costly, but not too costly to be worth doing, making concealment less costly produces a net benefit. In a world where concealing information is so costly that nobody bothers to do it, making concealment less costly increases the amount spent protect-

[9] This argument is proposed as a possible justification for trade secret law in David Friedman, William Landes, and Richard Posner, "Some Economics of Trade Secret Law," *Journal of Economic Perspectives* 5, no. 1 (Winter 1991): 61–72.

[10] One reason that the assumption may be correct is the difficulty of propertizing information. Suppose that keeping some particular fact about me secret benefits me at the expense of people that I deal with; for simplicity, assume that I get this benefit through a simple transfer with no net gain or loss. If you discover the fact, you have no incentive to keep it hidden, so you tell other people. You end up getting only a small fraction of the benefit, while I bear all of the cost, so I am willing to spend much more to conceal the fact than you would be willing to spend to discover it. This would not be the case if you could sell the information to other people who deal with me—as credit agencies, of course, do. But in many contexts such sales are impractical, due to the problems of transacting over information (briefly discussed below).

ing privacy, which is a net loss. More generally and precisely, lowering the cost of privacy reduces expenditures on privacy if the demand for privacy is inelastic, and increases them if it is elastic.[11]

This explanation also depends on another assumption—that the information about me starts in my control, so that facilitating privacy means making it easier for me to protect what I already possess. But much information about me comes into existence in other people's possession. Consider, for example, court records of my conviction on a criminal charge, or a magazine's mailing list with my name on it. Protecting my privacy with regard to such information requires some way of removing that information from the control of those people who initially possess it and transferring control to me. That is, in most cases, a costly process. There are lots of reasons, unconnected with privacy issues, why we generally want people to have access to court records, and there is no obvious nonlegal mechanism by which I can control such access.[12] If we do nothing to give people rights over such information about them, the information will remain public and nothing will have to be spent to restrict access to it.

B. Privacy as property

An alternative argument in favor of making privacy easier to obtain starts with a point that I made earlier: if I have control over information about me, but transferring that information to someone else produces net benefits, then I can give or sell that information to him. Hence, one might argue, by protecting my property rights in information about me, we establish a market in information. Each piece of information moves to the person who values it most, maximizing net benefit.

So far this is an argument not for privacy, but for private property in information.[13] To get to an argument for privacy requires two further steps. The first is to observe that most information about me starts out in my possession, although not necessarily my exclusive possession. Hence, giving anyone else exclusive rights to it requires somehow depriving me of it—which, given the absence of technologies that produce selective

---

[11] A demand is elastic if a 1 percent decrease in price results in more than a 1 percent increase in quantity demanded. A demand is inelastic if a 1 percent decrease in price results in less than a 1 percent increase in quantity demanded.

[12] There may be very costly ways of doing so. At one point during litigation involving conflicts between the Church of Scientology and discontented ex-members, information that the Church wished to keep private became part of the court record. The Church responded by having members continually checking out the relevant records, thus keeping anyone else from getting access to them. And I might preserve my privacy in a world where court records were public by changing my name.

[13] For a discussion of why it makes sense to treat some things as property and some as commons, see David Friedman, "Standards as Intellectual Property: An Economic Approach," *University of Dayton Law Review* 19, no. 3 (Spring 1994): 1109–29; and Friedman, *Law's Order*, chap. 10.

amnesia, is difficult. It would be possible to deprive me of control over information by making it illegal for me to make use of it or transmit it to others, but enforcing such a restriction would be costly, perhaps prohibitively costly.

The second step, following a general line of argument originated by economist Ronald Coase,[14] is to note that, to the extent that our legal rules assign control over information to the person to whom it is most valuable, they save us the transaction costs of moving it to that person. My earlier arguments suggest that information about me is sometimes most valuable to me (for example, when it protects me from a burglar), and sometimes it is most valuable to someone else. There are, however, a lot of different "someone elses." Giving each person control over information about himself, then, especially information that starts in his possession, is a legal rule that should minimize the transaction costs of getting information to the users that value it the most.

Stated in the abstract, this sounds like a reasonable argument. It would be one if we were talking about other forms of property. But there are problems with applying a property solution to personal information. The first problem is that transacting over information is often difficult, because it is hard to tell the customer what you are selling without giving it to him in the process. The second is that a given piece of information can be duplicated almost costlessly; thus, while the efficient allocation of a car is to the one person who values it the most, the efficient allocation of a piece of information is to everyone to whom it has positive value.[15] This implies that legal rules that treat information as a commons, such that everyone is free to make copies of it, lead to the efficient allocation.

This conclusion must be qualified in two ways. First, as we have already seen, legal protection of information may be a cheaper substitute for private protection; if the information is going to be protected because it is in someone's interest to do so, we might as well have it protected as inexpensively as possible. Second, you cannot copy information unless it exists. Thus we get the familiar argument from the economics of intellectual property, which holds that patent and copyright result in a suboptimal use of existing intellectual property, since they allow owners to sell the right to copy the protected material at a positive price even though the marginal cost of that right is zero. In exchange for this suboptimal *use* of existing intellectual property, however, patent and copyright allow us to get a more nearly optimal *production* of intellectual property.

---

[14] Ronald Coase, "The Problem of Social Cost," *Journal of Law and Economics* 3, no. 1 (October 1960): 1–44. See also Friedman, *Law's Order*, chap. 4.

[15] This assumes that A's possession of information does not impose a cost on B. But the argument generalizes to the case where the cost to B of A possessing information is typically lower than the benefit to A, which brings us back to the earlier discussion of reasons why privacy is likely to result in net costs.

Establishing rights to information in order to give an incentive to create that information is a legitimate argument for property rules in contexts such as copyright or patent. It is less convincing in the context of privacy. Information about me is either produced by me as a by-product of other activities, in which case I do not need any additional incentive to produce it, or else produced by other people about me, in which case giving me property rights in the information will not give them an incentive to produce it. It does provide an argument for privacy in some contexts, most obviously the context of trade secrets, where privacy is used to protect produced information and so give people an incentive to produce it.[16]

C. Privacy as an inefficient norm

Legal scholar Robert Ellickson, in *Order Without Law* (1991), argues that close-knit communities tend to produce efficient norms.[17] One of his examples is the set of norms developed by nineteenth-century whalers to deal with situations in which one ship harpooned a whale and another ship eventually brought it in. He offers evidence that those norms changed over time in a way that efficiently adapted them to the characteristics of the changing species of whales that were being hunted.

This story raises a puzzle. The reason the whalers had to change the species that they were hunting, and the associated norms, was that they were hunting one species after another into near extinction. That suggests that a norm restricting the catch would have produced sizable benefits. Yet no such norm developed.

My solution to that puzzle starts with a different puzzle: what is the mechanism that produces efficient norms? My answer begins by distinguishing between two different sorts of efficient norms. A *locally efficient* norm is a norm that it is in the interest of a small group of individuals to follow among themselves—for example, a norm of fair dealing. A *globally efficient* norm is one that it would be in the interest of everyone in the population to have everyone follow.

Locally efficient norms can be adopted by small groups. Since the groups benefit by adopting the norm, adoption of the norm will spread. Eventually everyone in the larger society will follow the norm. This mechanism does not work for a norm that is globally but not locally efficient, such as a norm against overwhaling. If some whalers follow it, it is in the interest of other whalers to take advantage of the opportunity by increasing their whaling efforts. Hence we would expect systems of private

---

[16] Friedman, Landes, and Posner, "Some Economics of Trade Secret Law."

[17] Robert Ellickson, *Order Without Law: How Neighbors Settle Disputes* (Cambridge, MA: Harvard University Press, 1991).

norms to be locally but not globally efficient, which corresponds to what Ellickson found for whaling.[18]

This brief sketch of norms provides a possible explanation for the widespread existence of norms of privacy, that is, norms holding that individuals are entitled to conceal personal information about themselves and that other individuals ought not to seek to discover such information. Such norms may well be locally efficient even if they are globally inefficient.

Why would such norms be locally efficient? Consider some piece of information about me: for example, my value for the apple in the earlier discussion of bilateral monopoly. If I am the sole possessor of that piece of information, I can either withhold it, to my benefit, or offer to sell it to my trading partner, supposing that there is some way in which I can prove to him that the information I am selling is truthful. If a third party is the sole possessor of the information, he can offer to sell it to either me or my trading partner, whoever bids more. But if several people possess the information, none of them can sell it for a significant price; anyone who tries will be underbid by one of the others, since the cost of reproducing the information is nearly zero. The logic is exactly the same as it would be in a situation in which we wished to maximize the revenue from a patent and were comparing the alternatives of having one owner of the patent or several, where in the latter case each owner could freely license to third parties.

It follows that if we are members of a close-knit group containing all of the people who can readily discover personal information about each other, and if we are also engaged in dealings with nonmembers of the group such that possession by them of personal information about one of us would make them better off at his expense, a norm of privacy is likely to be in our interest. Its effect is to give each of us monopoly ownership of information about himself, permitting each to maximize the return from that information, whether by keeping it secret or by selling it. To the extent that this return comes at the expense of the nonmembers with whom we are dealing, the norm may be globally inefficient. But it is locally efficient, which provides a possible explanation of why it exists.

D. Blackmail and privacy

If blackmail were legal, blackmailers and their customers (today called "victims") would enter into legally enforceable contracts whereby the blackmailer would agree for a price never to disclose the infor-

---

[18] A longer version of this argument can be found in David Friedman, "Less Law than Meets the Eye," review of *Order Without Law*, by Robert Ellickson, *Michigan Law Review* 90, no. 6 (May 1992): 1444–52.

mation in question; the information would become the legally protected trade secret of the customer.[19]

Laws against blackmail provide an interesting puzzle. Suppose you know something about me that I would prefer not to be public. I offer to pay for your silence. At first glance, the transaction seems obviously beneficial. I value your silence more than the money, which is why I made the offer; you value the money more than publishing my secret, which is why you accepted. We are both better off, so why should anyone object?[20]

One way to respond to this is to assert that by posing this question after you obtained the information, we have started too late in the process. The possibility of blackmail gives people an incentive to spend resources acquiring information about other people and gives potential targets an incentive to spend resources concealing such information. If blackmail is legal, I might spend a thousand dollars' worth of time and effort trying to conceal the information, and you might spend a thousand dollars trying to discover it. If you succeed, I would then pay you three thousand dollars to keep your mouth shut. This would leave us, on net, two thousand dollars worse off than when we started: you would be two thousand dollars better off, I would be four thousand worse off. If you fail, we would have each spent a thousand dollars, so again we would be, on net, two thousand dollars worse off than when we started. A law that made it impractical for you to profit by discovering such information thus provides a net benefit of two thousand dollars. We are back to the rent-seeking explanation of privacy.

An alternative reason why we might object to blackmail is that we ought to include more people in our calculations of costs and benefits. In particular, we ought to include the people to whom you are threatening to tell my secret. The reason I am willing to pay for your silence is that doing so makes me better off, possibly at their expense. Perhaps the secret is my record for fraud or malpractice; having moved from where my

---

[19] Richard Posner, "Blackmail, Privacy, and Freedom of Contract," *University of Pennsylvania Law Review* 141, no. 5 (May 1993).

[20] These issues are explored in an extensive literature, including: James Lindgren, "Blackmail: On Waste, Morals, and Ronald Coase," *UCLA Law Review* 36, no. 3 (February 1989): 597–608; Lindgren, "Kept in the Dark: Owens's View of Blackmail," *Connecticut Law Review* 21, no. 3 (Spring 1989): 749–51; Lindgren, "Secret Rights: A Comment on Campbell's Theory of Blackmail," *Connecticut Law Review* 21, no. 2 (Winter 1989): 407–10; Lindgren, "In Defense of Keeping Blackmail a Crime: Responding to Block and Gordon," *Loyola of Los Angeles Law Review* 20, no. 1 (November 1986): 35–44; Lindgren, "More Blackmail Ink: A Critique of Blackmail, Inc., Epstein's Theory of Blackmail," *Connecticut Law Review* 16, no. 4 (Summer 1984): 909–23; Lindgren, "Unraveling the Paradox of Blackmail," *Columbia Law Review* 84, no. 2 (March 1984): 670–717; Richard S. Murphy, "Property Rights in Personal Information: An Economic Defense of Privacy," *Georgia Law Journal* 84, no. 7 (July 1996): 2381–417; Posner, "The Right of Privacy"; Posner, "An Economic Theory of Privacy"; Posner, *The Economics of Justice* (Cambridge, MA: Harvard University Press, 1981), chaps. 9–10, pp. 231–309; Posner, *Overcoming Law* (Cambridge, MA: Harvard University Press, 1995), chap. 25, pp. 531–51; and Posner, "Blackmail, Privacy, and Freedom of Contract."

misdeeds were first unveiled, I may be looking for new, poorly informed customers. Perhaps the secret is what happened to my first wife; I may now be seeking to obtain a replacement. In these and many other circumstances, when a blackmailer accepts a payment for silence, he imposes an external cost on those who would otherwise have learned what he knows. Perhaps legal rules permitting me to buy his silence would make the society as a whole worse off, by keeping him silent and others ignorant.

As should be clear, these two arguments for banning blackmail are not only different, they are in an important sense inconsistent. If we assume that the same amount of information will be produced whether or not blackmail is legal—if, that is, we imagine that the typical blackmailer obtained his information by accident, not effort—then the rent-seeking argument vanishes, but the public-benefit argument replaces it. The potential blackmailer has the information; if he cannot sell it, he might as well give it away. If, on the other hand, we assume that the information on which blackmail is based is primarily obtained for that purpose, the rent-seeking argument is revived, but the public-benefit argument vanishes. If blackmail is illegal, the information will never be generated, so the public will never be warned.

At this point, we seem to have arguments against permitting blackmail both when blackmailers discover information by accident and when they deliberately search for it. This conclusion becomes less clear if we assume that the information a blackmailer discovers is not merely useful to other people in dealing with the victim, but is also discreditable to the victim—as we usually do assume when discussing blackmail. If we suppose that the blackmailer discovered the information by accident and will publish it—perhaps in the hope of a financial or reputational reward—if he cannot sell it to the victim, then laws against blackmail make sense, since they result in the potential victim being exposed for his misdeeds. If we permit blackmail, the victim still suffers—but his suffering takes the form of a payment to the blackmailer. The reason why the victim makes the payment is that it costs him less than it would cost him if his misdeed were revealed. Therefore, the result is a lower cost to the victim; furthermore, other people will never receive the information, and so will not be able to modify their behavior to take account of it, making them worse off than they would have been if the information had been revealed.

Suppose, however, that the incentive provided by the ability to blackmail people plays a major role in the discovery of the information. In that case, blackmail becomes a useful mechanism for the private enforcement of law.[21] If blackmail is legal, people have an incentive to look for evidence of other people's crimes and use it to blackmail them, thus impos-

---

[21] Posner has argued that laws against blackmail are desirable in circumstances where private law enforcement is for some reason inefficient. See, for example, Posner, *Economic Analysis of Law*, 5th ed. (New York: Aspen Law & Business, 1998), 660–61.

ing a punishment on criminals who would otherwise go free. The same argument applies if the information concerns violations of norms rather than laws, assuming that we believe the norms are efficient ones and that punishment for their violation is, therefore, desirable.

I previously pointed out that one argument for intellectual property law is that it provides an incentive to generate valuable information. Similarly here, the form of transferable property right that exists if blackmail is legal also creates an incentive to generate valuable information. The information, once generated, is suppressed, but there is still a benefit, since the process generates a penalty for the behavior that the information concerns, and blackmail is particularly likely to occur with regard to behavior that we would like to penalize.

E. Privacy and government

> It would have been impossible to proportion with tolerable exactness the tax upon a shop to the extent of the trade carried on in it, without such an inquisition as would have been altogether insupportable in a free country.[22]

> (Adam Smith's explanation of why a sales tax is impractical.)

> The state of a man's fortune varies from day to day, and without an inquisition more intolerable than any tax, and renewed at least once every year, can only be guessed at.[23]

> (Smith's explanation of why an income tax is impractical.)

Until now, I have ignored an issue that is central to much of the concern over privacy: privacy from government. The logic is the same as in the situations we have been discussing. If the government knows things about me—for example, my income—that permits the government to benefit itself at my expense. In some cases, it also permits the government to do things that benefit me—for example, pay me money because my income is low—but in such situations, privacy rights would leave me free to reveal the information if I wished.

However, privacy from government differs from privacy from private parties in two important respects. First, although private parties occasionally engage in involuntary transactions such as burglary, most of their interactions with each other are voluntary ones, which makes it less likely that someone else having information about me will result in an inefficient transaction. Governments engage in involuntary transactions on an

---

[22] Adam Smith, *An Inquiry into the Nature and Causes of the Wealth of Nations*, ed. Edwin Cannan (New York: Modern Library, 1937), bk. 5, chap. 2, pt. 2, art. 2.

[23] Ibid., bk. 5, chap. 2, pt. 2, art. 4.

enormously larger scale. Second, governments almost always have an overwhelming superiority of physical force over the individual citizen. It follows that while I can protect myself from my fellow citizens to a considerable degree by using locks and burglar alarms, I can protect myself from government actors only by keeping from them the information that they need to benefit the government at my expense.[24]

The implications of these differences for the value of privacy depend very much on one's view of government. If, at one extreme, one regards government as the modern equivalent of the Philosopher King, then individual privacy simply makes it harder for government actors to do good. If, at the other extreme, one regards government as a particularly large and well-organized criminal gang supporting itself at the expense of the taxpayers, individual privacy against government becomes an unambiguously good thing. Most Americans appear, judging by their expressed views on privacy, to be close enough to the latter position to consider privacy against government as on the whole desirable, except in cases where they believe that privacy might be used primarily to protect private criminals. Similar views are common among citizens of some, but not all, other countries, a difference that may help explain different national policies with regard to privacy. As a very rough observation, Europeans seem to be more concerned than Americans with privacy vis-à-vis private actors and less concerned than Americans with privacy vis-à-vis their governments. The quotations from Smith—when contrasted with current British practice—suggest that concerns with privacy against government may have declined over time, at least in Britain.

F. The weak case for privacy: a summary

Explaining why individuals wish to have control over information about themselves is easy. Explaining why it is in my interest that both I *and* the people I deal with have such control, or why people believe that this latter state of affairs is in their interest and act accordingly, is more difficult.

We have considered three reasons why privacy might be in the general interest, that is, why it might be efficient in the economic sense. One is that people want to control information about themselves, so the easier that this is to do, the less they will have to spend to do it. People also want information about other people, and the harder it is to get, the less they will spend getting it. As the odd asymmetry of the two sides of the argument suggests—in one case, lowering a price reduces expenditure; in the other, raising a price reduces expenditure—the argument for the efficiency of privacy depends on specific assumptions about the relevant

---

[24] Of course, I could also protect myself by engaging in political activity—for example, by lobbying Congress or making contributions to the police benevolent fund. For most individuals, such tactics are rarely worth their cost.

demand and supply functions. It goes through rigorously if the demand for one's own privacy is inelastic and the demand for information about others is elastic—which might, but need not, be true.[25]

Put in that form, the argument sounds abstract, but the concrete version should be obvious to anyone who has ever closed a door behind him, loosened his tie, taken off his shoes, and put his feet up on his desk. Privacy has permitted him to maintain his reputation as someone who behaves properly without having to bear the cost of actually behaving properly—which is why there is no window between his office and the adjacent hallway.

The second reason why privacy might be efficient is that property rights permit goods to be allocated to their highest-valued use. If protection of privacy is easy, then individuals have reasonably secure property rights over information about themselves. It makes sense to give such rights to the individual whom the information is about, because he is more likely to be the highest-valued user than any single other person— and if he is not, he can always sell the information to someone else. The problem with this argument is that information, unlike other goods, can be reproduced at almost no cost, making it likely that the highest-valued user is "everybody." Even if the transfer of the information from its subject to everybody produces net benefits, it may not occur, since once a few people have the information, it is hard to prevent them from reselling it, making it impossible for the original owner to collect its value from anyone else, and thus making it less likely that the information will be bought in the first place.[26]

The third reason why privacy might be efficient is that it provides a way in which individuals may protect themselves against government. The strength of that argument depends very much on one's view of the nature of government.

We also saw one argument against privacy—that it permits people to act badly while evading the consequence of having people know that they acted badly. This argument was worked out in the context of arguments for and against legalizing blackmail.

The conclusion so far is that the case for privacy rights—for the claim that it is desirable to lower the cost to individuals of controlling information about themselves—is a weak one. Under some circumstances, privacy produces a net gain, but under others it produces a net loss.

---

[25] Privacy might also be on net efficient if one of the two functions met the required condition and produced gains that more than outweighed the loss from the function that did not.

[26] This problem suggests a further point relevant to the issue of blackmail. The information that I am a swindler is worth more to my potential victims than it is to me. But since it is much easier to sell a single piece of information to one person than to many, the blackmailer can collect most of its value to me from me and has no way of collecting any significant fraction of its value to them from them. So he sells it to me instead of to them, which is an inefficient outcome—and one that may be prevented by laws against blackmail.

G. Other privacies

So far we have been talking only about informational privacy. The link between this sort of privacy and physical privacy is fairly obvious; if there is someone else in the room with you, he will probably notice when you loosen your tie and take off your shoes. Physical privacy is, among other things, a means to maintain informational privacy.

The link between informational privacy and attentional privacy is also obvious, but the implications are less clear. When someone sends me a message, such as a phone call or an e-mail, it costs me something to examine the message and determine whether it is of interest. In a world of uncertainty, some messages are of interest to me and some are not; neither I nor the sender knows for certain whether I am interested in a particular message until I have examined it.

Both the sender and I would prefer that the sender send me messages that are of interest to me; there is no point to calling someone up in order to sell him something that he has no interest in buying. Where we differ is in where we draw the line between messages that are or are not worth their cost. The sender wants to send messages if and only if the probability that I will be interested—and will respond in a way that benefits him—is sufficient to justify the cost to him of sending the message.[27] I want him to send messages if and only if that probability is sufficient to justify the cost to me of examining and evaluating the message. In a world where sending messages is expensive and evaluating them is inexpensive, I will receive inefficiently few messages, so I will buy additional messages by (for example) subscribing to magazines. In a world where sending messages is cheap and evaluating them is expensive, I will receive more messages than I want. Resolving that problem requires a negative subscription price, that is, a mechanism by which I can charge people for sending me messages.

The connection between attentional privacy and informational privacy exists because the sender needs information about me in order to decide whether sending a message to me is worth the cost to him. The implication of this is ambiguous because increasing the amount of such information available to him may make the outcome better or worse for me. In the limiting case of a world with complete information, potential senders know for certain whether I want to buy what they are selling, so I receive all the offers that I would want to receive and do not have to waste time

---

[27] Throughout this discussion, I am assuming that the purpose of messages is to propose voluntary transactions. I am, thus, ignoring cases such as harassment, where the benefit to the sender does not depend on the buyer deciding that the message is of value. I am also ignoring cases of e-mail bombing (flooding someone's mailbox in order to prevent him from using it), where the purpose of the message is to impose a cost on the recipient.

examining any that I do not want to receive.[28] In the limiting case of a world with no information (and in which the cost of sending messages is significant), it is never worth it to send a message. This latter outcome cannot be an improvement on other alternatives, since the other alternatives give me more choices, yet still permit me the option of ignoring all messages—cutting the bottom out of my mailbox and putting a waste basket underneath it.

More generally, increasing the information other people have about you can benefit you by making it easier for those who have offers that you are interested in to find you, and easier for those whose offers you are not interested in to discover your lack of interest and save themselves the cost of making the offers. If only all the world knew that I did not have a mortgage on my house, I would no longer be annoyed by phone calls from people offering to refinance it.

As this example suggests, one way of getting the best of both worlds is to have control over information about yourself and to use that control to make some information public while keeping other information private. I will return to that possibility in Section III, after discussing technologies that facilitate that approach.

Finally, it is worth noting that different societies have had different norms with regard to privacy, some of which surely reflect the differing value that individuals place on having information about themselves widely known. Consider the English upper class at the beginning of the nineteenth century, as depicted by Jane Austen. Every gentleman's income appears to have been a matter of public knowledge. One reason for this may have been that the information was crucial to families with daughters on the marriage market. A gentleman who went to some trouble to conceal his financial situation would be signaling not a taste for privacy, but an income below his pretended status.[29]

We are now finished with our theoretical discussion of privacy. One thing this discussion has made clear is that whether it is desirable for individuals to be able to control information about themselves depends on a variety of technologies—in the economist's sense, in which a technology is simply a way of transforming inputs to outputs. In particular, it depends on technologies for obtaining, concealing, and transmitting information—which will be the subject of the next part of this essay.

---

[28] This result is not quite as rigorous as it sounds, since the cost of evaluating an offer is already "sunk" at the point when you decide whether to accept it. Consider an offer that costs fifteen cents to evaluate and proposes a transaction that would produce a gain of ten cents for the individual receiving the offer. The receiver, having already paid the examination cost, accepts the offer and so produces a gain for the sender sufficient to more than cover the cost of sending. I will ignore such complications since I doubt they are of much real world importance.

[29] In modern-day Israel, judging by my observations, asking someone his salary is considered perfectly normal, whereas in the United States, it is a violation of norms of privacy. I have no good explanation for the difference.

III. The Technology of Privacy

Over the course of the past fifty years, a variety of technologies have been developed that substantially affect the cost of obtaining information about other people, concealing information about oneself, and transacting in information. For our purposes, they may be grouped into three broad categories: information processing, encryption, and surveillance.

A. Information processing

The earliest and best known of these technologies is information processing. Fifty years ago, a firm or government bureau possessing information on millions of individuals faced daunting problems in making use of it. Today, the average citizen can afford, and may well own, computer hardware and software capable of easily dealing with a database of that size.

One implication of this is that organizations that already have large-scale data collections are increasingly able to use them; privacy rights, in the sense in which I have been using the term, are therefore weaker. A second implication is that dispersed information that nobody found worth collecting in the past may be routinely collected in the future.

It is possible to hinder that development through the use of legal rules restricting the collection and sale of data, and such rules exist (for example, the Fair Credit Reporting Act[30]). But doing so is costly, and it is far from clear that it is useful. For the most part, dispersed information is collected in order to be used by private parties to facilitate voluntary transactions with others—an activity that typically produces net benefits.[31] Given that information is collected for this purpose, it is hard to design legal rules that prevent its occasional use for other purposes, such as locating potential targets for criminal activity. Furthermore, as the growth of the Internet makes it easier for individuals to transact with firms and individuals in other countries and, thus, moves more and more of the commercial activity relevant to U.S. citizens outside of the jurisdiction of U.S. courts, regulation of the collection and use of such information will become even more difficult.

An alternative approach is to give individuals control over information about themselves; this could be achieved through a combination of physical privacy and contract. Information about an individual is frequently produced by voluntary transactions, such as purchases of goods and

---

[30] The Fair Credit Reporting Act, 15 U.S.C. sec. 1681 et seq., regulates firms that produce consumer reports—information about an individual consumer used by a firm to determine whether to extend that consumer credit, to decide whether to hire him, or to accomplish some other legitimate business purpose. The text of the act is available on-line at http://www.ftc.gov/os/statutes/fcra.htm.

[31] Although it might under some circumstances produce net costs associated with attentional privacy.

services, and thus starts out in the possession of both parties to a transaction. If one party wishes that the information should be kept confidential, that party can specify this in the terms of the initial transaction, which is, of course, often done in a variety of settings. The same information-processing technology that makes it relatively inexpensive to keep track of large numbers of facts about vast numbers of people also makes it inexpensive to keep track of the conditions under which various pieces of information can be disclosed.

A more exotic and potentially more secure approach, which may become increasingly practical as a result of technologies to be discussed in the next section, is to engage in transactions anonymously. When an individual does this, relevant information about him is never put in the control of anyone else, not even the other party to the transaction. More generally, one possibility implicit in the combination of technologies for information processing and encryption is a shift to something more like a private property/freedom of contract model for personal information—a point we will return to in the next section.

B. Encryption

Many forms of modern communication, including e-mail and cellular telephony, are physically insecure; intercepting messages delivered via these media is relatively easy. In order to protect the privacy of such communications, it is necessary to make them unreadable to those who might intercept them. This is done by encryption—scrambling a message in such a way that only someone with the proper information—the key— can unscramble it.

The most important modern development in this field is public-key encryption.[32] An individual generates a pair of keys, two long numbers having a particular mathematical relation to each other. If one key is used to scramble a message, the other is required to unscramble it. In order to make sure that messages sent to me remain confidential, all I have to do is to make sure that one of my keys (my "public key") is widely available, so that anyone who wants to send me a message can find it. The other key (my "private key") is my secret, never revealed to anyone. Anyone who has my public key can use it to encrypt a message to me. If someone else somehow steals a copy of the public key, he can send me secret messages too. But only someone with my private key, which I need never make available to any other person, can read the messages.

The same technology solves a related problem: how to prove to the recipient of my message that it is really from me. In order to sign a

---

[32] For a much longer discussion, see David Friedman, "A World of Strong Privacy: Promises and Perils of Encryption," *Social Philosophy and Policy* 13, no. 2 (Summer 1996): 212–28.

message digitally, I encrypt it with my private key.[33] The recipient de-
crypts it with my public key. The fact that what he gets is understandable
text rather than gibberish demonstrates that the message was encrypted
with the matching private key, which only I have.

A digital signature not only demonstrates, more securely than an ordinary signature, that I really sent the message, it also demonstrates it in
a way that I cannot later deny. You now possess a digitally signed
message—the original, before decryption—which you could not have
created yourself. Thus, you can prove to interested third parties that I
actually sent the message, whether or not I am willing to admit it. Furthermore, since there is no way of changing the digitally signed message
without making the signature invalid, a digital signature, unlike a physical signature, demonstrates that the message has not been altered since
it was signed.

Encryption technology also has two other privacy-enhancing applications. One is an anonymous remailer. If I wish to communicate with
someone without the fact of our communication being known, I send the
message through a third party who is in the business of relaying messages. In order to preserve my privacy from both the remailer and potential snoops, I encrypt my message with the recipient's public key, add
to it the recipient's e-mail address, encrypt the whole package with the
remailer's public key, and send the package to the remailer. The remailer
uses his private key to strip off the top layer of encryption, permitting
him to read the e-mail address and forward the message. If I am concerned that the remailer himself might want to keep track of who I am
communicating with, I can bounce the message through multiple remailers, providing each with the address of the next. Unless all of them are
jointly spying on me, my secret is safe.

The second important application is anonymous digital cash. Using
encryption, it is possible for an issuer of money to create the digital
equivalent of currency. This permits a person, by sending a message to
someone else, to transfer claims against the issuer without either person
having to know the other's identity and without the issuer having to
know the identity of either of the two parties.

Consider a world in which all of these technologies exist and are in
general use. In such a world, it is possible to do business anonymously,
but with a reputation. Your cyberspace identity is defined by your public
key. Anyone who can read messages encrypted with that public key must
have the matching private key—which is to say, must be you. The same

---

[33] The process used for digital signatures in the real world is somewhat more elaborate
than this, but the differences are not important for the purposes of this essay. A digital
signature is produced by using a hash function to generate a message digest—a string of
numbers much shorter than the message it is derived from—and then encrypting the message digest with the sender's private key. The process is much faster than encrypting the
entire message and almost as secure.

is true for anyone who can sign messages with the private key that matches that public key.

One disturbing implication of this, which I have discussed elsewhere,[34] is the possibility of criminal firms operating anonymously, but with brand-name reputation. A more attractive implication is that, in such a world, the private property model of personal information becomes a practical possibility. If, when I buy something from you, neither of us knows the identity of the other, then neither of us can obtain the relevant transactional information—the fact that a certain other person bought or sold a particular good—without the cooperation of the other person. Hence, transactional information starts as the sole property of the person whom the information is about; that person is then free to suppress it, publish it, or sell it, whichever best serves his interests.

A second feature of this world relevant to the issues we have been discussing comes from a different use of the technology of encryption: technological protection of intellectual property.[35] It may soon become practical to distribute intellectual property in a cryptographic container, that is, as part of a computer program which controls access to its contents; IBM refers to this as a "cryptolope." Use of the contents will then require a payment, perhaps in digital cash, with the container regulating the form of use. Combining such technologies with the use of intelligent software agents that can negotiate on-line contracts, we have the possibility of a world where it will be practical to treat information as something close to ordinary property. One could, for example, sell or give away transactional data about oneself in a form that could only be used for specified purposes, or only in association with specified payments.

This set of possibilities represents one part of a more general pattern. The combination of encryption, information processing, and on-line communications will permit a much more detailed control over information flows—at least on-line information flows or flows of information that originate on-line—than has been possible in the past. Thus, to take an entirely different example, there is no technical barrier preventing the creation of an e-mail program that would permit someone who wished to protect his attentional privacy to charge a price for receiving e-mail—and to simply trash, without human intervention, any messages that came without an associated payment. Nor is there any barrier to making such software distinguish among senders, receiving messages for free if they are digitally signed by people from whom the owner of the software wants to receive messages.

For a less exotic example, consider the marketing of magazine subscription lists. With current transactional technology, the fact that a

---

[34] Friedman, "A World of Strong Privacy."

[35] See David Friedman, "In Defense of Private Orderings: Comment on Julie Cohen's 'Copyright and the Jurisprudence of Self-Help,'" *Berkeley Technology Law Journal* 13, no. 3 (Fall 1998): 1151–72.

transaction took place is known to both parties. Therefore, I cannot directly control access to the fact that I am a subscriber to a magazine—as I could if the transaction had taken place on-line between anonymous parties. But a magazine may, and some do, restrict its use of that information by contract, by promising not to make its mailing list available to others or by giving the customer the choice of whether or not to have his name and address sold to other merchants. Such contractual arrangements will become easier as more and more transactions shift to digital forms, where individualized contract terms are considerably less expensive to implement than they are under conventional contracting technology.

Suppose a magazine that you subscribe to lets you decide whether or not to be on the mailing lists that it provides to others. One option is to keep your name and address private; another is to permit it to be freely sold. A third option, which many might find more attractive than either of the others, is for the magazine to sell merchants access to its subscribers without revealing the subscribers' identities. This could be done easily enough by having the magazine operate its own remailer. Information about each subscriber would be provided to merchants interested in communicating with him. Merchants would get information about what the subscriber had purchased, and any other information the magazine had that was relevant to what the subscriber would want to buy; however, merchants would not get any information that could be used to identify the subscriber. The merchant would then send a message directed at that particular unnamed subscriber, which the magazine would forward to him.

Currently, mailing lists are usually not sold, but rented for a fixed number of uses. Modern technology makes possible a more sophisticated version of such a transaction. Ultimately, we could have third-party remailers holding large amounts of information on unidentified individuals in ways that would permit merchants to search for individuals possessing combinations of characteristics that make them attractive targets for specific offers; this could be done without permitting any outsiders to link this information with a particular identity. The same result could be produced even more securely—without having to trust the remailer—by having individuals interact via anonymous on-line personas. This would make the facts of transactions public, which would help customers attract desirable offers, but would keep the identity of the realspace person corresponding to a particular cyberspace persona private.[36] One thus abandons privacy sufficiently to permit voluntary transactions, which can

---

[36] For an early and still interesting fictional exposition of the idea of separating realspace and cyberspace identities, see Vernor Vinge's novelette "True Names," included (among other places) in Vinge, *True Names and Other Dangers* (New York: Simon and Schuster, 1987). A more recent fictional effort, picturing something much closer to what we are actually likely to see in a few decades, is Marc Stiegler, *Earthweb* (New York: Simon and Schuster [Baen Books], 1999).

take the form of an offer to an unknown identity, but retains it for protection against involuntary transactions. It is hard to burgle the house of a cyberspace persona when the only identifying information you have about him is his public key and a remailer address.

With the exception of fully anonymous e-cash (which we know how to do but which nobody has so far done[37]) and cryptolopes (which are still mostly in the development stage), the fundamental technologies I have described above already exist. Public-key encryption has been implemented in a variety of forms, including a widely distributed free program.[38] Anonymous remailers currently exist. Digital signatures are widely used. But for the most part, these technologies have been applied only to text, and so have affected only that part of private and commercial life that is embodied in text messages.

As computers become more powerful and the bandwidth of digital networks increases, that situation will change. Using wide-bandwidth networks and virtual-reality software, it will eventually be possible to create the illusion of any transaction that involves only the senses of sight and sound. Further in the future, we may succeed in cracking the "dreaming problem," figuring out how our nervous system encodes the information that reaches us as sensory experience. At that point, we will no longer be limited to reproducing only two senses. We will be able to create, by the transmission of information in digital form, the illusion of any interaction that could take place in realspace.

As more and more of our activity shifts into cyberspace, encryption and related technologies make possible a degree of control over both the creation and the transfer of information that is very much greater than that which we now have. Given this, the property justification for privacy, rejected in Section II, comes back into the argument.

What about the argument against privacy—that one reason I may wish to conceal information about myself is in order to defraud my trading partner? This becomes a less serious problem on-line, where encryption technology restricts parties to voluntary transactions. You can, of course, conceal information about yourself if that information is under your control, and you can attempt to defraud me with false information. But I can refuse to transact with you unless you agree to reveal the relevant information in verifiable form; if you decline, that fact signals something about the information that you are keeping private.

---

[37] There have been experiments with e-cash. Most notable of these experiments was that performed by the Mark Twain Bank of St. Louis, which worked with David Chaum, the cryptographer responsible for many of the fundamental ideas in the field. The currency was semianonymous, meaning that the issuing bank could identify one party to the transaction if it had the cooperation of the other.

[38] PGP (Pretty Good Privacy) is a freeware program (also available in a commercial version) for doing public-key encryption and decryption, and for keeping track of other people's public keys. It is available from, among other places, http://web.mit.edu/network/pgp.html.

C. Surveillance devices—toward a transparent society

While technological developments in on-line communication are moving us toward a high level of privacy in cyberspace, developments in surveillance technology may be moving realspace in precisely the opposite direction, for two reasons. One is that surveillance devices provide an inexpensive and effective way of reducing crime, one that is becoming increasingly popular. The other is that, as these devices become smaller and cheaper, it becomes more difficult to prevent surveillance. We may be moving toward a world in which video cameras with the size and aerodynamic characteristics of a mosquito are widely available.

Physicist and science fiction author David Brin, on whose book *The Transparent Society*[39] this section is largely based, argues that in the future, privacy will no longer be an option for most people. We will be limited to two choices: a world in which those in power know everything that they want to know about everyone, and a world in which everyone knows everything he wants to know about everyone. Brin, not surprisingly, prefers the latter. He envisages a future with video cameras everywhere—including every police station—all generating images readily accessible, via some future equivalent of the World Wide Web, to anyone who is interested.

If Brin is correct, physical privacy in realspace will vanish. Individuals will protect their informational privacy in the same ways in which people in primitive societies without physical privacy protect their informational privacy: by adopting patterns of speech and behavior that reveal as little as possible of what they actually believe and intend. This will represent a substantial rent-seeking cost, which must be added to the rent-seeking cost of individuals processing enormous quantities of public information in order to learn things about all those with whom they expect to interact.

Two qualifications are worth making to Brin's picture. The first is that he is assuming that the technology of surveillance is going to outrun the technology of physical privacy, that the bugs will beat the screens, that video mosquitoes will not fall victim to automated dragonflies. While he may be correct, it is hard to predict in advance how the balance will turn out. We might end up in a world where legal surveillance is cheap and easy, but where illegal surveillance is difficult; this would give us the choice of how much privacy we would have.

One possible compromise is for people to have privacy in private spaces, but not in public spaces. This would represent a further development along the same lines as computerized databases. What you do in public spaces, like the public records produced by your life,[40] has always been

---

[39] David Brin, *The Transparent Society: Will Technology Force Us to Choose Between Privacy and Freedom?* (Reading, MA: Addison-Wesley, 1998).

[40] There are a few exceptions created by the law, such as the rules under which a record of the criminal conviction of a minor may sometimes be expunged. (In Florida, for example, such a record may be expunged when the minor reaches twenty-six years of age. See Fla. Stat. chap. 943.0515, on the World Wide Web at http://www.leg.state.fl.us/citizen/documents/statutes/1994/CHAPTER_943.html.)

public in a legal sense. A video surveillance network, coupled to computers running pattern-recognition software and sorting and saving the resulting data, would simply put that public information in a form that would permit other people to find and use it.

A second qualification is that although the technology that Brin anticipates will produce information, it might not always be verifiable information. Suppose I am conducting an adulterous affair. My suspicious wife can use a video mosquito to obtain video footage of me in flagrante delicto with my paramour. That footage may be of very limited use in court, though, since it could have been produced just as easily if I were not conducting an affair—using video-editing software instead of a camera. To the extent that modern technology makes it easy to forge evidence, evidence without a provable pedigree becomes worthless. It may be easy to get a mosquito camera into my bedroom, but it is somewhat more difficult to also get a reliable witness in there to prove that that camera really took that film.[41]

Encryption technology provides one approach to solving this problem. Conceivably, a manufacturer could build a sealed, tamperproof camera, complete with its own private key. The camera would digitally sign and time-stamp[42] its films as it produced them, making it possible to prove at a later date that those particular films were created by that camera, at that time, and have not since been edited.

One difficulty with this approach is that a camera records not facts about the outside world, but facts about the pattern of light that comes into its lens. To defeat such a camera, I could build a lens cap capable of generating computer-synthesized holographic images. I would then put the lens cap on the camera and play whatever I want the camera to see; it would see the images and sign them, making them appear authentic. As this example suggests, figuring out the implications of technologies that do not yet exist, or that exist only in primitive forms, is not a trivial problem.

IV. Conclusion

In Section II of this essay, I sketched out an economic analysis of privacy. The conclusion was that increasing the ability of individuals to

---

[41] A human solution to the problem of forged data was proposed by Robert Heinlein in *Stranger in a Strange Land*: a body of specially trained "fair witnesses," whose job it was to observe accurately and report honestly. See Heinlein, *Stranger in a Strange Land* (New York: Putnam, 1961).

[42] One way of time-stamping a digital document is to calculate a *hash* of that document—a much shorter string of digits derived from the document in a fashion that is difficult to reverse—and post the hash in some publicly observable place. The document is still secret, since it cannot be derived from the hash. The existence of the hash at a given date can later be used to prove that the document from which it was derived—in our case, a digital video—existed at the time that the hash was posted. The fact that the hash function cannot easily be reversed means that one cannot post a random hash and then later create a suitable document that would be a source of that particular hash.

control information about themselves had both desirable and undesirable effects, making it unclear whether, on net, we were better off with more or less privacy. One argument that I considered and rejected was that increased privacy rights—at least over information that originates with the person that it is about—are efficient because they make it possible to convert such information into private property and then allocate it efficiently through market transactions.

That argument is harder to reject when applied to the information technology of a few decades hence. It may become possible to create transactional information in such a way that each piece of information originates in the possession of a single person. It may also become possible, given the much lower transaction costs of on-line transactions, to then use private transactions to allocate information to its highest-valued users. If these things occur, we would end up with a world in which information that is generated by cyberspace events—on-line transactions—is characterized both by a high degree of control by those whom the information concerns and by an efficient market for its creation and allocation.

There is no reason to expect the same to be true in realspace. If anything, the combination of improved surveillance technology and improved information-processing technology is likely to make increasingly large amounts of realspace information about everyone inexpensively available to everyone else. We then have both the advantages and the disadvantages of a low-privacy environment. Individuals cannot hide unattractive facts about their doings in realspace from those whom they transact with, which makes many forms of commercial and social fraud impractical. The cost of privacy becomes the cost of behaving in a way that reveals as little as possible about oneself.

If realspace is public and cyberspace is private, the amount of privacy that individuals have depends critically on the importance of each type of space, and on the links between the two. It does me no good to protect my messages with strong encryption if a mosquito camera is watching me type the unencrypted original. In extreme versions of this scenario, versions where both Brin's vision of realspace and my vision of cyberspace are realized in full, privacy depends critically on mechanisms for computer input that cannot be observed from the outside. The low-tech version of this is touch-typing under a very secure hood; the high-tech version is a link directly from mind to machine. If some such method makes it possible to protect cyberspace privacy from realspace prying, the balance between public and private then depends on how much of what we do is done in cyberspace and how much in realspace. It is going to be an interesting century.

Law, Santa Clara University

THE PRIORITY OF PRIVACY FOR MEDICAL INFORMATION

By Judith Wagner DeCew

I. Introduction: The Value of Privacy

Individuals care about and guard their privacy intensely in many areas. With respect to patient medical records, people are exceedingly concerned about privacy protection, because they recognize that health care generates the most sensitive sorts of personal information. In an age of advancing technology, with the switch from paper medical files to massive computer databases, privacy protection for medical information poses a dramatic challenge. Given high-speed computers and Internet capabilities, as well as other advanced communications technologies, the potential for abuse is much greater than ever before. At every stage in the process of collection and storage, dangers can arise, including entry errors, improper access, exploitation, and unauthorized disclosure. Secondary use and aggregation of data are all far easier, faster, and less expensive, and thus pose additional threats to an individual's control over the disposition of medical information.

As a moral philosopher, I have often defended the view that privacy acts as a shield to protect us in various ways, and that its value lies in the freedom and independence it provides for us.[1] Privacy shields us not only from interference and pressures that preclude self-expression and the development of relationships, but also from intrusions and pressures arising from others' access to our persons and details about us. Threats of information leaks, as well as threats of control over our bodies, our activities, and our power to make our own choices, give rise to fears that we are being scrutinized, judged, ridiculed, pressured, coerced, or otherwise taken advantage of by others. Protection of privacy enhances and ensures the freedom from such scrutiny, pressure to conform, and exploitation. We require this insulation that privacy provides so that as self-conscious beings we can maintain our self-respect, develop our self-esteem, and increase our ability to form a coherent identity and set of values, as well as our ability to form varied and complex relationships with others. Thus privacy is a shield protecting us from prejudice, pressure to conform, and the judgment of others.

---

[1] For a full defense of this view, see Judith Wagner DeCew, *In Pursuit of Privacy: Law, Ethics, and the Rise of Technology* (Ithaca, NY: Cornell University Press, 1997).

Loss of privacy leaves us vulnerable and threatened. We are likely to be more conformist, less individualistic, and less creative. Loss of a private sphere can be stifling. In the context of medical information, the possibilities of exploiting, aggregating, or misusing this information, including genetic testing results, drug test data, mental health records, information on pregnancy, and results from tests for sexually transmitted diseases and HIV status, to name just a few, make it obvious how important it is to preserve the protection that privacy affords individuals. In such cases, the potential harms from disclosure range from embarrassment, loss of self-esteem, social stigma, isolation, and psychological distress to economic loss and discrimination in such areas as employment, child custody, insurance, housing, and immigration status. Given these concerns, it is necessary to determine when and how much to defend privacy for medical information in an age of electronic medical records.

In this essay I examine three alternative public policy approaches to the protection of medical records and data: reliance on governmental guidelines, the use of corporate self-regulation, and my own hybrid view on how to maintain a presumption in favor of privacy with respect to medical information. I maintain that on this hybrid account, privacy is safeguarded as vigorously and comprehensively as possible, without sacrificing the benefits of new information technology in medicine. None of the three models I examine are unproblematic, yet it is crucial to weigh the strengths and weaknesses of these alternative approaches. As others have noted, "[h]itherto, the limited debate related to [electronic patient records] has tended to polarize between, on the one hand, those who see the health care sector as one big family within which impediments to data flow would be considered a detriment to effective patient care, and on the other hand those who see clinician-patient confidentiality as an absolute."[2] I shall defend the view that it is indeed possible to be a staunch privacy advocate without being an absolutist who believes that privacy trumps all social goals. It is possible to defend the priority of privacy and yet recognize that sometimes privacy should give way to other concerns.

Note first that at least one poll shows that Americans do not believe that they have adequate privacy protection over how medical information about them is used and circulated. Eighty-five percent of those questioned put a far higher priority on confidentiality of medical records than on providing universal coverage, reducing paperwork, and gaining better data for medical research on disease and treatments.[3]

---

[2] Michael Rigby, Ian Hamilton, and Ronald Draper, "Finding Ethical Principles and Practical Guidelines for the Controlled Flow of Patient Data" (paper presented at an international conference on "Electronic Patient Records in Medical Practice," Rotterdam, The Netherlands, October 7, 1998).

[3] Alan Westin et al., "Health Care Information Privacy: A Survey of the Public and Leaders" (survey conducted for Equifax, Inc., 1993), 23, cited in Lawrence O. Gostin, "Health Information Privacy," *Cornell Law Review* 80, no. 3 (March 1995): 454.

Second, it is worth noting that different perspectives on privacy in medicine may depend on existing health care systems. Perhaps there is more concern about privacy among individuals in the United States—where people still fear the possible loss of medical coverage, despite recent legislation intended to prevent such loss—than in countries with guaranteed national health care.

II. MEDICAL RECORDS AND ACCESS: THE SCOPE OF THE PROBLEM

Although some physicians maintain their paper files and may be resistant to the use of computers, it is clear that electronic medical records have largely replaced paper copies, and will continue to do so at an exponential rate. While paper records and copying machines have never been particularly secure, computerized records introduce new risks and new opportunities for abuse. Both the quantity and the nature of medical data have increased dramatically in recent years. In the United States, physicians and other primary health care providers such as hospitals and health maintenance organizations (HMOs) keep computer databases of the health information of individual patients. Increasingly, there are also statewide, regional, and national computer files of health information. There are, in addition, population-wide health databases that include information on genetic data and communicable diseases such as AIDS and tuberculosis, as well as "information on medical cost reimbursement programs such as Medicaid or Medicare, hospital discharges, health status, health policy research, utilization and cost effectiveness, specific diseases such as cancer, and immunization registries."[4] Most of these databases are controlled by federal departments, including the Department of Defense and the Veterans Administration.

Moreover, there are health database organizations (HDOs) that operate under the authority of the U.S. government; other HDOs operate under the authority of private or not-for-profit organizations. HDOs have access to massive databases of health information, and their central mission is the public release of data and of analyses performed on the data. These organizations usually serve specific geographic areas and hold comprehensive health status data on all persons in a defined population. HDOs acquire some data from individual health records currently kept by physicians and hospitals. They also collect information from many secondary sources: financial transactions (information on which is itself collected from private insurance companies and government programs); public health surveillance and tracking systems; epidemiologic, clinical, behavioral, and health services research; surveys conducted by government, academics, and private foundations; and numerous other data sources. The data collected may be general information, or it may specifically

---

[4] Gostin, "Health Information Privacy," 464–65, footnotes omitted.

identify a person by name or by some other type of identification.[5] Health database files include information on illness (especially communicable diseases), medications, test results, and even genetic blueprints from blood samples. Moreover, health agencies now gather behavioral data on "alcohol and other drug use, seat-belt and bicycle helmet use, smoking, exercise, and sexual practices. To assess environmental risks, health agencies also collect such data as pediatric blood lead levels, and the incidence of cancers, birth defects, and pulmonary diseases."[6]

Medical data is often stored in a form termed "personally identifiable." This refers to information that includes any uniquely identifiable characteristic such as a name, Social Security number, fingerprint, or genetic link. Some data may contain no such unique identifier, but may include sufficient information on age, sex, race, and other personal information to make connection with a specific individual possible; such data is thus viewed as personally identifiable data as well. All other stored data is viewed as "anonymous." However, there is a major difficulty in determining how to classify data that is not personally identifiable, but which is linked to a named person with a confidential code. If this code were somehow accessed, that data, which was previously anonymous, would become personally identifiable.

New computer technology makes rapid access, transmission, and even deletion of this mass of information fast, efficient, inexpensive, and relatively easy because the information can be downloaded and viewed from almost any location, often without detection. Because electronic records can be accessed in combination with other databases, and in diverse geographic locations, linking capacity makes it possible for data to be compared, matched, and aggregated so that even data with neither personal identifiers nor a confidential code can be linked with other data to get a profile of an identifiable person or population. The rapid and sophisticated ways that data can be updated, changed, and configured with no restrictions on its dissemination and use, combined with the difficulties of getting rid of data that is obsolete or inaccurate, make privacy concerns for medical information appear virtually intractable.[7] It is no surprise that people are becoming ever more distrustful of computerized medical records.

Beyond the problems posed by expanded electronic capabilities, there are additional concerns compounding the privacy problems associated

[5] Ibid., 464.

[6] Lawrence O. Gostin, Zita Lazzarini, Verla S. Neslund, and Michael T. Osterholm, "The Public Health Information Infrastructure: A National Review of the Law on Health Information Privacy," *Journal of the American Medical Association* 275, no. 24 (June 26, 1996): 1921.

[7] See James Moor, "Towards a Theory of Privacy in the Information Age," *Computers and Society* 27, no. 3 (September 1997): 27–32; and Charles Culver, James Moor, William Duerfeldt, Marshall Kapp, and Mark Sullivan, "Privacy," *Professional Ethics* 3, nos. 3 and 4 (Fall/Winter 1994): 4–25, for descriptions of the problems and for some general guidelines for establishing privacy protection guidelines.

with medical data. First, technological advances allowing easy access to such data make it difficult to determine who is the "owner" of the computer record. Many find it obvious that the patient owns his or her record and should continue to be named as owner. Others urge, however, that in an electronic world, especially when some data is compiled anonymously, privacy protection is needed from wherever the data may flow, without the designation of an owner with privacy rights.

Second, consider that access to most of these databases is virtually unlimited, and yet it is widely recognized that the risks of fraud and abuse of patient medical records come not from outside hackers, but mainly from those described as "authorized" users. Consequently, the perhaps obvious tactic of restricting access to medical records only to those with authorization is by itself unlikely to provide adequate safeguards.

Third, in the United States the legal protection of informational privacy in medicine relies heavily on a relationship view of doctor-patient confidentiality that is outdated in an era of HMOs and group practices. Most patients see a wide range of nurse practitioners, nurses, nutritionists, therapists, and specialists as well as their team of primary care physicians. Thus, while legal protection for informational privacy has not generally been as controversial as protection of privacy in other areas (such as the *Griswold* line of U.S. constitutional cases[8]), existing legal guidelines are nevertheless inadequate for medical data technology.

Fourth, note that most of the legislation that has been proposed in an attempt to provide some privacy protection for medical information in the United States forms a patchwork of guidelines with no consistency and many unfilled gaps. Such legislation often includes vague language giving health care professionals broad authority to disclose information without the patient's consent for purposes of treatment, reimbursement, public health, emergencies, medical research, and law enforcement (including warrants).

III. Governmental Guidelines

It is now well known that there is a major lack of informational-privacy protection in the United States compared to the detailed privacy guide-

---

[8] In *Griswold v. Connecticut*, 381 U.S. 479 (1965), the Supreme Court first announced and recognized a constitutional right to privacy when it overturned the convictions of the director of Planned Parenthood in Connecticut and a physician from Yale Medical School who violated a statute that banned the disbursement of contraceptive-related information, instruction, and medical advice to married persons. This privacy right, in some ways distinct from informational-privacy protection in tort and Fourth Amendment law, has since been invoked in a variety of other cases concerning decisions about marriage, family, and lifestyle. For example, it was cited in *Loving v. Virginia*, 388 U.S. 1 (1967), as a justification for overturning a Virginia statute that banned interracial marriage; in *Stanley v. Georgia*, 394 U.S. 557 (1969), as a major reason for allowing the possession of obscene matter in one's home; in *Eisenstadt v. Baird*, 405 U.S. 438 (1972), as a justification to allow the distribution of contraceptives; and in *Roe v. Wade*, 410 U.S. 113 (1973), as a reason to permit abortions at some points during a pregnancy.

lines endorsed by the European Union.[9] These privacy guidelines, currently being implemented by members of the European Union, were originally proposed to restrict carefully the collection and dissemination of personal data. These directives require companies to register all databases containing personal information, require that subjects be told and give consent before their personal data can be collected or used, and require that any information gained for one purpose not be used for any other purpose unless the subject consents to the sharing of the information. The guidelines also prevent the transfer of information from one country to another unless the latter country also has adequate protection of records, and they do not allow the collection of data on race, ethnic origin, political or religious affiliation, health status, or sexual orientation.[10] Many Europeans are astounded that there is no comparable protection or similar plan pending in the United States. Unfortunately, American corporations, far from embracing these sound ideas, are fearful that the rules will hinder their routine use of computer data. However, many European countries are threatening to prohibit business transactions with American companies that cannot ensure protections similar to those found in Europe. Thus the profit motive may actually boost these types of privacy protections in the United States.

Some believe that this American fear of regulating data is unwarranted. It has been argued that Germany's experience with careful control of electronic databases undermines the claims, made by U.S. corporate officials, that strict privacy laws will place unacceptable burdens on businesses. Today Germany is cited as having one of Europe's most successful direct-marketing industries, despite laws that forbid both collecting personal information on anyone without prior notification and withholding that information from the individual if he or she wants to review it. The German system also requires businesses of twenty or more employees to name an official to oversee the gathering of personal data. There are state and federal data directors as well.[11]

Sweden, which in 1973 was the first country to pass a national privacy law, provides a somewhat different example. It has a centralized govern-

---

[9] See DeCew, *In Pursuit of Privacy*, 151–52.

[10] John Markoff, "Europe's Plans to Protect Privacy Worry Business," *New York Times*, April 11, 1991, A1; and Larry Tye, "EC May Force New Look at Privacy," *Boston Globe*, September 7, 1993, 10. An excellent summary of the European approach is supplied in Paul M. Schwartz, "European Data Protection Law and Restrictions on International Data Flows," *Iowa Law Review* 80, no. 3 (March 1995): 471–96. On the domestic approaches in Germany and Sweden, see Colin J. Bennett, *Regulating Privacy: Data Protection and Public Policy in Europe and the United States* (Ithaca, NY: Cornell University Press, 1992). See also Charles E. H. Franklin, ed., *Business Guide to Privacy and Data Protection Legislation* (Dordrecht, Netherlands: Kluwer Law International, 1996), where the Council of Europe's guidelines, the guidelines of the Organisation for Economic Cooperation and Development (OECD), and the laws of several European nations are summarized and explained, with relevant portions translated.

[11] Larry Tye, "No Private Lives: German System Puts a Lid on Data," *Boston Globe*, September 7, 1993, 1.

ment file with the information that marketers want, and the file is used by about 9 percent of Sweden's direct-mail companies.[12] Sweden's system also includes a constitutional right for any individual to see what is in his or her own archive or file. Such a centralized database could be augmented with the formation of national privacy boards staffed with experts who have considered the issues from consumer, business, medical, political, philosophical, and economic viewpoints. These boards could oversee regulations such as those suggested by the European Union.

There is a common theme in these different approaches by the European Union, Germany, and Sweden. Each echoes a dominant thesis that I endorse: the initial *presumption* must be that privacy protection is important and that guidelines are essential. Moreover, each plan helps individuals retain control over information about themselves by providing them with knowledge about the data banks and access to the information, and by requiring individuals' permission and consent for collection or transfer of data about them.

As noted above, the European Union guidelines bar the collection of data on health status. Consider, however, the implications of applying these guidelines to medical records. Presumably there would be centralized medical data files, with the potential benefits of easier access to medical histories. This is the type of program that was proposed in the United States by the Clinton administration and Secretary of Health and Human Services (HHS) Donna Shalala; the plan required the use of a universal health care card. What was actually enacted in 1996 was the Kassebaum-Kennedy health insurance reform bill. The "Administrative Simplification" clause of this bill requires the creation of a national electronic data-collection and data-transfer system for personal health care information, and of a computer code as a "unique health identifier" to trace each citizen's medical history.

There are certainly benefits to such a program, including quality assurance in health care, monitoring of fraud and abuses, the ability to use tracking to evaluate access to health services, and lower health care costs. For patients who move or for other reasons change health care providers, centralized databases of medical records can also lead to better individualized medical care (for example, by decreasing the likelihood of problematic drug interactions and allergic responses, or by helping to track diseases more effectively in order to enhance prompt diagnosis and treatment). Indeed, without appropriate sharing of information, patients are at risk for uninformed and suboptimal care. Data can also aid consumers in making more informed choices regarding health care plans and providers. In addition, medical records in centralized databases aid society as a whole. They are particularly useful for medical labs and research on epidemiology, disease prevention, and treatments aimed at reducing un-

---

[12] Ibid., 10.

necessary mortality. Public health is enhanced when information allows health problems to be identified and publicized, and allows funding decisions to be well informed. Such a centralized data system is potentially even more of a boon to insurance companies, pharmaceutical companies, biotechnology companies, and employers. Moreover, if the European Union guidelines were applied to such a centralized system, they could require that individuals be told and give consent for their data to be collected in the database, bar the use of the data for any purpose other than that for which it was gathered, allow individuals access to their records, and so on. This would maintain the advantages of a presumption favoring privacy protection and individual control over their medical information.

Yet the "Administrative Simplification" clause of the Kassebaum-Kennedy bill is under attack,[13] and hearings by an HHS panel on the "unique health identifier" began in July 1998. Part of the reason for the uproar is that the U.S. program does not currently include any of the privacy safeguards endorsed by the European Union. Thus, for example, there is at this point no regulation barring the recent call by the Centers for Disease Control and Prevention (CDC) to enhance its HIV surveillance by tracking how and where the deadly virus strikes and by requiring reports of the names of all those who test positive for HIV. The CDC has always relied on the reporting of names for diseases such as syphilis and tuberculosis. With this new database, the CDC could link cases of the AIDS virus with cases in other databases (for example, to respond quickly to an outbreak of an HIV-related illness). However, critics of the program worry about the stigma and discrimination associated with the disease, and the complete lack of privacy protection—or even coding of the data—to protect anonymity for the individuals involved. These critics cite the likelihood that instead of promoting better health care, a program requiring a government list of names will discourage people from being tested for HIV, leading to a loss of lives rather than achieving the goal of saving lives.[14]

Moreover, there are serious disadvantages to storing medical information in a centralized database system with federal guidelines. One worry is that whether the individual health identifier is a Social Security number or a less traceable number, it will make it "even easier for [medical] claims information and pharmacy data to be linked to other data bases—like tax records, voter registrations, motor vehicle data and credit card records."[15] The linkage capacities of technological networks are already well established.

[13] Beverly Woodward, "Intrusion in the Name of 'Simplification,'" *Washington Post*, August 15, 1996, A19; and "Medical Identifier Hearings to Begin," *Boston Globe*, July 20, 1998, A5.

[14] Louise D. Palmer, "States Urged to Use Names in HIV Reports," *Boston Globe*, July 19, 1998, A1.

[15] Judy Foreman, "Your Health History—Up for Grabs?" *Boston Globe*, July 20, 1998, C1.

A related worry with this centralization of such sensitive information is that it places too much power in a single public agency. Although a statutory right to see one's files can place a check on the government, having *access* to information does not guarantee *control* over the information. Thus it is still necessary to have procedures for those who find erroneous information or want data eliminated from their record. Furthermore, even with the addition of careful guidelines for protecting privacy, other concerns remain, including questions about who or what group would oversee enforcement of the guidelines and how effective such enforcement could be.

In the United States there is a new National Committee on Health Information Privacy, funded by the CDC and the Carter Center, and chaired by Lawrence Gostin of the Georgetown University Law Center. It has recommended the adoption of some level of privacy protection, and has been drafting a model statute which incorporates some of the European guidelines. Thus it is a welcome attempt to find a compromise between the free flow of medical information advocated by public health practitioners and researchers, and the absolute privacy protection defended by those who believe that virtually all data collection and disclosure must be severely limited. Recommendations suggested include the development of state or regional data protection committees to review and correct data, to ensure that identifiable health data is collected only for "important" health purposes and disclosed only for purposes consistent with the original collection, to develop principles concerning consent for the use of information, to provide individuals with enough control to review and correct their data, and to oversee data protection and security systems such as audit trails and encryption.[16] Nevertheless, most of these regulations are intended to apply only to personally identifiable data, and hence the Committee acknowledges that access to most data would be granted to many, and thus, through database links and aggregation, privacy would be compromised. In sum, the European directives are viewed as placing too much emphasis on privacy protection. Gostin and others suggest that a unique health identifier, distinct from one's Social Security number and used only for the health care system, could adequately protect patient privacy. They urge further that ethical arguments for the importance of privacy protection are balanced by equally compelling arguments supporting a more efficient health information system. Most specifically, Gostin has allowed that "one of the burdens of achieving cost effective and accessible [health] care is a loss of privacy."[17] The Commit-

[16] Lawrence O. Gostin, "Making Tradeoffs Between the Collective Good of Human Health and the Individual Good of Personal Privacy" (paper presented at an international conference on "Electronic Patient Records in Medical Practice," Rotterdam, The Netherlands, October 6, 1998).

[17] Gostin, "Health Information Privacy," 515–16.

tee's suggestions are welcome for advancing the debate, but may well allow too much privacy to be sacrificed for administrative efficiency.

IV. CORPORATE SELF-REGULATION

The European Union, German, and Swedish approaches to privacy protection for most personal data tend to emphasize federally mandated regulations and review boards. The U.S. Kassebaum-Kennedy bill actually requires such a national system for medical records, but it has not yet been implemented. A second alternative focuses on corporate self-regulation, and this appears to be the model currently defended by the Clinton administration for computer and Internet technology, if not for medical records.

At a conference in May 1998, Ira Magaziner, special assistant to President Clinton, wryly observed that "government understands enough to know it doesn't understand developing technology."[18] Current U.S. policy in the communications field, he argued, treats privacy protection as a way of empowering people to protect themselves, for example, through the use of filtering software on computers that gives users choices, rather than mandating federal guidelines that deprive individuals of choice. Privacy guidelines, on the current view, (1) should be led by industry and the private sector, (2) should be market-driven and not regulated, and (3) should maximize consumer choice as well as governmental restraint. According to Magaziner, the U.S. government is generally too slow to make or change policies quickly enough to keep pace with the rapid changes in new information and communications technologies. Thus, he argued, when government does act, its role should be minimal and transparent. Magaziner envisioned the use of corporate and consumer pressure to develop privacy "Codes of Conduct," which could then be backed by some sort of enforcement agencies (though it was unspecified whether these agencies would be led by corporations or consumers). Nevertheless, the end result of his proposals is a defense of the private management of the Internet and other communications technologies.

Consider how this second model would apply in the field of medicine. Presumably it would reflect what is largely happening in the United States at this time: hospitals, health maintenance organizations, and insurance companies are basically left to regulate themselves in their handling of patient medical records. Although such private self-regulation has the potential benefit of enhancing patient choice over what data is collected and how it is stored, used, and accessed, the reality is that individual control is minimal. Usually personal medical files can be viewed

---

[18] Ira Magaziner, remarks made at conference, "ACM Policy '98," Washington D.C., May 10–12, 1998.

not only by doctors and nurses, but also by insurers, self-insured employers, and law enforcement officials, to name a few. In most systems there are virtually no patient controls over how personal health information may be used and disseminated.

While consumer activism has put considerable pressure on health organizations to publicize their privacy guidelines, there is no consistency, uniformity, or certainty of privacy protection. Indeed, medical data is largely unprotected in the United States, and what few protective measures there are form a complex patchwork of different regulations developed at the federal level, in different states, and in different organizations. For example, about thirty states currently require the reporting of names of individuals who test positive for HIV, about a half-dozen additional states are developing code systems to report that information, and the remaining states do not make such reports.[19] Even the National Committee on Health Information Privacy continues this patchwork approach in its recommendations by endorsing regional enforcement of its proposed privacy guidelines. There is no coherent policy on privacy and medical records, and "U.S. citizens often have no legal recourse if they are harmed by inappropriate disclosure of their medical records."[20] Health organizations and insurers may welcome the freedom from external regulations that they enjoy when the privacy of medical data is protected via a corporate self-regulation system. However, it seems clear that from the patient's point of view, the disadvantages of such a system far outweigh the advantages.

It may well seem, then, that federally mandated privacy guidelines are preferable to corporate self-regulation and will best serve our interests in enhancing privacy protection in an age of advancing technology. Moreover, as Marc Rotenberg of the Electronic Privacy Information Center (EPIC) has pointed out, studies show that the public is becoming more and more skeptical about the self-regulation model.[21] Nevertheless, U.S. reaction to the "unique health identifier" demonstrates that many people are equally distrustful of giving government more power, and perhaps more access to data, through the federal-regulation model. I shall therefore give an illustration defending my view that it is indeed possible to protect privacy stringently in the face of advancing information technologies. My illustration provides solid reasons to endorse a hybrid approach that requires some federal regulations in order to mandate the presumptive importance of privacy protection, but allows for individual choice within those guidelines. Nevertheless, there are difficulties with this approach for medical information as well.

[19] Palmer, "States Urged to Use Names in HIV Reports," 1.
[20] Don E. Detmer and Elaine B. Steen, "Shoring Up Protection of Personal Health Data," *Issues in Science and Technology* 12, no. 4 (Summer 1996): 76.
[21] Marc Rotenberg, e-mail correspondence with author, 1998.

V. A Hybrid Approach: Dynamic Negotiation

In my book, *In Pursuit of Privacy: Law, Ethics, and the Rise of Technology,* and elsewhere, I have used caller identification, or "caller ID," as an illustration to defend my approach to privacy protection in different technological contexts.[22] As is now well known, caller ID allows telephone callers to be identified by their names and phone numbers to whomever they call, even if the callers' numbers are unlisted. It seems clear that the service needs to be at least minimally regulated at the federal level rather than the local level, perhaps with worldwide guidelines to follow. This is necessary in part to coordinate the interstate and international calling patterns of consumers and businesses, as well as to harmonize the competing claims of individual privacy and commercial viability. Local and state regulations involving caller ID do not protect privacy uniformly, and have already led consumers to become frustrated or annoyed with a patchwork of different rules and options. Such frustration will only hinder the success of the technology. However, any federal or international guidelines must be supplemented to satisfy both the callers and the called parties in the privacy debate over caller ID. This can be accomplished in a way that allows people to negotiate dynamically the degree of privacy that they wish to sacrifice or maintain.[23]

Let me briefly describe how a system of dynamic negotiation would work with caller ID and then discuss such a system's implications for medical records. Initially, all phone subscribers' lines would, by default, block the release of the caller's number. Subscribers could choose to release their number on a per-call basis by dialing an unblocking code. Thus far, this is what is called per-line blocking. However, phones with caller ID displays could also be set up to refuse calls automatically when the number has not been provided by the caller. When this sort of anonymous call is attempted, the phone would not ring. The thwarted caller would hear a short recorded message explaining that to complete the call, the originating phone number must be furnished; this message would then instruct the caller what code to dial in order to give out the number. If the caller then chooses not to give out the number, the call would not be completed and the caller would not be charged. Thus, a caller would have the chance to decide whether a call is important enough to be worth surrendering his or her anonymity. This solution preserves choice and ensures privacy. Callers can control when to give out their numbers; call recipients can screen and refuse anonymous calls. The system remains voluntary. Through a dynamic and interactive process, both callers and

[22] DeCew, *In Pursuit of Privacy,* 159–60.
[23] The term "dynamic negotiation" was introduced by Ross E. Mitchell and first appeared in Ross E. Mitchell and Judith Wagner DeCew, "Dynamic Negotiation in the Privacy Wars," *Technology Review* 97, no. 8 (November/December 1994): 70–71.

call recipients are allowed to determine the extent to which their privacy is compromised.

Most callers, of course, will want to release their number when calling friends and associates. If such calls dominate their use of the phone, they might choose to change the default on their line so that their number is automatically released unless they dial in a blocking code. Thus, a dynamic-negotiation system may well lead many people to change from per-line to per-call blocking—precisely what the phone companies and the U.S. Federal Communications Commission (FCC) favor. Under a dynamic-negotiation system, however, when these customers change their default setting, they will know what they are choosing and why; they will be actively consenting to give out their numbers as a matter of course. Most businesses will want to take all calls, whether numbers are provided or not. Certain establishments, however, might want to reject anonymous calls—for example, florists or pizzerias that want incoming numbers for verification in order to avoid filling bogus orders. Most callers will happily unblock their numbers when such a business asks them to do so.

Some display units that can be purchased for use with caller ID are already able to reject anonymous calls, but they do not yet enable the dynamic-negotiation system described above. Rarely does a message tell callers how to complete a call. Moreover, with these caller ID units, every call, whether accepted or not, is considered to have been answered and is charged to the caller. However, a call that is rejected because of its anonymity should entail no charge. Solving this problem would require that the call be intercepted by the phone company's central office switchboard before it reaches the recipient's line. The technology for implementing dynamic negotiation for caller ID is already available. To begin this implementation, the FCC need only amend its 1996 ruling that merely allowed per-line blocking; privacy could be given presumptive protection via an amendment *mandating* per-line blocking as the *default* and requiring the necessary recordings and call interceptions. With this system of dynamic negotiation as the national norm, privacy concerns associated with caller ID would become self-regulating. The government need not micromanage the details, but neither can it be passive and allow total self-regulation as long as the telephone marketplace continues to be unwilling or unable to move to this position of dynamic negotiation without the government intervening.[24]

This system of dynamic negotiation can be applied to other telecommunications technologies, such as electronic mail.[25] There are, moreover,

---

[24] Such governmental regulation would be unnecessary if the telephone corporations implemented and enforced the system described here. Thus far, there has been no such corporate coordination or cooperation.

[25] With traditional mail, people have always had the right, and the ability, to send anonymous correspondence. Delivery of the envelope requires neither that the letter be signed

applications for Internet use being developed along similar lines (for example, software allowing interactive choices throughout one's use of the Internet). Clearly the technology for such systems is available.

It is obvious that dynamic negotiation cannot be applied to protecting privacy for medical records in either a simple or straightforward way. Only the traditional doctor-patient relationship, now relatively rare, mirrors the relationship of parties to a telephone conversation. Nevertheless, we can consider a system that incorporates and applies some of the main principles of dynamic negotiation to protection of medical records, and then can assess some of the advantages and disadvantages of this approach for medical information.

Dynamic negotiation would require federal guidelines mandating the priority of privacy, so that the collection, storage, and use of medical records would require maximal privacy protection as the default. Thus, as with caller ID, the presumption of privacy would be mandated; the prevailing assumption would be that one can get confidential medical care and that others' access to one's medical data would be limited. This idea is hardly new. As others have pointed out, "Physician commitment to confidentiality enables a patient to share sensitive personal information and increases the likelihood that the physician will have complete data on which to base clinical judgments. This improves the chances for accurate diagnosis and better clinical outcomes. At a more fundamental level, some patients will not even seek care unless they believe that a health care professional or organization will maintain confidentiality."[26]

The theoretical principles underlying governmental privacy guidelines would include commitments to preserving anonymity of data when at all possible, establishing fair procedures for obtaining data, requiring that proposed collections of data have both relevance and purpose, and specifying the legitimate conditions of authorized access. These principles would also demand commitments to developing systematic methods for maintaining data quality, mandating that data collected for one purpose not be used for another purpose or shared with others without the consent of the subject, and limiting the retention time of data to what is necessary for the original purpose of the data collection. Following these principles may also lead to other safeguards protecting the access to and control of medical data by the authors and subjects of the records.[27] Clear

---

nor that a return address be provided. On the receiving end, people similarly have the right to discard anonymous mail without opening it. If the principles of dynamic negotiation were applied to electronic mail, senders of e-mail would have the option to identify or not identify themselves. Recipients could reject as undeliverable any e-mail with an unidentified sender. The sender would then have the option to retransmit the message, this time with a return address. The users would negotiate among themselves.

[26] Detmer and Steen, "Shoring Up Protection of Personal Health Data," 74.

[27] These principles echo the European directives. See Michael Rigby, Ian Hamilton, and Ronald Draper, "Towards an Ethical Protocol in Mental Health Informatics," in B. Cesnick,

and public articulation of these principles is essential in order to emphasize that privacy is a fundamental part of a positive strategy for addressing health care information technology rather than merely a defensive and ad hoc reaction to threats. This will help restore public confidence in the use of electronic medical records.

Some might prefer to endorse proposals from the National Committee on Health Information Privacy that require privacy guidelines solely for identifiable data. Certainly, identifiable patient records pose the greatest risk and may need the greatest guarantee of privacy protection. Consider, for example, the companies called "pharmacy-benefit managers" that use pharmaceutical data in their work on behalf of health plans. They claim to use the data to aid patients directly by pinpointing dangerous overlaps in medications and by advising patients about generic drugs where they might be appropriate. They have also saved health plans billions of dollars in recent years. Given this link between health plans and pharmacy-benefit managers, it is no surprise that the parent companies of the three largest pharmacy-benefit managers are the prescription drug manufacturers Merck, Eli Lilly, and SmithKline Beecham; these drug manufacturers want their drugs—rather than those of other companies—to be used by HMOs and pharmacies. However, these pharmacy-benefit managers are not merely aiding and saving money for patients, health plans, and drug manufacturers. They have also shared with others, without consent and in alarming ways, the sensitive medical information that they acquire about individuals. For example, one woman in Texas who was taking antidepressants because of difficulty sleeping during menopause unexpectedly received a notice from her employer that she would be enrolled in a depression program, that her prescriptions would be monitored, and that she would be sent educational material on depression![28]

Nevertheless, there are dangers in focusing just on privacy for identifiable health records. The linkage potential described above, which allows nonidentifiable information to be aggregated and linked in ways such that it becomes identifiable, makes it imperative that privacy guidelines apply to databases of anonymous information as well, because this linkage potential eliminates any clear line between identifiable and nonidentifiable data. There is thus a false security in the apparent anonymous nature of information that lacks a name or other identifier.[29]

A. T. McCray, and J. R. Scherrer, eds., *MEDINFO '98: Proceedings of the Ninth World Congress on Medical Informatics* (Amsterdam, The Netherlands: IOS Press, 1998), 1223–27.

[28] Robert O'Harrow, Jr., "Plans' Access to Pharmacy Data Raises Privacy Issues: Benefit Firms Delve Into Patient Records," *Washington Post*, September 27, 1998, A1.

[29] Michael Rigby has suggested to me in correspondence that although the downloading of rich data sets of anonymous data should not be allowed, the use of such a database for public health research may be morally justifiable. This could occur if the simplicity of the data set or the large size of the study would preclude the indirect identification (or even the suspicion of such identification) of individuals in the database.

Furthermore, protecting all databases, rather than just those containing identifiable information, will enhance public confidence in the technological safeguards.

Others have described the details of a computerized system guided by the theoretical principles above. Such a system would require user authentication, different levels of access control, a method of data coding, a process by which to audit the trails of users, some type of cryptography, a system of data ownership that would allow authors of documents to set access controls and to shadow records, and so on.[30] Security would be provided through the technology, by using it to achieve all feasible, affordable, and reasonable steps to protect the collection, storage, and transmission of data. Once this is done, those security measures that prevent accidental disclosure or unauthorized dissemination or access could then be used to protect confidentiality and privacy.

Clearly the challenge is no longer technological, as the technology has already been developed. Rather, the issues are moral and political, namely, how to incorporate and implement the available privacy safeguards in the computer program designs and how to determine which features to include or exclude, prioritize, use as a default, and so on. For example, there are differences of opinion regarding whether a complete medical record should be released to anyone authorized to access it, or whether there should be "layering" or partial restrictions on access to very sensitive data items. The options need no longer be total access or total denial. Because well-designed computer systems can incorporate and differentiate customized access controls that would be impossible to establish for paper records, such systems may enhance security for medical records. Defenders of such systems believe that "[e]lectronic records are arguably more secure [than paper record systems] if the proper policies and best available technologies are in place."[31]

Principles mandating the priority of privacy would insist that privacy guidelines extend both to primary uses of medical records (namely, those used to provide delivery of health care) as well as to secondary uses by insurers, employers, public health agencies, medical researchers, educational institutions, and rehabilitation and social welfare programs. On this view, medical records data would not be completely unavailable to third parties; however, those parties would be expected to gain consent for the use of the data from the patient or to justify their need for the data to a supervisory committee or other comparable gatekeeper. The guidelines could also include provisions for access to the data in the case of emergencies.

---

[30] Randolph C. Barrows, Jr., and Paul D. Clayton, "Privacy, Confidentiality, and Electronic Medical Records," *Journal of the American Medical Informatics Association* 3, no. 2 (March/April 1996): 139–48.

[31] Ibid., 146.

The first and most distinctive feature of the principles underlying a system of dynamic negotiation is the requirement that overarching guidelines mandating privacy protection be the default. On this view, privacy protection is expected, and access and use of medical records must be justified and approved. The model takes patient privacy—rather than clinician needs, research needs, administrative efficiency, or convenience—as fundamental. This is in sharp contrast to dominant systems currently in use in the United States. For example, Boston's Beth Israel Deaconess Medical Center has implemented a system with over five thousand terminals used by staff doctors, residents, nurses, medical students, and others. The software designers clearly recognized the conflict between confidentiality and availability in the use of electronic medical records. When developing the system, the designers made two assumptions. First, they assumed that there were a large number of patients who faced high risks of receiving bad medical care as a result of inadequate information; second, they assumed that only a small number of patients were at risk for breaches of confidentiality. The system that they adopted, based on these assumptions, establishes *access* (rather than privacy) as the default. This system has some methods of securing accountability (audit trails, monitoring of records, etc.); unfortunately, these systems of accountability merely track privacy intrusions after the fact, and provide little protection over the information.[32]

Second, a major theme of a dynamic-negotiation system includes emphasis on patient choice through a negotiation, more accurately referred to as "counseling," between patients and their health care providers or others wanting or needing access to their medical histories and data. Parties with different stakes in the information, such as insurance companies, would be required to ask for access and demonstrate a need to know.[33] This might at first sound like the process known as "informed consent to disclosure of information," which includes telling patients what information is to be disclosed, ensuring that they understand what is being disclosed, and requiring that the patient is competent and willingly consents. However, dynamic negotiation goes further, not merely

[32] Charles Safran, "The Introduction of EPRs in the Beth Israel Deaconess Medical Center, Boston" (paper presented at an international conference on "Electronic Patient Records in Medical Practice," Rotterdam, The Netherlands, October 6, 1998). David Friedman has suggested to me that federally mandated systems have failed in the past to allow for experimentation with different solutions to problems. He urged that it would be preferable to have various systems of information control, in order to see what system is best. To the contrary, I believe we have already had years of experimenting with a patchwork of programs, and the Beth Israel system (as well as others) indicates that no self-regulating system has emerged that adequately protects patient privacy.

[33] For a defense of a "restricted access" view of privacy, see Ruth Gavison, "Privacy and the Limits of Law," *Yale Law Journal* 89, no. 3 (January 1980): 421–71; see also James Moor, "The Ethics of Privacy Protection," *Library Trends* 39, nos. 1 and 2 (Summer/Fall 1990): 69–82.

presenting patients with a consent form to sign, but requiring health care providers and secondary users to have an ongoing conversation or meaningful dialogue with patients (about the implications of allowing access, the importance of the research study for which data is needed, etc.) before gaining access to their data. That is, the goal is to educate patients so that they understand the benefits of the release of their data—not only for themselves, but for medical research or public health as well—so that they make the choice about how much or little they wish to withhold and thus that they release information voluntarily. This goal emphasizes the importance of autonomy by allowing patients to retain control over their health records.[34]

One technical program reflecting these principles of dynamic negotiation is a database called the Integrated Primary Care Information (IPCI) Project, which has been developed recently in the Netherlands.[35] A supervisory board oversees privacy protection for the database, even for direct patient care data without obvious name and genetic identifiers. Furthermore, an individual has two additional gatekeepers that can act to prevent unauthorized dissemination of his or her information: a general practitioner (or primary care physician) and an additional review board. Any of the three gatekeepers can reject a claim to access the information, but even if all three agree that the need for the information is reasonable and well justified, the physician, whenever possible, must still go back to the patient to gain consent to release the data. The computer program includes double-coding so that, like a bank safe-deposit box, two keys are needed to open and access the record, and the patient—or, if necessary, the physician—holds one of the keys. This may seem like an incredibly cumbersome system, yet many doctors in the Netherlands appear to prefer the protection rather than resenting it. It is ironic that this extraordinary level of privacy protection is deemed important, even essential, in a country where national health care is guaranteed, and hence the ill effects of privacy violations do not include the possible loss of medical care.

Third, a dynamic-negotiation system would insist on protection for physicians as well. Direct-care physicians and other caretakers could feel free to explain that they are unable to provide services for patients who refuse to divulge essential medical information, though it is likely

---

[34] See Tom L. Beauchamp and James F. Childress, *Principles of Biomedical Ethics*, 3rd ed. (New York: Oxford University Press, 1989), for their stress on four ethical principles, namely, respecting *autonomy*, beneficence, nonmaleficence, and justice (emphasis mine).

[35] Johan van der Lei, "The EPR as Catalyst for Change" (paper presented at an international conference on "Electronic Patient Records in Medical Practice," Rotterdam, The Netherlands, October 6, 1998). See also Albert E. Vlug and Johan van der Lei, "Postmarking Surveillance with Computer-Based Patient Records," in Robert A. Greenes, Hans E. Peterson, and Denis J. Protti, eds., *MEDINFO '95: Proceedings of the Eighth World Congress on Medical Informatics* (Edmonton, Canada: IMIA, 1995), 327–30.

that most or all patients would gladly release the information to gain care.

Fourth, control over the information would need to include the ability of patients to access their records or database information, as mandated by the European Union guidelines. As with credit bureau databases, the problem is often correcting misinformation or information that is incomplete and therefore misleading.

The advantages of such a system are similar to those that were illustrated in the discussion above about dynamic negotiation for caller ID. The presumption in favor of privacy is protected, and when patients choose to release their medical records and data, they will know exactly what they are doing and why. They will not be losing their privacy by default. Patient privacy is protected, and physicians are assured the medical information needed for any patients they treat.

The disadvantages of the dynamic-negotiation approach are not insignificant, however. First, there will be difficulties, similar to those arising for informed consent, concerning the ability of patients to understand, discuss, or consent meaningfully if they are infirm, confused, or unaware of the content of their medical records. This is especially true for vulnerable patients, such as those getting mental health treatment. However, it can even be a typical issue for those in a very normal state of anxiety upon being admitted to a hospital for surgery. Advocacy on behalf of vulnerable patients is often helpful, but there is always the worry that an advocate, often a relative or close friend, may have a vested interest in some information being hidden or revealed.[36] Thus, there is a need for guidelines concerning who or what supervisory group has custody or oversight of a record when a patient is unable to be consulted.

Second, there are the problems posed when one cannot gain consent to attain information due to the death of patients, or when gaining information would be unwise, because, for example, the fear caused in the patient would far outweigh the benefits one could derive from the information. The IPCI program allows the primary care physician to be more actively involved in such cases, with overview from the review board and the supervisory board.

Third, some doctors and secondary users of health information are better communicators than others. Even with forms to aid them, those with less-than-gracious bedside manners may find initiating the necessary counseling and conversations extremely difficult, and they may do a poor job. The end result may be neither a "negotiation" nor "dynamic." Note, however, that prompts and reminders for dialogue and consent can be built into the database programs.

---

[36] Rigby, Hamilton, and Draper, "Towards an Ethical Protocol in Mental Health Informatics," 1225.

Fourth, some system of enforcement will need to be developed, perhaps on the model of the Dutch IPCI program. Though not completely analogous to the release of medical files, cases involving the release of sealed juvenile criminal records may be instructive here. Once sealed, juvenile records are supposed to remain that way; in cases where courts or judges have released them, lives have been ruined and devastated. Examples like this emphasize the importance of a careful evaluation of justifications of the "need to know"; they also emphasize the importance of review boards or supervisory boards to oversee enforcement.[37]

Fifth, the time, effort, potential paperwork, and computer entries needed for a system of dynamic negotiation are likely to be eschewed by physicians, especially in the United States, where so many are used to the current system allowing the free flow of so much data. Physicians may also lack the time to educate patients—especially given the economic stresses of managed health care—even when the possibility of quick confirmations for consent are built into the computer programs. Some have argued that this will likely lead to (1) the authorizations approved in forms being substantially broadened so that physicians can avoid needing to track down patients later, and (2) doctors simply avoiding inconveniences by not attempting to get consent for the release of information for secondary purposes. Both outcomes would work to the detriment of medical research and public health.[38]

Sixth, some might argue that many individuals, even with the best information, will be comfortable sharing sensitive medical information with only some of the many people involved in their direct patient care—primary care doctors, specialists, nurses, covering physicians, therapists, residents, dietitians, etc.—who can help with their own personal health needs. They may also be unwilling to part with their data, even if encrypted, for research and public health studies, which doctors often feel are just as crucial for the medical profession as is individual patient care. If such unwillingness is common, research samples may be skewed and less useful than data collected without the restraint of patient consent. This may well lead to inadequate or statistically invalid research databases, and declines in other public health activities.

To the contrary, however, I believe that as in the case of caller ID, many or even most people, when educated, will be willing to share more data than is anticipated. It has been pointed out that in West Virginia, "some patients are allowing their physicians to put unencrypted data about their health on the Internet's World Wide Web to facilitate the sharing of records during consultations with other physicians and to make records accessible when patients arrive at hospitals. Patients involved in the project have

---

[37] I am indebted to Tom Beauchamp for emphasizing this point.
[38] Detmer and Steen, "Shoring Up Protection of Personal Health Data," 77.

indicated that the benefits outweigh the potential risks of privacy invasion."[39] Even this example should not lead one to draw the conclusion that most people would choose this course. Rather than paternalistically making the decision that such sharing should be allowed automatically and as a matter of course, it is preferable to endorse a public policy allowing individuals to decide for themselves whether it is worthwhile to relinquish some of their privacy for higher-quality medical care and the potential for future cures.

Interestingly, a recent proposal from the United Kingdom echoes the approach I have defended. A study by health planning and management experts recognizes the opportunities for "searching, processing, and presenting clinical information" with electronic medical records and yet takes seriously the privacy concerns raised by the uncontrolled sharing of health data. This study, which is guided by the moral view that privacy protection should be of paramount concern, focuses on mental health patients as one particularly vulnerable and dependent group. This is partly because of these patients' intrinsic need for protection, and partly because the authors believe that guidelines designed to protect the most vulnerable patients can apply to and protect the rest of the population. Some of the key principles endorsed in this proposal include controlled access (so that records are not open to all authorized system users, but only to clinicians involved in a case) and a requirement of patient consent for referral of data sets. Most interesting, however, is the computer logic program that the experts recommended. It presupposes an assumption of denial of access, specifically, that "the normal rule should be that access is denied unless a person can prove a legitimate responsibility for the patient which requires them to have access to the personal record."[40] Clearly the default of this system is denial of access, and hence it places a priority on privacy.

In sum, it is essential to weigh the benefits and drawbacks of these different public policy approaches. I do not believe that the disadvantages of the principles underlying a dynamic-negotiation system for health care information are fatal. If patients do often fail to consent to release their data, and if physicians do avoid the burdens and time needed for requesting it, then in the end public health and research needs may suffer. More public education can help minimize the loss, however, so that individuals will make choices more in line with those that doctors and researchers would have made on their behalf. I believe that the loss will diminish with time, education, and renewed faith in computer designs and encryption techniques, but that the short-term loss is necessary given the priority of patient privacy.

[39] Ibid., 78.
[40] Rigby, Hamilton, and Draper, "Finding Ethical Principles and Practical Guidelines for the Controlled Flow of Patient Data," 1.

VI. Conclusion

My fundamental presumption is that health information privacy must be viewed as a priority; its protection should be assumed to be necessary at the outset, and the technology designed for the use of electronic medical records should be adapted so that its use does not automatically require that one forfeit one's privacy. Several criteria guide the approach that I have defended: (1) the need to protect the privacy of sensitive health information for all individuals, (2) the value of emphasizing individual autonomy and education in designing and implementing computerized medical databases, (3) the importance of letting new information technology flourish to retain the benefits that electronic medical records bring both to patient care and to public health, and (4) the need to replace a conglomeration of conflicting state or local guidelines with national guidelines to provide consistency in medical practice. These guidelines must be set up with maximal privacy protection as the default so that patients and health care providers must then dynamically negotiate the extent of privacy protection and health care that they choose. Individuals—not their pharmacists, employers, or insurance companies—should determine the manner and extent to which they value the privacy of their medical information.

The approach that I have defended is not unproblematic and needs to be supplemented with more detail. Although I have recognized the clear benefits of electronic medical records, I have nevertheless argued that when technological advance clashes with privacy, it is imperative to seek a solution in which the technology does not dictate the extent of privacy protection, and in which patients and targeted individuals choose when and how much to protect or relinquish their privacy. The key idea is to have the government maintain the *presumption* in favor of privacy. That is, the government should begin with a default mandating maximal privacy protection, and then ensure that people are educated, consulted, and allowed to give consent or refusal before information is gathered or disseminated. They may then choose whether or not it is worthwhile for them to release personal medical information, whether it is in an identified format or not. This solution provides a balance that will protect privacy comprehensively, but not at the expense of medical technology. Our goal should be to manage new technologies and health information databases appropriately, not to impede or destroy them.

Philosophy, Clark University

GENETICS AND INSURANCE: ACCESSING AND USING PRIVATE INFORMATION*

By A. M. Capron

I. Introduction

Is information about a person's genome, whether derived from the analysis of DNA or otherwise, protected by the right to privacy? If it is, why and in what manner? It often appears that some people believe that the answer to this question is to be found in molecular genetics itself. They point to the rapid progress being made in basic and applied aspects of this field of biology; this progress has remarkably increased what is known about human genetics. Since knowledge of a particular person's genetic makeup entails a potential intrusion into that person's most private realms and exposes him or her to dire results if revealed to others, they argue, the law needs to protect "genetic privacy." There is nothing inherently wrong with this account, but it certainly presupposes that we know—and agree about—what it means to protect privacy and, indeed, what interests are implicated in the concept and why they matter. Rather than make this assumption, in this essay I first elaborate a concept of privacy before turning to the potential privacy implications that arise at the intersection of human genetics and the field of insurance. I argue that the core value here is self-determination broadly conceived—that control over one's genetic information may be important for achieving self-determination—but that at least in the context of contracts for life insurance, we should be reluctant to recognize "rights" that would permanently preclude the use of genetic data by insurers.

II. The Right to Privacy

One might well conclude that the right to privacy must be an ancient structure, so often is it portrayed as being worn down or assaulted by modern technological forces. "Among the wasting assets of modern society, privacy ranks high," declared J. Roland Pennock and John Chapman three decades ago, in their preface to a well-known collection on the subject. "The products of modern technology and some of the direct and

* This essay is based on research supported by a grant from the National Human Genome Research Institute (R01-HG00551). I thank Brian Shaw for his research assistance.

indirect effects of mass society combine to enhance its scarcity value."[1] Of course, as they acknowledged in an aside, privacy in many ways is a product of advanced society, rather than its victim. In an earlier era, privacy basically meant the protection of private property, embodied, for example, in the law of trespass and in the privilege to use reasonable force to repel invasions that interfered with an owner's right to possession and use.[2] The protection of property certainly served to enhance many of the interests associated with the modern privacy tort, but the two are not purely coincident. Property was then the primary basis for wealth and power. More than the sort of quiet isolation that modern city-dwellers associate with a country estate, the possession of property yielded the lord of the manor the products of the land, both cultivated and wild.

Today when we say that "a man's home is his castle," our thoughts run not to the backyard vegetable garden, but to the notion that within one's walls one is free to do as one wishes. In this sense, the right to be free both from being observed and from being controlled (that is, from having to adjust one's behavior to the expectations as well as the dictates of society) serves the basic human interest in having an autonomous life. In a liberal society, each adult is not only judge of which actions (conduct, associations, etc.) best serve his or her interests, but is also the author of his or her own being. Many critics of the modern world contend that any sense of self-authorship is a delusion, so pervasive are the influences of mass culture and especially of the electronic media. Moreover, the ability to shape one's life—never an absolute matter, for we are social animals and for the most part live our lives in relationship to one another—can be seriously compromised by economic, physical, or psychological limitations. Nonetheless, self-determination in this very personal, autobiographical sense seems to me to be the value that underlies our interest in protecting privacy.

It is a particularly American value. For many immigrants, escaping the Old World meant not only fleeing persecution or deprivation, but also breaking out of old structures and inherited strictures. The "land of opportunity" connoted not only an end point—material success—but also the process of becoming, the opportunity to start over again, free to be whom one could be, rather than just what was ordained by circumstance. With the development of the Western frontier, the chance to begin again remained even for people who were born in America, and the thought persisted even after the openness of the Western frontier ended, transferred to new embodiment in the cities and universities of a land that exalted freedom, change, and novelty. Of course, there are limits to this

---

[1] J. Roland Pennock and John W. Chapman, "Preface," in Pennock and Chapman, eds., *NOMOS XIII: Privacy* (New York: Atherton Press, 1971), vii.

[2] Beyond the protection of property, the interest in not being interfered with in a personal sense was embodied in the tort of trespass vi et armis and other doctrines that protected people's physical well-being.

ability to create oneself, as writers like Faulkner remind us. Yet even today, the description of a successful person as a "self-made man" conveys the optimistic view that we are authors of our own fates.

A. Autonomy and secrecy: in service of self-determination

In Section III, I will turn to the question of whether the findings of genetics are likely to unseat this view, but first I need to elaborate a little further on the argument that the essential interest served by a privacy right is to enable people to exercise personal self-determination. I recognize that this interpretation of the right may seem to overlook a great deal. As already noted, one way of looking at privacy would be to link it to private property; another way would be to link it to physical integrity. In both of these guises, privacy protects one's security, which is important for several reasons (especially in promoting economic efficiency), but we do not need a privacy right to achieve this protection. Instead, it comes about through other rules of tort, contract, and property law.

A more telling criticism of my position would be that the right to privacy is broader than my interpretation suggests because the right involves two separate interests that are violated by two different types of conduct. Elizabeth Beardsley describes these two types of conduct: the first is "conduct by which one person Y restricts the power of another person X to determine for himself whether or not he will perform an act A or undergo an experience E"; the second is "conduct by which one person Y acquires or discloses information about X which X does not wish to have known or disclosed."[3] The first type of conduct violates the "autonomy" norm, and the second violates the "selective disclosure" norm. I agree with Beardsley's description but believe that both norms are valued because they serve the same underlying interest, namely, personal self-determination.

The "autonomy" norm involves not only deciding what to do or what to experience as ends in themselves but also acting upon that decision as a means to the end of self-creation. Our actions are constitutive of our lives, in the sense that what we do and experience in life cumulatively *is* our lives. But those actions and experiences are not simply a path waiting to be trod. We must choose among paths and sometimes carve out new ones, and in doing both, we choose our course and destination in light of the terrain—the existing realities of the material world, including our own corporeal selves as well as the actions of other persons. Thus, our actions not only constitute our lives, but affect our lives by molding the preferences and felt needs that guide future choices and by placing us in positions from which we advance or retreat.

[3] Elizabeth L. Beardsley, "Privacy and Selective Disclosure," in Pennock and Chapman, eds., *Privacy*, 56.

Plainly, we are far from being the only (or sometimes even the major) determinant of our own actions. Autonomy does not depend upon or presuppose isolation but rather its opposite. Since our lives are lived in a web of voluntary and adventitious relationships with others—friends and family, business associates and strangers on the highway—our autonomy depends upon others being held responsible for their own conduct, as judged by expectations assumed by their relationships or imposed by society. Thus, autonomy not only rests on individual responsibility, but provides the moral justification for enforcing it. As autonomy is a characteristic of a moral agent, so past choices shape future ones. Self-determination is a process, not an act, and our past conduct and experiences matter not only for themselves but as determiners of our future conduct and experiences. To change the metaphor, our authorial choices in writing our own life stories are dependent on the chapters that we have already completed.

Beardsley's second norm, "selective disclosure"—our control over information about our lives—also derives its importance from its role in self-determination. By controlling information about myself, I not only protect my ability to choose what I do, free of the interference that could follow if people disapproved of my choices, but I shape who I am, since as a being who exists in time and space (and in greater or lesser relationship to my fellow human beings), my "self" has an exterior as well as an interior reality. That exterior reality resides in other people's perceptions of me. In controlling information, I can shape people's perceptions. The amount of control I am able to achieve in this regard depends in part on the degree of scrutiny and analysis to which I am subject (consider, for example, President Clinton during the year of the Monica Lewinsky scandal), and in part on how much I am willing and able to restrict my contact with others. It also depends very much on the extent to which society protects my power to exercise selective disclosure about myself and my life as an aspect of my right of self-determination.

In arguing that the essential interest served by a privacy right is self-determination, I do not mean to imply that self-determination is superior to other interests, nor do I adopt any particular stance on such empirical questions as whether most people live their lives conscious of their own role as self-creators or whether, if aware of this possibility, most people feel either a desire or an ability to act on it. Indeed, I recognize that for cultural or other reasons the whole notion of "self-determination" may seem alien to some Americans. In research on the effects of ethnicity on attitudes toward advance health care directives, undertaken by colleagues at the Pacific Center for Health Policy and Ethics, it was apparent that some ethnic groups did not regard decisions about care at the end of life as "belonging" to the patient.[4] Indeed, contradicting the usual common

---

[4] Leslie J. Blackhall et al., "Ethnicity and Attitudes Toward Patient Autonomy," *Journal of the American Medical Association* 274, no. 10 (September 13, 1995): 820–25.

law presumption, the typical Korean-American view appears to be that decisions about medical treatment should *not* be made by the patient.[5] This sort of departure from the usual model of self-determination is important in policy as well as clinical terms. For example, the "self-determination" protected in the United States by the federal Patient Self-Determination Act of 1990[6] is not the right to make a choice for its own sake. What is protected is the right to make a choice as a means of achieving a dying that is a continuation of the life one has lived, rather than being, for example, an experience shaped—or, more accurately, distorted—by medical technology that is deployed when and how others determine. Patients who, for cultural/ethnic reasons, do not embrace informed consent and advance directives can nonetheless shape for themselves a dying process that is consistent with the lives that they have lived, and this should help them to produce the sort of "life" that they want to leave in the memories of their relatives and friends.

B. *The legal contours of self-authorship*

The law has given considerable support to this process of authoring our own lives. The common law has long protected people's physical integrity, through the law of battery, and has prohibited intrusions into private space, through the law of trespass. Common law doctrines also protect people from analogous wrongs that occur with or without a physical invasion. One example of such a wrong is eavesdropping (that is, observing private conversations by standing close to a house, at the point where rain drops from the eaves, achievable today at a much greater distance through the use of electronic devices); another example is offensive shadowing in public. "These can be characterized as instances of distressing intrusion into the private domain of living or into the sphere of a person's autonomous movement."[7] Some forty years ago, courts expanded the

---

[5] Gelya Frank et al., "A Discourse of Relationships in Bioethics: Patient Autonomy and End-of-Life Decision Making among Elderly Korean Americans," *Medical Anthropology Quarterly* 12, no. 4 (December 1998): 403–23.

[6] The Patient Self-Determination Act requires that all hospitals, skilled nursing facilities, home health agencies, hospice programs, and HMOs that receive Medicare or Medicaid funding provide each patient at the time of entrance or enrollment with written information concerning:

> (I) an individual's rights under State law . . . to make decisions concerning . . . medical care, including the right to accept or refuse medical or surgical treatment and the right to formulate advance directives . . . , and
>
> (II) the written policies of the provider or organization respecting the implementation of such rights.

42 U.S.C.A. sec. 1395cc(a)(1)(f)(1)(A) (West Supp. 1999). The organization must also document in each person's record whether that person has signed an advance directive. The act also requires that each state develop written descriptions of relevant law.

[7] Paul A. Freund, "Privacy: One Concept or Many," in Pennock and Chapman, eds., *Privacy*, 182.

protection enjoyed by patients (as by all persons) against unauthorized or offensive touching into the modern doctrine of informed consent. Today, the doctrine draws less on its roots in battery than on the law of professional negligence and fiduciary duty. All of these legal doctrines provide direct or indirect support for individuals' control over their own lives and for individuals' rights to determine what they will experience and what they will share with others.

The publication in 1890 of Samuel Warren and Louis Brandeis's justly famous *Harvard Law Review* article on "The Right to Privacy"[8] pushed the law to move beyond these separate torts and recognize violation of privacy as a tort itself. Seventy years later, in another famous article— "Privacy"—William Prosser put the court decisions and statutes that had been inspired by Warren and Brandeis into four categories, which he described as:

1. Intrusion upon the plaintiff's seclusion or solitude, or into his private affairs.
2. Public disclosure of embarrassing private facts about the plaintiff.
3. Publicity which places the plaintiff in a false light in the public eye.
4. Appropriation, for the defendant's advantage, of the plaintiff's name or likeness.[9]

Prosser was correct that these "four distinct kinds of invasions," when viewed in strictly legal terms (elements, defenses, measure of damages, etc.) "have almost nothing in common,"[10] and, hence, that lumping them together has in some cases resulted in terrible confusion. Yet his concession that "each represents an interference with the right of the plaintiff, in the phrase coined by Judge Cooley, 'to be let alone',"[11] points back, I think, to the underlying interest that warrants erecting the protection. Why is it important for people to be left alone? Because interferences prevent them from constructing the life that they wish, not only injecting unwanted elements into their lives but also exposing their life choices to

---

[8] Samuel D. Warren and Louis D. Brandeis, "The Right to Privacy," *Harvard Law Review* 4, no. 5 (December 1890): 193.

[9] William L. Prosser, "Privacy," *California Law Review* 48, no. 3 (August 1960): 389. I focus in what follows on the first three of these categories of the right to privacy because the fourth (commercial appropriation of a plaintiff's name or likeness), while not unrelated to the core concept of self-creation that I argue is protected by the common law (subject to constitutional limitations designed to avoid chilling press freedom), is not very germane to the underlying topic of private genetic information. Cases falling into Prosser's fourth category typically involve individuals who have cultivated media attention to many— perhaps all—aspects of their lives and who merely object to others exploiting, and perhaps diluting, the commercial value that can attach to such celebrity.

[10] Ibid.

[11] Ibid., quoting Thomas McIntyre Cooley, *A Treatise on the Law of Torts, or, the Wrongs Which Arise Independent of Contract*, 2d ed. (Chicago: Callaghan and Company, 1888), 29.

the examination, and direct or indirect control, of others. Of course, sometimes people knowingly invite intrusions. A person who willingly chooses
to live next to a discotheque because she loves the music and crowds is
not thereby prevented from constructing her life just because the music
sometimes interferes with her activities. *Not* being left alone is in this case
part of her self-creation, just as it is (though probably more briefly and
with less commotion) in the life of a concert-goer at Lincoln Center in
New York who has chosen to hear music performed there rather than
listening at home to "the same performance" over the radio or on compact disc. In these ways, people use—and sometimes relinquish—their
privacy in order to shape and establish who they are, both to themselves
and to others, even when the tools of privacy do not rely on isolation
but on the anonymity that attaches to many actions in a busy urban
environment.

Recovery for the first of Prosser's four privacy categories—intrusions
upon the plaintiff's seclusion—stands on the firmest legal footing, namely,
in the law of trespass and such related wrongs as eavesdropping. What is
offensive about such acts[12] is that they disrupt the life that one wants to
live and, hence, change the path of that life, as well as altering the way
that one is perceived by others.

The ability of plaintiffs to recover for acts falling within Prosser's second and third categories—which both partake of the communication of
private information to the public but differ with respect to whether the
facts being publicized create a true or false impression—has been limited
on press-freedom grounds. The third category, called "false light," resembles defamation, though there are some differences in their elements. For
example, defamation can arise when a damaging statement is communicated to a single person, while false light requires "publicity" in the
ordinary sense. Similarly, the harm to reputation in defamation need
merely lower the plaintiff in the estimation of the community or deter
persons from dealing with him, while false light requires that the defendant cast the plaintiff in a light that "would be highly offensive to a
reasonable person."[13]

Because of the analogy to defamation, the Supreme Court, in *Time v.
Hill* (1967), applied to the false-light tort the requirement—imposed by
the First Amendment in defamation cases—that defendants may only be

---

[12] The offense has to be more than a common annoyance of life, as a result either of its
manner or its effect. For consideration of an offense's *manner*, see *Fowler v. Southern Bell
Telephone and Telegraph Co.*, 343 F.2d 150 (5th Cir. 1965) (wiretapping a phone conversation as
opposed to merely overhearing a conversation at the next table in a restaurant). For consideration of an offense's *effect*, see *Pinkerton National Detective Agency, Inc. v. Stevens*, 108 Ga.
App. 159, 132 S.E.2d 119 (1963) (ostentatious shadowing as opposed to mere observation on
a public street).

[13] Compare, in *Restatement (Second) of Torts* (1976), sec. 577 (What Constitutes Publication)
and sec. 559 (Defamatory Communication Defined) with sec. 652E (Publicity Placing Person
in False Light).

held liable if the statements were made with knowledge of their falsity or with reckless disregard of the truth.[14] In the subsequent case of *Gertz v. Robert Welch, Inc.* (1974),[15] the Court relaxed this high standard in defamation cases involving persons other than public officials and public figures, on the ground that the state has a legitimate interest in "the protection of private personality" as a manifestation of the U.S. Constitution's respect for "our basic concept of the essential dignity and worth of every human being."[16] Unlike those who have sought public office or celebrity, private individuals may not enjoy the opportunities to counter false statements and, in normative terms, deserve greater protection since they have not chosen to open their lives to the scrutiny of strangers.[17] Nonetheless, the Court declined to apply the lower burden of proof that private individuals face in establishing defamation liability to false-light cases involving such plaintiffs.[18]

Prosser's second category—public disclosure of embarrassing private facts—goes to the heart of people's interest in shaping their own lives through selective disclosure of private information. Warren and Brandeis had argued that even for public officers, the press's freedom should not extend to "the private life, habits, acts, and relations of an individual [that] have no legitimate connection with his fitness for a public office."[19]

---

[14] *Time v. Hill*, 385 U.S. 374 (1967). Actual events—the Hills being held prisoners in their own home by three escaped convicts—had been used by a writer in a novel, which was later made into a play. In an article about the play, *Life* magazine published photographs of the actors in the Hills' former home, which gave the photographs the appearance of reenacting actual events, when in fact both the novel and the play included some elements of fiction that the plaintiff claimed placed his conduct in a false light. The New York courts held the defendant liable to the plaintiff under a New York statute because of the false statements, but the U.S. Supreme Court held such misstatements to be privileged unless made recklessly or with knowledge of their falsity.

[15] *Gertz v. Robert Welch, Inc.*, 418 U.S. 323 (1974). The Court's holding, that "so long as they do not impose liability without fault, the States may define for themselves the appropriate standard of liability for a publisher or broadcaster of defamatory falsehood injurious to a private individual" (ibid., at 347), provides a classic example of the half-empty/half-full phenomenon. Justice Byron White dissented on the grounds that rather than liberalizing the stringent requirements of *New York Times Co. v. Sullivan*, 376 U.S. 254 (1964), and *Time v. Hill*, the majority had erected a new barrier—proof of negligence. In doing so, White claimed, the majority discarded "the contrary judgment arrived at in the 50 States that the reputation interest of the private citizen is deserving of considerably more protection," namely, a legal rule that "put the risk of falsehood on the publisher where the victim is a private citizen and no grounds of special privilege are invoked." *Gertz*, 418 U.S. at 389–90 (White, J., dissenting). Writing for the majority, Justice Lewis Powell responded that "[i]n light of the progressive extension of the knowing-or-reckless-falsity requirement . . . , one might have viewed today's decision allowing recovery under any standard save strict liability as a more generous accommodation of the state interest in comprehensive reputational injury to private individuals than the law presently affords." Ibid., at 348.

[16] Ibid., quoting *Rosenblatt v. Baer*, 383 U.S. 75, 92 (1966) (Stewart, J., concurring).

[17] The Court limited recovery, however, to compensation for actual injury proven by the plaintiff, "at least when liability is not based on a showing of knowledge of falsity or reckless disregard for the truth," in which case presumed or punitive damages might be allowable. *Gertz*, 418 U.S. at 349.

[18] See *Cantrell v. Forest City Publishing Co.*, 419 U.S. 245 (1974).

[19] Warren and Brandeis, "The Right to Privacy," 216.

The same limitation would apply perforce to private citizens, and the *Restatement (Second) of Torts* reflects this view by basing liability on a defendant giving publicity to information the disclosure of which "(a) would be highly offensive to a reasonable person, and (b) is not of legitimate concern to the public."[20] Courts have found that identifying people who have made a new life despite a criminal or disreputable past "usually serves little independent public purpose" beyond curiosity, while recognizing that it is a matter for determination by the trier of fact whether the attention given to a person or an incident has resulted in the person's having lost his or her control over publicity for all time.[21] In its landmark decision in *Sidis v. F-R Publishing Co.* (1940), the U.S. Court of Appeals for the Second Circuit extended the group of people who, as conceded by Warren and Brandeis, "must sacrifice their privacy and expose at least part of their lives to public scrutiny" from public officers to "any person who has achieved, or has had thrust upon him, the questionable and indefinable status of a 'public figure.'"[22] To test the claims of people like former prodigy William James Sidis—"a once public character, who has since sought and has now been deprived of the seclusion of private life"—the court adopted a newsworthiness test that still drew the line at revelations that are "so intimate and so unwarranted in view of the victim's position as to outrage the community's notions of decency."[23] The Supreme Court cited this standard with approval in *Time v. Hill*,[24] and subsequently gave constitutional dimension to the prevailing law that protection from liability for publishing private facts is absolute regarding matters already on the public record, such as the name of a victim set forth in a rapist's indictment, because the very fact of placing information

---

[20] *Restatement (Second) of Torts*, sec. 652D. The American Law Institute (ALI) was established in 1923 to promote the clarification and simplification of the law and to encourage and carry on scholarly work. The Institute drafts various *Restatements of the Law, Model Codes*, and other proposals for law reform; once reviewed by its sixty-member Council and approved by its membership (which consists of up to three thousand elected lawyers, judges, and law professors), these products are then published. The *Restatements*, which attempt to clarify the law by setting forth the prevailing rules as derived from judicial decisions, were the ALI's first undertaking. Between 1923 and 1944, *Restatements of the Law* were developed for agency, conflict of laws, contracts, judgments, property, restitution, security, torts, and trusts. In 1952, the ALI started the *Restatement (Second)*—new editions of the original *Restatements* that updated them, reflected new analyses and concepts, and expanded upon the authorities used in reaching the conclusions set forth. A third round of editions is now underway in a number of fields, including torts.

[21] *Briscoe v. Reader's Digest*, 483 P.2d 34, 39–40 (Cal. 1971).

[22] *Sidis v. F-R Publishing Co.*, 113 F.2d 806, 809 (2d Cir.), *cert. denied*, 311 U.S. 711 (1940). William James Sidis, who had been a famous mathematics prodigy, sued *The New Yorker* for breaching his right of privacy by publishing a profile of him in which his early accomplishments were contrasted, twenty-seven years later, with his withdrawn and unaccomplished existence.

[23] Ibid.

[24] *Time v. Hill*, 385 U.S. at 383 n. 7. Since it was decided on false-light grounds, *Time v. Hill* left open the question of whether a state could constitutionally proscribe the truthful publication of very private matters.

in the public domain indicates that the state has decided that the public interest in good government is served by unfettered access.[25]

C. Privacy as self-determination under the U.S. Constitution

The weighing of conflicting interests—a free press versus personal privacy—that is on display in the cases involving private defamation and privacy actions also emerges in a number of important Supreme Court decisions over the past third of a century. These decisions have attempted to articulate the limits of state control over "the most intimate and personal choices a person may make in a lifetime"—ones that are "central to personal dignity and autonomy."[26] In *Griswold v. Connecticut* (1965), the Supreme Court first gave a constitutional dimension to the interest in question by describing it as the right of privacy, a right found not in the "specific guarantees in the Bill of Rights" but rather in their "penumbras, formed by emanations from those guarantees that help give them life and substance."[27] In subsequent cases, the Court seemed for a while to give an ever wider scope to the protected "zone of privacy," which was not dependent on a private, physical space at all but went directly to protecting individuals' choices about important aspects of their lives. Recent cases have made clear, however, that the Court regards any broad "right of privacy" as a dead letter, and is unwilling to generalize from its cases on reproductive choice to other purported liberty interests. In judging proposed extensions of the right of privacy to new choices—such as the wish of terminally ill patients to obtain their physicians' assistance in ending their lives—judges must determine whether the liberty interest involved finds such support in our history as would justify the conclusion that the interest was implicit in the due process of law.[28]

---

[25] *Cox Broadcasting Corp. v. Cohn*, 420 U.S. 469 (1975).

[26] *Planned Parenthood of Southeastern Pennsylvania v. Casey*, 505 U.S. 833, 851 (1992).

[27] *Griswold v. Connecticut*, 381 U.S. 479, 484 (1965).

[28] In *Washington v. Glucksberg*, 521 U.S. 702 (1997), the Court upheld a Washington State statute that banned assisted suicide. The statute was challenged as it applied to mentally competent, terminally ill adults who wanted their physicians to be able to prescribe lethal medications with which they could take their own lives. The plaintiffs had succeeded in persuading the district and circuit courts that the statute deprived them of a liberty interest protected by the due process clause of the Fourteenth Amendment. The lower courts had not only relied on the Court's recognition in *Cruzan v. Director, Missouri Dept. of Health*, 497 U.S. 261 (1990), of a constitutionally protected interest in refusing medical interventions even when doing so could lead to death; the plaintiffs also pointed to the category of "intimate and personal choices" that were held under *Casey* to be central to personal autonomy. In *Glucksberg*, the Court made clear that not all personal choices qualified for Fourteenth Amendment protection simply because the choice to abort a pregnancy was so protected. Chief Justice William Rehnquist, writing for the majority, found the bans on assisted suicide were "not innovations" but "longstanding expressions of the States' commitment to the protection and preservation of all human life," a commitment that reflected "consistent and enduring themes of our philosophical, legal, and cultural heritages." *Glucksberg*, 521 U.S. at 710-11. In the companion case, *Vacco v. Quill*, 521 U.S. 793 (1997), the Court also held that New York did not violate the Fourteenth Amendment's equal protection clause by permitting physicians (without threat of criminal liability) to carry out patients'

III. Genetics and Privacy

The preceding section aimed to accomplish several things. First, I argued that many disparate threads of the privacy right are woven together in support of a basic interest of all persons to control their own lives: the direction and content of that life, the way in which they experience it, and the way it is perceived by others. Second, I suggested that this interest in self-determination serves important social interests, as it is the reciprocal to the principle of personal responsibility, which undergirds so much of our social and legal structure. Finally, I briefly reviewed common law and constitutional law regarding the right to privacy in order to identify the extent to which the interest in self-determination finds support in the law—which I would argue is large, despite the limitations imposed in the name of a free press.

A. Genes and fate

In Section II, I focused on those aspects of our lives that are subject to our selection, on those points where the paths of life choices branch off or present an opportunity to venture into the wilderness. Note, however, that our sense of being authors of our own fate would appear to come into tension with the increasing understanding of the role of genes in shaping who we are. In these early days of the age of molecular medicine, too much is probably ascribed to genetic factors; this tendency sometimes borders on espousals of genetic determinism, which, like all forms of determinism, is the enemy of free will and personal responsibility. I suspect that in the long run, our appreciation of the complicated interactions among multiple genes and between an individual's genome and his or her environment will leave the notion that we should "seek not in the stars but in our genes for the herald of our fate"[29] as little more than poetic rhetoric. Yet while the deterministic view of our genetic endowment may be unwarranted, genes do play an important role in our lives as we live them, as we experience them, and as others perceive them. Indeed, genes can be seen as analogous to our past conduct with respect to their role in influencing which existing or potential paths are available to us and how we go about choosing among them—with the difference being that we did not choose our genes as we (presumably) chose our conduct.[30]

---

wishes that life support be withdrawn while continuing to prohibit physicians (among others) from aiding in the suicide of terminally ill patients not dependent on life support.

[29] Robert Sinsheimer, "The Prospect of Designed Genetic Change," *Engineering and Science* 32, no. 7 (April 1969): 13.

[30] Should medicine ever develop the capability of making precise changes in an individual's genome (that is, through a refined version of today's "gene therapy" experiments), then the genes we live with might come to be more a matter of choice rather than chance. (We might ask, however, *whose* choice this would be—our choice, or that of our parents?)

Thus, the protections for privacy that aim to safeguard our ability to be self-creators are implicated in decisions about obtaining and using information about our genetic makeup. Just as losing control over private information about our thoughts and behavior exposes us to loss of our self-creative powers, so too loss of control over our "genetic data" could alter not only the choices available to us but also the way that we approach those choices. Whereas in the past the predictive value of genetic information (in the form of family histories of disease, for example) was often weak, much more precise predictions are already beginning to flow from genetic laboratories. More generally, the scientific project of mapping the human genome, initiated in 1990, will only accelerate this process. This project is an effort by scientists from around the world to locate the estimated 100,000 human genes on the chromosomes and then to determine the DNA sequences of the genes themselves.[31] Already, a number of tests for genetic susceptibility to diseases such as cancer have been introduced into medical practice, and many more are in the pipeline. Indeed, the notion that a single sample of one's blood or other tissue contains a "future diary" of one's life (with all the implications of privacy—indeed, secrecy—that attach to diaries), just waiting to be decoded by a molecular biologist, a physician, or even a lab technician, becomes less hyperbolic each day.[32] While the public thus far seems remarkably sanguine about the benefits of the collection of genetic material and information and genetic testing,[33] over recent decades the field of genetics "has provoked public excitement and terror, which in turn have engendered statutes, regulations, and court rulings" at "a rate that is disproportionate to the manifest consequences."[34]

---

[31] The Human Genome Project was begun in 1990 with a projected fifteen-year budget of $3 billion. Initially, the project was funded principally by the U.S. government (through the National Institutes of Health and the research division of the Department of Energy), with substantial additional support provided by the Howard Hughes Medical Institute and now by the Wellcome Trust of London. The funds are used by a consortium of laboratories around the world, among whom parts of the human genome have been parceled out for analysis. In June 1998, a private company, Celera, announced that, using a different method than that followed by the worldwide consortium, it should be able to complete the basic map of human genes within two years for a mere $200 million. Attempts by the leaders of the two groups to form a collaborative arrangement have stalled on the question of whether all results from all laboratories will be in the public domain, free of any patents or other commercial restrictions. Nicholas Wade, "Talk of Collaboration on Decoding the Genome," *New York Times*, November 14, 1999, sec. 1, p. 18.

[32] George J. Annas, "Privacy Rules for DNA Databanks: Protecting Coded 'Future Diaries,'" *Journal of the American Medical Association* 270, no. 18 (November 17, 1993): 2346–50.

[33] In one oft-noted public opinion poll, 68 percent of the respondents were "very" or "somewhat" likely to undergo genetic testing, even when no treatment exists for the disease in question, yet only 27 percent reported hearing or reading "quite a lot" about genetic tests. Harris Poll, no. 34, May 29, 1995.

[34] A. M. Capron, "Which Ills to Bear?: Reevaluating the 'Threat' of Modern Genetics," *Emory Law Journal* 39, no. 3 (Summer 1990): 665–66.

B. Protecting health-related information

Worries about privacy in the United States arise in many contexts, but especially in the context of health-related information. To overcome the problems that arise from our present patchwork of inconsistent and even contradictory state and federal laws,[35] the Health Insurance Portability and Accountability Act of 1996 (HIPAA, also known as the Kassebaum-Kennedy Act) required the Secretary of Health and Human Services to submit to Congress recommendations on privacy standards. Since Congress failed, by August 21, 1999, to pass legislation governing such standards for health data maintained in electronic format, the statute further mandated that the Secretary had to promulgate regulations that would create such standards.[36] The proposed rules, which were published for public comment on November 3, 1999, have generated heated debate on several points. The main dispute centers on whether the thrust of the rules increases patients' privacy rights or actually diminishes them.[37] Under the proposed rules, health plans must provide notice of their policies on using and sharing data about patients, but they are not required to secure the consent of patients for such use.

For all the detailed information contained in medical records, few things are more sensitive than genetic data.[38] As Francis Collins, the director of the National Human Genome Research Institute (NHGRI) at the National Institutes of Health, has observed, the Ethical, Legal and Social Implications (ELSI) Working Group established by the NHGRI has concluded that "two pillars of protection [are] necessary to prevent the misuse of genetic information. The first pillar consists of the enactment of anti-discrimination laws, especially in the realm of health insurance and employment, and the second focuses on the assurance of privacy protections for individuals involved in genetic testing."[39]

I shall address the "second pillar" here, and the "first pillar" in Section IV. The basic standard in ethics and law regarding medical information is that such information is to be regarded as private and subject to disclosure only with the consent of the patient, or under a policy allowing the release of such information for an important public purpose (such as to protect public health or safety, and even then only with individualized review by a disinterested decision-maker, such as a judge). In reality, this

[35] See Lawrence O. Gostin, "Health Information Privacy," *Cornell Law Review* 80, no. 3 (March 1995): 451.

[36] 42 U.S.C.A. sec. 1320-2 (West Supp. 1998). See generally Bartley L. Barefoot, "Enacting a Health Information Confidentiality Law: Can Congress Beat the Deadline?" *North Carolina Law Review* 77, no. 1 (November 1998): 283–360.

[37] See, e.g., Robert Pear, "Rules on Privacy of Patient Data Stir Hot Debate," *New York Times*, October 30, 1999, A1.

[38] U.S. Congress, Office of Technology Assessment, *Protecting Privacy in Computerized Medical Information* (Washington, DC: U.S. Government Printing Office, 1993), 28–29.

[39] Monique K. Mansoura and Francis S. Collins, "Medical Implications of the Genetic Revolution," *Journal of Health Care Law and Policy* 1, no. 2 (1998): 343.

policy of confidentiality is far from scrupulously followed. One major departure from the policy arises in institutional settings, where many more people have access to patient records than have any clinical need to see the information. A second occurs when excessive information is conveyed to health insurers (under a nominal "waiver" of rights by the patient): this occurs when the information provided goes beyond reporting which tests or procedures were conducted, and frequently involves the release of information from the medical record about the results of such interventions. Excessive disclosure sometimes occurs inadvertently, and sometimes because an insurer claims to need these data in order to decide whether the interventions were "medically necessary" and hence reimbursable.

Confidentiality problems involving inadequate protection of medical records within health care organizations are not unimportant: witness the special statutes and hospital policies that were adopted to better insure confidentiality of HIV tests as the AIDS crisis arose in the early 1980s. However, the major focus of concern about genetic data has arisen over the transfer of such data to insurers. The chief concern is that health insurance companies will, by policy or chance, accumulate genetic test data regarding specific patients, which will then be available to these companies (or, perhaps, to the entire industry) when these patients apply for new health, life, or disability insurance policies.

The latter is a real and important concern, one that is not now adequately resolved by the law. One response has been to suggest that genetic information needs special legal protections.[40] The disadvantage to this approach is that it requires special legislation and, more importantly, requires that all parties understand what constitutes "genetic data." The latter task would be difficult to implement practically and hard to defend conceptually. Instead, the special concerns that are now expressed about the misuse of genetic information should serve as an impetus to improve the protection generally afforded to medical data of all sorts.

There is another concern about the field of genetic medicine which, even if it might not justify a separate privacy protection, does serve as a reminder of the importance of adequately resolving the privacy concerns as they affect this field of medicine. This concern is that the elevated public sensitivity to the risks that might arise from misuse of genetic information will stand in the way of researchers advancing the field and physicians providing the clinical benefits that genetic medicine has already made possible. Even though most diseases are not yet susceptible to a true "cure," having information about an individual's particular genetic predispositions will allow the development of a tailor-made reg-

---

[40] George J. Annas, Leonard H. Glantz, and Patricia A. Roche, *The Genetic Privacy Act and Commentary* (Boston, MA: Boston University School of Public Health, 1995), available at http://www.bumc.bu.edu/www/sph/lw/gpa/GPA.htm [accessed October 1, 1998].

imen of preventive measures—from drugs and vaccines to changes in personal habits—that could aid that person. When combined with regular monitoring, such measures should greatly reduce the chance of many diseases occurring, or at least allow them to be detected at much earlier stages, when treatments stand a much greater chance of succeeding. Thus, there are many reasons why a patient would—and should—welcome the availability of molecular tests, such as those that indicate susceptibility to certain types of breast cancer by detecting mutations in the so-called BRCA1 and BRCA2 genes.[41]

Within our model of the self-created life, though, there are reasons why patients might have doubts about going ahead with testing. For some, the benefits simply seem small or nonexistent. A woman offered the breast cancer gene test after she has already been diagnosed with breast cancer, for example, would gain little from knowing that her lamentable situation is in part attributable to having the "genetic deck" stacked against her. Nor are concerns about the destructive effects of information ever completely absent from genetic testing. This is especially true when effective treatments do not exist for the predispositions in question, as is the case today for most predictive genetic screening (such as for BRCA) and even for older forms of gene detection (such as phenylketonuria screening in newborns, where dietary treatment forestalls some problems but does not cure the metabolic abnormality). Even when prevention works technically (as it does when pre-conception and prenatal screening for certain conditions provides useful, timely information that will allow a couple to decide whether to reproduce or to terminate an affected pregnancy), shame, recrimination, and other intrafamily difficulties are still potential harms. Physicians must weigh these harms against the benefits of knowledge in deciding when and how it is appropriate to offer genetic tests; patients must weigh the same factors when deciding whether to undergo a test that has been offered.[42]

Testing for BRCA and other genes that predispose one to adult-onset diseases generates, if anything, a less favorable benefit-to-risk ratio than do prenatal tests. Not only are the clinical benefits at present less clear, as just mentioned, but the steps that would provide these benefits—such as increasing the frequency of mammograms and other exams—could be in many cases implemented on the basis of a family history alone, without the complications of a gene test.[43] The less favorable ratio is also due in

[41] See generally Wylie Burke et al., "Recommendations for Follow-up Care of Individuals with an Inherited Predisposition to Cancer: II. BRCA1 and BRCA2," *Journal of the American Medical Association* 277, no. 12 (March 26, 1997): 997–1003.

[42] R. T. Croyle et al., "Psychological Responses to BRCA1 Mutation Testing: Preliminary Findings," *Health Psychology* 16, no. 1 (January 1997): 63–72; H. T. Lynch et al., "A Descriptive Study of BRCA1 Testing and Reactions to Disclosure of Test Results," *Cancer* 79, no. 11 (June 1, 1997): 2219–28.

[43] Among Ashkenazi Jews without a family history of breast or ovarian cancer, a finding of one of three specific BRCA mutations carries a risk of developing these diseases that is markedly higher than in the general population. Their risk level is lower, however, than that

large measure to the greater number of potential social and economic harms that may result from predisposition screening.[44]

IV. Issues in Using Genetic Testing for Insurance

A. Is it inherently unjust for insurers to use gene test results?

Now, I shall return to the ELSI Working Group's "first pillar": the need for antidiscrimination provisions to safeguard genetic (and other) medical information. The group's concern goes beyond protecting privacy in general; it extends to preventing the misuse of any medical information that is disclosed. Thus, a basic underlying issue is whether "policies that allow genetic information to be used to discriminate against individuals, families, or groups are unjust."[45] This view has an inherent appeal, especially if it is read to mean "*unfair* discrimination," which seems self-evidently wrong, a "misuse of genetic information."[46] Thomas Murray, the chair of the ELSI working group on insurance, links this view of unfairness with the involuntary nature of one's genetic condition: "An old maxim in ethics is 'Ought implies can.' You should not be held morally accountable for that which you were powerless to influence."[47] On closer analysis, however, the use of genetic information in the insurance context is not unjust simply because genes are inherited; judging whether a particular use amounts to unfair discrimination requires careful attention to a number of factors, to which we now turn.

Plainly, the issue of "fairness" is complex when it comes to insurance, a field in which discrimination—in the sense of being aware of differences when they are relevant to the question at hand—is not merely tolerated but desirable. The question of fairness, then, may be a question of relevance and relationship. On the one hand, the mere fact that certain people have different probabilities of experiencing a given outcome is not enough to make using that difference to appraise risk fair or even legally acceptable. If the effects of having or not having a particular genetic mutation have not been studied well enough to make us able to predict that mutation's effects on a relevant outcome (such as health care expenses or

---

faced by women from families with a disease history who are found to have BRCA1 and BRCA2 mutations; these women suffer from risk rates of 85 and 63 percent, respectively. J. P. Struewing et al., "The Risk of Cancer Associated with Specific Mutations of BRCA1 and BRCA2 Among Ashkenazi Jews," *New England Journal of Medicine* 336, no. 20 (May 15, 1997): 1401–8.

[44] See, e.g., Mark A. Rothstein, "Genetic Testing: Employability, Insurability, and Health Reform," *Journal of the National Cancer Institute* 7 (1995): 87–90; and Paul R. Billings et al., "Discrimination as a Consequence of Genetic Testing," *American Journal of Human Genetics* 50, no. 3 (March 1992): 476–82.

[45] Mansoura and Collins, "Medical Implications," 343.

[46] Ibid., 345.

[47] Thomas H. Murray, "Genetics and the Moral Mission of Health Insurance," *Hastings Center Report* 22, no. 6 (November/December 1992): 14.

longevity) reliably, then it would be wrong for an insurer, when writing policies, to use knowledge that a client has such a mutation. Moreover, even if the consequences were well established, if the mutation caused deviations from normal risk rates that were smaller than other deviations that are encompassed within the "standard" range, then basing insurance decisions on the genetic mutation would be unacceptable.

On the other hand, if a difference has actuarial significance (meaning that it can be accurately predicted to produce outcomes that vary enough on the relevant dimension to put people into distinct groups), the fact that the difference is inherited—and, indeed, inherent in a person's genome—does not necessarily make its use unfair, though such use may be prohibited by law in order to achieve another statutory purpose.[48] Of course, value judgments reside in all decisions about what to measure and how to group the resulting measures, but once the central judgments have been made (such as establishing the parameters of what constitutes "standard risk"), it is easier to see whether the outcome predicted from a particular characteristic falls outside the boundaries of the standard. It

---

[48] Consider, for example, the Supreme Court's decision in *Arizona Governing Committee v. Norris*, 463 U.S. 1073 (1983). In *Norris*, the Court determined that in enacting Title VII of the Civil Rights Act of 1964, Congress intended to prohibit employers from offering women lower monthly retirement benefits than men who have made the same contributions. In *Los Angeles Dept. of Water & Power v. Manhart*, 435 U.S. 702 (1978), the Court had held that an employer violated Title VII by requiring its female employees to make larger contributions to a pension fund than male employees in order to obtain the same monthly benefits upon retirement. In *Manhart*, the Court had opined that Title VII's "focus on the individual is unambiguous," since the statute prohibits an employer from treating some employees less favorably than others because of their race, religion, sex, or national origin (ibid., at 708). "[A]ny individual's life expectancy is based on a number of factors, of which sex is only one. . . . [O]ne cannot 'say that an actuarial distinction based entirely on sex is "based on any other factor than sex." Sex is exactly what it is based on.'" Ibid., at 712–13. Applying *Manhart*, the Court held in *Norris* "that the classification of employees on the basis of sex is no more permissible at the pay-out stage of a retirement plan than at the pay-in stage." *Norris*, 463 U.S. at 1081 (footnote omitted).

It is important to remember that *Norris*'s rejection of the use of accurate class-based predictions is solely a matter of statutory interpretation; the trial court had rejected the plaintiffs' claim that the retirement plan violated the equal protection clause of the Fourteenth Amendment. Because the McCarran-Ferguson Act of 1945 assigns the regulation of insurance to the states (except to the extent that a federal statute explicitly provides otherwise, which Title VII does not), *Norris* did not challenge Arizona's regulation of insurance practices, under which companies issuing annuity or insurance contracts were permitted to use sex-segregated tables. The heart of the difficulty, as Justice Lewis Powell pointed out, is that an employment statute that insists on individualizing each employee to ensure that he or she is not subject to group-based discrimination is fundamentally inconsistent with the business of insurance.

> Insurance and life annuities exist because it is impossible to measure accurately how long any one individual will live. Insurance companies cannot make individual determinations of life expectancy; they must consider instead the life expectancy of identifiable groups. Given a sufficiently large group of people, an insurance company can predict with considerable reliability the rate and frequency of deaths within the group based on the past mortality experience of similar groups. Title VII's concern for the effect of employment practices on the individual thus is simply inapplicable to the actuarial predictions that must be made in writing insurance and annuities.

Norris, 463 U.S. at 1103 (Powell, J., dissenting in part).

still remains open to argue that a company has been unfair if it chooses to measure the difference in question while choosing not to measure other characteristics that produce outcomes of greater magnitude. This argument on fairness grounds is particularly justified if the characteristic in question is associated with an existing group in society, particularly if that group is one that has been the object of other discrimination based on factors unrelated to what is measured by the difference in question.[49] Thus, if a particular gene variant were predominantly associated with African-Americans, the choice to deny insurance to or impose a substandard rating on individuals with the gene would be more likely to be characterized as unfair, even if the gene produces a large disease impact. The accusation would be even more telling if the insurer had also chosen not to utilize tests for other genes prevalent in non-African-Americans that produced comparable (or larger) costs for the company.

B. Genetic test results in insurance underwriting

When a physician and a patient with a family history of a particular disease, such as certain types of cancer, discuss the advisability of undergoing a test for genetic predisposition, the fear of an insurance-related consequence would probably enter the discussion. The patient would likely factor into his decision the risk that a person with a positive test result would be unable to obtain or renew health insurance or might even face cancellation of an existing policy. The stories told in the past decade in both the popular and the medical press about people being unable to get insurance or losing their coverage have primarily involved health insurance.[50] Yet for reasons of practicality, principle, and policy, health insurance is, in most instances, much less likely to be affected by genetic test results than is life or disability insurance. Understanding why this is the case involves examining the role that gene testing could play in any kind of insurance and the reasons for—and problems with—using the results of genetic tests to determine disease susceptibility in an insurance context.

How might the results of a genetic test affect an insurer's decision whether or not to issue a policy, or the price at which the policy would be written? The information could be used by the company's underwriters, in consultation with its medical director, just the way that other information in the application is now used to determine whether the likelihood an applicant will experience an insured event falls within the rather broad range that constitutes standard risk for insurance purposes. The informa-

---

[49] "The immediate and direct tie between genetics and ethnicity may make genetic testing a more blatant use of a potentially explosive and discriminatory social classification scheme." Murray, "Genetics and the Moral Mission of Health Insurance," 14.

[50] See, e.g., Geoffrey Cowley, "Flunk the Gene Test and Lose Your Insurance," *Newsweek*, December 23, 1996, 48; and Billings et al., "Discrimination as a Consequence."

tion provided by applicants typically includes data about insurance history (other coverage then in force, policies cancelled, other applications denied, etc.) as well as personal information, some of it of a medical nature. The medical information may include anything from the applicant's answers to a few simple questions about diseases for which treatment has been sought, to a form filled out by the applicant's physician involving a more extensive review of the applicant's medical history, to the results of tests conducted by a person working for or on behalf of the insurance company (such as a blood pressure examination or a blood sample to test for lipids, HIV, or hepatitis).

In addition, information that an applicant has provided to other companies is available to the insurer from the Medical Information Bureau (MIB), a data bank run by the insurance industry, which provides a means for insurers to see whether applicants have omitted important facts from their applications or have given answers about their health status that are inconsistent with prior data. The illness codes that an insurer gets from the MIB may prompt further research by the insurer, but the rules of the bureau preclude members from using the information to decline an application or charge a higher premium.[51]

Finally, underwriters sometimes rely on inspection reports from agencies that interview applicants and people who know them. While the primary focus of such reports is on lifestyle (hobbies, use of alcohol and drugs, financial matters, etc.), some medical information may also be produced. Political scientist Deborah Stone has suggested that part of an applicant's "unadmitted health history" that an underwriter may be able to construct from such an inspection report could involve "a family history of disease," because "it is very likely that [applicants] would discuss their [family's medical] concerns with friends and possibly some neighbors who are also friends."[52] Given the sensitivity of genetic diagnosis at the present time, however, it seems just as likely that family medical history is not something the average person would chat about to neighbors, especially if the information at hand did not involve a disease that was affecting the person's life at that moment but, rather, involved sus-

---

[51] Medical Information Bureau, Inc., *A Consumer's Guide to the Medical Information Bureau* (Westwood, MA: Medical Information Bureau, 1998), 7. Deborah Stone is skeptical that such forbearance occurs:

> In practice, there appears to be very little restriction on insurance companies' use of information obtained from the bureau in underwriting decisions. Moreover, although the MIB has procedures for individuals to correct information in their files, the procedures are cumbersome and it is often difficult for consumers to find out why they have been denied insurance in the first place.

Deborah A. Stone, "The Implications of the Human Genome Project for Access to Health Insurance," in Thomas H. Murray, Mark A. Rothstein, and Robert F. Murray, Jr., eds., *The Human Genome Project and the Future of Health Care* (Bloomington, IN: Indiana University Press, 1997), 143.

[52] Ibid., 144.

ceptibility to disease in the future. In sum, neither the MIB nor inspection reports are likely sources of genetic predisposition data for insurers.

Indeed, even when information emerges in answers to specific questions posed by an insurer as part of an application or in a physician's report, it is improbable, for a number of reasons, that such genetic data will enter into underwriting the average insurance application now or any time in the immediate future. First, since the nineteenth century, many of the basic tests that physicians routinely perform—such as measuring height, weight, and blood pressure—have been introduced into medical practice by insurance companies, because those companies' actuaries had found that certain test results were correlated with disease and hence with decreased longevity. Second, besides being useful in actuarial terms, the medical tests on which insurance companies now rely share several characteristics. They are typically simple, accurate, and inexpensive, and the results that they produce are already a part of the medical record that a physician would typically have for his or her patients. Thus, collecting this information in a reliable fashion is usually quite an easy matter for an insurance company with an application to evaluate. The results of molecular genetic tests, however, do not fit this pattern. The impetus for the use of these tests did not come from insurance companies but from physicians, researchers, patients with family histories of genetic disease, and, not least, from the companies that developed and market the tests. The tests are many orders of magnitude more expensive than those on which insurance companies now place major reliance, and one would not yet expect to find the results of such tests in most patients' medical records.

The third reason that genetic data is unlikely to play a significant role in evaluating insurance applications is predictability. Perhaps the most significant difference between the information in the medical sections of insurance applications and the sort of information that would be forthcoming from molecular genetic tests, is that the former is useful to insurers because it allows them to make reliable predictions about the likelihood that a person will experience an insured-against event during the policy period (and hence necessitate a payment by the insurance carrier). In contrast, information from most gene tests is still too new to be of much value in predicting the future life course of the person tested.

This problem is exacerbated by the fact that the present generation of genetic tests was typically developed through screening members of high-risk families in which a particular genetic disease reappeared through several generations. Thus, the implications of a positive test result for a person at lower family risk, or for someone whose positive test result emerged adventitiously from a screening of the general population, are even less certain. Might "high-risk" families actually carry other as yet unidentified risk factors not found in the rest of the population that contribute to the occurrence or severity of the disease? If so, even the best longitudinal data on persons with positive tests (who are likely at first to have been disproportionately from high-risk groups) may not be generalizable to what other, lower-risk individuals will experience. Moreover, a positive result on a gene test is actuarially ambiguous because being predisposed to developing a disease like breast cancer does not necessarily mean that death or disability will occur prematurely. A person found to have a BRCA mutation is likely to take steps that should result in earlier detection of tumors (and hence improved survival), and may even adopt a greater health consciousness and better preventive measures that could reduce her risk for a wide range of diseases and disorders. Furthermore, the very scientific advances that underlie the identification of a gene mutation also represent "an early step in the elucidation of the pathophysiology and the development of treatments and/or cures."[53] What this means is that an actuary's prediction of the likelihood and timing of breast cancer in the person with the BRCA mutation will likely be invalidated by the radically improved ability of medicine to respond therapeutically in the future.

V. Health Insurance: Not the Focus for Gene Testing

All three factors discussed in Section IV explain why genetic testing may not have as great an immediate impact on insurance as some have expected. However, the third point—that future therapeutic advances will likely provide dramatic improvements in the treatment of diseases that can be predicted through today's gene tests—does logically suggest that to the extent that gene data *are* relevant they would have an impact on health insurance. In this type of insurance, the insurer faces substantial costs when medical treatment is required by one of its policyholders. Nor are the insurer's outlays diminished—as would be the case for life insurance—if a predisposition to disease does not eventuate in the expected fatality. Until good longitudinal data have been accumulated, predictions about death and disability that are based on gene test results may be no more than guesses, which rules out such results serving as a useful part of underwriting for life and, perhaps, even for disability insurance. Yet even without the long-term studies, the genetic conditions to which a policyholder is susceptible will almost certainly generate medical treatment expenses. Despite this logic, genetic data are less likely to play a role in health insurance for three reasons—practicality, principles, and policy.

A. Practical reasons

Gene testing will not be a major feature in health insurance simply because most of this insurance is not individually underwritten; most

---

[53] Mansoura and Collins, "Medical Implications," 333.

people obtain health insurance coverage either through a public program (such as Medicare or Medicaid) or through group policies connected with their employment.[54] For many years, group policies—such as those written by Blue Cross and Blue Shield—were "community-rated," meaning that the premiums for those policies were set based upon the risks faced by the general community of which the groups were a part, with the same rates being offered to all groups. Today, even nonprofit insurers have largely followed the commercial insurers in "experience-rating" the groups that they insure. In this fashion, risk factors enter into the rates charged for group insurance, but rather than being underwritten based upon the disease-disposition of the individuals included, the insurance carrier bases the group's rates for the coming year upon the group's prior years' claims. Rates are also adjusted for changes in unit costs of treatment (e.g., increases or decreases in physician charges for a particular unit of service) and any extensions of coverage to new treatments (e.g., a formerly "experimental" breast cancer treatment that is now considered "medically necessary" and, hence, reimbursable).

Insurance purchased by individuals or by small groups usually undergoes basic underwriting, often not to set "substandard rates" or to decline to write the policy, but rather to write an "exclusion waiver" that precludes payments for treating a particular condition for an individual or the whole group. But overall, employment-based coverage—whether purchased from an insurance carrier or provided on a self-insured basis by the employer—makes little use of data that is predictive of an individual's future health risks. Thus, insurers would not have a means of adding gene test results to an ongoing process of setting premiums and limiting or declining coverage.[55]

There are additional practical reasons why genetic data are less likely to be used than other medical information. First, the medical information about employees that employers have to include on the group's master application—so-called "risk-finder questions"—concerns whether any employees or their dependents have had substantial claims during the several years prior to the application. (This is just the sort of information that an existing carrier would have in its own records for the group when setting premiums for the coming year.) Yet such risk-finding questions,

---

[54] "About 85–90 percent of health insurance is currently purchased through group plans which accept all full-time employees and dependents without evidence of insurability." *Report of the ACLI-HIAA Task Force on Genetic Testing* (Washington, DC: American Council of Life Insurers and Health Insurance Association of America, 1991), 6.

[55] Deborah Stone argues that the industry position disguises the amount of medical underwriting that takes place because about a third of all workers are at firms employing twenty-five or fewer employees (a size at which underwriting commonly occurs), and that "over the last decade or so there has been a trend toward using individual underwriting with even larger employee groups." Stone, "Implications of the Human Genome Project," 145.

whether framed in terms of claims history or the employer's knowledge about medical problems among employees and dependents, are very unlikely to produce any data from genetic testing, since by definition the feature that makes such data different from data about illnesses that have already become symptomatic is that the gene tests reveal susceptibilities to *future* disease.

Furthermore, such data would be substantially irrelevant, at least for large groups of insured persons, because the risks that such gene tests would reveal are already expressed in the claims experience of the population on which the insurer already relies in experience-rating the group. Unlike AIDS, which, as a new disease, played havoc with existing actuarial tables, the genes that predispose certain people to certain diseases are not new factors. To the extent that such genetic variations are responsible for diseases that give rise to medical expenses, they can already be seen in the group's claims experience. Therefore, gene test results would add no information that is not already present in more relevant form. Of course, this conclusion only holds when the law of large numbers is at work. Underwriting can still be useful for companies providing insurance for small groups, in which the chance occurrence of several individuals having the same rare risk factor could lead to results that are out of line with actuarial expectations. This is why it makes sense for small companies to come together in buying-cooperatives to purchase insurance jointly at lower rates.

Finally, even when underwriting takes place, insurers must balance the costs of the process—including the expense of obtaining the results of tests that are not a regular part of applicants' files—against the gains that they will receive by fine-tuning the coverage that they are willing to write for a particular premium.[56] At the moment, it probably does not make economic sense to perform gene tests on all applicants for individual or small-group health insurance who appear to be at no greater risk than general members of the population for any particular disease: the cost of obtaining the additional information will far exceed the value of that information. Thus, as a practical matter, the relevance of gene tests to

---

[56] As Justice Powell observed in his dissenting opinion in *Arizona Governing Committee v. Norris*:

> The most accurate classification system would be to identify all attributes that have some verifiable correlation with mortality and divide people into groups accordingly, but the administrative cost of such an undertaking would be prohibitive. Instead of identifying all relevant attributes, most insurance companies classify individuals according to criteria that provide both an accurate and efficient measure of longevity, including a person's age and sex. These particular criteria are readily identifiable, stable, and easily verifiable.

Norris, 463 U.S. at 1104 (Powell, J., dissenting) (citing George S. Benston, "The Economics of Gender Discrimination in Employee Fringe Benefits: *Manhart* Revisited," *University of Chicago Law Review* 49, no. 2 [Spring 1982]: 499–501).

health insurance is likely to be limited to situations in which an applicant for an individual policy is identified as "high risk" because of a family history of a condition that is associated with great likelihood of large medical expenses. For example, an applicant whose family has a history of Huntington's disease may offer to an insurer a negative test result to establish that the gene for Huntington's has not been inherited, and hence that he or she should be regarded as "standard risk."

B. Reasons of principle

While at the moment it seems unlikely that tests for genetic predisposition to adult-onset, non-Mendelian diseases[57] will be utilized widely (if at all) by health insurance companies, there are also reasons of principle for why such tests ought not to be used in determining health insurance coverage. The primary reason arises from comparing the purposes of health insurance with those of life insurance (and probably disability insurance as well); the reason is that an inability to obtain health insurance is a much graver harm to people than an inability to purchase life (or disability) insurance.

Plainly, all insurance is designed to cushion or avoid the economic harm associated with the occurrence of certain adverse events: health insurance with illness (and hence the cost of treatment); life insurance with death (and hence the loss of support for dependents and onerous estate taxes on large and illiquid estates); and disability insurance with loss of function (and hence a decrease in one's work-related income). These harms are not all of equal concern, for at least two reasons: first, the interests associated with health are of special importance; second, with respect to ensuring that the relevant interests are met, private health insurance is necessary in more cases than are life or disability insurance.

While one hears criticism of the extreme differences in income and wealth that the "free market" has produced in recent decades in the United States, and while government efforts that are supposed to redistribute funds from the very rich to the (deserving) poor enjoy at least nominal popular support, by and large, our society seems not only to be comfortable with but even to exalt such differences both as "just rewards" for ingenuity and hard work and as appropriate incentives for efforts to

---

[57] Most Mendelian disorders—those whose manifestation follows the classical pattern associated with point mutations in dominant or recessive genes—are very rare. Especially in adults, the inherited genetic mutations associated with common diseases such as cancer or heart disease are better described as creating susceptibilities or predispositions, the manifestation of which is non-Mendelian because it depends on other inherited or acquired genetic variations and on other factors in the person's environment. "The majority of genetic diseases are polygenic and multifactorial." Mark Rothstein, "Protecting Genetic Privacy by Permitting Employer Access Only to Job-Related Employee Medical Information: An Analysis of a Unique Minnesota Law," *American Journal of Law and Medicine* 24, no. 4 (1998): 455.

increase the national stock of goods and services. Differences also arise in access to health care, largely as a derivative of the disparities in income and wealth, but differences in health care access are neither as widely accepted nor as easily justified. Even though the public was persuaded in 1994 that it did not want to authorize a new government health care program to overcome some of the barriers to access, most Americans probably still strongly agree with the conclusion of the President's commission on bioethics. In 1983, the commission stated that "society has an ethical obligation to ensure equitable access to health care for all,"[58] and that this obligation (which is met for many people through their participation in private rather than public forms of health insurance) exists even in the absence of a societal obligation to ensure access to other important goods such as food, clothing, or housing.[59]

In explaining the ethical justification that lies behind this instinctive sense of obligation, the President's Commission reasoned that it "derives from the special importance of health care in promoting personal well-being by preventing or relieving pain, suffering, and disability and by avoiding loss of life."[60] Health care also broadens one's range of opportunities—"that is, the array of life plans that is reasonable to pursue within the conditions obtaining in society"[61]—and it provides the "ability to relieve worry and to enable patients to adjust to their situation by

---

[58] President's Commission for the Study of Ethical Problems in Medicine and Biomedical and Behavioral Research, *Securing Access to Health Care* (Washington, DC: U.S. Government Printing Office, 1983), 1:4. The commission was authorized by an act of Congress in 1978. Pub. L. 95–622, 42 U.S.C. sec. 300v-1. The original eleven members were named by President Carter in 1979 and sworn in at the White House in January 1980. By the time the commission's report on access to health care—one of eleven reports, most of which responded to specific mandates in the commission's authorizing statute—was released in March 1983, eight of its members were appointees of President Reagan, while three of Carter's appointees remained.

[59] Richard A. Epstein takes a more skeptical view of such claims in *Mortal Peril* (New York: Addison-Wesley, 1997).

[60] President's Commission, *Securing Access to Health Care*, 16:

Health, insofar as it is the absence of pain, suffering, or serious disability, is what has been called a primary good, that is, there is no need to know what a particular person's other ends, preferences, and values are in order to know that health is good for that individual. It generally helps people carry out their life plans, whatever they may happen to be. This is not to say that everyone defines good health in the same way or assigns the same weight or importance to different aspects of being healthy, or to health in comparison with the other goods of life. Yet though people may differ over each of these matters, their disagreement takes place within a framework of basic agreement on the importance of health.

[61] Ibid., 17:

The effects that meeting (or failing to meet) people's health needs have on the distribution of opportunity in a society become apparent if diseases are thought of as adverse departures from a normal level of functioning. In this view, health care is that which people need to maintain or restore normal functioning or to compensate for inability to function normally.

supplying reliable information about their health."[62] Moreover, "health care has a special interpersonal significance: it expresses and nurtures bonds of empathy and compassion."[63] Finally, not only is the need for health care often a matter of chance (largely beyond individual control or planning), but this need—unlike that for other basic necessities such as food, housing, and clothing—is highly variable among individuals and over any individual's life course. Given the potentially great expense that health care entails, it is beyond the ability of most people to "budget" or to pay for it in full with their own funds at any particular moment. For all of these reasons, health care is distinctively important, and the failure to ensure that everyone has access to an adequate level of care without bearing excessive burdens is a matter of greater ethical concern than are other inequities in society.

Given the relative importance of the interests involved, to what extent do social programs obviate the need for private insurance in order to ensure that the interest in question is adequately protected? While no public program fully replaces the income stream that is lost upon death or disability, Social Security's benefits for one's surviving spouse and children, and the coverage the program provides for persons who are totally and permanently disabled, are adequate for survival. Thus, it is not surprising that a minority of the adult population carries individual life or disability insurance. Such insurance is primarily of interest to high-income individuals whose standard of living (or that of their dependents) would be seriously eroded if they had no more income than that provided by Old Age, Survivors, and Disability Insurance (OASDI).

In contrast to the near-universal coverage for income lost through death or disability, the public programs covering medical expenses are limited to certain groups: principally, those age sixty-five years and older; those who are totally and permanently disabled; and those whose income falls

---

[62] Ibid.:

> Although health care in many situations may . . . not be necessary for good physical health, a great deal of relief from unnecessary concern—and even avoidance of pointless or potentially harmful steps—is achieved by health care in the form of expert information provided to worried patients. Even when a prognosis is unfavorable and health professionals have little treatment to offer, accurate information can help patients plan how to cope with their situation.

[63] Ibid.:

> [H]ealth care takes on special meaning because of its role in the beginning of a human being's life as well as the end. In spite of all the advances in the scientific understanding of birth, disease, and death, these profound and universal experiences remain shared mysteries that touch the spiritual side of human nature. For these reasons a society's commitment to health care reflects some of its most basic attitudes about what it is to be a member of the human community.

below an amount specified in relation to the "poverty level" and who meet other categorical criteria. These programs are, thus, of no applicability to most nonelderly Americans, at least until they have expended all of their assets and have little or no income. Furthermore, the most pervasive effect of being uninsured is not the inability to pay for care, but rather that in order to gain access through "the front door" to good quality health care (that is, not through the emergency room or in a public clinic), one needs proof of insurance. It is not that hospitals, physicians, and other care providers think that most uninsured people will be unable to pay for ordinary medical care. Instead, providers worry that a few of the people who become their patients will need extensive and very expensive treatment; the providers know that once treatment has begun, it is well-nigh impossible to refuse to continue it, even if the patient is unlikely to be able to pay more than a fraction of the total cost.

On the level of principle, then, if the results of genetic testing were to make private insurance unobtainable for some people, their inability to obtain health insurance without an excessive burden would be a matter of greater ethical concern than their inability to obtain life or disability insurance. It is, thus, not surprising to find that on the policy level, both the government and insurance companies have been much quicker to protect health insurance from the effects of "genetic discrimination" than other forms of insurance.

C. Policy and prudential reasons

The reasons why gene test data are unlikely to be used in the near future by health insurers go beyond practical impediments and principled objections to include reasons of public policy—which also happen to largely coincide with the prudent strategic interests on the part of insurance companies. In addition to the barriers to using gene tests already erected by a number of state and federal laws, insurance companies themselves probably favor restrictions (both in the law and in the policies of testing companies) that make it less likely that they will face competitive pressure to decline coverage for persons whose genotype places them at elevated risk of developing a disease. Any sizeable increase in the number of persons unable to obtain private health insurance at an affordable price is very likely to create renewed interest in expanding public coverage or, at the very least, in restricting the freedom of private insurers to set the terms of both the coverage they write and their decisions to decline to cover certain risks.

Already, over the past decade, state and federal legislators have taken a number of steps either to regulate or to ban (permanently or through a time-limited moratorium) the use of genetic information by health insurers in rating or denying applicants. At the federal level, HIPAA seeks to overcome the problem of people becoming unable to obtain adequate health insurance—or of being "locked into" their present job because they fear that they would be unable to get insurance at a new job—because they or an insured member of their family has a "preexisting condition."[64] The statute limits the exclusion period that an insurer or plan may impose for such conditions—with the statute defining "preexisting conditions" in very broad terms—and makes clear that conditions identified through "genetic information" cannot be treated as "preexisting conditions."[65] HIPAA has several limitations, however. First, the rules on genetic information apply only to coverage under group plans, not to the individual market, where applicants are most at risk for discrimination in health insurance because companies are more likely to do medical underwriting for individual policies. Second, HIPAA does not forbid premium adjustments, only denials or exceptions in policies. Third, the implementation of protections is likely to vary a great deal, because HIPAA will only be enforced by the U.S. Department of Health and Human Services in states that have not adopted comparable portability and access legislation.

Thus, it is hardly surprising that 1997 saw a rush of state laws aimed at preserving state jurisdiction over group health plans. In addition, in 1997 the "number of states that prohibit genetic discrimination by health insurers more than doubled, to 23 states."[66] States have long required that insurance companies not engage in arbitrary decision-making when setting their rates or processing applications; the usual benchmark is that actions must be actuarially sound, that is, correlated with significant, demonstrable differences in risk. Furthermore, since the 1970s, a number of states have even protected persons with genetic conditions from actuarially sound determinations. Early statutes along these lines were aimed at discrimination based on sickle-cell anemia and several other genetic diseases or carrier states. An extension of this approach can be seen in a 1989 Arizona statute that brought "genetic conditions" generally within the prohibition on unfair discrimination, while permit-

[64] *Health Insurance Portability and Accountability Act of 1996*, Pub. L. No. 104–191, 110 Stat. 1936 (1996).

[65] Sec. 101 of HIPAA (which amends the Employee Retirement Income Security Act of 1974) contains language at sec. 701(a)(1) that defines a "preexisting condition" very broadly as "a condition (whether physical or mental), regardless of the cause of the condition, for which medical advice, diagnosis, care, or treatment was recommended or received within the 6-month period ending on the enrollment date," but sec. 701(b)(1)(B) excludes "genetic information" from the definition of preexisting condition "in the absence of a diagnosis of the condition related to such information." (The same effect is achieved in the Public Health Service Act, and other provisions of federal law relating to different types of health insurance, through amendments that parallel those made to ERISA.)

[66] M. S. Yesley, "Protecting Genetic Difference," *Berkeley Technology Law Journal* 13, no. 2 (Spring 1998): 656. By the end of 1998, thirty-five states had legislation that imposed at least a temporary ban on insurers' use of genetic information to determine eligibility or premium level for health insurance, and twenty-five states had restricted insurers' ability to impose conditions on insurance based on genetic information.

ting insurers to consider those genetic risks that substantially affect actuarial predictions.[67]

The strongest type of anti-genetic-discrimination statute is illustrated by one that became effective in Wisconsin on July 1, 1992. Not only does the statute apply to the molecular tests that are at the frontier of genetic testing, but it forbids health insurers (as well as employers who self-insure) from either requiring genetic tests or requesting information about prior tests.[68] Furthermore, coverage may not be conditioned upon having a genetic test, nor may rates be predicated upon test results.[69]

A middle approach—more specific than Arizona's but less restrictive than Wisconsin's—can be seen in a Florida statute adopted in April 1992 that, when it was in effect until 1998, did not restrict insurers' ability to determine eligibility and rates on genetic grounds.[70] Instead, that statute was primarily concerned with making sure that insurance companies use gene tests accurately. The law required informed consent for gene tests, and insisted that the person tested be the one to authorize any disclosure of test results.[71] As of October 1999, Georgia was the only state with a statute that relies solely on this approach to combat genetic discrimination by insurers.[72]

Proposed by researchers at the Boston University School of Public Health, the Genetic Privacy Act of 1995 (GPA), takes a similar approach to protecting the genetic information of insurance-company customers from misuse.[73] The GPA set out to preserve the confidentiality and privacy of individuals' genetic information from misuse by unauthorized parties. Its provisions require that anyone collecting or analyzing genetic samples must obtain written informed consent from the sample's source prior to DNA collection or analysis. Individuals also have the right to limit the types of genetic tests performed on samples of their own DNA and to order the destruction of the DNA samples. Written informed consent from the individual is also required for storage, usage, and disclosure of genetic information. Furthermore, the GPA grants property rights in the DNA samples to the sample's source. Currently, a few states have incorporated some of these provisions within their insurance antidiscrimination statutes. The

---

[67] Ariz. Rev. Stat. sec. 20–2301 (1999).

[68] Wisc. Stat. Ann. sec. 631.89 (West 1998).

[69] This statute resembles the recommendations endorsed by the Hereditary Diseases Foundation; the National Institutes of Health; the Department of Energy Working Group on Ethical, Legal, and Social Implications of the Human Genome Project; and the National Action Plan for Breast Cancer to prevent genetic discrimination in health insurance. *Statement on Protection Against Genetic Discrimination* (1995), available at http://www.hdfoundation.org/testread/discrim.htm [accessed August 17, 1999].

[70] In 1998, Florida moved beyond this approach and enacted a statute that prohibits insurers from using genetic information to cancel, limit, or deny coverage, or to establish premium rates based on such information. Fla. Stat. chap. 627.4301 (1998).

[71] Fla. Stat. chap. 760.40 (1998).

[72] Ga. Code Ann. sec. 33–54–3 (1999).

[73] Annas, Glantz, and Roche, *The Genetic Privacy Act and Commentary.*

medical and research communities have criticized the GPA, however, arguing that it would impose significant financial burdens on the practice of medicine and research, primarily from the requirements to obtain and document informed consent and to counsel patients or subjects.[74]

It appears that the movement among state legislatures is toward the Wisconsin model. As of June 1999, thirty-five states have adopted statutes that prohibit insurers from using genetic information to determine eligibility for health insurance coverage, and nineteen states have adopted statutes prohibiting insurers from requiring applicants or family members to provide genetic information as a prerequisite to being offered coverage. In thirty-five states, it is illegal for health insurers to charge a higher premium, or even to set the premium rate, based on an individual's genetic information. Twenty-five states prohibit insurers from imposing different conditions on health coverage based on genetic information (for example, by excluding genetic disorders from an applicant's coverage because he or she has tested positive on a gene test). Twenty-seven states do not allow genetic information to be the basis of the determination of a "preexisting condition," unless the condition has been diagnosed clinically. Only nine U.S. jurisdictions (including Puerto Rico and the Virgin Islands) still lack a statute designed to protect against genetic discrimination in health insurance.

Exactly what information are health insurers prohibited from using under HIPAA and the state statutes? While the state laws all encompass the results of molecular tests for disease-susceptibility genes, their definitions vary greatly in how widely they reach beyond such gene tests. For example, the California statute that governs health insurance discrimination includes—in addition to "any scientifically or medically identifiable gene or chromosome"—the broad category of characteristics derived from a family member, which would seem to prohibit the use of family medical history as a source for insight into an individual's genetic risks.[75] Two states, Florida and Tennessee, do specifically "exclude family medical history, and several states exclude routine tests such as blood and urine analysis done in the course of a physical examination, unless the tests were conducted specifically to identify a genetic anomaly."[76]

The interim rules for HIPAA, which took effect in July 1997, define "genetic information" as:

[74] See, e.g., Philip R. Reilly, "Panel Comment: The Impact of the Genetic Privacy Act on Medicine," *Journal of Law, Medicine, and Ethics* 23 (1995): 379; and Edwin S. Flores Troy, "The Genetic Privacy Act: An Analysis of Privacy and Research Concerns," *Journal of Law, Medicine, and Ethics* 25 (1997): 266.

[75] Cal. Health and Safety Code sec. 1374.7(d) (West 1998) and Cal. Ins. Code sec. 10123.3(d) (West 1998). Note that with respect to life and disability insurance, the California Insurance Code uses a narrower definition of "genetic characteristic." Cal. Ins. Code sec. 10147(b) (West 1998).

[76] Yesley, "Protecting Genetic Difference," 660 (citing statutes in Florida, Georgia, Illinois, Minnesota, New York, Tennessee, and Texas).

information about genes, gene products, and inherited characteristics that may derive from the individual or a family member. This includes information regarding carrier status and information derived from laboratory tests that identify mutations in specific genes or chromosomes, physical medical examinations, family histories, and direct analysis of genes or chromosomes.[77]

This language would appear to protect virtually all genetically relevant information or, one might say, to treat a great deal of medical information (virtually all?) as genetic.[78] Thus, the effect of the expansive definition of genetic information will be to prevent insurance carriers from placing in their policies a "preexisting condition exclusion" involving a presymptomatic disease that has some genetic component—provided that the patient has no clinical signs from which a diagnosis could be made.

While it might be thought that insurance companies would resist such extensive prohibitions on the use of genetic data by health insurers, that is not necessarily the case. As already noted, insurers recognize the public sensitivity to the danger that increased genetic testing for predisposition to an ever wider range of diseases could leave a growing number of people unable to find affordable insurance. Such an outcome—or even the prospect of its occurrence—definitely increases the pressure for more public programs or, in the short run, for greater government regulation of health insurance. This is something the industry certainly wants to avoid, whether it would mean more oversight of health insurance arrangements or broad restrictions on the use of genetic information that could spill over into other insurance lines, particularly life insurance.

At the same time, insurers recognize that a prohibition on the use of genetic information undermines their ability to detect individuals whose purchase of health insurance is prompted by having found out that they are at higher-than-average risk of needing medical care. This risk of "adverse selection" is of concern to the industry as a whole, but is a much greater concern to any insurance company that decides not to screen out certain risk factors while competitors engage in such screening.

Beyond legislation, this same policy objective comes through in the apparent willingness of health insurance companies to agree with a major player in BRCA-predisposition testing, like Myriad Genetics, that the insurers that cover the cost of the test (which runs about $2,400, plus the

---

[77] 26 C.F.R. sec. 54.9801-2T, 29 C.F.R. sec. 2590.701-2, 45 C.F.R. sec. 114.103.

[78] As will be explored in the following section, the result could be that members in group health plans will be better off when a disease is seen as "genetic" rather than as "environmental": coal miners, for instance, would hope to have their risk of developing lung disease classed as "something that runs in the family" rather than as "something that all miners have." Mark Rothstein argues that reasoning of this sort would also support prohibiting insurers from using any genetic information. If no insurer is allowed to use such information in underwriting, then the cost of adverse selection would be shared equally among all insurers. Rothstein, "Protecting Genetic Privacy."

fees of the physician running the test, the fees of the genetic counselors interpreting the results, etc.) will not ask Myriad to reveal the results to the company. Each company is safe from "targeted adverse selection" as long as all other companies agree to the same terms, even though the industry as a whole will experience adverse selection since the total pool of people seeking private health insurance will contain a greater proportion of people at risk for developing breast cancer (and other conditions related to the BRCA genes) than would otherwise be the case. This industry-wide problem is rendered more manageable if the ex ante risk is spread fairly evenly and all insurers lack one important piece of information (the BRCA test result) that is available to some insurance applicants and that, if available to some insurers, *might* lead them to treat these applicants differently.

D. Not discriminating in favor of genetic disease

The upshot of this analysis is that DNA testing is not likely to play a major role in health insurance decision-making, either because it is precluded by statute or because insurers are willing to forgo the collective advantage of avoiding adverse selection in order not to provoke more restrictive legislative responses. Nevertheless, health insurers do engage in one practice that some critics have labeled "genetic discrimination,"[79] though what turns out to be at issue are medical conditions, not genetic predispositions.

Insurance is, almost by definition, not available for a harm that has already occurred: you cannot insure a burning house. Insurance is available for risks that are collectively predictable but individually unpredictable. This principle provides the justification for insurers not writing health coverage for a person with a "preexisting condition" or limiting coverage to conditions other than the one for which the person is already being treated. In ethical terms, it would be unfair for those who are already experiencing a loss to climb belatedly into the same boat with people who have been pooling their funds to cover a loss that is still, for them, a matter of chance rather than certainty. The occurrence of the loss may still be "unfair" to those experiencing it (in the sense that the loss is not something that they could have avoided or for which they are otherwise responsible), but that does not give them any claim to a pooled fund to which they did not contribute when their risk was purely hypothetical.[80]

---

[79] See, e.g., Billings et al., "Discrimination as a Consequence."

[80] HIPAA acknowledges this principle because it provides that the maximum length of a "preexisting condition exclusion" that a group health plan may impose on a new participant—which is twelve months (or eighteen months for a late enrollee)—will be reduced "by the aggregate of the periods of creditable coverage" that the participant had through a prior group or other form of health insurance. Thus, HIPAA and comparable state statutes aim principally at allowing people who are already insured to continue to have health care coverage when they move to a new position; such "portability" suggests that the person is not waiting until he or she knows "the house is on fire" before getting insurance.

Many instances of alleged genetic discrimination in health insurance seem to be garden-variety applications of these basic precepts. Individuals who already manifested their diseases faced denial of their insurance applications not because of their genotype but because they were already in need of medical care. The fact that their disease may have had genetic components is adventitious. To include these people within the ambit of protection, on the ground that they are suffering an unfair genetic discrimination, would be unfair to all those sick people whose conditions happen not to be regarded as "genetic." There is no reason to favor a disease—in public policy terms—simply because its etiology is described in one fashion rather than another. Public policy recognizes this in statutes like HIPAA, which, for example, excludes from the category of conditions defined by their "genetic information" those that have already led to a diagnosis.

VI. Life Insurance: Can—and Should—Genetic Risks Be Treated Differently?

We have already found several bases for differentiating life insurance from health insurance. First, unlike health insurance, life insurance does not protect an interest regarded as a primary good, nor is it necessary to possess this form of insurance in order to achieve an adequate existence. Hence, society's ethical obligation to ensure equitable access to an adequate level of health insurance does not arise for life insurance, and society is not obligated to ensure access to life insurance beyond that provided through fair treatment under public programs. Second, unlike health insurance, most life insurance is individual-issue and undergoes an underwriting process, in which all the factors and sources of information previously described come into play. The extent of medical testing and information-gathering depends on several considerations, a principal one being the size of the policy; the company's greater exposure with a large policy justifies the company expending more money and utilizing tests that have a lower expected payoff.

At the moment, DNA-based tests, such as the BRCA1 and BRCA2 tests that are offered by several gene testing companies, are much more expensive than the tests typically employed in the insurance application process. Furthermore, as previously described, the high correlation of disease incidence with positive test results is not yet matched by proof that such results are an equally reliable predictor of longevity for asymptomatic individuals. It is thus unlikely that life insurance companies will make testing for BRCA or comparable disease-predisposition genes a routine part of the insurance application process in the near future. However, insurance companies are likely to ask applicants about the results of any gene tests that they have undergone. Moreover, applicants who know that their family history (which is a routine part of the application) reveals a pattern of a disease—such as breast cancer—for which a molecular test exists may actually take such a test in order to be able to overcome the negative impact that their family-disease pattern might have on their ability to obtain life insurance, at standard rates or at all.

A. Will predictive medicine doom insurance?

In certain situations, then, genetic information—whether obtained from a family history, from interpretation of clinical findings, or from a gene test—fits into life insurance underwriting like any other information about an applicant: it will be used to the extent that it reliably predicts the risk of premature death, and it will affect decisions to issue policies when this predicted effect is sufficient to place applicants outside the normal range for longevity. What this means at the moment is that, outside of a few single-gene diseases with dramatic effects on lifespan (such as Huntington's disease), it is unlikely that the results of gene tests will be a major part of insurance underwriting in the near future. It is also unlikely that significant genetic information in an applicant's file will result in a substandard rating (leading to a higher premium) or in denial of coverage.

There is, however, an interesting dilemma facing the life insurance industry that is, in effect, parallel to the dilemma of health insurers. If health insurers use genetic information (especially if they were to bring it into the process of rating group plans), they could end up, for competitive reasons, having to deny coverage to so many people as to threaten the very viability of the private insurance market. The problem facing life insurers is that, taken to an extreme, the information about individual genotypes that they will eventually be able to obtain from gene tests could provide such detailed predictions about life prospects as to threaten the very premise on which insurance rests. Insurance depends on applying the law of large numbers to a population whose collective age-adjusted longevity is well known and all of whose members are ex ante at equal risk. The smaller the group, the less reliable the predictions, and the more individuals know about their individual risk, the less likely the group is to conform to expected data. Provided that the decision to join the group is voluntary, those who can reliably predict that their need for insurance is lower than average will be less likely to sign on, while those who believe themselves to be at greater-than-average risk will be more likely. Assuming their predictions are accurate, the actual losses experienced by the insurance pool will exceed expected losses, meaning that to protect its solvency, the pool will have to raise the price of entrance. This will make entrance even less attractive to low-risk individuals, fewer of whom will be interested in joining, which will further skew the composition of the enrolled group, and so on.

It will, of course, be some time before tests (especially relatively inexpensive ones) become available for all known deleterious genetic mutations or before individual genotyping becomes routine. Even when the genetic data are in hand, their actuarial significance will take even longer to establish. Yet, while genetic knowledge has not accumulated quite as rapidly as some forecasters predicted twenty years ago, the day when these things become reality probably lies within the lifetime of biomedical scientists now working. At that point, some optimists have tried to suggest, genetic discrimination will cease because we will all see (indeed, with precision) that everyone carries a number of harmful genetic mutations. Further, since the hope and expectation of clinical geneticists is that the arrival of that day will permit much more precise and useful advice about preventive measures and lifestyle changes, the optimists suggest that such measures will further obviate the use of genetic information to predict longevity because the genetic findings will be less predictive of particular outcomes. Yet by thinking in terms of averages, this rosy view misses the real consequences of the expansion of genetic knowledge. It is one thing to say that "each of us has an estimated five to fifty serious misspellings or alterations in our DNA." It is quite another to know what those mutations actually are, which would then mean that while "we could all be targets for discrimination based on our genes,"[81] some of us would be much bigger targets than others. Once the effects are known— not just of individual mutations, but of sets of mutations as well—it will be possible to refine predictions about longevity a great deal.

In the end, the fact that each person is genetically unique (including monozygotic twins, once their experiences have led to immunological differentiation and the acquisition of genetic mutations) could be the undoing of insurance. Human uniqueness is not new—what is new are the medical predictions that will be made from the substrate of that uniqueness, as revealed through genotype analysis. Of course, how one dies is less important for life insurance purposes than when one dies, so even detailed predictions of future disease states and their known effects on longevity (individually and in combination with each other) may still yield data on the basis of which insurance applicants can be grouped because of common life expectancy. The groups are still likely to be smaller, however, which will necessitate greater conservatism in rating them. Likewise, the fact that individuals will also have this knowledge about their genotype is likely either to skew the pool of applicants toward those with much shorter life expectancies, or to lead insurers to offer a much larger variety of "preferred" groupings so as to continue to have a product that is priced to appeal to individuals who want to insure against unpredictable causes of death despite the long life that their genotypes promise them. This, then, is the dilemma facing life insurers: If they ignore genetic information, they are at risk of adverse selection (especially of the targeted variety, to the extent that competitors employ genetic-based rating).

[81] Mansoura and Collins, "Medical Implications," 343.

If, instead, they utilize the results of gene tests that predict future diseases, they may bring about hyper-differentiation of their product, which would eventually make the product financially untenable to the insurers and highly unattractive to their customers. Both of those problems would emerge because risk would be spread over too small a pool; the outcomes among individuals in a given pool would be too similar ex post.

In addition to this dilemma—which will not manifest itself in the near future, if ever—life insurance companies face another one which is very real and very immediate. It is manifest in the tension between a company's sales arm and its underwriting office. On the one hand, the company relies on the underwriters to keep it from making improvident decisions about whom to insure; lax underwriting can spell doom if those who ought to be treated as substandard risks or not accepted at all are rated as standard risks. On the other hand, underwriting that is too cautious will deprive the company of contracts from which it could earn a reasonable profit. Moreover, beyond the applications actually denied or set at high premiums (which typically results in their not being accepted by the applicant), cautious underwriting discourages the sales force by making their job that much more difficult. When independent brokers are involved, such restrictive underwriting may simply drive away business, as the company earns a reputation for a high rate of rejections. Thus, while firms will differ in how they manage this tension, success seems to lie with honing the underwriting process so that it singles out the few exceptional cases and accepts most applicants at standard rates. (Life insurance companies typically rate 90 to 94 percent of their applicants at the standard rate, with the remainder divided between denials and applicants whose premiums are set at one-and-a-half to two times the standard rate.) The situation that all companies want to avoid, however, is having a "blind spot" to a particular category of risk. If independent agents discover that a particular company overlooks certain risks, they are likely to submit applications that present those risks to that company, to increase the probability of acceptance at a standard rate. If the risk skews outcomes in a significant fashion, the insurer stands to lose money. Conversely, what insurers want to find is a special niche where they can recognize a group of lower-than-average risk applicants and draw their business by offering reduced premiums; this is the way that "preferred rates" for nonsmokers were introduced, a bet—made on skimpy data— that paid off handsomely.

B. Don't ask, do tell

While life insurers are unlikely to institute gene tests on their own (certainly not for the average applicant without manifest illness, and usually not even for individuals with family histories of disease), insurers' fear of a blind spot and of the resulting adverse selection is increased when applicants have access to predictive information of the sort that gene tests may provide. This worry exists even if the amount of reliable information that these companies have about the actuarial effects of most mutations that these tests detect is not enough for the companies to promulgate sound rules for rating and declining applications. The absence of reliable information could mean that applicants who bought life insurance sooner or in larger amounts than they otherwise would have because they got a positive result on a disease-predicting gene test end up being just as profitable for insurers as their average customer. Nonetheless, this is not the sort of gamble that insurance companies like to take, especially when there is reason to think that the effects of a positive result on life expectancy may not be precisely known but are likely to be more than marginally negative. This is particularly true when the people most likely to be tested are those who have a family history of the disease in question, and even more so when that disease is associated with premature death.

To respond to the risks of adverse selection that arise in this sort of situation, the companies will want to adopt a "don't ask, do tell" stance — namely, that they will not test applicants, but will require that applicants disclose the results of any gene tests, just as they must disclose (or authorize others to disclose) other medically relevant information as a condition of applying for a policy. Plainly, the first part of such a policy — "don't ask" — is ethically desirable for many reasons. Requiring a person to undergo a test that in some sense predicts the future course not only of his or her own life but, to some extent, of the lives of close relatives goes far beyond what private parties are permitted to do now. It forces information on a person that could result not merely in emotional harm but in an involuntary redefinition of that person's self-identity. Thus, if gene testing became much less expensive and yielded much more valuable information, there would still be strong reasons of public policy to prevent insurers from instituting such testing as a routine part of a medical examination for insurance.[82]

The same objections do not arise regarding the "do tell" part of the policy, since the information from the gene test was not forced on the person. (The choice to have the test, however, may have been an instance of "constrained freedom." If the person was tested in response to family pressure, a sense of obligation, or — more germane to the present topic — in order to avoid the adverse result that might arise in insurance underwrit-

---

[82] Those reasons may diminish as gene tests become a more familiar part of medical care, as the range of information they supply increases, and as the treatments available from "molecular medicine" become more available and efficacious. In sum, those reasons may diminish as the mystery and dread that now attach to this type of testing abate. People will then overcome the simplistic genetic determinism that lies behind this thinking and come to see that genetic information does not supply a map of one's destiny or a measure of one's worth.

ing due to an uncontradicted risk revealed by a family history of disease, then the decision to be tested is not a completely unconstrained one.) The principal difference that might set a gene test apart from other tests that are routine, accepted parts of the insurance application process (like a blood pressure test or an HIV test) is that the information has, by implication, significance for the health status and longevity of close relatives as well. Of course, that does not distinguish the gene test results from a family's disease pedigree; indeed, the latter, precisely by identifying (perhaps by name) the applicant's relatives and their degree of risk of developing the disease, is actually more pointed in its implications for at-risk family members. But the assumption about gene tests—indeed, the whole reason why insurers would want to know the results—is that they allow more precise predictions than do the family histories that insurers already collect. Thus, requiring applicants to give full and truthful answers about the results of gene tests as a condition for obtaining a valid insurance policy[83] makes them reveal information that could be harmful to others. Nonetheless, since these relatives would not have standing to object to an applicant's voluntarily disclosing such information, the only effective response to this problem lies in controlling how insurers store and save data. In particular, insurers should be prohibited from entering genetic data collected from one person in relatives' records or using the information in making decisions about the relatives' insurance applications.

C. Making decisions about insurance risks from gene testing

It is unlikely that many people will in the near future seek out a gene test specifically for insurance purposes, although that will occur occasionally when a person with a family history of a dominant disorder with high penetrance and dire effects (such as Huntington's disease) decides to be tested in the hopes of being able to demonstrate to an insurer that he or she has not inherited the gene and, therefore, should be eligible for life insurance at standard rates. The major issue in such circumstances is making clear to the person that if the test results are positive, the person will be faced with having to reveal this information and, perhaps, having it become a permanent part of his or her medical record. Furthermore, if the person seeks to have the costs of the test covered by health insurance now, the fact that the test was taken will be part of his or her health insurance file even if the company's life insurance branch does not seek the results at this time.

A familiar part of all medical interventions is the mutual process of disclosure and agreement between health care professional and patient

---

[83] False statements on an application can void a policy, though this is a penalty that typically only has teeth if the insured-against event occurs during the "contestability period" within a year or two after the application.

that is called "informed consent." At its worst, this is nothing more than a ritual in which the "informed consent" consists solely of a patient's signature on a consent form. The process can be much more, meaning that the form itself is merely a memorandum recording the process, a memorandum which may even be inadequate at that.

Many physicians are pressed for time, poorly reimbursed for "talking" as opposed to "doing," and less than fully acquainted with all relevant clinical background about a gene test or the potential meanings of its results (much less with all the psychosocial dimensions). For these physicians, the informed-consent process may consist of providing the patient with a brochure from the test company and then answering questions after the patient has reviewed a standardized consent form drawn up by the company. It is difficult for the patient to understand the various aspects of such a form, since the way a particular issue is understood will depend upon the context in which it is discussed and the manner in which related factors are set forth. For example, in the case of BRCA testing, the major testing firm, Myriad Genetics, distributes to patients a three-paged, single-spaced pamphlet, "Informed Consent for Genetic Susceptibility Testing for Breast and Ovarian Cancer." The pamphlet sets forth the purpose of the test, an explanation of the diseases, the procedures involved, and the range of possible results (including a nebulous one described as a "genetic change of uncertain significance"). Also discussed are risks, limitations, and benefits of the test.[84]

Outside of testing conducted for insurance purposes, what effects on insurance can be expected to flow from the results of gene testing done

[84] The section on risks includes the following language:

Myriad Genetic Laboratories will strive to keep the results of your test confidential. It will release your test results only as directed by you (or a person legally authorized to act on your behalf) in writing. Despite the company's best efforts, there is a small chance that a staff member will inappropriately disclose your test results to a third party.

If you learn that you have a genetic predisposition to breast and/or ovarian cancer you will have knowledge that you may be forced to disclose to third parties. For example, as insurance companies learn more about hereditary risk for cancer, they may ask about the results of genetic tests of those who have or apply for coverage.

In most states, life and disability insurers may ask such questions and use the answers in underwriting decisions. In less than half the states, there are laws that restrict the uses that health insurers may make of such information. These laws are not comprehensive and may not protect you. Knowledge that you have a genetic predisposition to breast and/or ovarian cancer may compromise your ability to obtain or maintain insurance coverage.

Because this is a new test and there is much to learn about findings that suggest increased risk, some states may define it as investigational.

Myriad Genetics, "Informed Consent for Genetic Susceptibility Testing for Breast and Ovarian Cancer," available at http://www.myriad.com/patient/choiceform.html [accessed October 1, 1998]. Myriad has now replaced the consent form with a multipart website devoted to genetic testing for hereditary breast and ovarian cancer. This site includes educational materials for patients, information for professionals, and a glossary. See http://www.myriad.com/gt.html [accessed December 10, 1999].

for clinical reasons? At this early stage in the development of gene testing, these effects cannot be simply stated: they will vary by the disease for which the test is performed, by the confidence with which we can predict a particular outcome from the test results, and by the clinical point at which the test is done. Other variables include the type of insurance sought, the manner in which it is obtained, and even the state in which the applicant resides. As a general matter, gene test results are likely to have a greater impact on insurance that is purchased on an individual basis than on that purchased on a group basis (especially as part of an employee benefit plan). This is mostly because group insurance is subject to less adverse selection (in terms of the timing of purchase) and is less likely to take into account an individual's disease risks (beyond those that are already manifest as conditions for which medical intervention has recently been sought).

Correlatively, as I have argued, at least in the near term, the impact of gene test results will be greater on life (and disability) insurance than health insurance. This is both because a larger proportion of the latter is obtained on a group rather than an individual basis and because insurers are less likely to seek—and society is less likely to allow—restrictions on health insurance, which is more of a necessity for a decent life than is life insurance.

VII. Conclusion

The right of privacy protects a basic human value, our interest in having control over our lives and how others perceive them. Information related to our health is among that which people regard as particularly private, and among health information, that relating to our genes— particularly the results of DNA-based tests for genetic mutations that predispose us to future diseases and disorders—constitutes especially sensitive material. Consequently, if the right to privacy protects anything, it ought to provide individuals with maximum control over information about their genome.

However, this conclusion runs into several difficulties, beyond any lacunae in the legal protection of privacy. The main difficulty that I have examined in this essay arises when genetic information would be actuarially relevant to an insurer in deciding whether to issue or to "rate" a new policy. On the one hand, the potential harm to individuals in being unable to obtain an insurance policy (at least at standard rates) underscores why the right of privacy to insurance data seems so important. On the other hand, when genetic factors place an applicant outside the expected range of risks of illness, disability, or death, the value to the insurer of having this information is obvious. I have suggested that, for various reasons, these conflicting interests will likely play out differently with respect to different lines of insurance. Insurers should not, and probably will not, rely on genetic testing in offering health insurance policies in the foreseeable future. Because of different forces in the life insurance market— principally, the important role of underwriting and the need to avoid adverse selection by applicants—genetic testing may play a greater role there. It would be unwise for government to restrict the operation of this market, that is, the freedom of companies, agents, and applicants to arrange for the use of genetic test results as part of the underwriting process.

Nonetheless, applicants continue to have privacy interests, which dictate that the use of genetic test information be restricted to those circumstances in which the risk of adverse selection is greatest—namely, when the applicant possesses genetic data that the insurer does not. Limiting insurers' ability to impose gene tests as part of the insurance application process, while insisting that insurers be given access to the results of gene tests that the applicant has already had performed—"don't ask, do tell"— accommodates the principal interests of both parties. To the extent that this formula were made a part of statutory law, it would constrain the more powerful party in the bargaining process—the insurer—from imposing genetic testing on applicants who have chosen to preserve their sense of an "open future," but still protect insurers from the worst effects of adverse selection.

Finally, there is the problem of the leaky nature of many "confidential" medical records—a condition that additional legislation aimed at protecting the privacy of health or genetic information is unlikely ever to remedy fully. Yet the moratoria adopted by many states in the latter half of the 1990s to restrict the adverse uses of genetic data seem appropriate. These moratoria seem difficult to enforce—how is it possible to be certain whether such information was taken into account by a decision-maker, or whether all private genetic information had remained confidential? However, the moratoria will at least provide some time for society to appraise the impact of these new genetic tests.

Law, University of Southern California

THE RIGHT TO PRIVACY AND THE RIGHT TO DIE

By Tom L. Beauchamp

I. Introduction

Western ethics and law have been slow to come to conclusions about the right to choose the time and manner of one's death. However, policies, practices, and legal precedents have evolved quickly in the last quarter of the twentieth century, from the forgoing of respirators to the use of Do Not Resuscitate (DNR) orders, to the forgoing of all medical technologies (including hydration and nutrition), and now, in one U.S. state, to legalized physician-assisted suicide. The sweep of history—from the Quinlan case in New Jersey[1] to legislation in Oregon[2] that allows physician-assisted suicide—has been as rapid as it has been revolutionary.

Although generally treated as an account of the development of the legal protection of the poorly delineated idea of a right to die, the history

---

[1] *In re Quinlan*, 70 N.J. 10, 355 A.2d 647 (1976). This case involved a brain-damaged patient in a coma. In the face of active opposition from the hospital, the physicians, state and local authorities, and a lower-court guardian *ad litem*, the New Jersey Supreme Court held that it is permissible for a person's guardian to direct a physician and hospital to discontinue all extraordinary measures in order to allow a person to die. After a lengthy legal battle, the parents of Karen Ann Quinlan obtained a court order allowing them to remove the respirator that was keeping their daughter alive. The court ruled that the Quinlans could disconnect the mechanical ventilator so that the patient could "die with dignity." Unable to communicate with anyone, she lay comatose in a fetal position for ten years, with increasing respiratory problems and bedsores; her weight dropped from 115 to 70 pounds. Several Catholic moral theologians advised the parents that they were not morally required to continue the medical nutrition and hydration used to keep their daughter alive or the antibiotics used to fight her infections. However, the Quinlans believed that the feeding tube did not cause pain and that the respirator did.

[2] Oregon, *The Oregon Death with Dignity Act*, Or. Rev. Stat. secs. 127.800–897 (1994). Measure 16 was first approved by Oregon voters in a November 8, 1994 referendum. Under its provisions, a terminally ill patient who wants to utilize physician-assisted suicide must wish to escape unbearable suffering and must request a physician's prescription for lethal drugs three times. The doctor then must wait fifteen days after the first request before writing a prescription for the requested lethal drugs. In late December 1994, a federal judge in Eugene, Oregon, issued a preliminary injunction that prevented the implementation of the new law indefinitely. Three years later, on November 4, 1997, voters rejected Measure 51, which would have repealed Measure 16, by a 60–40 margin. This reaffirmed the voters' previous support for legally allowing physicians to provide lethal medication. The 9th U.S. Circuit Court of Appeals had, one week previously, lifted an injunction that had kept Measure 16 from going into effect. A few weeks after its decisions in *Vacco v. Quill*, 117 S.Ct. 2293 (1997), and *Washington v. Glucksberg*, 117 S.Ct. 2258 (1977) (see below), the U.S. Supreme Court refused to hear an appeal involving the injunction in *Quinlan*, and Measure 16 was shortly thereafter reaffirmed by the voters of Oregon and became the law of their state. (Note: The 9th Circuit case mentioned above was from the state of Washington, not Oregon.)

of these right-to-die issues reveals a powerful struggle in law, medicine, and ethics over the nature, scope, and foundations of a variety of autonomy and privacy rights. Early legal cases involving the right to die attempted to ground claims about the right in privacy rights,[3] but recently liberty rights have been the favored category. I offer no judgments here about foundations in law or about legalization or institutional policy. My interest is in moral questions: chiefly, whether privacy and liberty protections justify requests for active forms of aid-in-dying.

Before we can appropriately address legal and policy issues about the emerging frontiers of the right to die, especially voluntary active euthanasia and physician-assisted suicide, we need to determine whether these acts are morally licit. I maintain that their moral licitness is grounded in rights of autonomy and privacy. In morals, unlike American law, there is no competition for justificatory supremacy between privacy rights and liberty rights. Indeed, they are mutually reinforcing, and their use in moral reasoning does not present the problems that have beset privacy-rights doctrine on the right to die in the law.[4]

II. Legal and Historical Background

Though my analysis is not rooted in law and policy, I start with a discussion of the brief period of recent legal history that has motivated moral theorists to address issues about the right to die in terms of rights of autonomy and privacy. Prior to the findings in *In re Quinlan* (1976), few judicial cases and effectively no public policy set the contours of decision-making rights for seriously ill or injured patients. However, in *In re Quinlan*, in the face of active opposition from a comatose patient's hospital, physicians, state and local authorities, and a lower-court guardian *ad litem*, the New Jersey Supreme Court held that it is permissible for a patient's authorized guardian to direct a physician and hospital to discontinue all extraordinary measures and disconnect a respirator in order to allow that patient to die.[5]

In the opinion's principal section on "Constitutional and Legal Issues," the first and only fundamental value cited by the court was "the constitutional right of privacy," a right it grounded in the U.S. Constitution.[6] The court recognized that the right to privacy is not absolute and must be balanced against state interests in continuing life, preventing suicide, and

---

[3] In *Griswold v. Connecticut*, 381 U.S. 479, 486 (1965), and various subsequent U.S. Supreme Court decisions, the right of privacy is held to arise from the "penumbra" of several amendments to the U.S. Constitution. The thesis is that a personal right to privacy exists because these amendments imply it.

[4] These problems are examined in Carl E. Schneider, "*Cruzan* and the Constitutionalization of American Life," *Journal of Medicine and Philosophy* 17, no. 6 (1992): 589–604.

[5] *In re Quinlan*.

[6] Ibid., 70 N.J. at 38–42, 355 A.2d at 662–64.

protecting the practice of medicine. In a celebrated statement, it said that "the State's interest *contra* [the right to privacy] weakens and the individual's right to privacy grows as the degree of bodily invasion increases and the prognosis dims. Ultimately there comes a point at which the individual's rights overcome the State interest. It is for that reason that we believe [the patient's] choice, if she were competent to make it, would be vindicated by law."[7]

The court thus brought decision-making rights in these intimate family affairs under the umbrella of privacy rights. Justifying the former rights in terms of the latter is unfortunate, but understandable. The court was reconstituting the language of privacy that had been invoked to protect the contexts of marriage, family, and procreation. The court was also attempting to thwart an unsuitable reach by law and medicine into private affairs. During the case, the physicians had presented the preposterous claim that judgments about the removal of medical technology were *medical* in nature and, hence, the province of physicians alone. In this circumstance, the court looked to the right to privacy to undergird its conviction that the patient's rights and judgment should prevail over the physician's judgment in decisions made at the end of life. The news from New Jersey was that decision-making authority resides in the privacy of patient and family deliberations, not in the authority of the physician, the medical profession, or the hospital.[8]

In the 1980s, the issues were broadened, and the question became whether *all* medical treatments that are used to sustain life are optional. Several courts continued to invoke the right of privacy in their decisions,[9] though the focus was rapidly shifting to liberty rights. The leading moral and legal issues had been in effect already answered by the time the first relevant U.S. Supreme Court decision, *Cruzan v. Director, Missouri Dept. of Health*, was handed down in 1990.[10] In *Cruzan*, the Court held that the right to refuse treatment is protected by the U.S. Constitution and that there are circumstances under which nutrition and hydration may be justifiably withheld from incompetent persons.[11]

---

[7] Ibid., 70 N.J. at 41, 355 A.2d at 664.

[8] Ibid., 70 N.J. at 22–29, 35–42, 355 A.2d 653–57, 661–64.

[9] See the string of cases from *Superintendent of Belchertown State School v. Saikewicz*, 373 Mass. 728, 737–40, 370 N.E.2d 417, 424–25 (1977) through *Bouvia v. Superior Court*, 179 Cal. App. 3d 1127, 1144, 225 Cal. Rptr. 297, 306 (1986).

[10] *Cruzan v. Director, Missouri Dept. of Health*, 110 S.Ct. 2841 (1990).

[11] Ibid. Twenty-five-year-old Nancy Cruzan had been in a persistent vegetative state for over three years. Her parents petitioned for permission to remove her feeding tube, knowing that if this were done, their daughter would die. The Missouri Supreme Court ruled that no one may order an end to life-sustaining treatment for an incompetent person in the absence of clear and convincing evidence of the patient's wishes, and the U.S. Supreme Court upheld this decision. The Supreme Court decision was followed by a hearing before a county probate judge at which three friends of Nancy Cruzan provided sufficient additional evidence that she had expressed a clear and convincing preference not to live "like a vegetable" connected to machines. This new evidence led the judge to accept the parents'

Like various state courts before it, the Supreme Court spurned the language of privacy in addressing these issues. It held that the right to refuse treatment is protected by the U.S. Constitution in virtue of the liberty interest of the patient against unwanted medical interventions, not in virtue of a right to privacy.[12] The Court had previously limited privacy claims to affairs of marriage, procreation, childrearing, and family;[13] it reaffirmed this position in *Cruzan* without incorporating decisions made at the end of life under the same doctrine. The Court commented that at least as early as *In re Storar*,[14] a 1981 New York case, a trend had emerged in the courts of basing the right to refuse treatment on the informed-consent doctrine[15] and on liberty rights, rather than on a constitutional privacy right. The Court also noted that in the case of *In re Conroy*,[16] even the New Jersey Supreme Court—the leading supporter of the privacy basis—elected to base its decision on the common law right to self-determination and informed consent.

It is beyond reasonable doubt that acceptance of passive euthanasia (that is, intentionally letting people die when it serves their best interest) became part of the social consensus in the United States between 1976 and 1990. Exactly fifteen years after *Quinlan*, the nation was poised for the next stage of the discussion, which would be about so-called *active* forms

---

request to remove the feeding tube, and thirteen days after it was removed, Nancy Cruzan died. Yet, the U.S. Supreme Court had not granted the Cruzan family precisely the relief that it had sought; the Court had declined to find a constitutional right to die, only a right of competent persons to decline life-sustaining treatments. The Court also held that it is constitutionally permissible for states to impose procedural precautions when third parties make decisions for incompetent patients. See *Cruzan*, 110 S.Ct., esp. at 2852.

[12] *Cruzan*, 110 S.Ct. at 2851. The Court noted that a constitutionally protected liberty interest in such matters could be inferred from its previous decisions that reached back as far as 1905. "Freedom," "liberty," and "self-determination" are the terms used to ground the argument in *Cruzan*. The Court also noted that the Supreme Court of Missouri had recognized a right to refuse treatment that was embodied in the common law doctrine of informed consent, but had declined to read a right of privacy into the state constitution and had expressed doubt as to whether such a right existed under the U.S. Constitution. *Cruzan v. Harmon*, 760 S.W.2d 408, 416–18 (Mo. 1988) (en banc), *cert. granted*, 109 S.Ct. 3240 (1989).

[13] See the Court's own explicit statement on the limits of privacy claims in the subsequent case of *Planned Parenthood of Southeastern Pennsylvania v. Casey*, 505 U.S. 833 (1992).

[14] *In re Storar*, 52 N.Y.2d 363, 376–77, 420 N.E.2d 64, 70 (1981).

[15] Informed consent is not an ancient concept with a rich medical tradition. The term "informed consent" first appeared in a public case in *Salgo v. Leland Stanford, Jr., University Board of Trustees*, 317 P.2d 170 (1957). The *Salgo* court suggested that there is a duty to disclose the *risks and alternatives* of a proposed treatment, which is a logical extension of the well-established duty to disclose the treatment's *nature and consequences*. Serious discussion of the doctrine of informed consent began only around 1972 in *Canterbury v. Spence*, 464 F.2d 772 (D.C. Cir. 1972), and *Cobbs v. Grant*, 104 Cal. Rptr. 505, 502 P.2d 1 (1972). These courts moved in the direction of a more patient-oriented standard of disclosure in which the patient's right of self-decision requires that the patient be given sufficient information to make an intelligent choice. As the idea of informed consent evolved, discussion of appropriate guidelines moved increasingly from a narrow focus on the physician's or researcher's obligation to disclose information, to the quality of a patient's or subject's understanding of information and right to authorize or refuse a biomedical intervention.

[16] *In re Conroy*, 98 N.J. 321, 486 A.2d 1209 (1985).

of aid-in-dying. Fifteen years is but a fleeting moment in the history of the subject of how to treat the dying, but during this period, North American society had experienced an extraordinary transformation in its conception of rights of privacy and autonomy regarding end-of-life decisions. We migrated from a pre-*Quinlan* fear of any form of intentional hastening of death to a confidence that it is permissible under a variety of conditions to intentionally forgo life-sustaining technologies of all types. What was unthinkable or at least bitterly contested before *Quinlan* became routine in medicine and protected in law.

The hitherto unthinkable unraveled further in 1996 when two favorable decisions supporting a constitutional right to limited physician-assisted suicide were handed down in successive months by the Ninth and Second U.S. Circuit Courts.[17] Their decisions were reversed, however, by the U.S. Supreme Court's 1997 decisions in *Vacco v. Quill* and *Washington v. Glucksberg*. The Court held that there are no constitutional rights to physician aid-in-dying and that each state may set its own policy on the issue. There is no mention in the decisions of a right to privacy and no serious consideration given to liberty rights as a constitutional basis for the right to request aid-in-dying. The Court's prior invocations in *Cruzan* of a "constitutionally protected liberty interest in refusing unwanted treatment" are mentioned, but only in the course of insisting that there is no "right to hasten death" and that the right to refuse treatment in *Cruzan* was "grounded" in "well established, traditional rights to bodily integrity and freedom from unwanted touching."[18]

One consequence of the *Vacco* and *Glucksberg* decisions was realized in Oregon, where voters reaffirmed what they had three years previously passed—the initiative known as Measure 16 (see footnote 2 for a complete explanation of the history of this initiative). Under the provisions of this act, a terminally ill patient may seek to escape unbearable suffering by requesting a physician's prescription for lethal drugs. This Oregon act reflects the new frontier of the social and legal acceptance of expanded legal rights to control one's death. The cutting edge has shifted from *refusal* of treatment to *requests* for aid-in-dying.[19]

---

[17] *Compassion in Dying v. State of Washington*, 79 F.3d 790 (9th Cir. 1996); *Vacco v. Quill*, 80 F.3d 716 (2d Cir. 1996). In the latter, at 723–24, see the court's conclusion that a right to physician-assisted suicide could not be included within the scope of the right of privacy.

[18] *Vacco*, 117 S.Ct. at 2300–2301; *Glucksberg*, 117 S.Ct. at 2269–70.

[19] Many believe that Dr. Jack Kevorkian has been the most significant figure in bringing these issues to public attention, though his influence is highly controversial. His acts of assisted suicide eventuated in several court decisions as well. In the same month as the *Glucksberg* ruling, a court in Michigan acquitted Kevorkian of charges that he violated the state's newly enacted law on physician-assisted suicide by administering carbon monoxide to a patient. A jury decision in this case found that Kevorkian did not have the relevant *intention* to be in violation of the Michigan law, which exempted physicians whose intent is to relieve pain or discomfort rather than to cause death. The jury found that Kevorkian had only intended to relieve the suffering of his patients. Only after he performed a direct mercy killing was Kevorkian found guilty of a crime (second-degree murder).

Though the law has led us to this point, the law is poorly positioned to grapple with the moral and social issues that have emerged from its own history. The upshot of the aforementioned legal decisions is that, excepting the jurisprudence of individual states, the right to privacy has been eclipsed by the right of self-determination as a basis for a right to refuse medical treatment. However, neither *legal* right now stands to help us resolve social issues of physician aid-in-dying. Constitutional law is barren when it comes to normative guidance on these frontier moral issues. The question I will now address is what the law should be, not what it is.

III. "KILLING" AND "LETTING DIE"

To introduce the moral issues, I begin with the enormously influential distinction between killing and letting die.[20] My motivation is simple: it has long been the presumption in law and medicine that assisted suicide and active euthanasia at the request of the patient are wrongful acts of killing or assistance in killing, and that a request for assistance from an individual who seeks death provides neither a justification nor an excuse for having provided it. This presumption is now being called into question by lovers of liberty and privacy. The question of whether killing is warranted in these circumstances has become the centerpiece of discussion.

I believe that construal of this debate as a doctor's dilemma about killing would be a moral misconception. Killing should not be at the center of this debate; the debate's core should be the liberty and privacy rights of patients. Moreover, I maintain that the distinction between killing and letting die must itself be understood in terms of liberty—in particular, when it is valid to refuse medical care. If I am right, then issues about active euthanasia at the request of the patient and physician-assisted suicide should not be focused on the morality of killing, but rather on the scope and limits of liberty rights and privacy rights.

A. Liberty in letting die

It is a reasonable presumption that the conditions under which it is acceptable to let a person die are the logical place to look for an already established liberty right to die. "Letting die" is (prima facie) acceptable in medicine under one of two justifying conditions: (1) a medical technology is *useless* (medical futility), or (2) a medical technology has been *validly*

---

[20] See Bonnie Steinbock and Alastair Norcross, eds., *Killing and Letting Die*, 2d ed. (New York: Fordham University Press, 1994); Tom L. Beauchamp, ed., *Intending Death* (Upper Saddle River, NJ: Prentice Hall, 1996); H. M. Malm, "Killing, Letting Die, and Simple Conflicts," *Philosophy and Public Affairs* 18, no. 3 (Summer 1989): 238–58; Jeff McMahan, "Killing, Letting Die, and Withdrawing Aid," *Ethics* 103, no. 2 (January 1993): 250–79; and Lawrence O. Gostin, "Drawing a Line Between Killing and Letting Die: The Law, and Law Reform, on Medically Assisted Dying," *Journal of Law, Medicine, and Ethics* 21, no. 1 (Spring 1993): 94–101.

refused. Condition (2) honors a refusal of a useful treatment when it is known that the refusal will be fatal; it is an instance of letting die, not of killing. The classification of an action as a killing or a letting die can, thus, depend entirely on whether a valid refusal of medical technology had been made.

In the medical context, then, letting a patient die is *acceptable* if and only if the condition of futility or the condition of a valid refusal of treatment is satisfied. "Killing" in medicine, by contrast, has been conceptually and morally tied to *unacceptable* acts. The conditions of medical practice render this verdict sensible, but it breaks down in the world beyond medicine. In general, the term "killing" does not entail a wrongful act or a crime, and the rule "Do not kill" is not an absolute rule. Standard justifications of killing include such grounds as self-defense, killing to rescue a person endangered by the immoral acts of others, and killing by misadventure (that is, accidental, nonnegligent killing while engaged in a lawful act). These grounds prevent us from prejudging an action as wrong merely because it is a killing. Applying the label "killing" to a set of events outside of medicine will, therefore, not determine whether an action is acceptable or unacceptable.[21] Within medicine, in contrast, morally justified killing has never had a foothold, because it had been thought that no exceptions to a general proscription against killing should be tolerated. However, issues about physician aid-in-dying have compelled us to rethink this dogma on pain of begging the essential question: can certain active interventions by doctors that cause death ever have moral warrant?

Killing may, of course, generally be wrong and letting die only rarely wrong, but, if so, this conclusion is contingent on the features of particular cases. The general wrongness of killing and general rightness of letting die are not surprising features of the moral world inasmuch as killings are rarely authorized by appropriate parties (cases of capital punishment excepted), and cases of letting die generally are validly authorized. Be that as it may, the *frequency* with which one kind of act is justified, by contrast to the other kind of act, is not relevant to the moral (or legal) justification of either kind of act. An unjustified forgoing by a physician that lets a patient die can be both as intentional and as immoral as an action that in some more direct manner takes the patient's life (and both can be forms of killing).

Questions of the justifiability of "killing" and "letting die" should, therefore, be left open when we consider forms of physician aid-in-dying such as active euthanasia by request and physician-assisted suicide. Whether letting die is justified and whether killing is unjustified are

---

[21] Cf. James Rachels, "Active and Passive Euthanasia," *New England Journal of Medicine* 292, no. 2 (January 9, 1975): 78–80. See also his *The End of Life: Euthanasia and Morality* (Oxford: Oxford University Press, 1986); and Dan W. Brock, "Voluntary Active Euthanasia," *Hastings Center Report* 22, no. 2 (March/April 1992): 10–22.

matters in need of moral analysis, not matters that have been resolved by medical tradition and legal prohibition.

B. Causation and causal responsibility

Many believe that problems of the justification of physician aid-in-dying must be approached through a curiously influential doctrine. Under this doctrine, when a physician intentionally forgoes the use of a medical technology for his or her patient, this act qualifies as an instance of letting die, rather than one of killing, if and only if an underlying disease or injury causes the patient's death. When medical technology is withheld or withdrawn, according to this doctrine, a natural death occurs, because natural conditions do what they would have done if the technology had never been initiated. By contrast, killings occur when acts of persons, rather than natural conditions, cause death.[22]

Despite the venerability and wide acceptance of this attempt to isolate the causal conditions that pinpoint responsibility for death, this doctrine of a natural death is wholly unsatisfactory in this bald form. To obtain a satisfactory account, it must be added that for a death to be considered an instance of letting die, the forgoing of the medical technology must be *validly authorized* and for this reason *justified*. If the physician's forgoing of technology were unjustified and his or her patient subsequently died from "natural" causes of injury or disease, the result would be unjustified killing, not an instance of justified letting die.

A valid authorization determines which conditions in a causal chain are responsible for death; it is not the case that some inherent feature of a natural causal chain determines whether a decision to cause death is valid. Thus, the morality of the action is determined by the validity of an authorization, not by some independent assessment of causation. To bring out this point, consider a thought experiment. Two patients are in their beds in a semiprivate hospital room; both have the same malady and both require a respirator to survive. One wants the respirator removed; the other wishes to remain on the respirator. A physician intentionally flips a master switch that turns off both respirators. The two patients die in the same way, at the same time, of the same physical causes, and because of the same physical action of the physician.

Though both patients die of the same physical causes, they do not die of the same causes of interest to law and morals, because the proximate cause—that is, the cause responsible for the outcome—is not the same for the two otherwise identically situated patients. The physician justifiably

---

[22] See Daniel Callahan, "Vital Distinctions, Mortal Questions: Debating Euthanasia and Health Care Costs," *Commonweal* 115, no. 13 (July 15, 1988): 397–404; Daniel Callahan, *The Troubled Dream of Life* (New York: Simon and Schuster, 1993), chap. 2; and several articles in Joanne Lynn, ed., *By No Extraordinary Means* (Bloomington, IN: Indiana University Press, 1986), 227–66.

let one patient die, but unjustifiably caused the death of and killed the other patient. In the first case, the physician forbeared from treating the patient and did not perform an action that caused the death; in the second case, the physician's action caused the death. Since causation in law and morals, unlike causation in many other fields of inquiry, is structured to identify responsibility for an outcome, locating the "cause of death" involves inquiry into who or what is causally responsible for death.

In law and morals, there can be no assessment of responsibility and liability for negative outcomes without a preexisting system of duties. Without an assigned duty, no causal responsibility or liability exists. If a physician has no duty to treat or a duty not to treat, then forbearing to treat does not breach a duty *and* does not cause death, even though death is an inevitable result. Authorized withdrawal of treatment is such a forbearance, and the physician's forbearance to treat under such circumstances is not causally connected in law and morals to the death. (Alternatively, we could say that there is causation but not causal responsibility.) Absent a duty to treat, the relevant cause of death is a preexisting disease, system failure, injury, or some other condition in the patient; there is no proximate cause in the sense of an act responsible for death.

Consider again our physician who intentionally shut down the respirator that was sustaining a patient who wanted to continue living. It would be absurd to say, "The physician did not cause the patient's death; he only allowed the patient to die of an underlying condition." By "letting" this patient die a "natural" death, the physician failed to discharge a duty and was the proximate cause of the patient's death; indeed, he unjustifiably killed the patient. However, if the patient had authorized the same sequence of events, the sole relevant cause of death would have been the physical condition of the patient.

Although I have thus far been considering only patients whose death is physically caused by so-called "natural" conditions of illness or injury, in many cases of withdrawing or withholding a medical treatment, death is not physically caused by an underlying condition of illness or injury. For example, removing a patient's nasogastric tube in order to abate nutrition leads to death from malnutrition, not death from an underlying condition of disease or injury. A disease or injury *motivates* and *justifies* the decision to forgo treatment, but does not cause death. Here, a natural condition of disease or injury that counterfactually would have eventually caused death plays a role in the justification of forgoing treatment, but the disease or injury does not itself cause death.

From both a legal and a moral point of view, one reason why physicians do not injure, maltreat, or kill patients when they withhold or withdraw medical technology and thereby physically cause death[23] (often with the

---

[23] It is not absurd to say that a physician's actions physically cause death even when he or she forbears from treatment as a result of a patient's refusal. The actions of physicians are commonly necessary parts of sufficient conditions of a death as it occurs. For example, to withhold nutrition and hydration so that a patient dies of malnutrition is a necessary part

intention of bringing about death) is that a physician is morally and legally obligated to recognize and act upon a valid refusal, irrespective of the causal outcome of doing so. Since a valid refusal of treatment binds the physician, it would be absurd to hold that these legal and moral duties require physicians to cause the deaths of their patients—in the legal and moral sense of "cause"—and thereby to kill them.

I conclude that the particular form or mode of causation of death is not the relevant matter in moral and legal issues about the justification of aid-in-dying when the case involves forgoing treatment. Moral problems about forgoing treatment and letting die in medicine are not fundamentally causal problems about who or what caused death. As long as a refusal of medical technology constitutes a valid authorization to stop treatment, there is no problem involving responsibility for the death that ensues or about the justification of the action.

With this account of *refusals* of medical treatment before us, we can now ask whether, in a parallel manner, a *request* for aid-in-dying validly authorizes a physician's assistance.[24]

C. Valid requests

Clearly the two types of authorization—refusals of treatment and requests for aid-in-dying—are not perfectly analogous. A doctor is obligated to honor an autonomous refusal by a patient of a life-prolonging technology, but he or she is not obligated to honor an autonomous request for physician aid-in-dying. This difference does not, however, cut to the heart of the problem, because the issue is not about whether physicians are *obligated* to lend assistance. The issue is whether valid requests render it *permissible* for a physician to lend aid-in-dying. Refusals in medical settings have a moral power that requests lack, but requests are not powerless to confer on another a right to act in response.[25]

---

of a sufficient condition of death at the time and in the way the death occurs. The doctor is not a sufficient cause of death but is a necessary part of a sufficient set of conditions of death. If the patient is suffering from conditions such as severe brain damage or cancer, these conditions are neither necessary nor sufficient conditions of death in the way it comes about. In many cases, both a physician's intervention *and* a disease, system failure, or injury are joint causal conditions of death. In a few more uncommon cases, multiple causal conditions may be relevant, each forming an independent causal sequence that is sufficient to cause death. That is, any one of several distinct sequences of causally linked events may be sufficient to cause death.

[24] On the importance of the refusal/request distinction, see James L. Bernat, Bernard Gert, and R. Peter Mogielnicki, "Patient Refusal of Hydration and Nutrition," *Archives of Internal Medicine* 153, no. 24 (December 27, 1993): 2723–28; Gert, Bernat, and Mogielnicki, "Distinguishing between Patients' Refusals and Requests," *Hastings Center Report* 24, no. 4 (July/August 1994): 13–15; and Gert et al., "The Distinction between Active and Passive Euthanasia," *Archives of Internal Medicine* 155, no. 12 (June 26, 1995): 1329.

[25] A physician who in principle accepts the permissibility of active aid-in-dying may legitimately refuse to honor any particular request for aid-in-dying for various reasons. For example, a sympathetic physician willing to assist a patient at a crisis point may refuse a patient's request for lethal medication if that request is premature.

A physician's precise responsibilities to a patient may depend on the nature of the request made and the nature of the preestablished patient-physician relationship. In some cases of a physician's compliance with a request, the patient and the physician had previously agreed upon the patient's best interest, with an understanding that the physician would not abandon the patient or resist what they jointly had determined to serve the patient's best interest. In some cases, patients in a close relationship with a physician both refuse a medical technology *and* request a hastened death in order to lessen pain or suffering; in these cases, refusal and request are parts of a single plan. If the physician accepts the plan, assisted suicide (or possibly euthanasia) grows out of the preestablished relationship.

From this perspective, a valid request for aid-in-dying frees a responder of all moral culpability for a death, just as a valid refusal of treatment precludes culpability. This logic underlies Oregon's Measure 16 and helps explain why its opponents fought it so fiercely: the measure conspicuously subscribes to the principle that valid requests for aid-in-dying are licit and that physicians may respond affirmatively to such requests without fear of legal liability. This Death with Dignity Act is drafted throughout in the language of "request" and "voluntary informed choice." The form legally authorizing a request for aid-in-dying is referred to as the "Form of the Request," and the form itself is entitled "Request for Medication to End My Life in a Humane and Dignified Manner."

Next, I will consider a variation of my earlier example of two respirator-dependent patients in a semiprivate room. A doctor has two terminally ill patients who are afflicted with the same condition. Both are competent to make medical decisions when alert, but both must often be sedated nearly to unconsciousness to escape their pain. One patient requests that sufficient drugs be made available to cause death; the other patient wishes to live as long as possible. However, the physician believes that they have both suffered enough and leaves each patient a quantity of drugs sufficient to cause death. The first patient understands the physician's intention, takes the drugs, and dies. The second patient does not understand the physician's intention; thinking that the drugs are simply a new means of controlling pain, this patient ingests them and dies.

The doctor has unjustifiably killed the second patient, but what about the first patient? By the logic of the argument I have been developing, the doctor has not killed the first patient; whatever the physician's precise causal role in bringing about death, he or she bears no moral or causal responsibility of the sort that invites censure or punishment. I can conceive of no moral grounds for restricting the liberty of any competent individual to make the request made by the first patient. The only serious question is whether physicians are obligated not to implement such requests under certain conditions, such as when a patient is in a depressed state of mind that has not rendered him or her incompetent. It is beyond reasonable doubt that physicians sometimes have sufficient moral reason to refuse to comply with such a request, even when they are permitted to comply.

From this argument, the next logical step would be to consider a case of requested causation of death—a case of active euthanasia rather than a case of physician-assisted suicide. But taking this next step would simply require extending the same logic used previously, and would raise few questions that have not already been considered.

IV. LIBERTY AND PRIVACY

A. Liberty

My arguments suggest that causing a person's death is morally wrong, when it is wrong, not merely because the death is caused by someone, but because the unauthorized intervention thwarted or set back a person's interests. Death is bad for a person only if it entails a deprivation of opportunities and goods.[26] However, if a person freely elects and authorizes death and makes an autonomous judgment that his or her death would constitute a personal benefit rather than a setback or deprivation of opportunities, then active aid-in-dying (killing, as some would insist) at the person's request involves no harm or moral wrong.

Accordingly, if instances of letting die based on valid refusals do not harm or wrong persons or violate the rights of persons who die earlier than they otherwise would, how can assisted suicide or voluntary active euthanasia harm or wrong persons who make autonomous choices to die earlier than they otherwise would? In each case, persons seek what for them, in their bleak circumstances, is the best means to the end of quitting life. The person in search of assisted suicide, the person who seeks active euthanasia, and the person who forgoes life-sustaining technology to end his or her life may all be identically situated in regard to prognosis and suffering. They simply select different means to end their lives.

Assisting an autonomous person at her request to bring about her death is, from this perspective, a way of showing respect for the person's autonomous choices. Similarly, denying the person access to other individuals who are willing and qualified to comply with the request shows a fundamental disrespect for the person's autonomy. These are the liberty interests that we have come to value so highly in refusal-of-treatment contexts. Yet our liberty (and privacy) interests in averting unwanted medical interventions are not necessarily more substantial than our interests in requesting interventions by medical officials that will ease and hasten death. From a *social and legal* perspective, there may be good

---

[26] Cf. Allen Buchanan, "Intending Death: The Structure of the Problem and Proposed Solutions," in Beauchamp, ed., *Intending Death*, 34–38; Thomas Nagel, "Death," in Nagel, *Mortal Questions* (Cambridge: Cambridge University Press, 1979); and F. M. Kamm, *Morality, Mortality*, vol. 1 (New York: Oxford University Press, 1993), chap. 1.

grounds for more zealously protecting one type of patient than another, but why, from a *moral* perspective, should we protect one patient's right to make an autonomous choice more than that of another patient? What basis could give one type of patient a liberty right and privacy right weightier than the liberty right and privacy right of the other type of patient?

Many principles have been advanced as valid moral grounds for the limitation of individual liberty, including preventing harm to others, preventing harm to self, and preventing immoral behavior. It is difficult to see how any liberty-limiting principle other than hard paternalism (that is, overriding a person's autonomous preferences in order to protect the person from causing harm to himself) could be applied to forbid instances of physician-assisted suicide or voluntary active euthanasia. If accepted, however, hard paternalism would apply equally well to refusal-of-treatment cases, and would thus endanger this aspect of our liberty rights. Moreover, if cases of assisted suicide and voluntary active euthanasia do not involve harming oneself, as I have maintained, then no form of paternalism would apply. Therefore, paternalism cannot provide a justification for preventing these methods of aid-in-dying. Would the paternalist have us believe either that all acts of assisted suicide and voluntary active euthanasia are intrinsically immoral because patients should never be allowed to consent to their own killing, or that such choices are never freely made by competent persons?

B. Privacy

When considering cases of aid-in-dying, a privacy interest is no less evident than is a liberty interest. A factor in the tragic suicide of Nancy Cruzan's father, Joseph Cruzan,[27] was the way in which law, medicine, and the media intruded into what he and his family thought were private affairs. As guardian of his comatose daughter, who was in a persistently vegetative state, Mr. Cruzan was ultimately given (by a state court) the freedom to choose the time and manner of her death, a choice he exercised by withdrawing nutrition and hydration. But he was never allowed to make choices under more than a thin veneer of privacy. Even the television set in his living room was a constant source of information about his own private affairs. His pathetic death epitomizes both how privacy in making choices may be as important as the freedom of choice itself, and how we wrong people by not leaving them alone.

In moral, legal, and political literature, interest in privacy, and ultimately the right to privacy, emerged in contexts in which there was a need to protect the individual from public inspection, particularly from the reach of law and public officials. The much disputed question of the

---

[27] Several years after Nancy Cruzan died, Joseph Cruzan killed himself. He had suffered a long period of depression.

definition of privacy[28] cannot be explored here, and I will simply assume for the purposes of this essay that privacy is a state or condition of physical or informational inaccessibility. A loss of privacy thus occurs if others gain access by intervening in regions of intimacy, secrecy, anonymity, seclusion, solitude, and the like.[29]

If it turns out that the primary moral justification of a right to privacy resides in a right of liberty or in the principle of respect for autonomy, nothing will be lost to my argument. Moral rights of privacy are valid claims against access whether or not they have their justificatory basis in a liberty right to authorize or decline access.[30] However, it is confusing to think of the right of privacy as nothing more than a right to be free to do something or a right to act autonomously. One has to be able to act freely in the absence of the watchful gaze of others. Nowhere is this clearer than in decisions about one's own death or about a death in one's family. Just as sexual intimacy, reproductive decision-making, and family planning have become paradigmatic instances of the importance of privacy in American law, so an individual's decisions at the end of his life ought to become paradigmatic instances in morals of the importance of privacy in decision-making. (What *should* happen in law is a question I leave open, though I reiterate that there is nothing morally objectionable about the law concerning aid-in-dying in Oregon.)

What more intimate and private moments can we expect to encounter in life than decision-making about our death? Are matters of marriage, procreation, childrearing, and family any more private or due more moral protection than decisions made about the end of life? Privacy in choosing a course of death could be of the highest importance to a patient, and

---

[28] Some definitions of privacy center on a narrow range of conditions under which intrusions constitute losses of privacy, whereas other definitions center on a broader range of conditions. Some definitions view privacy as a condition of the person, others as a condition of control by the person over access to information. Some definitions place a value on privacy, others do not. See Madison Powers's survey of several definitions of privacy in "A Cognitive Access Definition of Privacy," *Law and Philosophy* 15, no. 4 (November 1996): 369–86; and Anita L. Allen's examination of restricted-access definitions in *Uneasy Access: Privacy for Women in a Free Society* (Totowa, NJ: Rowman and Littlefield, 1988). See also Alan F. Westin, *Privacy and Freedom* (New York: Athenaeum, 1967); and the critique by Ferdinand David Schoeman, "Privacy: Philosophical Dimensions of the Literature," in Schoeman, ed., *Philosophical Dimensions of Privacy: An Anthology* (New York: Cambridge University Press, 1984), 3–4.

[29] Cf. Ruth Gavison, "Privacy and the Limits of Law," *Yale Law Journal* 89, no. 3 (January 1980): 428. (Gavison's article is reprinted in Schoeman, ed., *Philosophical Dimensions of Privacy*, 346–402.)

[30] Suffice it to say, here, that personal autonomy carries over the ideas of a region of sovereignty for the self and a right to protect it by restricting access, ideas that are closely linked to the concepts of privacy and the right to privacy. Cf. Joel Feinberg, *Harm to Self*, vol. 3 of *The Moral Limits of the Criminal Law* (New York: Oxford University Press, 1986), chap. 19. The idea that certain forms of self-determination are immune from social control has made the legal right of privacy controversial throughout its history. The U.S. Supreme Court has sometimes hinted that the right to privacy is primarily a right of self-determination in decision-making, a right on which clear boundaries must be placed. See *Whalen v. Roe*, 429 U.S. 589, 599–600 (1977).

there is no reason to expect that other parties will be harmed or otherwise negatively affected by the patient's decision.

Leon Kass has argued that "[t]he attempt to ground a right to die in the so-called right to privacy fails . . . [because a] right to make independent judgments regarding one's body in one's private sphere, free of governmental interference, cannot be the basis of the right of someone else, appointed by or protected by government, to put an end to one's bodily life."[31] This clever assessment misses the moral context. Privacy rights and liberty rights work together. The chief liberty right in this context is the right to request aid-in-dying, and it is this request that authorizes another party to act. The right to privacy, by contrast, is the individual's valid claim not to have to endure what the Cruzan family had to endure.

V. THE PUBLIC AND THE PRIVATE

Even if my moral arguments are sound, they are plainly insufficient to justify laws or social practices that permit active forms of aid-in-dying. My goal has been to present moral arguments to justify acts, not to promote policies or legalization. I have been clarifying foundational moral questions about active aid-in-dying; I have not attempted to peer beyond those arguments to theorize about their implications for social policy. Nor have I speculated about the conditions under which it is legitimate for physicians or other parties to balk at honoring requests for aid-in-dying. These questions are not entirely independent of the questions I have posed, but they do raise fresh issues and need to be addressed by distinct arguments.

Therefore, my thesis that acts such as voluntary active euthanasia and physician-assisted suicide are morally justified for some patients does not entail that the government should legally permit voluntary active euthanasia and physician-assisted suicide under the conditions that these patients suffer. Factors such as the costs of controlling abuses and the possibility that institutional standards of care will deteriorate are deservedly considered in assessing the merit of legalization, but they should play no role in judging the morality of aid-in-dying. If it turns out that DNR orders, say, have pernicious or other detrimental effects in an institution, that fact might be grounds for not allowing such orders in that institution, but it does not follow that it is immoral for a patient to request that a physician not resuscitate her.

The theoretical backbone of public resistance to physician-assisted suicide and voluntary active euthanasia has long been slippery slope and

[31] Leon Kass, "Is There a Right to Die?" *Hastings Center Report* 23, no. 1 (January/February 1993), reprinted in Tom L. Beauchamp and LeRoy Walters, eds., *Contemporary Issues in Bioethics*, 5th ed. (Belmont, CA: Wadsworth, 1999), 352 n. 10.

potential abuse arguments.[32] These arguments portend that some acts that are acceptable in one type of circumstance will, if legalized, inevitably be performed in circumstances in which the acts are morally unacceptable. For example, particular acts of aid-in-dying may be acceptable in the context of a long and affectionate patient-physician relationship. However, if legalized, aid-in-dying might be used in circumstances in which the serious risks of abuse would, on balance, outweigh the benefits to society of accepting the practice. The concern is that restrictions initially built into legislation will eventually be revised or ignored, increasing the possibilities for unjustified killing.[33]

If the dire consequences envisaged in these slippery slope and potential abuse arguments would result from the legalization of physician-assisted suicide or voluntary active euthanasia, we would have a very powerful reason for resisting legalization of these practices. Perhaps there is good reason for believing that assisting in suicide and euthanasia should constitute manslaughter and second-degree murder, respectively, as they do in several American states. However, the evidence that would help us decide such matters is still out, and we should be careful not to engage in speculative, telescoped analogies to events in such contexts as the Netherlands, where active euthanasia is de facto legal, and Northern Australia, where its legal status was rescinded.

Social controversies about active aid-in-dying have been fueled by a strong sense that decisions to end a human life are inherently public matters, just as murder and manslaughter are. The focus and priority has been on the public interest rather than on liberty and privacy interests,

---

[32] Cf. James Rachels, *The End of Life*, chap. 10; John Arras, "The Right to Die on the Slippery Slope," *Social Theory and Practice* 8, no. 3 (Fall 1982): 285–328; Wibren van der Burg, "The Slippery Slope Argument," *Ethics* 102, no. 1 (October 1991): 42–65; Ruth Macklin, "Which Way Down the Slippery Slope? Nazi Medical Killing and Euthanasia Today," in Arthur L. Caplan, ed., *When Medicine Went Mad: Bioethics and the Holocaust* (Totowa, NJ: Humana Press, 1992), 173–200; J. A. Burgess, "The Great Slippery-Slope Argument," *Journal of Medical Ethics* 19, no. 3 (September 1993): 169–74; and Douglas Walton, *Slippery Slope Arguments* (Oxford: Clarendon Press, 1992).

[33] See Peter A. Singer and Mark Siegler, "Euthanasia—A Critique," *New England Journal of Medicine* 322 (June 28, 1990): 1881–83; Joanne Lynn, "The Health Care Professional's Role When Active Euthanasia Is Sought," *Journal of Palliative Care* 4, nos. 1 and 2 (May 1988): 100–102; Susan Wolf, "Holding the Line on Euthanasia," *Hastings Center Report* 19, no. 1 (January/February 1989): S13–S15; Leon R. Kass, "Neither for Love Nor Money: Why Doctors Must Not Kill," *Public Interest* 94 (1989): 25–46; H. Hendin and Gerald Klerman, "Physician-Assisted Suicide: The Dangers of Legalization," *American Journal of Psychiatry* 150, no. 1 (January 1993): 143–45; Alan D. Ogilvie and S. G. Potts, "Assisted Suicide for Depression: The Slippery Slope in Action?: Learning from the Dutch Experience," *British Medical Journal* 309, no. 6953 (August 20–21, 1994): 492–93; Raymond J. Devettere, "Slippery Slopes and Moral Reasoning," *Journal of Clinical Ethics* 3, no. 4 (Winter 1992): 298; David Orentlicher, "Physician Participation in Assisted Suicide," *Journal of the American Medical Association* 262, no. 13 (October 6, 1989): 1844–45; and C. Everett Koop and Edward R. Grant, "The 'Small Beginnings' of Euthanasia: Examining the Erosion in Legal Prohibitions against Mercy-Killing," *Notre Dame Journal of Law, Ethics, and Public Policy* 2, no. 3 (Spring 1986): 585–634.

but this perfectly sensible emphasis loses all sense when we are assessing the *morality* of aid-in-dying.

VI. Conclusion

My interest in this essay has been in moral rather than legal questions—chiefly, whether privacy and autonomy rights justify requests for active aid-in-dying. I noted that a health professional is obligated to honor an autonomous refusal of life-sustaining technology, but is not obligated to honor a request for physician aid-in-dying. This difference does not, however, capture the core problem, because the issue is not the *obligation* to lend assistance in dying. The issue is whether valid requests render it *permissible* for a physician to lend aid-in-dying.

I have defended the view that some acts of physician-assisted suicide are morally justified, but that empirical uncertainties render it unclear whether legalization is morally justified. My position is premised largely on autonomy and privacy rights. We know that, at least for now, no U.S. federal constitutional right to aid-in-dying is recognized, and that one state, Oregon, has given its citizens a limited legal right to request such aid. We can now observe how well Oregon fares, which will give us more empirical evidence to factor into future legal and public policy decisions.

As we watch developments in Oregon and other states, we will need to attend to an unresolved problem of public policy that I have treated only briefly: In the United States, we constitutionally protect the forgoing of life-sustaining technologies, whereas every state except Oregon criminally prohibits physician-assisted suicide. This social policy seems incoherent if, as I believe, there is no morally relevant difference between forgoing treatment and requesting assistance when both are used as methods to end one's life.

Philosophy, Georgetown University

CAN PUBLIC FIGURES HAVE
PRIVATE LIVES?*

By Frederick Schauer

I. The Distractions of the Word "Private"

A rash of very public scandals, of which the behavior of President Clinton and the activities of the late Princess Diana are merely the most famous examples, has raised the question of the appropriateness of the disclosure, or the newsworthiness, of the so-called "private" lives of so-called "public" figures or "public" officials. That is the question I address in this essay.

The scare quotes that I use around the words "private" and "public" are designed to suggest that the typical references to the private lives of public figures have a quality about them that might indicate that these terms are what some might call "ascriptive" rather than descriptive,[1] what others might characterize as "thick descriptions,"[2] and what many of the rest of us might simply see as question-begging. Far too often, once a characteristic or an activity—whether it be a medical condition, cheating at golf, or cheating on one's spouse—is described as "private," a presumption appears to attach that the activity is inappropriate for disclosure to or knowledge by the population at large. Conversely, once a

* Research for this essay was supported by the Joan Shorenstein Center on the Press, Politics, and Public Policy at Harvard University, which also provided the ideal forum for fruitful discussion and debate of the ideas presented here.

[1] An ascriptive term is one that, in the guise of description, is largely evaluative. For example, a jury verdict of "guilty" not only says that the defendant engaged in certain behavior, but also that it is appropriate for the defendant to be punished for that behavior. On ascriptive terms, see H. L. A. Hart, "The Ascription of Responsibility and Rights," *Proceedings of the Aristotelian Society*, n.s., 49 (1949): 171–82. See also Hart, "Definition and Theory in Jurisprudence," in Hart, *Essays in Jurisprudence and Philosophy* (Oxford: Clarendon Press, 1983), 21–44; and G. P. Baker, "Defeasibility and Meaning," in P. M. S. Hacker and J. Raz, eds., *Law, Morality, and Society: Essays in Honour of H. L. A. Hart* (Oxford: Clarendon Press, 1977), 26–52. For useful criticism (which Hart later acknowledged and accepted in his *Punishment and Responsibility: Essays in the Philosophy of Law* [Oxford: Clarendon Press, 1968], vi), see P. T. Geach, "Ascriptivism," *Philosophical Review* 69, no. 2 (April 1960): 221–25; and George Pitcher, "Hart on Action and Responsibility," *Philosophical Review* 69, no. 2 (April 1960): 226–29.

[2] A thick description is one whose moral evaluation of the conduct is inseparable from the description itself; the classic example of this is the word "rude." See Philippa Foot, "Moral Arguments," in Foot, *Virtues and Vices and Other Essays in Moral Philosophy* (Oxford: Clarendon Press, 1978), 96, 102–5; Judith Jarvis Thomson, *The Realm of Rights* (Cambridge, MA: Harvard University Press, 1990), 10–20; and Bernard Williams, *Ethics and the Limits of Philosophy* (Cambridge: Cambridge University Press, 1985), 129.

person—whether a head of state, a football star, or a television chef—
is described as "public," a presumption again appears to attach that the
person's activities should be available for widespread inspection. The
question whether the private lives of public figures should be open to
newspaper reporting is so close to self-answering as to be an unhelpful
characterization. Too much of the normative and conceptual work is
elided by the terms "public" and "private," which turn out to have the
attributes of normative conclusions masquerading as descriptions or
analytic tools.

The use of superficially descriptive language to mask contested or
contestable normative conclusions is a problem with most of the language
of privacy, and not only with the particular dimension of privacy that
concerns me in this essay. Consider, for example, the issues of abortion,
contraception, sexual orientation, medical records, genetic codes, computer databases, electronic snooping, or police searches, among many
others. With respect to these issues, "private" is typically the label we
attach to those activities and domains in which, for previously decided
normative reasons, there is a justified interest in excluding someone else
or in establishing a right to exclude someone else, often (but not necessarily) including the government. Conversely, "public" is the word we
typically use to mark situations in which we have concluded, for reasons
that are antecedent to the application of the label "public," that an individual's preferences should not be indulged, including a preference that
information not be disclosed. Yet because the words "private" and "public" serve this ex post labeling function, they often occlude analysis of
which domains, activities, facts, and behaviors are appropriate for the
labels and which are not.

In addition, the word "privacy" is commonly used to refer to a very
diverse range of activities and issues. For example, "privacy" is often
involved in discussions of: the right to choose whether to have an abortion; the right to bring a lawsuit against a newspaper that accurately
reveals an embarrassing fact about one's past; the right to prevent a credit
reporting agency or insurance company from amassing and disseminat-
ing data about one's consumer behavior, driving habits, or medical history; and the right to keep the police out of one's home unless they have
first obtained a search warrant. However, the connections among these
issues are arguably a great deal looser than the invocation of a common
label would indicate. When we employ a word that encompasses such a
wide range of arguably diverse activities, we run the risk of thinking,
prior to analysis, that the activities have more in common than it turns
out that they actually do.

As a result of these possibilities for conceptual confusion, I will attempt
to avoid using the terms "public" and "private" in this essay. Instead, I
will deal directly with the question of the conceptual and normative

dimensions of revealing facts about well-known people or government employees[3] that they would wish not to be revealed. This definition of the problem is thus wide enough to deal not only with presidents who cheat at golf or on their spouses, or candidates for office who wish to conceal their medical histories, but also with all the facts that the full range of people who work for the government, influence policy, or are widely known would prefer not to have publicized about themselves. Some of these categories of people, and some of the conclusions that attach to them, may overlap, but we will never approach a proper understanding of the problem if we remain too promiscuous at the outset about using the terms "public" and "private."

II. Preferences for Information and Preferences for Secrecy

I want to focus primarily, even if not exclusively, on the case of elected governmental officials, such as the president of the United States, the governor of Georgia, or a member of the school board in Woodstock, Vermont. Analogously to the U.S. Supreme Court's decisions on constitutionalized questions of libel and slander, what we think about the central case of the elected official can inform our thinking about nonelected governmental officials; about those in the nongovernmental for-profit and nonprofit sectors who may still be involved in policymaking and the discussion of social issues; and about those who, like the pop music star Madonna and the basketball player Dennis Rodman, are simply famous.[4] Insofar as the elected governmental official is the paradigm case, getting clear about this case will enable us to think more carefully about cases bearing some, but not all, of the properties of the case of the elected governmental official.

---

[3] The confusion to which I refer is underscored by the terms "public official" and "public figure." Not all government employees are well known (although many are, such as the President of the United States and the Prime Minister of Australia), and not all well-known people are government employees. Despite this, there are issues about the extent to which even government employees who are not well known have less of an interest in keeping secret facts about their lives than do ordinary citizens. There are also issues about the extent to which even well-known people who are not employed by the government (including television personalities like Martha Stewart and sports stars like Michael Jordan) should be thought of as having relinquished a degree of control over the facts about their lives that is greater than that relinquished by the rest of us. As a result, the topic I address covers discussions of well-known government employees, government employees who are not well known, and well-known people who are not government employees. I may quite possibly reach different conclusions for each group.

[4] On the issues surrounding the extension of *New York Times Co. v. Sullivan*, 376 U.S. 254 (1964), which was a libel case about governmental officials, to libels of "public figures" who are not government employees, see *Curtis Publishing Co. v. Butts* and *Associated Press v. Walker*, 388 U.S. 130 (1967); *Gertz v. Robert Welch, Inc.*, 418 U.S. 323 (1974); *Time, Inc. v. Firestone*, 424 U.S. 448 (1976); *Wolston v. Reader's Digest Ass'n, Inc.*, 443 U.S. 157 (1979); and *Hutchinson v. Proxmire*, 443 U.S. 111 (1979).

The issue surrounding the disclosure of facts about elected governmental officials (or candidates for governmental office) that those officials (or candidates) would wish not to have disclosed[5] could plausibly be analyzed in strictly utilitarian or consequentialist terms. If we were doing so, we would include within a utilitarian calculus people's preferences about what information they desired and the pleasure or other forms of utility that they would gain from getting it, as well as people's preferences about the pain they would feel if facts about themselves were exposed. We would also consider a host of second-order consequences, such as the one most commonly discussed in this context—the extent to which the possibility of disclosure will discourage more-qualified people from running for public office, leading to less-qualified people running for and then holding those same positions. This list of factors is hardly exhaustive, and identifying fully all of the factors to be included would be a worthwhile exercise, as would engaging in the difficult but important empirical work of trying to measure the full array of positive and negative consequences. However, because the strictly consequentialist analysis would require so much empirical speculation (a long phrase for guessing), and because the right to privacy, even more than most other rights, is so often understood in nonconsequentialist terms, I propose to focus on the question largely from a nonconsequentialist perspective.

Framed in a nonconsequentialist way, we might understand and formulate the question as follows: even if many people prefer to discover facts and secrets about elected officials and candidates for governmental office, and even if that preference is moderately important or intense to the people who desire the information, and even if that preference is a justified one,[6] and even if the negative consequences of disclosure—measured in consequentialist terms—are small,[7] it nevertheless might be wrong for people to try to satisfy or indulge that preference and for journalists and authors to cater to it. Thus, the question I address is whether an elected public official or a candidate for public office has a right to nondisclosure that operates as a genuine side-constraint or trump on what might otherwise be a justified interest on the part of the electorate in obtaining the information.

---

[5] The locution "would wish not to have disclosed" is of course an oversimplification. Previous policy fiascos would also fit under the heading of facts that officials or candidates would wish not to have disclosed, as would criminal convictions for bribery and election fraud, but in neither of these cases is there a plausible argument for nondisclosure. As is obvious, my attention is solely on the facts and activities that are often claimed to be "nobody's business."

[6] I do not mean that it is justified *all things considered*, but rather, I mean to focus on the fact that moral side-constraints are most important not when they constrain illegitimate or unjustified preferences, but when they constrain otherwise legitimate or justified ones.

[7] This assumption may be counterfactual, but I will deal with this issue presently.

At this point I am not concerned about the structure of this right. If there is such a right, it might be legally enforceable against those who would seek to disclose some piece of information—as when the British royal family obtained from a French court an injunction preventing the publication in France of surreptitiously taken photographs of Princess Diana—or it might simply be grounds for legitimate criticism. In the United States, First Amendment doctrine makes it implausible to imagine that the British royal family or an elected official could have obtained an injunction against publication in such circumstances,[8] or could have collected damages after publication. That does not mean that it would be impossible in the United States to violate the royal family's moral rights, or impossible to criticize disclosers on the grounds that they violated the moral rights of others. Consequently, the central question is the existence of a moral right, held in the paradigmatic case by an elected public official or by a candidate for elective office, against the disclosure of certain facts about the right-holder that the right-holder believes are not any of the public's business.

III. The Question of Relevance

In most of the debates about the issue of disclosing facts about the lives of candidates or officeholders who wish to keep those facts secret, the issue is framed around the question of the *relevance* of the facts at issue. Typically, as with the 1992 debates about the extramarital sexual activities of President Clinton or about his alleged drug use or other "minor" crimes that took place in the distant past, some people argue that facts ought not to be disclosed when they are irrelevant to an individual's performance of a job. Regardless of whether people want the information, the argument goes, information that is not relevant to job performance has no place in public discussion of political candidates.

Such claims of irrelevance mask a host of deeper and more difficult issues. Chief among these are contestable issues about what the given job actually *is*, and equally contestable empirical issues about what facts indicate an ability to do the job so understood. Following a distinction that is well known in the law of evidence, I will refer to the former set of issues as *materiality issues* and the latter set of issues as *relevance issues*. In this usage, a fact is immaterial to a conclusion if what the primary fact tends to indicate has no bearing on the decision to be made. Thus, even if it is true that there is a correlation between being unfaithful to one's

---

[8] See *Virgil v. Time, Inc.*, 527 F.2d 1122 (9th Cir. 1975); and *Hall v. Post*, 323 N.C. 259, 372 S.E.2d 711 (1988). See generally Richard C. Turkington and Anita L. Allen, *Privacy Law: Cases and Materials* (St. Paul, MN: West Group, 1999), 449–95; and Diane L. Zimmerman, "Requiem for a Heavyweight: A Farewell to Warren and Brandeis's Privacy Tort," *Cornell Law Review* 68, no. 2 (Spring 1983): 291–363.

wife and being unfaithful to one's religion, knowledge of an individual's infidelity will be *immaterial* for anyone who believes that being faithful to one's religion has no bearing on holding public office. And even if someone believes that being faithful to one's religion *is* a part of holding public office, being unfaithful to one's wife will be *irrelevant* if it turns out that there is no empirical relationship between being faithful to one's spouse and being faithful to one's religion. With this distinction in hand, I will first address the question of materiality, and then turn to the issue of relevance.

Douglas Ginsberg, then (and now) a judge of the U.S. Court of Appeals for the District of Columbia, was nominated in 1987 by President Reagan to be a justice of the U.S. Supreme Court. Shortly thereafter, it was disclosed, largely by reporters relying on unnamed sources, that Ginsberg had been in the past a frequent user of marijuana. This fact, which led to the withdrawal of Ginsberg's nomination, was thought by some to be material to the job of Supreme Court justice; others, however, thought that Ginsberg's past drug use was immaterial.[9] Even assuming that Ginsberg was not going to be smoking marijuana while hearing arguments, writing opinions, or deciding cases—and assuming as well that there is no causal relationship between one's smoking marijuana in the past or on off-hours and one's current ability to hear arguments, write opinions, and decide cases—some still objected to Ginsberg's nomination. They argued that the job description of a Supreme Court justice was not limited to deciding cases and writing opinions, but extended as well to being a role model by showing the importance of obeying even those laws with which we disagree. Because violating the marijuana laws was an example of disobedience, and because obedience was itself part of the job, so the argument went, the fact that Ginsberg had previously disobeyed the law was material to Ginsberg's qualifications.[10]

This argument against Ginsberg was repeated some years later in the wake of several nominations by President Clinton. In 1993, Clinton unsuccessfully nominated Zöe Baird and then Kimba Wood to be attorney general of the United States; a year later, Clinton successfully nominated Stephen Breyer to be a justice of the Supreme Court. After each nomination, it came out that the nominee had not complied with certain portions

---

[9] They might have thought otherwise if, for example, it had been alleged that Ginsberg had been using LSD or other hallucinogenic drugs regularly for a period of ten years prior to becoming a judge.

[10] The argument would, of course, also extend to Supreme Court nominees who exceed the speed limit while driving, who cross the street against the "Don't Walk" signs, or who, when such activity was unlawful, removed the label describing the contents from their mattresses and pillows. The fact that some of those who opposed Ginsberg's nomination on obedience-to-law grounds did not express a willingness to oppose a nominee who had engaged in these other forms of unlawful behavior does cast doubt on their sincerity, but the disingenuousness of some or many proponents of the argument does not address the soundness of the argument itself.

of the immigration and social security laws in hiring domestic employees. In each case, the argument was made that the jobs to which the nominee had been nominated were ones in which obedience to law was part of the job description.

In all of these cases, the argument was not that no one should disobey the law. Rather, it was that people occupying certain kinds of public offices—Supreme Court justice and attorney general of the United States, for example—should have an exceptional proclivity to obey the law just because it is law. Their proclivity to do this, it was argued, should be greater than that we would expect from other citizens, and greater than that we would or should expect from people holding public office in general. It is, of course, possible to debate the materiality question of whether this exceptional obedience to law *simpliciter* should be part of the job description of a Supreme Court justice or the attorney general of the United States, but I do not want to get bogged down in the particulars of this case. Rather, my point is a general one: that a claim of immateriality presupposes some standard of materiality, and a standard of materiality in turn presupposes a conception of the position to which the asserted trait is either causally or indicatively related.[11] While we may have debates over which conception of some position is the correct one, it is nevertheless the case that denials of materiality often mask narrow conceptions of the position and its responsibilities, conceptions with which others might reasonably disagree. The claim that marital infidelity is immaterial to the office of president of the United States presupposes that the role of president should not include the role of being an exemplar of marital fidelity. Many people claim that it should not, but many others claim that it should, and debates about its materiality to the job are commonly smoke screens for debates about just what it is that the job really entails.

Even when there is agreement about what the position is and what traits are required to perform it, there remain issues about what *other* traits might be causally or indicatively relevant to those required traits, or about what other pieces of evidence would be relevant to those traits. Take an example that I suggested at the opening of this essay. It is widely

---

[11] To make a *causal* claim is to claim that the trait or behavior at issue bears a causal relationship (including a probabilistic causal relationship) to the existence of the genuinely relevant trait or behavior, as when it is claimed that marijuana use increases the likelihood of heroin use. The *indicative* claim is that the trait or behavior at issue is evidence of the genuinely relevant trait or behavior, even when or if there is no causal connection. One example of an indicative claim is the claim that the incidence of heroin use among the population of marijuana users is higher than the incidence of heroin use in the population at large, making evidence of marijuana use some indication of heroin use. In the present context, the claim is more likely an indicative one, with the argument being that one who has disobeyed some laws presents a greater likelihood of disobeying other laws than is one of whom there is no evidence of disobedience.

known that President Clinton cheats at golf.[12] Although it is clear that playing golf is not part of the job description of president of the United States (even though a high percentage of American presidents over the past fifty years have played the game with some enthusiasm), many people believe that maintaining certain high standards of veracity are indeed part of the job description. If that is the case, then the empirical question is presented whether evidence of cheating at golf is some evidence of (that is, is relevant to) a likely failure to maintain high standards of veracity in public pronouncements. It is possible that the answer is no, and that there is neither a causal relationship nor even a correlation between the existence of the trait of cheating at golf and the existence of the trait of being abnormally dishonest in one's public and political dealings. But it is also possible that the answer is yes, and that a cheater at golf, holding everything else constant, is more likely to be dishonest in public statements than is a person who does not cheat at golf. If this latter alternative is in fact the case, then the argument that golf behavior is "private" or none of the public's business becomes a somewhat more difficult one to maintain. Although there may be a fair amount of agreement on the abstract proposition that irrelevant information ought not be disclosed, it is hardly clear that the range of irrelevant information is as narrow as is often claimed to be the case.

IV. Democracy and the Determination of Relevance

Implicit in the foregoing discussion is a particular view about democracy, and it is worthwhile at this point to bring that view to the surface for closer inspection. Under this view, the public has a legitimate interest in knowing about those traits that are relevant to determining the plainly material qualifications of the people for whom they are considering voting.[13] Thus, if some trait or some item of behavior is relevant to a properly understood conception of the job under consideration, then the arguments that militate in favor of the right to vote in the first instance are

---

[12] For those readers who are golfers, I point out that it is well known that President Clinton's cheating at golf goes quite a bit beyond winter rules, mulligans ("do-overs") on the first tee, and other rule modifications that are common among casual golfers. By all accounts, Clinton has a disregard for the rules of golf that is uncommon even among casual golfers of his skill level, a disregard that would lead many golfers to question whether the game he plays ought to be called "golf" at all. ("Is it chess without the queen?") For a sampling of the published accounts, see Tim Tucker, "Shooting a 60 with President Mulligan," *Atlanta Constitution*, August 16, 1999, 1D; Melinda Henneberger, "Tom DeLay Holds No Gavel, But a Firm Grip on the Reins," *New York Times*, June 21, 1999, A1; R. Cort Kirkwood, "Worst of All, He Cheats at Golf," *Ottawa Sun*, January 10, 1999, C4; Jonathan Rosenblum, "Bill's Problem and Ours," *Jerusalem Post*, February 6, 1998, 9; Glenn F. Bunting, "Game Fits President to a Tee," *Los Angeles Times*, November 13, 1997, E1; and *CNN Newsroom Worldview*, July 6, 1998, transcript 98070600VO5.

[13] Constitutionalized American libel law reflects this view. *Monitor Patriot Co. v. Roy*, 401 U.S. 265 (1966).

likely to militate as well in favor of an interest in obtaining the information that is relevant to voting in an intelligent fashion.[14]

But this is too easy. In the foregoing, I have assumed that there is some agreement about the proper conception of the job or position at issue. Although it may be the case that there is often an excessively impoverished understanding of the nature of the job (as with the claim that the only job of a member of Congress or Parliament is to vote on proposed legislation), the discussion thus far has still assumed away the possibility of disagreement about what the position entails. When such disagreement does exist, the issue becomes more difficult, because then the question emerges of when it is appropriate to make widely available a piece of information that only *some* voters might think is relevant to their voting decision, under circumstances in which the information is indeed relevant to *their* voting decision based on criteria that *they* take to be material.

Let us continue with a hypothetical example based on the behavior of President Clinton. Suppose that some people believe that how a male president treats women is material to their decision about how to cast their ballot in a presidential election. Suppose further that many of these people believe, arguably correctly, that a male supervisor's willingness to propose or engage in sexual relations with one of his employees is negatively correlated with his likelihood of treating women with respect in

---

[14] I describe the interest in voting as an interest and not as a right because I want to bracket, at least for now, questions about how that interest might be enforced or effectuated. One way to enforce that interest is by giving people an enforceable right (a *claim* in the strict Hohfeldian sense) to obtain information from others that those others would prefer not to disclose. We can imagine, in theory, something like a Freedom of Information Act against political candidates, by which members of the public might claim access to various documents and various forms of information that a candidate possesses, just as a claimant under the Freedom of Information Act can enforce a demand for documents that are in the possession of the government.

Although this is one (extreme) way in which the interest in getting information relevant to a voting decision might be effectuated, there are others as well. For example, the institutional press could be given the enforceable claim-right just discussed, which it could exercise on behalf of the public. Alternatively, the institutional press could be given a Hohfeldian privilege against interference with its obtaining and publishing of such information. (This is reasonably close to the current state of American law, although in practice the privilege is extended to all, and not only to the institutional media.) Another possibility is the use of a statute or regulation requiring affirmative disclosure of certain information by all candidates. (This possibility has often been raised in the context of proposals to require all candidates to disclose their medical histories, and was made with particular frequency in 1991 and 1992, when the late Paul Tsongas, who had been treated in the past for cancer, was campaigning to be the Democratic nominee for president of the United States.) Note also that the law could be entirely uninvolved, but there might still be a norm, according to which candidates who do not disclose certain information (such as their past use, if any, of illegal narcotics and other controlled substances) would be subject to criticism for their nondisclosure, and under which journalists who locate and disclose the information would likely be the recipients of prizes rather than excoriation.

There exist other possibilities for effectuation of the informational interest, but my point here is only that the identification of a legitimate interest, which is what I address here, is largely agnostic on the question of which legal or other devices might best be employed to give effect to that interest.

other contexts. Finally, suppose that other people disagree about the materiality of the trait of treating women well and/or with the empirical claim about the relevance of propositioning subordinates to that trait. Under these conditions of disagreement about materiality and/or relevance, what is the correct approach to the question of the legitimacy of disclosing facts about a candidate's sexual behavior with subordinates?

This question is made more difficult by the special nature of information. Unlike some number of other commodities, information—especially information of the variety we are now considering—is difficult to restrict to those who have, from their lights, a legitimate need for that information. In the case of pharmaceuticals, for example, the prescription system is moderately effective in keeping many pharmaceuticals out of the hands of those whose need for the product is less important or less legitimate than it is for those who have a medical need certified by a competent physician. In contrast, information that is made available to some is inevitably made available to all. If the information is to be made available to those for whom it is indeed relevant to the criteria that *they* employ in voting, then the same information will ordinarily be available to those who have nothing other than a salacious interest. If it is impossible to provide the information to the former group without at the same time also providing it to the latter, then what standards should be employed to determine the legitimacy of disclosure?

The example above, involving a male presidential candidate's sexual exploits with subordinates, might seem a bit strained, even though it reflects the factual situation that nearly resulted in the removal of President Clinton. Much less strained, however, and no less real, is the example of a disclosure of the sexual orientation of a candidate for public office, against the presumed wishes of the candidate. Although many of us believe that sexual orientation is both immaterial and irrelevant to job performance in all or virtually all public sector and private sector settings, it is unfortunately (from my perspective) the case that not everyone agrees. For a not insignificant proportion of the population in most countries in the world, having a gay, lesbian, or bisexual sexual orientation is immoral, and having a heterosexual sexual orientation is not only morally commanded, but is also a necessary qualification for holding public office or other positions of substantial responsibility.

If we were to put aside questions of democratic theory, the question of whether people should have information about a person's sexual orientation is not a difficult one. If the question is whether the president of General Motors ought to be able to know about the sexual orientation of prospective General Motors employees, it seems moderately easy, for those of us who reject the materiality of sexual orientation to job performance, to answer the question in the negative. This negative answer would be based on the moral argument that sexual orientation is immaterial to what General Motors *ought* to be looking for in their employees, regardless of what they are in fact looking for in their employees. If the actual practice of General Motors diverges from what is morally correct, then it is only a short step to the conclusion that the morally unacceptable tastes of the hypothetical General Motors president ought not be indulged.

When we leave General Motors and enter the realm of voting and democratic theory, however, the issues becomes substantially more difficult, even from the same moral perspective. For now we are forced to confront two questions. First, in a democracy, are there constraints on the array of factors that people might employ in deciding what they consider to be a material qualification for holding public office? Second, what traits are relevant in determining whether a particular candidate satisfied this material qualification? To put it differently, in a democracy there appears to be a right to base one's voting decisions on criteria that other people take to be wrong.

In order to address the question of when people may have a right to the information that would be useful to them in making a decision on what others think to be the wrong grounds, it is useful to draw two distinctions. The first is a distinction between morally permissible and morally impermissible minority tastes in a candidate's or an official's qualifications. This distinction is designed to capture the difference between those criteria with which we disagree but that we believe people may legitimately employ, and those criteria that we believe may not be legitimately employed by anyone. According to this distinction we could say, for example, that viewing marital fidelity as a necessary condition for holding public office is morally permissible—even though many of us would consider such a condition inadvisable and unrealistic—but that viewing heterosexuality, whiteness, maleness, or American birth[15] as a qualification for holding office is morally (and in some cases legally) impermissible, regardless of the preferences of some of the electorate. In these latter cases, there exist moral side-constraints on voter preferences and voter-employed criteria, and thus in some cases factors that some voters believe to be relevant and material to their voting decisions would and should be treated as out of bounds because of the moral impermissibility of permitting those factors to be part of the voting calculus of even an otherwise autonomous voter.

This distinction is more problematic in practice than it is in theory, because journalists—normally the ones who produce and disseminate the information that creates the problem of "privacy" in the first instance—

---

[15] Note that this qualification would only be impermissible for offices other than those of president and vice president of the United States; for those two positions, American birth, however morally problematic, is constitutionally mandated. U.S. Constitution, art. 2, sec. 1, clause 5. For a valuable critique of this provision and what it represents, see Randall Kennedy, "A Natural Aristocracy?" in William N. Eskridge, Jr., and Sanford Levinson, eds., *Constitutional Stupidities, Constitutional Tragedies* (New York: New York University Press, 1998), 54–56.

are especially loath to admit that they are making moral judgments, and are also especially prone to defending their disclosure practices on the basis of the "people's right to know." Indeed, much that I say in this section can be seen more as a response to the "right to know" argument than as anything else. For if the people have a "right to know" *simpliciter*, then it is presumptively hard to see what in the "right to know" argument provides the justification for journalists refusing to provide information to voters that those voters wish to have for use in their own voting decisions. But if journalists were more willing to acknowledge that moral limits exist on the people's right to know—even in cases of things that (some of) the people wish to know—and if journalists were more willing to take responsibility for identifying and enforcing those moral limits, then some of the issues created by the category of morally impermissible voter preferences might be lessened.

It is not only journalists, however, who are uncomfortable with journalists making these kinds of moral decisions. Thus, my second distinction is precisely about how to determine which factors are morally permissible voter preferences and which factors are morally impermissible. Under one view, determining the factors that are morally impermissible is antecedent to the electoral and deliberative process, and no additional complications are raised. Under the other view, these are just the kinds of issues that ought to be the subject of public deliberation.[16] The threshold problem, therefore, is that for the latter, deliberative view of democratic decision-making, which includes deliberative decision-making even about profound moral matters, the very fact of engaging in public deliberation eliminates the possibility of nondisclosure as a product of that deliberation. It is not possible for a public deliberation to yield the outcome that some of the public deliberation should not have taken place in public; such an outcome would be like unscrambling scrambled eggs.

In response to this problem—again generated by the comparative ease of information flow compared to the flow of most other things that people might desire—one could imagine a two-stage public deliberation. Under this procedure, deliberation about the permissible criteria for electoral choice and the legitimate qualifications for candidates would take place in the abstract, or by way of hypothetical examples, prior to the specific elections in which specific candidates with specific characteristics and specific pasts would run for office. We know, however, that this is not a realistic option. Instead, the electoral process is itself the public deliber-

---

[16] See, for example, Amy Gutmann and Dennis Thompson, *Democracy and Disagreement* (Cambridge, MA: Harvard University Press, 1996). See also James Bohman, *Public Deliberation* (Cambridge, MA: MIT Press, 1996); James S. Fishkin, *Democracy and Deliberation* (New Haven, CT: Yale University Press, 1991); Alan Hamlin and Philip Pettit, eds., *The Good Polity* (Oxford: Basil Blackwell, 1989); and David M. Estlund, "Who's Afraid of Deliberative Democracy? On the Strategic/Deliberative Dichotomy in Recent Constitutional Jurisprudence," *Texas Law Review* 71, no. 6 (October 1993): 1437-54.

ation, and thus is itself the process by which the polity decides which characteristics are or are not legitimate qualifications for office, legitimate factors for voter decision, or legitimate topics for public discussion. Given this, it may turn out that the disclosure of traits that some deliberators believe to be morally immaterial or empirically irrelevant will nevertheless properly be part of the process by which a polity decides collectively, under a deliberative view, what its moral criteria will be. The result of this is that it may, as a practical matter, be impossible to have an effective public deliberation about what factors ought not to be part of public deliberation, whether in the electoral context or anywhere else.

Under either a deliberative or a nondeliberative view of moral decision-making, there remains an additional sticky question. This is the question of the degree of legitimate public interest that is necessary to surpass a threshold of legitimacy for disclosure. Let us put aside the question of moral antecedence and consider an election in which 10 percent of the population treat some fact, which a candidate wishes to keep secret, as a factor that is relevant in a morally acceptable way to their voting decisions, which are based on their morally acceptable criteria for office. Putting aside the question of the indifferent middle, assume that the other 90 percent believe the factor to be immaterial to the office. This 90 percent, therefore, believe that the factor is appropriately within the domain of things that the candidate need not disclose, and appropriately within the domain that journalists and others ought not disclose, at least under penalty of public disapprobation.[17]

Under these circumstances, it is tempting to conclude that the majority should prevail, and that disclosure should be deemed inappropriate. But given that we are considering the information necessary for exercising the franchise, it is hard to distinguish the view that the majority should prevail here from the view that the majority should be able to limit the information available to the minority. This latter view is, to put it mildly, in some tension with a common conception of the roots of the American understanding of freedom of speech and freedom of the press.[18] Moreover, the issue presents an even broader problem with respect to majoritarian control of the "devices of democracy" more generally.[19] Whether it be the style of the ballot, the structure of voting (first-past-the-post or

[17] It is possible that previous use of controlled substances is a good example of this sort of situation. Although a majority of the population might disagree with those who think that unlawful drug use ten or fifteen years ago is properly a factor in a current voting decision, the majority would be hard-pressed to conclude that the minority who disagreed with them were voting immorally.

[18] See especially Alexander Meiklejohn, *Political Freedom: The Constitutional Powers of the People* (New York: Harper and Row, 1965). See also Frederick Schauer, *Free Speech: A Philosophical Enquiry* (Cambridge: Cambridge University Press, 1982), chap. 2; and Cass R. Sunstein, *Democracy and the Problem of Free Speech* (New York: Free Press, 1993).

[19] See Frederick Schauer, "Judicial Review of the Devices of Democracy," *Columbia Law Review* 94, no. 4 (May 1994): 1326–47.

proportional representation, for example, or single-member as opposed to multimember districts), the eligibility of voters, or a host of other questions, this question of the limits of majoritarian rule needs to be resolved. One view maintains that these are just the kinds of decisions that should be made by the majority. Another, however, maintains that these decisions should be antecedent to and immune from majority control, partly for the practical reason that majorities would be too likely to attempt to limit the voting power of minorities, and partly for the deeper reason that the idea of majority rule itself—as well as the set of procedures necessary to make it work—exists logically and temporally prior to majority decisions and thus ought to be out of reach of majoritarian modification.[20] If these reasons are correct, then they would suggest that there is something deeply problematic about majorities deciding that information relevant to the voting decisions of a minority ought in some formal or informal way to be made unavailable to that minority.

These conclusions are somewhat against the grain of what, at the time of this writing, appears to be a rising tide of sentiment that there is too much disclosure of so-called private facts. But the conclusions that I have reached, although hardly unassailable, do at least suggest that there is a nonutilitarian argument from democracy which, under some circumstances and under some assumptions, would provide support for the view that indulging the preference for the kinds of information under discussion is more central to democratic theory than is commonly supposed. If one dimension of democracy—or at least one dimension of the majoritarian dimension of democracy—is that the people have a nonutilitarian right to decide not only which candidates meet predetermined criteria for holding public office, but also what those criteria are to be in the first instance, and if another dimension of democracy is that the right to vote may entail the right to make many of these decisions on an individual and not on a societal basis, then it turns out that there are stronger arguments for the "anti-privacy" side of the debate about the private lives of public figures than is ordinarily understood.

V. "Private" Facts and the Clash of Rights

Although there are moral arguments on one side of the private-lives-of-public-figures debate, including moral arguments from the right to vote that are not often recognized, there are moral arguments on the other side as well. Chief among these is the argument that control over the information about one's life is itself a central part of what is sometimes referred to as personhood or personal autonomy, and that there is no

---

[20] This issue is a variant on the well-known *paradox of democracy*. See Karl R. Popper, *The Open Society and Its Enemies*, 5th ed. (London: Routledge & Kegan Paul, 1966), 265–66.

good reason why a person should be required to relinquish this right of personal autonomy simply to enter the public domain.

Yet if personal autonomy is the basis for the right of nondisclosure, it may be hard to distinguish this right from all of the other autonomy rights that one must forgo—or at least exercise in a particular and constrained way—in order to enter the public arena. One has the right to speak or to remain silent, the right to live where one pleases, the right (sometimes) to work where one pleases, as well as a host of other rights that are commonly and properly thought relinquishable by one's voluntary decision to stand for public office or to operate in the public domain more generally.[21] Insofar as there are arguments for overriding the full range of autonomy rights with other rights of the public, or by an aggregation of a sufficiently large quantity of interests,[22] these arguments appear no less applicable to overriding what would otherwise be a public figure's or official's right to privacy about information about himself or herself. At times, the arguments for overriding will be based on empirical and pragmatic concerns, and the very real possibility that good people will be dissuaded from public life must be weighed in the balance. At other times the arguments for overriding will be based on others' countervailing rights. There has been little discussion of countervailing rights in this context, except for the journalists' tiresome and self-serving incantations of the public's right to know.

One way of understanding the argument of this essay, therefore, is as an attempt to add some flesh to the skeleton of the abstract idea of the public's right to know. Thus, if there is a right to vote, and if the right to vote carries with it the accessory right to obtain the information that is relevant to a voter's decision (based on a voter's own conception of the morally permissible criteria that are material to an office), then both the pragmatic and the rights-based arguments against disclosure must confront a rights-based argument in the other direction. The person who wishes to have information about a candidate's marital infidelity, for example, or previous use of controlled substances, can be understood as

---

[21] The argument from *waiver* appears to go nowhere. When confronted with the argument that one has the right not to be evaluated by race or gender, but that one waives this by choosing to enter public life, a proper response is that it would be wrong to make people waive this right just to enter public life. Many ambitious politicians would agree to have their pinky finger or little toe amputated if that would assure them of election to higher office, but it would, nevertheless, be wrong to make them waive their right not to have this done to them. An argument from waiver, therefore, is parasitic on an antecedent determination of what it would be reasonable or right to make people waive, and thus cannot avoid this central substantive moral question.

[22] I have dealt with the calculus of all of this elsewhere. See Frederick Schauer, "A Comment on the Structure of Rights," *Georgia Law Review* 27, no. 2 (Winter 1993): 415–34; and Schauer, "Can Rights Be Abused?" *Philosophical Quarterly* 31, no. 2 (July 1981): 226–32. See also Alan Gewirth, "Are There Any Absolute Rights?" *Philosophical Quarterly* 31, no. 1 (January 1981): 1–16; Robert Nozick, "Moral Complications and Moral Structures," *Natural Law Forum* 13 (1968): 1–50; and Judith Jarvis Thomson, "Some Ruminations on Rights," *Arizona Law Review* 19, no. 1 (1977): 45–60.

arguing that, in a democracy, the determination of the nature of a job and its qualifications are, at least within certain moral boundaries, for each voter to determine individually and autonomously.

The issue is sharpened, of course, when we are dealing with informational preferences held by a minority of voters, of which information about marital fidelity is an example. Thus, one way of framing the question of what information should be disclosed is in terms of minority informational preferences that are nevertheless rights-based. Consequently, the argument that "the people" have decided that they do not want certain information must, nevertheless, confront the argument that the information an individual needs to make his or her own voting decision cannot be subject to majority control.[23]

Where the information desired is within the realm of what some of us consider morally inappropriate criteria—sexual orientation and physical handicap are good examples—then if we place impediments on obtaining that information, we base that action on a moral view of what it is morally permissible and impermissible for people to want to find out. In this case, the moral impermissibility of taking certain factors into consideration can be understood as trumping[24] the moral right to make decisions about the criteria to be used in evaluating candidates for public office. That the moral calculus is made in this way seems entirely appropriate. That the moral calculus is hidden under the common pronouncement that certain things "are not relevant" seems less so, because that claim obscures far more issues than it illuminates.

VI. Conclusion

In much of this essay, I have cast aspersions on journalists' favorite incantation: the "people's right to know." On closer inspection, however, this idea of the people's right to know may have something to be said for it, at least if we understand it as a permissible moral adjunct, under appropriate empirical conditions, to a moral right to vote and to be involved in policy in other public ways. If there is such a right to vote, and if voting decisions are essentially individual decisions that embody an important dimension of individual autonomy, then it seems wrong to

[23] There are interesting questions about when a minority interest is large enough to "count." Under one view, consistent with the argument that I make here, the informational preferences of even one person are sufficient to justify disclosure. But given the impossibility of restricting the information to those who need it, as I argued above, it is unrealistic to suppose that it is wrong to fail to indulge the informational preferences of just one person. In contrast, requiring that the information be actually and legitimately desired by the majority is inconsistent, as I have argued, with the idea of the right to vote itself. The difficult task, therefore, is determining where, above one voter and below a majority, one should draw the line.

[24] Ronald Dworkin, *Taking Rights Seriously* (Cambridge, MA: Harvard University Press, 1978), 190–94.

contend that the information that some voters require for making their voting decisions should be subject to majoritarian control. If I have made my case, then informational preferences that the majority or journalists find immaterial or morally problematic may, nevertheless, have to be indulged, for exactly the same reasons that indulging preferences that some of us find wrong is central to autonomy more generally.

Law, Harvard University

INDEX

Abortion, 4, 137, 145 n. 16, 158–59
Ackerman, Bruce, 182
Agency, 39–40, 51–53, 55, 61–63
Agreements, 60–61, 124, 132
Aleinikoff, T. Alexander, 179
Americans with Disabilities Act (1990), 23, 89
Anarchy, State, and Utopia (Nozick), 45
Anderson, Elizabeth, 108–9
Anthropology, 71, 73–75
Aristotle, 30
Arizona Governing Committee v. Norris (1983), 251 n. 48, 257 n. 56
Association, 125, 131, 139; freedom of, 136, 147
Authority, 129 n. 22; governmental, 123–25, 127, 131, 135, 138–40; moral, 120, 123–25, 130, 133, 135, 138–40; and religion, 126, 135
Autonomy, 5, 25, 30, 31–35, 37–42, 44, 55–58, 62–64, 91–92, 128, 141–42, 144–45, 162, 165, 306–9; and medical information, 230, 237–38; and the right to die, 277, 280, 287–89, 292

Bargaining, 125, 133, 140, 190–91, 275
Beardsley, Elizabeth, 237–38
Benn, Stanley, 38–39, 41
Berger, Raoul, 172
Bickel, Alexander M., 180–81
Bill of Rights, U.S., 91, 172–73, 175
Black, Charles L., Jr., 165, 173, 176–77
Black, Justice Hugo L., 166, 168–70, 174
Blackmail, 196–99, 201
Blackstone, Sir William, 8
Blasi, Vincent, 177
Bobbitt, Philip, 143 n. 10, 177
Bork, Robert H., 167, 170–71
Boundaries, 7, 64, 92, 105, 109, 124, 308
Boyd v. United States (1886), 178–79
Brandeis, Justice Louis, 29, 84, 90, 91, 104, 136–37, 240, 242–43
Brennan, Justice William J., Jr., 166, 168, 170
Brin, David, 210–11
Bureaucracy, 107
Burger, Chief Justice Warren, 137, 153

California v. Ciraolo (1986), 153
California v. Greenwood (1988), 152, 154
Carter v. Carter Coal Co. (1936), 30 n. 14
Causation, 1–2, 31 n. 17, 283–87, 299–300

Chapman, John, 235
Choice, 37, 55, 63–64, 103, 139, 229–30, 239, 246, 288
Citizens, 129–32
Civil Rights Act of 1964, 251 n. 48
Civil society, 129, 139
Clinton, President William, 297, 298, 300–302
Coase, Ronald, 194
Coercion, 55–56, 128
Cohen, G. A., 108–9
Commitments, 58
Common Law, The (Holmes), 2
Commons, 11
Communication, 1
Communitarianism, 128 n. 16, 181
Community, 30–31, 32, 34, 35, 39–42 passim, 125–26, 143, 181–82; moral, 127–28; political, 128
Compensation, 3, 6–7, 10; workers', 2
Competition, 12–13, 20–21, 81–82
Confidentiality, 16, 214, 217, 226, 228–29, 248, 263, 273 n. 84, 275; duty of, 20
Consent, 6, 8, 12, 28, 30, 55, 57, 66, 218, 230, 232–33, 247; and authority, 123–25, 129 n. 22, 131, 133, 135–36, 138–40; informed, 229, 231, 239–40, 263–64, 273, 279. *See also* Voluntariness
Consequentialism, 94–95, 98–101, 105, 110, 116–17, 296
Constitution: the Netherlands, 155 n. 54; United States, 2, 25, 26, 29, 90, 137–38, 141–42, 144, 147–48, 155–56, 163, 165–78, 181–85, 242, 277–79
Constitutional theory, 165–85
Constitutionalism, 154, 163–64, 176
Contractarianism, 183
Contracts, 5, 83, 120; freedom of, 21–22, 24; hypothetical, 134; and law, 20; and privacy, 4, 24, 125; and the United States Constitution, 2–3
Control, 28, 34, 39, 60, 66, 181, 213, 245; and information, 45, 48–50, 57, 59, 63, 70, 83–84, 89, 141, 144, 150, 187–212 passim, 219–22, 228–31, 235, 238, 246, 306
Conventionalism, 143–44, 149–50, 152–64, 168
Conventions, 26–27, 30, 38, 42, 60, 92, 104–5, 111, 143–44, 154–57. *See also* Norms; Practices

311